Candy M

W9-BVE-085

mod	Proper modification? Dangling? Misplaced?	pp. 418–419
[	Move to left (or] right)	
Numbers	You must follow conventions in use of figures.	
? ∧	Something left out here?	
⌗ ?	Should there be a paragraph indentation here?	
ǁ ism	Faulty parallelism.	pp. 420–422
Pn	Punctuation	
	General remarks	pp. 422–424
∧	Period	p. 424
∧	Comma	pp. 425–427
∧	Semicolon	pp. 424–425
∧	Colon	p. 427
	Dash	p. 427
	Quotation marks	pp. 427–430
Ref	There is a faulty reference here between a pronoun and its antecedent.	pp. 430–431
R.O.	Run-on (fused) sentence	p. 431
Sp	Misspelled word here? Write it five times correctly in the margin of your paper.	pp. 431–436
Stet	Ignore the correction; I was wrong.	
Title	You have not followed the appropriate convention re the handling of titles.	pp. 436–437
∼	Transpose. Reverse order for more effective expression?	
∗[	Very effective section. Good for you!	
W	Wordy. Condense this expression into fewer words.	

If you consistently have trouble read the appropriate general remarks:

Grammar	pp. 395–404
Punctuation	pp. 422–430
Spelling	pp. 431–436

How did I know.

Candy Mountjoy   EKU
308 Sullivan   Richmond, Kentucky
Box 99

COLLEGE WRITING

Mrs. Nims
A3

Candy Mountjoy

COLLEGE WRITING

The Rhetorical Imperative

HARRY H. CROSBY

GEORGE F. ESTEY

Boston University

Harper & Row, Publishers

New York, Evanston, and London

COLLEGE WRITING: The Rhetorical Imperative

Copyright © 1968 by Harry H. Crosby and George F. Estey

Library of Congress Catalog Card Number: 68-12275

ACKNOWLEDGMENTS

ADVANCED PLACEMENT PROGRAM: ENGLISH. Reprinted with permission from ADVANCED PLACEMENT PROGRAM: ENGLISH, published in 1965 by College Entrance Examination Board, New York.

Janet Agle, "Come Back Detroit, All Is Forgiven." Copyright © 1966 by Harper's Magazine, Inc. Reprinted from the May, 1966, issue of *Harper's Magazine* by permission of the author.

Marion Walker Alcaro, "Colleges Don't Make Sense." Reprinted by permission of *Woman's Day Magazine*. Copyright © 1946 by Fawcett Publications, Inc.

Anonymous, "The Compulsive Drinker." Copyright © 1959 by The Atlantic Monthly Company, Boston, Mass. Reprinted with permission.

Maurice Beebe, LITERARY SYMBOLISM, edited by Maurice Beebe. © 1960 by Wadsworth Publishing Company, Inc., Belmont, California. Reprinted by permission of the publisher.

Family Circle Magazine, "The Adolescent." Reprinted by permission.

George R. Farnum, "Reverence for Life Magazine." Reprinted by permission of the New England Anti-Vivisection Society.

E. M. Forster, ASPECTS OF THE NOVEL. Copyright, 1927, by Harcourt, Brace & World, Inc.; renewed, 1955, by E. M. Forster. Reprinted by permission of Harcourt, Brace & World, Inc., New York, and Edward Arnold (Publishers) Ltd., London.

Nancy Hale, "The First Day of School." Reprinted from *The New Yorker*, February 19, 1955, by permission of the publisher.

Lou LaBrant, "The Dynamics of Education." Reprinted from *Saturday Review*, September 12, 1959, by permission of the publisher and the author.

Daniel Lang, "The Hot Phone." Reprinted from *The New Yorker*, February 12, 1955, by permission of the publisher.

Mell Lazarus, MISS PEACH cartoons, November 20, 1966, July 4, 1967, and July 24, 1967. Courtesy Publishers-Hall Syndicate.

Donald Lloyd, "Snobs, Slobs and the English Language." Reprinted from *The American Scholar*, Summer, 1951, by permission of the author.

Dwight Macdonald, "The String Untuned." Reprinted from *The New Yorker*, March 10, 1962, by permission of the publisher. "A Theory of Mass Culture." Reprinted from *Diogenes*, Summer, 1953, by permission of the Conseil International de la Philosophie et des Sciences Humaines.

Ashley Montagu, "The Annihilation of Privacy." Reprinted from *Saturday Review*, March 31, 1956, by permission of the publisher and the author.

Raoul de Roussy de Sales, "Love in America." Copyright © 1938 by The Atlantic Monthly Company, Boston, Mass. Reprinted with permission.

THE SMALL SOCIETY cartoons, December 9, 1966, and January 17, 1967. © Washington Star Syndicate, Inc. Reprinted by permission of King Features Syndicate.

"Sweet Tooth, Sour Facts." Courtesy *Time;* copyright Time, Inc., 1958.

Roul Tunley, "America's Unhealthy Children." Copyright © 1966, by Harper's Magazine, Inc. Reprinted from the May, 1966, issue of *Harper's Magazine* by permission of the author.

E. B. White, "This is New York." Abridged from HERE IS NEW YORK by E. B. White. Copyright 1949 by E. B. White. Reprinted by permission of Harper & Row, Publishers.

Forrest P. White, "Will Norfolk's Schools Stay Open?" Copyright © 1959 by The Atlantic Monthly Company, Boston, Mass. Reprinted with permission.

CONTENTS

PART II.   PERSPECTIVES

PART III.   "NUTS AND BOLTS"

PREFACE

There *is* a New Rhetoric. Its terminology is not yet completely defined nor its concepts standardized, but just as students profit from the discoveries of the New Math and the New Linguistics, so can students of Freshman English profit from recent discoveries and assumptions. We hope that this textbook provides such rewards.

In recent years, there has come to be a broader perception of the writing process, partly as a result of the renewed interest in such classical writers as Quintilian and Aristotle. Instruction in writing is now seen to include the thinking that must be done before a person sits down to write. In other words, it is now seen to be more than the correction of sentences or the construction of paragraphs. Hence, a rhetoric textbook must be more than a grammar handbook that guides a student through the intricacies of language conventions. It must be more than a style book. It must cover the writing process from the first thought to the final revision.

Part I of this textbook deals with the whole process of writing from the pre-thinking and head-scratching stages to the last polishing. Chapter 1, "The Writer's Obligation: The Rhetorical Imperative," helps a student get at the source of significant ideas; it suggests the kinds of questions he must carry around in his head if he wants to happen upon the discoveries that make a difference in the world, the thoughts that are worth communicating. Chapter 2, "The Controlling Concept: Purpose," shows how a significant idea, once captured, has its own dynamism. It tells the writer what he must do and what he must write. The sentence, "That girl deserves her shady reputation," is a *generative* one—that is, it is the kind of sentence that would generate a dialogue, if a listener were present. It is the kind of sentence a student can learn to analyze in order to anticipate a listener-reader's questions: "What girl? What reputation? How has she deserved it?" When a student learns to analyze generative, provocative, and significant ideas, he can anticipate the issues his writing will raise, the content he must provide, and the language he must use. Chapter 3, "The Implied Structure: Organization," describes the sentence qualities that are the bases for extended communication and outlines the basic questions that must be answered to form the structure of a written composition. Chapter 4, "The Predicted Content: Development," describes how framework questions should be answered if a piece of writing is to be clear and persuasive. Chapter 5, "Proper Words, Proper Places: Style," shows how appropriate expression grows out of the analysis of a total writing situation that includes not only the message, but also the writer and the audience. When a professional writer discusses his craft, he almost always focuses upon the time-consuming, worrisome, muscular, rewarding process of revision, excellence in which, almost more than any other trait, marks the effective writer. Some professional writers admit to making as many as eighty revisions after their first draft. The total writing process, no matter how few or how many revisions it entails, is always more than a polishing of diction and a check on spelling. Besides the usual attention to grammar, spelling, and punctuation, Chapter 6, " 'Hard Writing': Revision," helps the student ask himself again, "Is what I am writing worth writing?" and describes the steps whereby he can achieve coherence, completeness, and artistry.

The New Rhetoric's emphasis on breadth and perspective justifies the presence of Part II, "Perspectives," which is based on the postulate that a student, if he is to excel as a writer, must have a clear understanding of the tools of writing, language and logic. Chapter 7, "Language: Past, Present, and Future," is primarily concerned with the arbitrary, developing nature of language as it grows and adapts to fit man's needs and personality. Chapter 8, "Epistemology and Logic," is more than a study of common fallacies and Aristotelian logic; it traces the history of the Western mind and shows how systematic thought processes change with society's needs and as a response to current philosophies. It describes the kinds of thought man has to come to trust and the kinds he has learned to question. It outlines the conditions that must be developed to ensure and promote sound thought. Part II should contribute to the student's total writing skill; it should help teach him what he must know about language and logic if he is to have a sound liberal and general education. When he converses with intelligent, educated persons, this information is assumed of him. Without a general understanding of logic and language, he may miss the point of a joke or a nuance in a play or novel. He may even lose the respect of his audience, or his employer. If he does not get this information in Freshman English, he probably will not get it anywhere, and he is poorer for its absence.

Part III, "Nuts and Bolts," is not exclusively a journeyman's section. Admittedly, there comes a time when a writer must master certain pedestrian techniques: how to do research, how to set up a manuscript, how to use the conventions of grammar, spelling, and punctuation. We have tried, however, to avoid saying "Do this" and "Don't do that" and, instead, have tried to show what techniques and conventions apply in certain situations—not what is "correct" or even "standard," but what accomplishes the writer's purpose. To this end, for instance, we have resurrected the almost dead word "amphiboly" because this term from the classical rhetorician's tool kit describes the ambiguity or confusion that occurs when a convention is violated.

We detect in the New Breed of student a new desire. He is inquisitive. He wants to know more—more about what truth is and how it is verified. He wants to know how to go beyond the classroom and beyond his teacher; he wants to do his own studying. He cannot expect to learn everything in a classroom, but he deserves to be shown how he can learn what he does not know. Chapter 9, "The Library Research Paper," should give him substantial help in answering some of the questions he poses.

The New Breed of student, in spite of his rejection of authority and in spite of his haircut and clothes, often has a sense of convention, for he realizes that conventions can be the tools of revolution and protest. If he uses language in a conventional way, his message will be the more forcefully received. Shunning the bizarre and the vague, the really effective young writer masters manuscript techniques, grammar, spelling, and punctuation—and moves the world with his important ideas.

This discussion of student attitudes brings up the problem of mind set. Many writing teachers, as they look back on their careers, realize that their greatest triumphs have been attitudinal. Those students who learned to write best and perhaps even went on to important positions where writing ability was basic to their success almost inevitably have come to have tremendous respect and enthusiasm for the process of writing. The feeling for language that prompted Winston Churchill to refer to the English sentence as a "noble thing" is paralleled by the Rhodes Scholar who credits his success to his ability to write. The writing teacher who helps his students through the study of the thought and language behind great literature and great science may be the teacher who "takes their hearts and sets them on fire."

We admit that we have never recovered from the pleasure of our discovery that a study of the writing process can be exciting. We admit still being awed by what a man can do if he can write well. We admit keeping notebooks in which we jot down sentences or phrases that we find particularly well tailored or well expressed. We hope that a little of this fervor and excitement has crept into our textbook. Freshman English is usually not the most popular course in college, and more's the pity, for you may look long and far before you find a course that is more important. You may look long and far before you find a process or discipline more challenging than writing. You may look long and far before you find a skill that, when even reasonably mastered, is more rewarding. We hope this textbook opens the door to this pleasure and profit.

Acknowledgments

Rarely is a book a completely original document. Certainly this textbook is not. We are very much aware of the many indeterminate and now indescribable influences on us, but we hope we have not failed to credit the appropriate sources. We are aware that, unwittingly, we may have adopted some quotation or teaching device years ago, and, while using it effectively, have forgotten its source. If, here or there, a sentence or example appears that is reminiscent of a source we have not cited we can only apologize and hope that we have squared matters by providing ideas for subsequent textbook writers.

While on the subject of citations, it seems appropriate to note that we have used formal footnotes very sparingly, crediting our sources either in the text or by name, title, and date immediately following a quoted excerpt. This seeming contradiction of our own instruction results from the requirements of publishers from whom we secured permissions. In the bibliographies at the ends of chapters we have diverged from the usual practice of citing the classic and original works in the field and have cited instead materials that are interesting and ranging in the hope that students might be induced to continue their study of language and writing. When possible we have cited inexpensive editions in the hope that students might add them to their own libraries. In every possible instance we have cited collections of essays on the subject. These admirable anthologies are one of the exciting new developments in modern publishing history.

There is credit we can and must give here. We are products of the Rhetoric programs at the University of Iowa and the University of Illinois; we therefore thank John Gerber and Charles Roberts for their contributions during our formative years.

Re-examinations of classical rhetoricians, especially Aristotle, Cicero, and Quintilian, as presented by Richard Hughes, P. Albert Duhamel, John Rycenga, Joseph Schwartz, Arnold Tibbets, Donald Lemen Clark, Dudley Bailey, and Edward P. J. Corbett, have been provocative and valuable. Our first chapters reflect their concepts of "invention." To Kenneth Pike we are indebted to his concern for new "perspectives." To A. L. Becker and Paul Rodgers, and very greatly to Francis Christensen, we owe much, especially regarding paragraph and sentence "texture." The concept of the generative sentence and its effect on organization and development is our own (at meetings of the Conference on Communication and Composition and of the National Council of Teachers of English we called it "macro-rhetoric"), but we owe Josephine Miles, Wayne C. Booth, Martin Steinmann, and neurosurgeon H. Russell Meyers much for their early germinal ideas. To Dr. and Mrs. Roger Jeanloz of the Harvard Medical School, we are indebted for their suggestions about international and scientific English. Admittedly there is a traditional tinge in this textbook to our handling of problems of grammar, but we must mention our debt to Harold Whitehall and Paul Roberts, especially regarding our treatment of punctuation. To James Sledd we owe much for our study of the dictionary.

To the present and former faculty of the College of Basic Studies of Boston University we are greatly indebted, especially to Agnes Moreland, Frank Fletcher, and Aija Zarrella, and to Dean Horatio La Fauci, and we express our appreciation. To our students, past and present, we owe a vote of thanks. We would be remiss if we were not to express our appreciation to two members of the Harper & Row staff, to Chris Jennison, for his quiet encouragement and no-nonsense common sense, and to Firth Fabend, for her annoying exactness and flashes of humor that made the "hard writing: revision" of this book almost pleasant.

Finally, we extend our gratitude and affection to our wives, Jean Crosby and Barbara Estey, for their cooperation and encouragement.

H.H.C.

G.F.E.

Boston, Massachusetts

THE DYNAMICS
OF RHETORIC

I

Students should be taught, not to "write"—that is, to apply the standard principles and conventions—but, rather, to "compose"— that is, to start with an idea and let it dictate the appropriate content, organization, and diction. BERTRAND EVANS.

CHAPTER 1

THE WRITER'S OBLIGATION:
THE RHETORICAL IMPERATIVE

I know what I want to say, but I don't know how to say it. A STUDENT.

The function of rhetoric

Some ideas are simple to communicate, and once they are expressed, there is no need to elaborate on them. If a man were to say, "My name is James Adair," or "This watch weighs one ounce," he would be making a final, conclusive, definitive statement. His listener needs nothing more for complete understanding. But if the man says, "That girl has a shady past," the finality is gone. "Oh?" says his listener. "What girl? What did she do?" After such a sentence, more must be said, for if a sentence is "a group of words expressing a complete thought," the statement about the girl with the shady past is, in a sense, not a sentence at all. It is incomplete, elliptical. It leads you on. It is a tease.

Characteristically, such a sentence creates questions, and to a great extent we can predict those questions.

1. *The Sentence:* "John has a bright future."
   The Response: "He has? What makes you think so?"

2. *The Sentence:* "A scientist in Cambridge, Massachusetts, has discovered a cure for arthritis."
   The Response: "What's his name? What is the cure?"

3. *The Sentence:* "Winston Churchill's success began with an early, calamitous mistake."

3

The Response: "It did? Success in what? What was the mistake?"

4. *The Sentence:* "There is a way to end war."
The Response: "You really think so? How?"

These sentences vary in importance, complexity, breadth, and vagueness, but they are alike in that they generate questions that must be answered if their total message is to be communicated. We say that they have *predictive content;* by the way they are expressed they hint at what must be said next.

Literature exists because writers in the past had significant ideas and, anticipating what readers needed to know about them, fulfilled the obligation of explaining them. The extent of the obligation dictated the size of the composition. Edward Gibbon required six volumes to show that four factors led to the decline and fall of the Roman Empire. Karl Marx needed one volume to explain his belief that economic conditions determine history. Because other ideas need less development, we have shorter units of literature. Ralph Waldo Emerson needed thirty pages to recommend self-reliance. Montaigne needed one paragraph to justify vigorous conversation. William Faulkner needed only five words to describe the major function of the artist.

If it were possible to commission some omnipotent scientist to develop a pill that would make us all great writers, it would have three powers. It would give us the significant ideas that are at the core of all great writing. It would give us the ability to analyze those ideas and make them clear, interesting, and convincing. And it would provide us with the writing ability to fulfill that obligation. Fortunately or unfortunately, scientists have not yet provided us with pills for instant genius, and we must look elsewhere for all three powers. This is the purpose of studying rhetoric.

The source of significant ideas

When Galileo Galilei, at the age of eighteen, was bored by a lecture in the cathedral of Pisa, he began to wonder about a lamp swinging above him. He timed its arc by his own pulse beat, noticed that all the arcs, regardless of their span, took the same amount of time, and thus discovered the basic laws of harmonic motion. As Isaac Newton, at about the same age, napped under a tree in Cambridge, an apple hit him on the head, and he suddenly perceived that all particles of matter in the universe exert attraction for each other. From this observation he deduced the law of gravity. Were these developments genius or luck? They probably were a little of both, for Galileo was already wondering about the characteristics of time before he entered the cathedral, and Newton was already curious about falling bodies before he took his nap. Sir Alexander Fleming discovered penicillin by accident, but he had been seeking a way to prevent infection for several years before he noticed that a mold on one of his bacterial cultures had caused germs to disappear. Dr. Jonas Salk searched from 1939 until 1955 before he found a vaccine to prevent poliomyelitis.

THE INQUIRING MIND

As these incidents illustrate, if significant ideas occur at all, they occur to people who carry important questions in their heads. Professional researchers carry specific questions related to their special training, but most people carry questions that are equally important. All responsible people are, to some degree, concerned with general questions of philosophy. What is the nature of man? Is he basically good or evil? Can all men be educated for any activity? What is the nature of society? Does society help the individual or enslave him? What is the nature of God? Does He direct man and society? What are the functions of government, nature, science, religion, art, education, mass communication? What is good? What are the legitimate sources of knowledge? What is the Good Life? These questions preoccupy, more or less consciously, all men.

Although he may not put the idea in words, a pawnbroker indicates his perception of the nature of man when he covers his shop windows with a steel gate at night. A state makes a commentary on mankind and the value of education when it provides colleges and universities at low cost for all its young citizens. The pawnbroker and the state comment on the action level, whereas the man of ideas, the intellectual, *thinks* about these questions and comments on them in words, spoken or written.

Any factual information that contributes to man's perception of his problems is important. Observations about any man can be made important if they provide insights into philosophical questions. A high-school student notices that his friend, whose father graduated from Harvard Medical School and whose mother was a Phi Beta Kappa at Wellesley, seems to have inherited her parents' intelligence, but refuses to study at school. Why? The student to whom the question occurs may develop an important answer.

Many thinking people are upset about the state of values in our day. Time is really out of joint, they say. A planeload of ministers flies to Mississippi to force desegregation on southern schools, but in their own city there is *de facto* segregation that is supported by majority vote. Although children are taught that murder is immoral, on almost any evening they can see television heroes in war and spy programs kill dozens of human beings—and then be rewarded for their deeds at the end of the program. A bartender may earn two or three times as much as a registered nurse. Much more money is spent by Americans on cigarettes, liquor, gambling, warfare, or cosmetics than on education and health.

Whatever your stand, we can all agree that these are matters of our time about which we must ask questions. Fortunately, many of these questions are asked by serious books and by such magazines as *Atlantic Monthly, Harper's Magazine, The American Scholar, Saturday Review, Foreign Affairs, Dædalus,* and *The New Yorker.* Daily newspapers pose the same questions. In the last decades, newspapers have had headline stories about the military responsibility of the United States toward France and Germany, Korea, Hungary, and Vietnam. Particularly since World War II, we have questioned whether people in one country should be concerned about the welfare of people in other countries. In general, current events stimulate the thinking person to have significant thoughts. A man kills a policeman. Does society have the right to electrocute the murderer? One fourth of the students at an Ivy League college drop out to take time off for military duty, a trip, or a rest. Should this pause, a kind of *Wanderjahr,* become a formal part of education?

Admittedly, it would be convenient to have a pill that gives us significant ideas, but we don't. Clearly, however, one step toward such ideas is to ask questions such as those we have been discussing. There is another step.

THE OPEN MIND

After Aristotle, people believed that if you dropped a ten-pound weight at the same time you dropped a one-pound weight, the larger one would fall ten times as fast as the smaller. When Galileo reputedly dropped two cannon balls from the Leaning Tower of Pisa and proved Aristotle wrong, he was dismissed from the University by his incensed associates. For almost two thousand years blood was believed to be composed in the liver from digested foods—another Aristotelian theory. In 1628 William Harvey announced that blood in the human body circulates from and to the heart. The common trait of Galileo and Harvey—as well as of every other person who gets a significant new idea—is that they were not content with the knowledge that preceded them. They did not rebelliously reject all wisdom and custom; rather, they had open minds that questioned error, myth, and legend.

New significant ideas will come to those people whose minds are open, and the college years—almost more than any other—provide opportunities for the open mind. In science classes you will hear that man can control his environment and even breed health and wisdom into his offspring. Is this good? In social science classes you will learn that the state can inject money into the economy and avoid depressions—if the individual gives up certain freedoms. Is the gain worth the loss? In your literature, art, and philosophy classes you will meet whole new ways of looking at problems. The importance of the questions that will arise—"Is that moral?" "Who was to blame, Hamlet or his times?"—will be enhanced if your mind is open and if you take advantage of your new experiences. Your new associates, the odd professor in your psychology class, the Frenchman down the hall—"He eats snails!"—and the Minnesotan who always says what she thinks, will all raise questions, and if you keep your ears open and your eyes wide and unblinking you may find that your psychology professor makes sense and that you too like snails. You will be exposed to new sports, new places to walk, new sounds, and new tastes, and if you consider them you may find them agreeable.

THE INFORMED MIND

To be the source of significant ideas, an inquiring, open mind must also be an informed mind, for you cannot pour out of a bucket what is not in the bucket. Great scientific ideas come, obviously, to people who know a great deal about science. Great novels are written by those who have observed people and life. The importance of being well informed in one's subject field is so obvious that it should require no restatement. Yet all too often the expert in, say, nuclear physics, pontificates on, say, the economics of rice production in Southeast Asia, without first acquainting himself with the facts. Do not fall into this trap. Read. Study. Observe. Profit from your years in college. The more you know, the more ideas you will have—and the sounder your ideas will be.

• Invention: the "thing-idea-word" relationship

We cannot acquire important ideas by merely knowing how they develop. Even so, there is a good reason for knowing their nature and origin: one of the obvious ways to persuade someone to accept what we believe is to explain how we came to have the conviction ourselves. Therefore, if we hope to write clearly and convincingly, we need an insight into the source of our ideas. This branch of learning is called *epistemology*.

We will not find out what an idea is from the dictionary. Since 1755, when Samuel Johnson's *A Dictionary of the English Language* was published, people have been amused by its definition of *network:* "any thing reticulated or decussated, at equal distances, with interstices between the intersections." Obviously, a reader who did not know what a network was would not know the meaning of the words used in the definition. We would hope that in the past two hundred years lexicographers would have improved their technique and could tell us what an idea is. We are in for disappointment. In one of today's standard desk dictionaries, for instance, *idea* is defined as "any conception existing in the mind as the result of mental apprehension or activity. . . . a concept developed by the mind (if empirical, in close connection with sense perception)." This definition is of little help, but we cannot blame the dictionary. Ideas are complex, and very little is known about how they develop.

Of all the aspects of speaking and writing discussed by rhetoricians in classical and medieval times, the one they knew least about was *inventio*, the origin of an idea. Aristotle, Cicero, and Quintilian agreed that the first step was to survey the available facts, but they had little to say about what to do next. Thomas Hobbes resorted to a metaphor to describe the process. He compared the search for an idea to a hunter ranging a field in quest of a bird. He has his bow pulled, his arrow ready. Suddenly, perhaps from an unexpected part of the field, a bird flies up, and the hunter recognizes it as the quarry he seeks.

This analogy suggests much that is included in modern epistemological theory. The fact that the hunter is in the field at all suggests that he has a "felt need," the state of mind conducive to receiving an idea. The fact that he has the right bow and the right arrow suggests an adequate intelligence. That he is in a flat, grassy field, the natural habitat of the pheasant he is pursuing, suggests that he has assembled the proper facts about his prey. But the analogy leaves a great deal unexplained.

A profitable approach to finding out how ideas develop began with Aristotle and has been followed by modern semanticists I. A. Richards, Leonard Bloomfield, Thurman Arnold, Wendell Johnson, and Kenneth Burke. The process that interested them is *abstraction*, or what some semanticists call the "thing-idea-word" relationship. All animals experience "things." By sight, taste, touch, hearing, and smell, we perceive objects to which we react. We walk across our lawn and bump into a tall something, slender at the bottom but big at the top. In our kitchen, we put a hand out to pick up an object. It has been on top of something that is glowing red. The object is in a state we cannot endure, and we quickly withdraw our hand, our fingers stinging in pain.

Like all animals, we get "thing-ideas" almost instinctively. We learn to avoid a bump on the head by walking around anything large in front of us. When we see something that has once burned our fingers, we realize we should not touch it again. An idea of this sort is simply a relationship: (That particular something) plus (touch) equals (hurt).

There are *hurt* ideas; there are *pleasure* ideas. A small child learns very early that if she takes a thing out of another thing (the stopper out of her mother's perfume bottle), she gets a smell that she likes, pleasure. Unless she spills the perfume and gets spanked, all her ideas about perfume are pleasure ideas. The child gets many pleasure ideas, about food that satisfies its stomach, the blanket that keeps out the cold, even the bandage and caress that seem to make a wound feel better.

As long as we stay on the thing-idea level, we are demonstrating animal mentality. Man, however, is not content to stay on this level, and he enters the world of verbal abstraction. Although we say that "experience is the best teacher," that is, we must bump into a tree ourselves to learn our lesson, we spend millions of dollars and man-hours each year on education because we believe we can convey ideas effectively with language. We tell a child to watch out for the tree or not to touch the pan because it is hot. We can do this because the words *tree, pan, hot,* and *"Don't touch!"* conjure up more or less the same picture in the mind of the mother and the child. An idea to a human being, therefore, is not just a thing-idea relationship. More often, there is a thing-idea-word relationship.

Since the complexity of the ideas we can get varies greatly, the language used to express the ideas must also vary. To understand the different patterns of language, we must understand the process of abstraction and the classes of statements that express various kinds of ideas. As a verb, *abstract* means "to separate as an idea either a quality or an attribute." You may have noticed that, at certain times, water, pans, and a stove have something in common: when you touch them, you get hurt. This quality, you learn, is called "heat." Something possessing the quality is called "hot." You now have a method of communicating the concept. Without ever going near one, you can understand that a volcano also gets "hot." Although the fabulous gryphon never existed, we can shudder at the thought that its fiery breath was very "hot" indeed.

To be sure that you understand the process of abstraction, identify the common qualities or attributes in each of the following groups.

1. Grand Canyon, Cassius Clay, *Hamlet,* a Rolls-Royce

2. Grand Canyon, Elizabeth Taylor, a seascape, a male cardinal

3. Cassius Clay, a lion, the Golden Gate Bridge, black coffee

4. a Rolls-Royce, a Republican banker, a simple black dress worn with pearls, a home in Evanston, Illinois; Palo Alto, California; Westport, Connecticut; or Wellesley, Massachusetts

5. Hamlet, a teen-ager, traffic in Paris, a blob of mercury

Depending upon your experience, taste, and imagination, there will be some abstractions apparent to you that would be similar to the abstractions of other readers. The first list suggests *superiority;* all are tops in their field. The second list suggests *beauty;* the third, *strength;* the fourth, but less definitely, *wealthy conservatism.* The fifth list would suggest unpredictability to many people. Hamlet could not make up his mind, and many adults think that teen-agers share this quality; Paris traffic, even to those who have only read about the city, is maddeningly confusing. Mercury flows every which way; the word *mercurial,* which means "flighty, fickle, changeable, unpredictable," touches upon this abstraction.

Several objects may have one abstract quality in common, but one object may have many abstract qualities. A peach, for instance, has sweetness, juiciness, fuzziness, ripeness, and roundness.

Although we have succeeded only in saying that abstractions pop out at us without our really knowing how, we can see that they appear to us in certain patterns.

Kinds of ideas

Ideas fall into the following categories: *observations, classifications, generalizations, judgments,* and *causal relationships.*

OBSERVATIONS

The first class of idea might be called no idea at all, since it requires so little mental activity. The *observation* is simply a statement of what has happened. The writer makes no comment about the source of the observation; he may have derived it from his own sensory perceptions, or he may have learned it from some other source. It may be true or false; if it is true—that is, if it can be verified by some acceptable standard and if people generally agree with it—it legitimately is called a *fact*. The following sentences are observations.

1. Lew Alcindor played basketball for an eastern high school before he enrolled at U.C.L.A.

2. I burned my finger.

3. Antoine Lavoisier was admitted to the French Academy of Sciences in 1768.

4. The amino-acid analysis revealed a trace of an amino sugar.

The observation takes hardly any abstraction. It is definitive. Rather than starting a dialogue, rather than being generative, the observation tends to be used to explain and support parts of the more complex types of ideas.

CLASSIFICATIONS

Suppose we say, "John F. Kennedy was a man." What we have said in the technical language of a logician is that "The thing called 'John F. Kennedy' is included in the class of things called 'man.'" Suppose we say, "Los Angeles and San Francisco are cities in California." We have placed the two in a class, that is, "cities in the state of California."

Whenever we "label" something, we classify it. When we say, "The automobile is a classic Pierce Arrow," we have classified it. If we say, "That crooked politician should be impeached," we have expressed the following two classifications.

1. That politician is in the class of people called "crooked."

2. He is a member of the class of people who should be impeached.

Often these labels are matters of opinion or judgment, which will be discussed later, but the strict classification is communicated with relative ease. All we need to do to be understood is to be sure that our audience understands and agrees with the definition of the class. In the sentences above, our audience must agree with us about the meaning of *John F. Kennedy, man, cities, California, crooked,* and *impeached.* The total communication required is really only a retracing of the thinking process by which we derived the idea. We decided upon the abstract qualities of the class, and we observed or stated that the specific example fitted the class.

Often when we classify we do not communicate, because there

may be less agreement about the class than we think. Take the simple statement, "Pete is an adult." It seems clear enough, but is it? On Friday night, Pete goes to the movies. Since he is sixteen, he pays an adult price for his ticket. On Saturday, the picture changes, and he goes again. Outside the theater he sees a huge poster with a half-naked girl and an "Adults Only" label on it. Confidently he lays down his adult fee, but the ticket seller stops him.

"Are you eighteen?" she asks.

Pete realizes that on Friday he was an adult, but on Saturday he is not.

This simple example illustrates that when we use a sentence containing a classification we have an obligation to define our terms. You can imagine the responsibility we assume when we use amorphous labels or classes like liberal, conservative, democratic, and so on.

GENERALIZATION

In the sentence, "The water is hot," the definite article *the* indicates that we mean some specific water, the water in a certain tea kettle, perhaps. We have made an observation. If we were to say simply, "Water is hot," we would be implying that we mean all water, even though we did not say it in so many words. Whenever we state that some idea is true of a class of things, we are making a *generalization.*

1. Newspapers print news.

2. Americans are materialistic.

3. Men are better drivers than women.

4. Apples are sweet.

5. Salt is a compound of nitrogen and glycerin.

6. Reading is good for the mind.

These six statements are generalizations. They also all contain classifications. Newspapers are included in the class of things that print news. Americans are included in the class of things that are materialistic, and so on. But, because they assert what is claimed to be true about a group, they are also generalizations.

You may have noticed that the fifth statement is not true. Salt is a compound of sodium and chloride. The false sentence was included to demonstrate that a statement can be either true or false and still be a generalization.

In the generalizations above, since no exceptions are mentioned, the word *all* is implied at the beginning of each sentence; truly or falsely, the last sentence, for instance, says that (all) reading is good for the mind.

We can, in addition, make generalizations about *one* object or phenomenon by making an assertion about all the actions or qualities of one thing.

1. John is dependable.

2. That dog does not bite.

3. The sun rises in the east.

All of these statements are classifications, but since they are also generalizations the word *always* is implied: the sentences seem to say that John is *always* dependable, that the dog *never* bites, and—whether it is true or not—that the sun *always* rises in the east. Unless a *qualification*, like "some" for the first kind of generalization and "usually" for the second kind, is used, there are no exceptions admitted.

Now that we are reminded what a generalization is, let us see how we come to have them. Ideally, we would make a generalization about a group only when we have observed every member of the group. We could have a really dependable belief about all newspapers only if we had seen *all* of them; the same is true about Americans, men, apples, salt, and reading. We can make a generalization about John, that dog, or the sun only if we have observed them under every relevant circumstance.

Since this total experience is patently impossible, human beings have come to accept some generalizations based on only a sample of occurrences. Although we do not read every newspaper, in the course of our lives most of us do see enough newspapers to be able to make some general observations about them. We could not generalize about their quality, their political bias, their editorial or advertising policy, because in all of these aspects of newspapers we have seen contradictions, but we can say that all newspapers print something we have come to call "news."

We can make reliable generalizations only if the following requirements have been met.

1. We have sampled enough of the group about which we generalize. This number, of course, varies.

2. We have found no contradictions.

3. The condition in the generalization can be determined according to the terms implied by the generalization.

By now the concept of predictive consequence may be beginning to emerge. A person who writes a sentence containing a classification unavoidably assumes the obligation of showing how the classification is justified. Now we can see that the person who writes a generalization assumes an obligation to show how the generalization is appropriate. In other words, he must fulfill the predictive consequence of his generalization by showing how the generalization fits the three requirements just listed.

JUDGMENT

The definition of the next kind of idea is indistinct. In the sentence "Apples are sweet," in addition to the labeling and classification, the writer made a *judgment*. The word *sweet* is inexact; the writer had to decide whether apples fit the standard or not.

Suppose, as we idly observe two boys mowing lawns, we notice not only that one boy is moving much more rapidly than the other, but that his mowing is neater. We decide that his mower, the one powered by a small engine, is better than the other, powered only by the muscular legs of the boy. This thought is a *judgment*. All judgments demand a standard or a measuring device. In judging the two mowers, we abstracted out the quality of "goodness" and said, perhaps too hastily, that one is better than the other. Reflecting again, we realize that what we thought of as goodness was based on two standards, speed and neatness. In these two respects, which might add up to the abstraction of "effectiveness," the power mower is definitely to be preferred. But for the general judgment of "better," the mower must be superior in all respects. What about cost? What about durability? We know that power mowers, which often cost over a hundred dollars, have a distressing habit of wearing out in about three years; a hand mower will easily last for ten. These convictions are based on observations of some specific incidents. We have seen advertisements in the newspaper that indicated prices of both types of mowers, and we remember the length of time our family power mower lasted. To make the broad judgment of "better," we must consider all the criteria.

In the sentence "This pan is hot," the abstraction is relatively basic, but the semantics is not. We can easily understand the relationship between the two concepts: something included in the class of things called "pan" is included in the class of things called "hot." What is meant by "pan"? Which pan? What kind of pan? Unless the statement is accompanied by a gesture to indicate "this" pan or "that" pan, your audience will be confused. And what is meant by "hot"? A hot day, hot spices, hot coffee, and a hot pan all suggest quite different temperatures. What we are now talking about is the kind of judgment in which both the abstraction process and the language can be confusing.

A man asks a waiter if the coffee is hot.

"Yes, sir, it is hot."

The customer puts the cup to his lips, takes a sip, and burns his lips. "It is not hot," he rages, "it's boiling!" Sitting at a table next to this customer is another customer who is quite mystified. He has a cast-iron tasting apparatus, and he really likes his coffee "hot." He finds the coffee "hot" to be sure, but just right.

Judgments differ. Elizabeth Taylor is beautiful, or disgusting? (How many times has she been married?) The Grand Canyon is magnificent, or useless? (It doesn't grow one ear of corn!) Ronald Reagan is completely unacceptable. Richard Nixon is a better candidate than Lyndon B. Johnson. A person can believe in Christianity, but question Roman Catholicism. He can call Mary a "lovable" person and John a "likable" one.

If you become a literary critic (or an English major) you may write, "Ernest Hemingway was America's greatest novelist of the twentieth century." Or you may write, "Ernest Hemingway was highly overrated." Whatever you become, you will make such judgments as, "The Cadillac is the best car; I think we should buy one." Or "The Cadillac is a terrible car; I would never buy one." Whichever of these judgments you make, you can predict your defense of it, for to have made the judgment you should have asked yourself:

1. What is the standard of judgment?

2. Does the specific case, example, or instance fit the standard?

3. Is the judgment reasonable?

Your argument undoubtedly would retrace the mental path you took to arrive at the judgment and the path would be along the lines suggested by these tests.

CAUSAL RELATIONSHIP

The final class of idea is one that, according to some historians, has been particularly important to Western civilization. When we say that B is the result of A, we have indicated a *causal relationship*. We have mentioned how touching something hot causes pain and how running into a tree causes a different kind of pain. Clapping your hands makes a noise. Usually these relationships can be explained by physical or chemical laws. Heat burns or oxidizes tissue, which irritates nerve endings, which in turn causes a pain response in the brain. Clapping your hands causes violently oscillating sound waves that vibrate your ear drums, which ac-

tivate nerve ganglia and send messages to the brain where they are translated into sound.

Other causal relationships are not so easy to explain. A new football coach is hired by your college, and the school starts winning more
games. Is he the cause, or did the school suddenly start getting better
material? Or did other schools field poorer teams?

A causal relationship between A and B, or—using technical
terms—between an antecedent and a consequence, would be established
if the following points could be proved.

1. Every time A was present, B happened.

2. When A was not present, B did not happen.

3. B did not happen when other events besides A were present.

4. The reason B took place when A was present is explainable by
   some natural law, i.e., gravity or a chemical process. In the absence of natural law, some other explanation, logical or psychological, should be possible.

Causal relationship is one of the most complex of ideas, and the burden
of proof is often heavy for the writer.

The dynamics of ideas

However significant ideas are derived, they have one characteristic that is all important in the study of rhetoric. They start a dialogue.
In conversation, when a speaker comments that "John has a bright future,"
he is guided in his next comments by the questions of his companion:
"He has? What makes you think so?" The conversation proceeds alternately
between speaker and audience. When the speaker does not make a point
clear, he is stopped: "Wait a minute. What do you mean?" If the speaker
fails to prove an assertion, his audience may interrupt: "Hold on. I do
not agree. I happen to know something to dispute your point." The speaker
must then refute his companion's argument and buttress his own point
with further evidence.

The writer has no such recourse. He must look out at his unseen
audience of one or one million and presuppose what its questions will be.
He must decide what assertions need proof, what terms need clarifying.
He has no puzzled expression, no smile, no reaction of any sort to guide
him. Fortunately, however, he does not always have to guess. Most ideas
fit into certain categories, and by their nature these categories give the

writer clues about what he must say to express them. The definitive sentence is concrete, verifiable, and exact; it completes an idea. After it is expressed, the reader usually has no question to ask. In contrast, the sentence that expresses the broader, more complex idea is almost invariably a leading sentence. Depending upon the category of which it is a member, it predicts what questions a reader would ask if he had the opportunity.

The notion that a writer turns to inanimate words on a page for instruction about what he must subsequently write may seem fanciful, but ideas do have their own natural dynamism, and a writer becomes sensitive to it. If every idea had a different kind of predictive content, the writer would be at a loss, but fortunately they do not; ideas fall into certain classes, and each member of the class makes approximately the same demands as any other member. The sentences that start a dialogue may appear as the basic ideas of books, essays, and paragraphs, or they may appear within paragraphs. Because they stimulate questions, we call them *generative sentences.* When we analyze the generative sentence that is the central message of our whole communication, the questions arise that will be the basis for our organization. When we answer those questions, we will get generative sentences of a level lower than our main sentence, and we will see what information we need within paragraphs. A thorough analysis of generative sentences at all levels will help us select appropriate sentence and language patterns. Sentences are generative usually because of their nature, and our task will be to learn what development, organization, and language are required by each type of idea.

We must also remember that the situation in which the sentence is uttered is directive. Surely, you might think, merely to tell your name and address would be definitive. No conversation would start. Usually this is true, but there are occasions when even this statement is generative and inevitably sets up questions. Take the sentence, "My name is Auchinauchie." The student who has this name calls it a "conversation piece." He says, "If I write it, I'm asked how to pronounce it. (It is 'o-HINE-a-hee.') If I pronounce it, I have to spell it." This circumstance is a capsule illustration of the predictive content of an idea. The instant you utter some statements, you take on a responsibility—or obligation—you must fulfill. In Auchinauchie's case, the utterance itself sets up the obligation. But suppose a college freshman is asked where her home is, and she answers, "Seattle, Washington." If she is a student at the University of Washington, she does not start a dialogue, but if she is attending the University of Alabama, she is immediately asked, "Why did you come way down here to school?" In this case, the situation, not the utterance, provided the predictive content.

What we are looking for in our study of rhetoric is a formula. We want to be able to say that, if we have a particular writing task, we will use a certain type of development, organization, and expression. If we have another kind of an idea to communicate, we will use the development, organization, and expression appropriate to that idea. We are looking for the type of equation that is symbolized by the logician's horseshoe, $\supset$, which means, "If you have one thing, you must have another." $P \supset q$ means "If you have p, you must have q." "Clouds $\supset$ rain" means "If there are clouds, there will be rain." "Touch me $\supset$ I will scream," means "If you touch me, I will scream." What we are looking for in our study of rhetoric is this equation:

$$\text{Idea} \supset \text{Technique}$$

The equation would be translated, "If you wish to express this idea clearly and convincingly, you use this technique." This equation must be based on an understanding of the origin, nature, and category of generative ideas.

The double responsibility of people with ideas

We have been discussing the idea that when we work with complex thoughts we inevitably assume a responsibility. Every generative utterance thus contains a kind of prediction; it foreshadows what probably will be forthcoming in subsequent lines and pages. The generative sentence looks forward in the sense that it makes this prediction, but it also looks backward in that it is a kind of written guarantee that in the past the writer has gone through certain processes of thinking.

Whenever you write a complex or general "generative" sentence, you have taken on two responsibilities: first, you should have had certain experiences and thoughts before you were justified in writing the sentence; and, second, whenever you write such a sentence you must provide all the information, organized and expressed properly, necessary to make your sentence clear and convincing. This double responsibility we call the *rhetorical imperative*.

The guarantee you have made when you write an observation, classification, generalization, judgment, or causal relationship is that you have had the experiences, found the evidence, and done the thinking implicit in the statement. This guarantee is in the form of an *implied logical history*. Each of your ideas must have a history that will stand scrutiny. If a person says, for instance, "I like *Hamlet*," he implies that he has read or seen the play and assigned it to the class of things that he likes. Under this kind of scrutiny we realize that we are limited in the generalizations and judgments we can make. We can make very few about large groups, because we will rarely have sufficient samples. Who could say, for instance, that "X makes the best coffee in town?"

About judgments we must be careful, especially if they involve a superlative. Seldom can we fulfill the obligation that they place upon us. Only with great care can we decide that something is "first" or "best." The following claims were taken at random from a magazine.

1. "X is the best whiskey America has to offer." (Has the advertiser tasted all the whiskey in America? We would hope not.)

2. "X aircraft is the best way yet to find new executives." (Has the claimant tried all ways?)

3. "Great Smoky is the most beautiful National Park." (How is this quality measured?)

4. "X is the world's finest cigarette." (Set aside the advertiser's enthusiasm. How do you measure "finest"? Has the advertiser smoked all of the world's cigarettes—or even a sufficient portion of them?)

If you were the author of these assertions, would you like to answer the questions that would arise if your audience could talk back to you?

Repeatedly in the study of rhetoric we are confronted with evidence that communication requires responsibility. Every man is entitled to his opinion, but we can justifiably feel uncomfortable when a man's opinion is not based on careful consideration and research. When a man says, "Socialized medicine has not worked in England," he is entitled to his opinion, but his listeners have the right to downgrade their evaluation of it if he has not done the mental homework necessary to support it. We respect the political commentator or the literary critic who does the research to back up his sweeping assertions, but we have little respect for the newscaster who makes such statements as "Joe and Josie Celebrity are pffffft" or "Have you noticed that the little dancer at the Copacobunco has needle marks on her thigh?" The gossip columnist is hinting that the girl is a narcotics addict, whereas she may be a diabetic taking insulin regularly.

After being exposed to all these warnings about the seriousness of thought, its responsibility, and the dangers of error, you may come to question most of your beliefs. This is good. As Socrates said long ago, the unexamined life is not worth living. More to the point, many savants define a good education as the process of coming to know a great deal

She unexamined life is not worth living.

and of learning the limits of that knowledge. You should question extravagant claims involving terms like "the best" and "the first" and "the finest." You should question any ideas based on a priori evidence—that is, premises or basic beliefs that are supposed to be self-evident. A political conservative may think it self-evident that it is better for an individual to settle his own problems than for the state to do it for him, whereas the liberal may be equally sure it is self-evident that it is better for a group of people to work together to get a job done.

The principles discussed in this chapter have limitations. They work in the realm of natural science, where all evidence is empirical—that is, verifiable by measurements observable through sense perceptions. They work rather less well, however, in the field of human relations, because events cannot be exactly duplicated to check any conclusion we have about them, and because human beings, involved as they are in their emotions, their limited knowledge, and the effects of their government, are unpredictable. In matters of taste in art and literature, Horace's dictum *de gustibus non disputandum est* (concerning taste there is no arguing) affirms that standards are based on emotions and impressions. The principles discussed in this chapter must therefore be very carefully applied in the realm of cultural matters.

In the field of religion there is justifiable argument about whether these principles work at all. The scientist may look at natural phenomena and deduce that there is a good God, as the eighteenth-century deists did when they looked at "the smoothly-running universe" and inferred that there must indeed be a "Maker." A social scientist may look at a number of civilizations and, observing that almost all have believed in a Supreme Being of some sort, may accept this as proof positive that He exists, a special reversal of Descartes' *Cogito, ergo sum* that might be stated, "They think He is; therefore He is." A theologian who believes that reason and faith are based on different types of thought might feel that one's perceptions about God should be based on faith, not reason. He might look upon the scientific religious arguments of the deist and the anthropologist as irrelevant and even arrogant.

This is not to say that any one of these groups is wrong. The problem, rather, is to make sure we know what game we are playing before we decide on the rules. Playing basketball with lacrosse regulations is ridiculous. Nevertheless, in our modern world, so oriented toward material, empirical thinking, we are inclined to demand of the social scientist that his conclusions about people and society be as infallible as those of the chemist about sodium chloride, forgetting that the social scientist usually deals with trends and tendencies, which are not so amenable to analysis as NaCl. Likewise we cannot expect the man of religion to present scientifically verifiable proof that God exists and that He would have us run our world in exactly such and such a way.

All these considerations about thinking have a bearing on how we communicate ideas. When we talk about the phenomena of natural science, we use the terms "laws" and "certainties." When we are in the realm of the sociologists, however, we are apt to talk about exceptions, limitations, and possibilities, and to qualify our statements with such terms as *some, many, usually,* and *often.* Regarding the arts, our enthusiasm undoubtedly will lead us to be just as positive as in our judgments about science, but we must be aware that we are basing our opinions on taste and other subjective criteria that are difficult to define and often quite uncommunicable. Our religious convictions are usually based not on pure reason, but on faith and on the testimony of authorities acceptable only to members of the same persuasion.

Thus, the predictive content of our ideas, besides giving us a responsibility, sometimes gives us pause. When we see what we must do to convince others, we may decide we have gone too far in our conclusions. We may work backward. We may revise our beliefs, and the qualifications we insert may permit us to discharge our responsibility more thoroughly. For this reason we can understand what Francis Bacon meant when he said "writing makes an exact man."

Projects

1. As a study guide, prepare a one-page outline of this chapter. Be sure to include a summary of the thing-idea-word relationship, the types and tests of ideas, and a brief explanation of the implied logical history of each type of idea. Use this guide as a checklist for the projects listed below.

2. Comment on the amount of mental energy implied by the following verbs. Rearrange the list, putting the words in order according to the amount of thinking required. Begin with the word requiring the least amount.

notice	assume
observe	hypothesize
discern	judge
perceive	suppose
interpret	believe
abstract	

3. Using your dictionary, ascertain the degree of certainty and confidence expressed by the following terms. (For instance, "notion," de-

fined as "a more or less general, vague, or imperfect conception or idea of something," expresses relatively little certainty.)

canon	I know
law	I believe
theory	opinion
principle	conviction
perception	knowledge
apprehension	faith
cognition	assumption
recognition	error
notice (verb)	common sense
note (verb)	obiter dictum
assertion	

4. Using terms discussed in this chapter, define the following expressions. (For instance, "a fact is the statement of an idea which has been verified. It can be a direct observation, a classification, a generalization, or a judgment.")

theory	heresy
notion	orthodoxy
assertion	hypothesis
thought	protocol
faith	manifest
reason	a priori evidence
assumption	

5. Classify the following statements according to whether they are observation, classification, judgment, generalization, or causation.

a. He arrived at ten o'clock.

b. Romney is a Latter-day Saint.

c. Charles II (1630–1685) of England had no legitimate offspring, but he did have a number of illegitimate children by his various mistresses.

d. If you hire more employees, they'll find work that requires still more employees. (Parkinson's Law)

e. If a Latin word begins with *p,* often its English equivalent begins with *f;* for instance, *piscis* means "fish," and *pes* means "foot."

6. Infer the logical history of the following ideas. Tell what facts were necessary and how the facts might have been assembled; explain what process of thought took place; and tell what probably could be some convincing verification. Indicate the training and experience necessary for the maker of the statement. Indicate how and on what basis the terms are defined.

a. I'm going to vote against Bilgewater.

b. Vote for Bilgewater.

   c. Lysergic acid diethylamide (LSD), unless used under the supervision of a qualified medical authority, is exceedingly dangerous.

   d. Excessive smoking seems to be a cause of lung cancer.

   e. "Stanford, Michigan, and Harvard, in that order, have the three most effective departments of psychology in the United States." *Time Magazine*.

   f. Since "in a democracy, dress and grooming are dictated by good taste and pride in one's appearance" and since "a child's behavior is most often a reflection of the way he dresses," a student's hair must not be so long [that] it touches his eyes, ears, or shirt collar." Paraphrased from a Pennsylvania high-school handbook.

   g. I love Lucy.

   h. God is dead.

   i. I want to marry Lucy.

   j. I want to be a doctor.

   k. My son wants to be a doctor.

   l. Robert Frost is a better poet than John Donne.

   m. John's dad is rich.

7. Indicate the way the following ideas could be tested for causal relationship. If appropriate after your analysis, rephrase each into a form you think might be more sound.

   a. Infectious mononucleosis is caused by kissing.

   b. Candy and gum cause cavities in teeth.

   c. Spontaneous combustion causes fires.

   d. Absentee ownership of stores in a racial ghetto leads to tension.

   e. Drinking a glass of water cures hiccoughs.

   f. If Americans move their troops out of that country, either the Red Chinese or the Russians will move in.

   g. Bad money chases good money out of circulation. (Gresham's Law)

   h. Decreasing the volume of a gas increases its pressure. (Boyle's Law)

8. Infer the training and experience a speaker should have for the following testimony to be trustworthy.

   a. Mother, I want to buy a teeny, weeny bikini. Everyone, simply everyone, is wearing one these days.

   b. Red China is not on the verge of revolution, but there is evidence of strain and doubt.

   c. Isometric exercises will build your muscles.

   d. Micro-cal will reduce your weight safely.

   e. Adams is the right man for governor.

   f. Testimony at the Salem witch trials was mostly false.

9. Listed below are some myths and superstitions that, if not dis-

credited, are at least questioned. Infer what must have happened to cause them
to be originally accepted and then to lose favor.

  a. Toads cause warts.
  b. The Aryan will conquer the world.
  c. Jesse Owens, the Negro track star who distressed Adolf Hitler
     during the 1936 Olympics by winning the 100-meter dash, the
     200-meter dash, and the broad jump, was a great athlete because
     he had an extra bone in each toe.
  d. People speak different languages because God did not want
     people to build the Tower of Babel so high they could reach heaven.
     He therefore caused the builders to speak different languages so
     they could not discuss the construction.
  e. Phlogiston is released during combustion.
  f. The sun rises in the east.
  g. An echo is an answering voice.
  h. Thunder is caused by Mars, the war god, driving his chariot
     across the sky.
  i. New York City is the largest city in the world.
  j. The Titan Prometheus molded a clay figure in the image of the
     gods and breathed life into him; thus began Man.
  k. Most Norse gods were good and kindly, but one, named Loki, was
     very mischievous and wicked. For a joke, he taught man to sin,
     and man learned quickly.
  l. George Washington cut down a cherry tree and proved his truth-
     fulness by admitting that he had done so.

10. Theme topics

Write a 500-word theme in which you trace the origin of an idea you
hold. For example:

  a. My high school produces (good) (bad) college students (athletes).
  b. Being a member of the Boy Scouts (or similar organization) was
     fun, but the experience means little (or much) later.
  c. There is a God.
  d. I generally approve of the Republican (or Democratic, or liberal,
     or conservative) point of view.

List all the misconceptions, superstitions, myths, and false beliefs you
can. Then write a 500–750 word theme in which you classify these myths and
generalize about how myths originate.

Select a stranger—perhaps a salesclerk, a waitress, a dean, or a professor—and observe him briefly. Then, at a place from which you cannot see your
subject, list everything you know about him. Now separate what you have
said into fact (verifiable by any other observer), inference (perhaps based on
observation and the entire situation and your previous experience), and judgment. Write a 200-word summary of your conclusions.

Repeat the exercise, either with the same subject or with a different one, after considering your total observation as analyzed above. Has your ability to perceive changed in any way?

Further reading

BENNETT, ARNOLD. "Seeing Life," *Writer to Writer*, ed. FLOYD C. WATKINS and KARL F. KNIGHT. Boston: Houghton Mifflin, 1966, pp. 93–105.

BRUNER, JEROME S., GOODNOW, JACQUELINE J., and AUSTIN, GEORGE A. "Categories," *A Study of Thinking*. New York: John Wiley, 1956.

FOGARTY, DANIEL, S.J. *Roots for a New Rhetoric*. New York: Teachers College, Columbia University, 1959. (See especially "I. A. Richards' Theory," pp. 28–55, and "The General Semantics Theory," pp. 88–115.)

MILL, JOHN STUART. "Of the Four Methods of Experimental Inquiry," *Essays on Rhetoric*, ed. DUDLEY BAILEY. New York and London: Oxford University Press, 1965, pp. 173–192.

RUBY, LIONEL. "Are All Generalizations False?," *The Art of Making Sense*. Philadelphia: Lippincott, 1954.

CHAPTER 2

THE CONTROLLING CONCEPT: PURPOSE

A speech has two parts. You must state your thesis, and you must prove it.
ARISTOTLE.

Most of the writing in serious magazines, in military, professional, political, scientific, and literary reports, in college term papers, and in all other forms of nonfiction prose is composed of a mixture of definitive and generative sentences. Each composition has at its core a generative sentence that is the broadest or most complex idea in the work. It is this sentence that gives unity and purpose to the total effort.

    That prose literature has unity is easily seen by examining almost any book or magazine article. Thomas Macaulay, in *The History of England from the Accession of James II* (1849–1861), does not merely present a vivid and detailed history of England from the reign of James II to the death of William III; he tries to prove that England under the influence of a Whig government and the Protestant religion was the best of all possible worlds. Another famous work of history, Frederick Jackson Turner's speech at the American Historical Association's meeting in Chicago in 1893, "The Significance of the Frontier in American History," set out to prove that America is the product of a series of developments accompanying the new type of frontier.

    Almost invariably the central idea is expressly stated. The monu-

26

mental *Main Currents in American Thought,* by Vernon L. Parrington, contains in its introduction this sentence:

> I have undertaken to give some account of the genesis and development in American letters of certain germinal ideas that have come to be reckoned traditionally American—how they came into being here, how they were exposed, and what influence they have exerted in determining the form and scope of our characteristic ideals and institutions.

This is Professor Parrington's purpose statement; it controls the entire work. The work is divided into three volumes, and each volume is broken into books. Part One of the first book in Volume I is called "The Puritan Heritage." Preceding it is a brief introduction that ends with the book's thesis or generative statement: "The Puritan was a contribution of the old world, created by the rugged idealism of the English Reformation; the Yankee was a product of native conditions, created by practical economics."

Thorstein Veblen's *The Theory of the Leisure Class* (1899) attempts to prove that the leisure class represents a continuing maladjustment of modern institutions that causes a reversion to an archaic scheme of life. He expresses this idea in a thesis sentence in the first chapter of his work.

Shorter prose literature also has the characteristic of stating the central idea. Francis Bacon's essay "Of Studies" begins, "Studies serve for delight, for ornament, and for ability," thus giving the reader cause to anticipate three reasons why study is valuable. "The Method of Scientific Investigation," an essay by Thomas Henry Huxley, contains in its introduction the sentence, "The method of scientific investigation is nothing but the expression of the necessary mode of working of the human mind"; the rest of the essay describes the scientific method and shows why the human mind must use the method to arrive at sound ideas. In an article in the *Saturday Evening Post* (July 13, 1957), a testy English baron, Lord Conesford, put his thesis in his title, "You Americans Are Murdering the Language," and you can anticipate what followed. In a *New Yorker* article (December 16, 1950), John Hersey wrote, "This conference caused frightful headlines all over the world about the possible use of the atomic bomb in Korea and China, and it also provided a hair-raising example of how bad news can be manufactured." Hersey's statement is another example of the generative sentence that predicts and obligates the rest of the article.

This characteristic of good writing is known to skilled readers. According to Mortimer Adler and almost every other reading expert, the first requirement of effective reading is that you must be able to put in a single sentence the central message or thesis of the material you are reading. Very often, when skilled students read a book, they underline certain passages. This is a good technique—if the proper sections are selected. Too often, students underline only the sections they find interesting. The single sentence that should be underlined is the thesis or purpose statement of the book, its generative sentence. Almost every author, either in the introduction, the first chapter, or the final chapter, sums up his central idea. When you locate the sentence you aid comprehension. Take, for instance, the very difficult *Education of Henry Adams*. Many readers start out with Chapter 1; instead, they should begin with the preface, for in it are found these two sentences: "Except in the abandoned sphere of dead languages, no one has discussed what part of education has, in his personal experience, turned out to be useful, and what not. This volume attempts to discuss it." From these sentences the reader has a frame on which to hang all subsequent material. Reviewers frequently have misunderstood Adams's purpose; in spite of its title, they have perceived his book to be an autobiography and have criticized it because it makes no reference to such personal matters as his marriage and the suicide of his wife.

As Walter Pater has said, one of the delights of reading worthwhile prose is to detect the point of the composition and then to follow an orderly mind through the content that must follow. If the thesis is not established and the content does not fulfill its obligation, we do not have effective, valuable writing.

Types of purpose indicators

When Aristotle commented that every speech has a point at which a speaker announces his central idea, he did not necessarily mean that there is only one way of doing it. Actually there are four general ways that the speaker, or writer, may indicate his purpose. He may do so with a thesis statement, a statement of purpose, a controlling question, or by announcing his topic.

THE THESIS STATEMENT

An extended communication usually has somewhere a sentence that summarizes the main idea the writer wishes to convey. Very often it is found at the end of the introduction, and very often it is restated in the conclusion. This sentence is called the "thesis statement" or, simply, "the thesis." The following sentences are famous thesis statements.

The man who has in full, heaped and rounded measures all these splendid qualifications is the present grand and gallant leader of the Republican party . . . James G. Blaine. NOMINATING SPEECH BY ROBERT G. INGERSOLL, 1876.

It is the English-speaking race that has moulded the destiny of this continent; and the Puritan influence is the strongest influence that has acted upon it. GEORGE WILLIAM CURTIS, "THE PURITAN PRINCIPLE: LIBERTY UNDER THE LAW," 1876.

To those of my race who depend upon bettering their condition in a foreign land, or who underestimate the importance of cultivating friendly relations with the Southern white man, who is their next-door neighbor, I would say: "Cast down your bucket where you are"—cast it down in making friends in every manly way of all the people of all races by whom we are surrounded. BOOKER T. WASHINGTON, "ADDRESS AT THE OPENING OF THE ATLANTA EXPOSITION," 1895.

I ask that the Congress declare that since the unprovoked and dastardly attack by Japan on Sunday, December seventh, a state of war has existed between the United States and the Japanese Empire. FRANKLIN D. ROOSEVELT, "WAR MESSAGE TO CONGRESS," 1941.

The thesis statement is the indicator used most often. A speaker often shows its importance by emphasizing it in volume, inflection, or rate. A writer does not have this opportunity, but by positioning it near the end of the introduction and by obviously leading up to it, he can often guarantee that it will be recognized by the reader.

THE STATEMENT OF PURPOSE

Occasionally a writer feels the need to make absolutely sure that his audience catches his purpose. Scholarly articles in professional journals often begin, "It is my purpose in this article to prove that . . ." and the writer finishes the sentence with his thesis. Examples include:

It is the purpose of this paper to point out that a critical theory to support a new approach has been available since 1944. . . . JOHN DENNIS HURRELL, *College English*, MAY, 1965.

It will be the purpose of this survey to report several representative studies in the following areas: using language in life; teaching grammar and usage; teaching writing, speaking and listening; and integrating the communication skills. OSCAR M. HAUGH, *Education*, MARCH, 1952.

In this paper we report that cholesterol is metabolized by
Digitalis purpurea to several products, among them preg-
nenolone.   E. CASPI, D. O. LEWIS, D. M. PISTOK, AND A. WINTER,
Experimentia, AUGUST 15, 1966.

The statement of purpose is mechanical, but it is effective. It is
apt to be used when a scholar is talking to his interested peers, when
clarity is more important than grace, or when, in a highly controversial
situation, a writer wishes to avoid any possible confusion about his central
purpose. A writer uses a purpose statement when he has no reason to avoid
expressing it bluntly and immediately. It is appropriate when the writer is
explaining a process; for instance, "Today I wish to show you how to do
the diagonal sum," or "The purpose of this paper is to show you how
Keynesian economics has influenced federal fiscal policies."

THE CONTROLLING QUESTION

There are times when a writer elects to use neither the thesis nor
the statement of purpose. In a situation where he faces an antagonistic
audience, he may prefer to delay indicating his own opinion until he has
conditioned his audience by reducing their prejudices or by producing
evidence that will make them more favorable to his thesis. At the beginning, he will ask a controlling question that he proceeds to answer in
the rest of his presentation. On June 24, 1788, while the New York Convention debated whether to ratify the Federal Constitution, an amendment
was suggested that would have limited federal powers. With sentiment
running strongly against him, young Alexander Hamilton rose to speak
against the amendment. Instead of incurring opposition at once by stating
his thesis, he asked, "Now, sir, what is the tendency of the proposed amendment?" He then showed how the amendment would make the U.S. Senate
an unstable "vassal." His evidence was great, and at its end the Convention accepted his conclusion, "It is necessary that . . . we eradicate the
poisonous principle from our government." Had he advanced his unpopular
view first, it is conceivable that an aroused Convention would hardly have
listened to his argument—and the federal government would have been
reduced in power forever.

THE ANNOUNCEMENT OF TOPIC

Besides asking a controlling question in the introduction, writers
have another way of delaying an expression of their own point of view without losing the opportunity to unify their message. The writer may merely
announce his topic. He may use this technique because he wishes to delay
a stand so controversial or so surprising that it needs evidence in advance,

or because his stand may already be known and his purpose is to explain or justify it.

In 1837, when Ralph Waldo Emerson was asked to give the Phi Beta Kappa address at Harvard, he planned to condemn American reliance on European thought and to request intellectual independence. He did not begin with this controversial thesis; instead he announced his topic: "I accept the topic which not only usage but the nature of our association seem to prescribe to this day,—the American Scholar."

A few years ago, during a convocation at Occidental College, a speaker began,

> This morning I'd like to talk to you as informally as I can. . . . I'd like to tell you some things about education—and in particular about liberal education—that I wish someone had told me when I was in college. THEODORE O. YNTEMA, "A LIBERAL EDUCATION," AN ADDRESS GIVEN AT OCCIDENTAL COLLEGE, LOS ANGELES, MAY 10, 1957.

The announcement of topic is often used in straight exposition; for instance, a sociology teacher might announce, "Today I will discuss fascism." Though this approach has its merit, it has a great drawback. Too often it is used as license to wander: a speaker or writer announces a broad topic and then proceeds to ramble all over the place. In contrast to the thesis statement, the statement of purpose, and the controlling question, all of whose predictive obligations are very exact, the announcement of topic provides little discipline. The first three guide the writer and tell the reader what he can expect. The announcement of topic, unfortunately, does too little of either.

The function of purpose

The importance of purpose cannot be overstated because it represents, in the simplest terms, what you want to say to your audience; it tells you what you need to write, and how to write it. Although the same is true, to varying degrees, of the statement of purpose, the controlling question, and the announcement of topic, the thesis statement best fulfills five very important functions.

1. *The thesis statement summarizes the writer's message.* For any of a number of reasons, including inattention, poor reading ability, or a man's natural inclination to find what he wants to find instead of what the author intended, it is important for the reader to be able to locate somewhere a precise and exact synopsis of what the writer is trying to say.

2. The thesis statement dictates to the writer what explanation or evidence he must provide. Throughout this text much is made of the generative sentence, a sentence that almost shouts out that there is more to be said. In any essay, the most heavily loaded sentence of all is the thesis statement. If the thesis is "There were many reasons for South Carolina's belligerence before the Civil War," the writer inevitably has his subsequent content dictated: he must explain what the reasons were. The predictive content of a thesis statement tells the writer what information he must provide and what he must avoid.

3. The thesis statement indicates what structures will be appropriate. Besides having predictive content, the thesis statement has an *implication of structure.* Besides indicating what content is necessary, the thesis indicates the way it should be arranged. In the thesis just mentioned, "There were many reasons for South Carolina's belligerence before the Civil War," the structure implied is obviously a list of reasons. If the writer indicates that he will discuss a process or an operation, he usually will discuss it in chronological order.

4. The thesis statement indicates the nature of the language that will be used. Obviously, if the thesis indicates that the essay will be highly technical, the language will be equally so. If, however, the paper is to explain the art of flower arranging to a ladies' club, the language would inevitably be less technical. The purpose indicates the tone of the paper —and the language may be either humorous or somber. It indicates the degree of conviction—and the language may be either bland or insistent.

5. The thesis statement indicates whether the essay will be exposition or argumentation. All serious nonfiction prose can be divided into two classes. The classification is based upon whether the writer intends to explain or convince. If a writer wishes to explain cybernetics, the objective correlative, or the quantum theory, he will write exposition. If he wishes to convince his audience that Jean-Paul Sartre is the most important thinker of the twentieth century or that a new school building should be constructed, he will write argumentation. This distinction is extremely important because it dictates the nature of the development needed in the essay. The development required for expository writing is called *exposition;* the development required for argumentation is called *evidence.* Just as development differs for exposition and argumentation, so do the organization and language that are required.

There are several types of argument, and when the writer indicates his purpose, he also indicates what type of argument he is using— and what evidence, structure, and language are required. A writer may argue for *agreement* with his thesis. The following sample theses should clarify the nature of this type of argument.

1. Immanuel Kant successfully refuted Wolff, Leibnitz, and Hume.

2. Harry S. Truman was one of the ten greatest Presidents of the United States.

3. Instead of baseball, basketball deserves to be called America's national sport.

All these theses are controversial; therefore to defend them would be to write argumentation. It is a characteristic of this type of argumentation that, if the writer succeeds, at the end the reader responds, "I agree."

Another kind of argument is *argument for action.* Rather than being content to have his audience agree with him, the writer hopes that his readers will act differently as a result. The following theses are examples of *argument for action.*

1. You should date Betty more often.

2. The United States should adopt the essential features of the British Broadcasting Company.

3. Noisy motorcycles should be outlawed.

4. *De facto* segregation should be eliminated in the public schools.

When a reader finishes this type of argument, the writer has succeeded if the reader responds, "I agree; I will *act.*" Since the action does not always come immediately, but is intended, this form is sometimes called *argument for policy.*

Argument for agreement and argument for action have different ends, and they require different development, organization, and language. These elements will be discussed in the next chapters.

Technically speaking, all argument is based on sound reasoning. It follows the rules of logic and evidence, and it ignores the emotions, bias, and prejudices of either writer or reader. However, since writers and readers are human beings, pure argument never exists. Therefore, when we study *argument,* we refer only to logic and reasoning; when we include emotional appeals, the subject is called *persuasion.* When a writer deliberately or unconsciously uses techniques that appeal to the emotions of his audience, he is writing persuasion. As might be expected, persuasion has its own development and organization. It also has its own language. This, too, will be discussed later.

Purpose versus creativity?

A student of writing may fear that the concept of purpose limits spontaneity and imagination. The concept does discipline the writer, but it is not a strait jacket. The sonnet and the villanelle are restricted in length, meter, and rhyme, but some of the world's most original poetry has been written within these forms. The prose writer has as many strings as the violinist, as many colors as the artist's palette. The influence of purpose on writing is not so much a Procrustean bed as it is a natural framework which has followed man's way of thought and has been worked out and accepted by writers in the past who tried the framework and found it effective. It is based on the way people think and the way they understand.

Narrowing the subject

SUBJECT TO TOPIC

Before a writer sets down his thesis on paper, he very likely has gone through several preliminary procedures. He probably started out with a broad subject and then narrowed it. As a writer in college, the three reasons for narrowing your subject are that (1) you only have so much space, (2) you need to reduce the subject to a topic that you either know about or have time to learn about, and (3) you need to reduce your broad subject to an aspect that will be significant or interesting to your audience.

The two most obvious ways to narrow your subject to manageability are in time and space.

Time. Frequently you do not have complete freedom in the selection of your topic. Your instructor may give you a broad heading from which you must select a subject. Suppose you are asked to write about "language." As we know, there are whole shelves of books in the library on this subject, and you must cut this wealth of material down to manageable proportions. You remind yourself that you know little of the historical background of languages; even if you do the library research—for which you have very little time—you can only rearrange some facts. On the other hand, having done some basic study of language processes, you have some thoughts about your own language experiences. In short, you will limit your subject *in time;* you will limit it to contemporary—in fact, *very* contemporary—language.

Space. You may decide you will limit your subject *in space* to the language spoken at the hospital where you worked last summer. Thus, you satisfy one of the requirements of a good topic: you know something about it. Since you are narrowing substantially, you are approaching another requirement; you are getting close to having something you can handle in the number of words permitted. You believe your readers are interested in slang; perhaps you can interest them in another contemporary language—professional jargon.

You have now limited your subject in time and space: your topic will be the jargon used in the Cook County Hospital last summer. Good.

SELECTION OF THE CONTROLLING QUESTION

Now comes the real job of limiting: choosing your controlling question. This step, more than any other, will tell you exactly what information is relevant and how it should be organized. Ask yourself, "What question shall I answer in my paper?" The answer to this question will be your thesis. You think for a while. You remember there is much jargon used: "O.B." for obstetrics; "jin" for gynecology; "prep" for preparing a patient for an operation, and the like. You decide that your controlling question will be, "Why is so much jargon used at the hospital?"

Instead of merely writing *about* jargon in the hospital, you will answer the controlling question. You can phrase your thesis; you will say, in an extended and fully developed manner, that "Although some of the jargon in the hospital is used simply to save time, most of it is used to avoid unpleasantness." Instead of saying "cancer," the term "C.A." is used; instead of "bowel movement," "B.M." You can think of many more examples.

Here, in one illustration, you have a demonstration of the whole process of narrowing from subject to topic, to controlling question, to thesis. The generative concept, the force that will help you select the appropriate organization, development, and diction, is established. Since the organization, development, and language of the body will be discussed later, and since the concept of purpose is especially related to introductions and conclusions, the rest of this chapter will be devoted to the mastery of these two parts.

The introduction

When discussing writing, the question of whether the body or the introduction is written first constantly comes up. Many writers do the first part last. At the top of the first page of their rough draft, they write their controlling question or thesis. Then they set about to organize and write the body of their paper. When they have the body in some order, they return and write an introduction with its two essential parts, the *appeal step* and the *establishment of purpose*. The introduction of a paper has two functions. One of them is obvious enough; it must indicate the purpose of the paper. As we have said, the information left unsaid by the thesis should cause the reader to want to read on; the writer, however, must not be satisfied with the innate or timely interest of his topic; he should make an effort to stimulate the interest of the reader, to show him why he must read on. The device by which he makes this attempt is called the *appeal step*.

Describing the appeal step is difficult because it is nearly impossible to discuss in general terms what people are interested in. We do know that there are topics of what we call current interest. At the time of an international crisis, almost any newspaper article about it will have interested readers. You must learn to be sensitive to such topics. A free-lance magazine writer makes his living from this sensitivity. For winter issues he may, in June, write articles about skiing and Christmas presents; for the summer issues, in January, about camping.

There are also topics of what we call general interest. Any mother will usually read an article about babies. College students will read about college problems. War, calamity, sex, and violence furnish a number of topics of general interest. Almost invariably, an article that starts out to prove that an important person is wrong about something will attract an audience. We like to read about Jack in conflict with the Giant. In fact, we will read almost any article about a controversy.

The trick in making your appeal, then, is to take advantage of current or general interest. The following articles demonstrate this technique.

> There is at large among us today an unholy number of people who make it their business to correct the speech and writing of others. When Winston Churchill says, "It's me," in a radio address, their lips purse and murmur firmly, "It is I," and they sit down and write bitter letters to the *New York Times* about What is Happening to the English Language. Reading "I only had five dollars" they circle *only* and move it to the right of *had*, producing "I had only five dollars" with a sense of virtue that is

Exploiting our interest in conflict, the author describes his opposition in lively detail. Perhaps the appeal is identification with the author and antagonism toward the purist.

beyond the measure of man. They are implacable enemies of "different than," or "loan" and "contact" used as verbs, and of dozens of other common expressions. They put triumphant exclamation marks in the margins of library books. They are ready to tangle the thread of any discussion by pouncing on a point of grammar.

If these people were all retired teachers of high school English, their weight in the community would be negligible; but unfortunately, they are not. They are authors, scholars, businessmen, librarians—indeed, they are to be found wherever educated people read and write English. And they are moved by a genuine concern for the language. They have brought us, it is true, to a state in which almost anybody, no matter what his education or the clarity of his expression, is likely to find himself attacked for some locution which he has used. Yet their intentions are of the best. It is only that their earnest minds are in the grip of two curious misconceptions. One is that there is a "correct" standard English which is uniform and definite and has been reduced to rule. The other is that this "correct" standard can only be maintained by the vigilant attention of everybody concerned with language—indeed, by the whole body of educated men and women. DONALD LLOYD IN "SNOBS, SLOBS AND THE ENGLISH LANGUAGE."

Apparently his opposition is quite formidable.

He throws down the gauntlet. "How," we wonder, "can the author be right against so many?" We are involved. We read on. The introduction is a success.

Notice that the third sentence from the end indicates that the article will discuss two "misconceptions." The next two sentences indicate what these misconceptions are and give a strong hint that the author will discuss them in that order. This technique is called "framing"; if it is accomplished in one sentence, it is called an "organizing sentence."

Here's another example:

One of the favorite targets for the viewer-with-alarm these days is the frenzy of the teen-ager over "acid rock" and "message" music. Adults are certain that the younger generation will all be deaf by the time they begin to vote; if not, they will all have tin ears.

The writer, a college student, is working toward her subject, how young people develop an interest in serious music.

In succession, high schoolers turn to weirdly-named groups, to The Cream, The Rolling Stones, the Grateful Dead, Moby Grape, The Electric Canary, The Jefferson Airplane, The Paupers, Love, The Supremes, The Animals, The Yellow Banana, The Pretty Things, The Who, The Byrds, The Yardbirds, The Mothers of Invention, The Cowsills, The Buffalo Springfield, and The Nickel Bag. Few of these "musicians" last long; a singer starts a group, cuts a pop seller, is on Ed Sullivan's show and in a couple of weeks he's back in Nowhere, playing in the high school gym, and he doesn't know what hit him. But he has done his harm.

She hopes her reader will be interested in the perennial conflict between the generations.
She establishes her topic.

She hopes her reader will be amused and caught by these ridiculous names.

She hints at the nature of the adults' complaint.

Adults are disturbed *somewhat* by the lyrics of rock and soul music. To be sure, Janis Ian sings that she loves God—but she messes it up by adding that some of her best friends are gods. Simon and Garfunkel defend all the old Judaic-Christian virtues. They sing "Blessed are the meek for they shall inherit" and "Blessed is the lamb, whose blood flows" but they end cynically, "Blessed are the sat upon, the spat upon, the ratted on. . . . Oh, Lord, why have you forsaken me?" But parents let that pass. After all, who listens to words?

Here she teases the reader just a bit; she is delaying. She is off the track, talking about something that disturbs the adult only "somewhat." She hints that something worse is coming.

She blithely dismisses the minor issue.

What *really* bugs adults is the rambam jangle-jam of the heavy beat music, the sour (to them) discordancies,

There is something worse— and here it is.

and the "nasal emissions" (I quote) of the singers. Adults (whose worry-apparatus is not all gone from worry about free love, drug jags, and drop-outs) worry about the musical taste of their young ones. Adults who are so unfortunate as to be dragooned into chaperoning a high school party are absolutely numbed by the outpourings of the electric guitar, the bongo drums, and the console. A mother grates her teeth at the moaning of a longhaired youth who used to be in her Cub pack. "His musical taste," adults lament, "will be ruined forever. Kids will never like really good music."

They are wrong.

Now she is identifying the real enemy. This is the state of mind she is going to oppose. She is trying to make her role the more appealing, the role of the person with a strong opponent.

Here she throws down the gauntlet This, opposed to the preceding thought, is her thesis.

Most readers are interested in teen-agers. Most of us, too, are interested in the human psyche. The following article thus has a double claim on our attention.

A fifteen-year-old-boy was brought to a psychiatrist because, his parents reported, he was acting strangely. One moment he was laughing and turning handsprings; the next he was in his room, brooding and inaccessible. On a Monday he loved his parents, on a Tuesday hated them. He criticized his mother for not wearing lipstick and called his best girl a creep when she did. He spent a month's allowance buying his father a birthday gift, then roared that Pop was a tyrant and darned if he was going to be treated like a baby.

The psychiatrist talked with the boy privately and emerged to report with a twinkle in his eye, "Your son seems to be afflicted with adolescence."

The transition from childhood to adulthood, experts agree, produces great storm and stress, anatomical

Enter the popular duo—psychiatrist and adolescent.

Here the writers set

change, and emotional upheaval. Outwardly, the adolescent may appear carefree, egotistical, selfish, and so insistent he has all the answers that even a doting parent has a wild desire to wring his grimy neck. Or he may seem loaded down with woe, be self-conscious, miserably convinced he has two left hands, a gargoyle face and no brain cells whatever. Either way he's a worrier, for the hallmark of adolescence is worry.

Chances are the teen-ager will eventually learn to face his problems with equanimity and balance. Meantime, as never before, he needs understanding parents. *Family Circle.*

out a problem we realize is important.

Interested to know how parents can help, we read on.

This *Time* article, besides demonstrating the appeal step and the thesis statement, shows how the latter controls the whole composition.

In the basement of Harvard's School of Dental Medicine, biochemist James H. Shaw and his assistants worked for more than ten years with cages full of white rats and cotton rats, with sugar-rich and sugar-free chow, with test tubes and dissecting boards. The twofold aim: to find out how certain sugars promote tooth decay, then to find a way to forestall it. The Sugar Research Foundation, Inc., set up by the sugar industry, bankrolled the project for a total of $57,000. Now in the *Journal of the American Dental Association,* Dr. Shaw reports his findings.

Tooth decay is caused only by food remaining in the mouth—proved by feeding rats through stomach tubes. Even sugar, fed this way, causes no decay.

Sugar, in solution, causes little decay: granulated sugar (as sprinkled

The opening sentence makes plain that the problem is important enough for some men to work ten years on it. This is the appeal step.

The thesis statement indicates that the article will answer two questions: (1) What causes decay? (2) How can it be prevented? This ends the introduction.

The first answer begins here.

on fruits and cereals) causes much more.

Of the various kinds of sugar, fructose (from most fruit), glucose (from grapes and starch foods), sucrose (table sugar from cane or beets), lactose (from milk), and maltose (from beer) are all precipitators of decay. So is a high-starch diet, even when relatively low in sugar. It does no good to substitute raw for refined sugar, but blackstrap molasses causes a marked reduction in cavities.

Saliva is a good tooth protector. Removal of successive salivary glands gave a progressive increase in decay.

The second answer begins here.

Penicillin and chlorotetracycline (aureomycin) are effective anti-decay agents, as are urea and dibasic ammonium carbonate; other antibiotics and chemicals tested (among them, many of those now commonly blended into toothpastes) do little or no good.

The two answers constitute the body of the report.

Dr. Shaw's conclusion: "We should cut down on sugar consumption, particularly candy. We should be careful about sugar in forms that remain in the mouth because of their physical properties." Along with his findings, Dr. Shaw also reported that his work has stopped. Reason: the Sugar Research Foundation withdrew its support.

This is the conclusion.

While reading the following passages, you can sharpen your reading and listening skills. A good student soon detects the thesis of an instructor's lecture. If an organizing sentence appears, signals flash in his mind, and he sees how he will outline the material that follows. As you read these five introductions, ask yourself what organizational patterns will follow.

(1)

To speak of a "social atom" is to take liberties with scientific terms. Yet the figure of speech is justified if it can awaken

the public imagination to the vast unreleased power for learning which is imprisoned within the millions of children who
grow up in American families belonging to those groups
whom I shall call the alienated. JOHN H. NIEMEYER, *Saturday Review*, SEPTEMBER 12, 1959.

(2)

Since sputnik, words on education have grown to be a flood-
tide. Much of the discussion has been either angrily negative
or stubbornly defensive, with most writers advocating either
more or less: less adjustment, less training in method; fewer
educators, more academics; more mathematics, English,
science, and languages; more rooms, pay, teachers; more,
more; less, less. Perhaps because many of the critics have
been persons who have not sat in a public-school classroom in
years, only a few have dealt with new concepts within
courses. But a solution by mere addition, subtraction, or
multiplication is an oversimplification of a complex problem.
At the risk of increasing confusion we might think about a
deeper change. LOU LABRANT, *Saturday Review*, SEPTEMBER
12, 1959.

(3)

February 2, 1959, was a day to remember in my city of
Norfolk, Virginia. On that day six formerly all-white junior
and senior high schools, closed since the previous summer,
opened their doors to seventeen Negro students. As this
desegregation began amid the crumbling ruins of Virginia's
"massive resistance" program, reporters and photographers
from over fifty different newspapers and wire services were
on hand to record the event. They had a rather dull day.
The students arrived, went to school, went home again, and
that was that.

It all looked simple, yet those of us who had worked for six
months to get the schools opened could see how amazing it
was, and how close it came to not happening. We face now
an even bigger question, and a longer struggle; will our
schools stay open, and will they continue to be good schools?
FORREST P. WHITE, *Atlantic Monthly*, SEPTEMBER, 1959.

(4)

I can't remember when I first realized I had begun to loathe
my sports car. Like most high-octane romances, mine was
all-consuming and, I dare say, somewhat embarrassing to my
friends. Certainly they tended to drop away from me during
the height of my passion, but—as is typical in such affairs—

I failed to notice their defection. I had a small but steadily growing group of new friends, ones who spoke my language: other sports-car owners. If our world was hemmed in by smugness and limited in scope, none of us was aware of it— not then, at least. JANET AGLE, *Harper's Magazine*, SEPTEMBER, 1959.

(5)

"Our Father, Who art in heaven, Hallowed be Thy name. . . ." At the end of my first Alcoholics Anonymous meeting the words of the old prayer came suddenly alive. Black despair melted into a glimpse of health and a good life, of relief from suffering, remorse, anguish—just a ray of hope, but enough to enable me to square my shoulders in new determination. These fine people had given me something I badly needed at that moment. They had shown me a way out of the abyss of alcoholism. ANONYMOUS, *Atlantic Monthly*, SEPTEMBER, 1959.

CAVEATS ABOUT INTRODUCTIONS

You can sensitize yourself to the generative nature of purpose by studying the introductions of articles you read in newspapers, magazines, and books. Notice that almost all of them indicate their purpose, usually in a direct assertion. If the thesis is not expressed directly, ask yourself why it is being delayed. Consider the possibility that the author is trying to put something over on you. Determine the method the author uses to enhance your interest in his topic.

As you write the introduction to an article of your own, try to avoid the following pitfalls.

1. *Avoid a thesis that promises too much.* Since the thesis makes a promise that you must fulfill, you are limited by a number of factors related to the body of the paper. In almost every writing experience—or speaking experience—you will be limited as to space and time. Sometimes the limitation will be expense, as when you are making a telephone call or sending a telegram. The college student writing a theme is limited by the number of words assigned or permitted by the instructor. After graduation, the limitation most often will be the difficulty of holding the attention of your audience. The human attention span is distressingly short. How long did you listen the last time you were at a lecture before your mind wandered away? Don't set out to do more than you have space and time for. You must not, as Mrs. Henry Adams wrote, "chew at more than you can bite off." You cannot, in a 500-word theme, tell your reader how to bowl, but you might tell him how to score. You cannot discuss the

causes of the Civil War, but you might show why General McClellan was relieved of his command. You cannot tell the whole history of your home town, but you might tell how it got its name. You cannot write a complete autobiography, but you can tell what experience has most influenced your life.

2. *Do not expect the impossible of your appeal step.* Your appeal step can show your reader that your topic is important only if it really is. If your topic is trivial and your thesis banal, and you do compose a sensational appeal step, the letdown will only irritate your reader. A proverb is appropriate here: don't beat a horse that is already dead. If your reader already knows your topic or is convinced of your thesis, you waste his time and yours by further discussion. Observe this unfortunate collection of sentences:

> War is a topic that is forced on our thinking constantly. It is a topic that most of us would prefer to forget but in these days that happy solution to the problem is impossible. War arises from a number of causes, some good and some bad. Some nations covet territory and riches other nations have, and so incite a war of aggression. Those nations which are attacked have no choice but to defend themselves. War brings untold hardship and suffering. Men are maimed and killed. Unfortunately the innocent must suffer too. Women and children lose their homes, grow hungry, and often die in bombing raids from which there is no escape. Future wars promise to be even more horrible. Atomic bombs and hydrogen bombs have the potentiality of destroying our civilization as we know it. No, war is nothing we like to contemplate but it is a subject we must contemplate in days like these.

This introduction is nothing more than a series of truisms. Nothing can be done to give it appeal.

3. *Avoid, in your thesis statement, announcing that you are going to "talk about" something, or "discuss" something.* Occasionally, a speaker stands up in front of a group and makes an announcement like, "Today I am going to talk about my trip to Peru." He then relates anecdotes about his trip, usually organized chronologically and with the details chosen only because they come to his mind by free association. Though he may entertain his audience, this speaker will not provide them with as memorable an experience as if he had decided in advance that he would develop a point of view. Perhaps his point of view, his basic idea, or his thesis, could have been "My experiences in Peru convinced me that there is money to

be made there by American businessmen," or even "Our trip to Peru was a wonderful experience for my family." If he had a point of view on which to hang his speech, he could have organized it more effectively and chosen more relevant details.

4. *Avoid starting out with an unrelated joke.* Doing so reveals a misunderstanding of the appeal step. You may have heard the story of the man who, before he sold his mule, said that it was easy to control; all it needed, he said, was a "soft word." When the buyer tried to work the mule, however, he could not get the mule to move. The seller, called in for help, took a long, heavy club and proceeded to beat the stubborn beast across the rear. At first the mule paid little attention and then turned his head around slowly and looked at his former master. At this point the man picked up the reins, spoke softly, and, sure enough, the beast went to work willingly.

"But you said this mule is easy to control. All I thought I needed was a soft word."

"You are right. That's what I said."

"Then why the beating?"

"Well, first you have to attract his attention."

This joke is more or less related to introductions, especially to the appeal step, and it conceivably could have been used in the opening of this chapter. Another story on another subject might have been quite inappropriate. The joke should, however, do more than "attract attention"; it should focus attention on your subject, or, better, it should illustrate dramatically your whole thesis.

5. *Avoid stereotyped and mechanical beginnings.* Whenever a speaker or writer begins, "According to Webster, such-and-such is such-and-such," he displays an insensitivity to the boredom threshold of his audience. Almost any reader or listener has heard such an introduction too many times. It is a cliché.

There are many such trite beginnings. You should watch out for expressions that have lately been used and overused by every newspaper, advertiser, and speaker. Any student who starts his theme with such expressions as "In this day and age . . ."; "In our world today . . ."; or "In our modern times . . ." has immediately achieved one purpose: he has more than half-convinced his audience that he is either too lazy to think or simply cannot produce an original thought and an opinion of his own.

6. *Avoid referring to your title in the text of your essay.* Well-written magazine and newspaper feature articles customarily open with zest. They do not sound like a carry-over from anything, even from the title. If the title of an article is "The Last Hurrahs Are Fading," the first

sentence might be, "Say it, say it—of course you are going to vote for a Republican. Sometimes party loyalty asks too much." Almost never would a skilled author begin with a reference to the title, "This idea is becoming increasingly evident." Nor would he refer to it later on in the article. After years of conditioning, readers may notice a title, but they do not think of it as part of the article itself. Their attention is caught by the title, but they rarely have it in mind as they read.

The conclusion

Theoretically, if you wrote a clear enough introduction and an effective body for your paper, you would not need a conclusion. You would have stated your thesis, and you would have explained it or proved it. Almost invariably, however, a conclusion is helpful. It is your last opportunity to demonstrate that you have fulfilled the obligation generated by your thesis or purpose statement.

A simple analogy may clarify. Suppose you have a rope in your hand, and you wonder why it is so strong. You look at the rope and see that it has three strands. You twist the rope slightly and look at each separate strand carefully for a moment, discovering that the strands are made of different fibers that are treated differently to develop resistance to snapping, shearing, and slow pull. You realize that, without any one of its strands, the rope as a whole would be weaker. To evaluate the rope as a whole, to generalize about its total strength, you let the three strands twist back together again so you can survey it as a whole. In the same way, the writer, at the end of his essay, in order not to leave the reader with the impression that his last subtopic is more important than any other part of his essay or, indeed, than his essay as a whole, returns to his thesis —and thus forms a conclusion.

Just as the introduction has two functions, so does the conclusion. A good conclusion should re-emphasize the thesis and help the reader to remember it.

The obvious, perhaps too obvious, procedure is to begin your last paragraph with "In conclusion, . . ." and end with an outlinelike summary. You may certainly restate your thesis, and you may summarize the body of your paper, but you probably should do either or both with some degree of subtlety. The following two conclusions, written by students who were asked to assist in designing a college building by giving their reactions to an existing classroom, both summarize the writers' objections, yet neither of them employs the words "in conclusion," or "in summary."

(1)

Only when these three factors—writing boards, acoustics, and seating—are remedied, will Room 205 become a decent classroom.

(2)

So now you have a headache as a result of attempting to take notes with poor lighting, jangled nerves from straining to hear and not being able to, and a backache from a cramped seating position. These are the rewards you receive from trying to obtain knowledge in Room 205.

Whether your conclusion contains a summary or not, make sure that it is an *integral part of the theme* and that it does not refer to a point you have not previously discussed.

There are as many possible conclusions as there are writers. What will effectively conclude one student's theme will not necessarily be effective or even acceptable in another. Use the following suggestions as a guide.

1. The conclusion should arise naturally out of what has been said in the theme.

2. The conclusion should be smoothly related to the theme body.

3. The conclusion should, in some way, bring out the main point or points of the theme.

4. The conclusion should make a strong impression on the reader and, consequently, cause him to remember your whole paper.

5. The conclusion should be consistent in tone with the rest of your paper. For instance, a frivolous conclusion will ill fit a basically serious paper.

The various ways of making a conclusion effective—the unusual or unexpected ending, the rhetorical question, a strong statement of intent or belief, a variation in the length and rhythm of your sentences—will be effective only if they fulfill the five basic requirements listed above.

One particular way of closing a theme that merits separate discussion is known either as "completing the cycle" or "closing by return" and consists of returning to an image, an idea, or a statement that occurs in the introduction. The first of the three examples below, which are all from student themes, contains a return to the same image that was employed at the beginning of the theme. The other two examples present a return to the same idea.

(1)

Introduction. Every fall, while trees and flowers are dying, a form of America's artificial beauty comes to life: the automobile is reborn. Out of the factory sprouts the stem of our leisure time with all its branches, displaying various different shapes, sizes, and colors. Each model has its own gadgets, its own improvements, its fancy name, and most of all, its price tag. . . .

Conclusion. Every summer, when trees and flowers are in their bloom, the young automobile is dying. It leaves behind a year of enjoyable driving, and now it is either ready for a trade-in or for the junk yard. Before it dies, however, it brings the birth of this year's new models. Once again, the cycle is completed.

(2)

Introduction. "May I help you, Madam?" "Yes, I'd like to see a 15 white-on-white, with a pin collar, please." "Surely, I'll see if I have it." To anyone who has ever worked in a department store, these are familiar words. They come from a salesperson, selling his wares, in this case, a shirt. For the past two and a half years, I have been employed by a large Boston department store, selling everything from children's shoes to men's furnishings. . . .

Conclusion. Here it is, two and one-half years later, and I'm still with the Company. On any Monday, Wednesday, or Saturday, I can be found waiting on and diligently answering the questions of my customers. "Could you help me out, sir?" "Certainly, Madam, which way did you come in?"

(3)

Introduction. Elevators, escalators, cashiers, shopping carts, and basement bargains are all part of the shopper's world of today, and this world is certainly a far cry from its general store origin. This shows that the life of a shopper has markedly changed with the growth of the general store into large-scale shopping plazas and department stores and that the purchase of a pair of pants today is no longer the simple operation that it used to be in the days of our ancestors. . . .

[In the body of the theme, the author discusses several kinds of changes that the old-time general store has undergone over the years until it was ʰurned into the department store of today.]

Conclusion. During the era of the general store, a man could run into the store, find a pair of pants his size and buy them. Today, if a man wants to buy a pair of pants, he must mill through racks and racks of clothes, find his size, choose one of the many colors and styles, try them on, and have the tailor fiddle with the cuffs. Then he pays for the pants, and leaves the store with nothing more than an alteration pick-up ticket.

Closing by return is one of the most effective ways of concluding a theme or paper, but it is also dangerous, for if you repeat a bad introduction at the end of your paper, your theme has two weak spots instead of one.

The additional responsibility of making the thesis memorable—of providing some remarks in the final paragraphs that will attach special significance to the message—is not easy to fulfill. Once, at a luncheon meeting of a businessmens' club, a young army private gave a speech detailing his experiences under fire. When he finished, he said, "The one lesson I learned more than any other is that General William Tecumseh Sherman was right in what he said about war." And then he sat down. Half of the audience knew the profane remark by the Civil War general and smiled. The other half did not, and there was a momentary buzz of conversation, and then the whole audience knew, and all smiled. The private had succeeded in giving his speech an extra fillip, thus adding to its success. His audience will be more likely to remember his thesis.

A single, dramatic incident, chosen because it illustrates most importantly the thesis, may be effective. A testimonial statement by an accepted authority may be useful. Restating a complex thesis in a short, pungent, aphoristic statement may be valuable. An appropriate, amusing anecdote, a joke, or an analogy may be an effective last-minute dressing.

Since the nature of the conclusion depends so heavily upon the nature of the previous parts of the paper, only general suggestions can be given here, but a study of conclusions that appear in anthologies of good prose models and in quality magazines is instructive. Although Aristotle was convinced that all conclusions—he called them "epilogues"—should contain the summary, most writers work for a more lively variety. Few effective writers look at the conclusion as nothing more than, "I've said everything on the subject so I will close." Almost all of them look at the conclusion as the last opportunity to demonstrate that they have completely fulfilled the obligation they assumed when they first announced their purpose.

The essay question

Probably no other form of writing so thoroughly epitomizes the concept of purpose as the answer to an essay question. The essay question is the ultimate generative sentence.

Geology Professor Sherwood Tuttle of the University of Iowa once made a study of examinations and found that his students were more likely to do badly on their exams because of their inability to write answers for essay questions than because of their ignorance about geology. In post-test conferences, he learned that 65 percent of the points lost in the examination was the result of the students' inability to focus on the question. Students did not fulfill the generative obligation of the test questions.

There is a technique for writing an answer to an essay question. In order to keep on the question, many students make a point of rephrasing the question in the first sentence of their answer. Thus, a rephrasing of the controlling question is their thesis statement.

In an examination in American history, a teacher asked his class to describe the major advantages held by the North on the eve of the Civil War. Among 110 others, he received the following four answers.

(1)

Good resources like money, etc. Manufacturing and commerce were centered in Northern cities instead of south. This gave north quite an advantage. (It seems to me that this question is unfair since the material was never covered in class.)

(2)

The North possessed the following advantages:
1. It had a larger population on which to draw (22,000,000 as against 9,000,000).
2. It held a commercial and financial advantage (foreign commerce and banking capital).
3. It had almost a complete monopoly on production of war materials (iron, steel, etc.).

(3)

To the student of American history nothing is more interesting than our own Civil War, or—as the Southerners like to call it—the War between the States. This was a war that had been brewing for a long while, all the way back to the Missouri Compromise, or, if one wanted to be really precise, all the way back to 1619 when the first slave was imported into Virginia. This is a long time. In spite of the attempts of many honest people to resolve the differences. War came, and with it great change. The Four Horsemen (death, famine, etc.) really rode rough-shod. On the eve of this war both sides held certain advantages but we are particularly interested in the advantages of the North. The North was a more populous area. The result was that many people lived in the North, and thus the North had a greater population upon which to draw. Besides this, it had almost all the steel and iron mills in the country in cities like Pittsburgh, etc. This meant that the North could have the "mostest" even if it didn't get there "fustest." (Indeed, the South during the early years usually got there "fustest.") The advantages of the South were not to be despised.

(4)

On the eve of the Civil War the North held at least three major advantages. In the first place, it had a larger population to draw on for army service. In 1860 there were roughly 22,000,000 in the North whereas there were only 9,000,000 in the South. The difference was even greater than these figures would indicate because more than one-third of the South's nine million were slaves and were thus not especially fitted for army service. In the second place, the North held certain important commercial and financial advantages. For example, it controlled most of the foreign commerce, since trade had centered in ports north of the Potomac River. Even foreign goods destined for the South had poured through Northern warehouses. Finally, the North had an almost complete monopoly on the production of war materials. Not only were almost all the iron, steel, textile, and munition factories in Northern possession, but almost all of the technicians and skilled laborers were also there.

Answer #1 is no answer at all. Since one reason for having an essay examination is to give the student a chance to demonstrate his power of expression, the first answer would lose credit not only because it provides so little information, but also because it is phrased so badly. Answer #2 is faulty because it ignores the operative word in the controlling question, *"Describe."* Answer #2 is not a description at all; at best, it is a list. The author of Answer #3 is a "snow artist." Instead of answering the controlling question, he sets down a lot of drivel about how interesting the War was. Two thirds of the way through the composition, he comes briefly back to the controlling question, but he is soon off again. In 229 words he does not answer the question nearly as well as the author of Answer #4 does in 163. Notice that Answer #4 starts out with a thesis. A rephrasing of the question, the thesis summarizes the main idea of the answer. The student can check his answer to make sure it is complete by asking himself, "Have I really described the three major advantages?"

Often essay examination answers are paragraphs. The original question, rephrased as a declarative sentence, is the topic sentence; the development is the content obligated by the generative nature of the controlling question and the topic sentence.

Projects

1. Since so much of the rest of this book depends upon the concept of purpose, guarantee your understanding by defining the following terms.

definitive sentence	exposition 32
generative sentence	evidence
assertion	argumentation
development	expository writing
thesis statement	argument for agreement
statement of purpose	argument for action
controlling question	persuasion
announcement of topic	appeal step
narrowing the subject	predictive content
implied structure	

2. Either in an anthology or in prose models in a serious magazine, locate the indicators of purpose in a group of essays. Classify the essay as to whether it is exposition or argument, and classify the purpose indicator as to whether it is a thesis statement, statement of purpose, controlling question, or announcement of topic. If the essay is argument, determine whether it is argument for agreement or action. Try to decide why the particular type of indicator was appropriate for the immediate purpose of the essay. Infer the logical history of the thesis of the essay and analyze it for predictive content and implied organization. Then compare the actual content and organization with what you predicted.

3. Throughout this chapter, much attention was paid to purpose as the unifying factor for a single extended communication, be it a book or a short essay. Sentences of lesser importance in a book or essay—that is, sentences that are not thesis statements or statements of purpose—may be "generative sentences" in that they have an implied logical history, predictive content, and structural implication. Such a sentence may introduce a chapter, or a

subtopic in a chapter, a paragraph, or even a section in a paragraph. Read the quotations given below and answer the following questions: (a) What must have been the thinking by the author before he phrased the sentence? (b) What development will the sentence need? (c) How will the content be structured? (d) By what method is the purpose established? (e) Does the quotation suggest exposition or argumentation?

a. "It is natural to believe in great men." RALPH WALDO EMERSON, IN "USE OF GREAT MEN."

b. "I shall therefore endeavor to refine upon it [a history of the art of political lying] by adding some circumstances of its birth and parents." JONATHAN SWIFT, IN "A MODEST PROPOSAL."

c. "When a person dies, who does any one thing better than any one else in the world, which so many others are trying to do well, it leaves a gap in society." WILLIAM HAZLITT, IN "THE DEATH OF JOHN CAVENAUGH."

d. "It has . . . been the peculiar lot of our country to be visited by the worst kind of English travellers." WASHINGTON IRVING, IN "ENGLISH WRITERS ON AMERICA."

e. Under the title "What Is a Classic?," Charles Augustin Sainte-Beuve discussed ". . . a delicate question, to which somewhat diverse solutions might be given according to times and season. An intelligent man suggests it to me, and I intend to try, if not to solve it, at least to examine and discuss it face to face with my readers, were it only to persuade them to answer it for themselves, and, if I can, to make their opinion and mine on the point clear."

f. "When the wise man brings his list of our genuine admirations, will intelligence be one of them?" JOHN ERSKINE, IN "THE MORAL OBLIGATION TO BE INTELLIGENT."

g. "And yet, for all its size and all its wealth and all the 'progress' it babbles of, it [the Southern part of the United States] is almost as sterile, artistically, culturally, as the Sahara Desert." H. L. MENCKEN, IN "THE SAHARA OF THE BOZART."

4. The following is an abstract from a chapter in Jane Jacobs' *The Death and Life of Great American Cities*. Thesis: "A city street equipped to make a safety asset out of the presence of strangers, as successful city neighborhoods always do, must have three main qualities." Body: "First, there must be a clear demarcation between public and private spaces. . . . Second, there must be eyes upon the street, *eyes* belonging to what we call its natural proprietors. . . . And third, the sidewalk must have users on it fairly continuously, both to add more effective eyes and to induce plenty of people in buildings along the street to watch the sidewalks." Write an introduction for a 500-word theme written with the sentences above as an outline.

5. Write three introductions, each approximately 150 words in length, on a subject that you think may interest your classmates. Be sure each introduction has an appeal step and a clear indication of purpose, each indicator being a different kind. Later you will complete one of the introductions, the choice being made either by your instructor or your classmates after your introductions have been read to them. In the class discussion, your classmates will be expected to tell what thinking you have experienced, for what development you have obligated yourself, and what structure the introduction seems to suggest.

Further reading

ARISTOTLE. *Rhetoric*. Book III, Chapter 13, ed. FRIEDRICH SOLMSEN. New York: Modern Library, 1954.

CHAPTER 3

THE IMPLIED STRUCTURE: ORGANIZATION

Good writing, like a good house, is an orderly arrangement of parts. Each major part has a certain amount of independence. . . . It may have an interior structure of its own. But it must also be connected with the other parts—that is, related to them functionally—for otherwise, it could not contribute its share to the intelligibility of the whole. MORTIMER ADLER, *How To Read a Book.*

At this point in the study of rhetoric, we are undoubtedly in agreement that some ideas are more complex than others. Some may be communicated in one word; others need more than fifty thousand. It is a truism to say that, when we are dealing with ideas of sufficient complexity that they take over a hundred words or so, we cannot throw all the ideas at once at our reader. Point One in the case for organization is that, on some basis or other, we have to decide on the order of the words.

Point Two rests on the nature of the human mind. A psychologist once read a list of twenty-one ideas to some listeners and asked that they be recalled. Most listeners could recall fewer than eight. The psychologist then put the ideas in three groups and gave each group a label. The mere act of classification nearly doubled the number of ideas his audience could remember. When he put the three classes into an order based on a spatial

55

scheme, he secured still further improvement in retention. Similar tests have shown that, besides understanding organized material better, readers are able to remember it better. This is Point Two in the case for organization.

Organization provides a path by which the writer can lead his reader through a maze of information and arrive at the conclusion desired. At first, it seems that the obvious way to do this is for the writer to reproduce the information in the order that he himself encountered it. Since the writer arrived at a given conclusion, presumably the reader will do likewise. There is much merit to this suggestion because every idea does have its own history. When a reader comes upon an idea written by one of his favorite political observers, he may uncritically accept it. Why? He accepts it because, perhaps unconsciously, he thinks, "The reporter must have gone through the research and thought necessary for him to believe this." The reader assumes that the idea has a legitimate and defensible history. Retracing this history would seem to be a good way to explain or prove it.

Synthesis

Of all the work that goes into a respectable article or book, that which is least obvious to the reader is what is called *synthesis*. This loose term covers all mental processes during the research—note-taking, head-scratching, mumbling, puzzling, writing down and tearing up, putting in and taking out—all the thinking that precedes the moment when the writer finally perceives the central message he wishes to convey. If we are to consider basing a pattern of organization on this process, we must know something about it.

CASE HISTORY 1. THE STUDENT WHO LIKED TO RIDE ON TRAINS

A student was asked to write a paper in which he was permitted to take any approach or use any tone, but he had to write on the merits of any one system of transportation. Since travel by air is modern and popular, the student began to do research on its advantages. He read about the speed, efficiency, and luxury of this form of travel, and he accumulated statistics about how air travel has boomed in the last three decades. The more he read, the less enthusiastic he became. He decided that he just was not personally enthusiastic about air travel, and he could not sincerely defend it. He preferred to travel by rail. He knew he would have a difficult time writing a convincing paper about the advantages of rail travel, but he decided that he would try. He felt that his honesty and sincerity might make up for the fact that his paper would oppose a majority viewpoint. As he began to plan his paper, he realized that he really did not know why he preferred the railroad. He thought for a while and decided that, if he was to be honest, he must confess that he preferred surface transportation because he was afraid to fly. Second, he realized that at this stage of his life he really did not care much whether a trip took four hours or twenty. What he did not like was all the trouble and expense of getting out to an airport, standing in line to select seats, gambling on the weather, and then, at the end of his flight, having to spend two more hours to get to his actual destination. If anything, instead of streaking through the air on a trip, he preferred each journey to be a "between-two-worlds" experience, a break in which he could talk to people, relax a bit, and enjoy doing nothing. He saw that his preference was made up of personal inclinations, and he doubted whether he could persuade anyone to accept his viewpoint. He came across a poem by Ogden Nash and an essay by E. B. White and learned that they too liked to travel by train, and he decided that his approach would be to write a personal essay about his own preference, the tone of which would be whimsical. He would jest at those hurried people who rush from airport to airport; he would ruefully admit to being a coward; he would show how rail travel gave him a chance to rest. In short, he would admit that he just felt a great deal more comfortable traveling by railroad.

CASE HISTORY 2. "WHAT WAS NATURALISM?"

A student taking a writing course for which the textbook was an anthology of selections by Thomas Malthus, Charles Lyell, Karl Marx, Herbert Spencer, Thomas Huxley, Hippolyte Taine, Emile Zola, Arthur Schopenhauer, Herman Melville, Hamlin Garland, Stephen Crane, Jack London, Frank Norris, and Theodore Dreiser was asked to write a paper explaining the philosophy uniting these writers. The instructor explained that these writers had some ideas in common that have come to be called "naturalism." The student was not even sure what a "philosophy" was, but some inquiries to his instructor and a session with an encyclopedia informed him that a systematic philosophy tends to be based on notions about the nature of God, man, society, and the relationship among them. The student began to reread his anthology to secure answers to these questions. He noticed that the writers varied widely in their views about the exact nature of God: Marx seemed to be an atheist and Huxley an agnostic; Spencer seemed to be a determinist, believing that God wound up the universe and let it go in directions that He was able to predict. All the writers agreed that God does not interfere in the day-to-day activities of man. They seemed to agree also that there are no events that take place in an inexplicable fashion, no miracles, no random developments. History is, for these writers, the result that can be expected from the laws of physical science and the laws, both legal and psychological, of man's institutions and innate nature. With these perceptions the student put together an extended definition of Naturalism.

CASE HISTORY 3. "THE MANUFACTURE OF PENICILLIN"

In a science class a student was required to write a term paper on penicillin. This was strictly a research project; the student did not have a clue as to what he would write. He went through the appropriate steps to get a bibliography, and he began to read and take notes. He put his note cards into four piles that formed naturally because these were the directions taken by his sources: the chemical structure of penicillin, its properties, the story of its discovery, and its manufacture in large quantities for marketing. As the piles grew, he realized he must limit his subject; he rejected the first two piles because the structure and properties of the compound were rather more technical than he felt he could handle and because these two subjects were mechanical and routine. He could see nothing that he could contribute to them that would demonstrate any originality on his part. He rejected the third pile also, because the story of the discovery of penicillin has been told so many times in popular magazines. He preferred the fourth pile, about manufacturing procedures, because it was timely: pharmaceutical companies were still trying to refine their techniques. He examined the notes in the appropriate pile, and he shuffled them into new piles based on the headings, (a) the preparation of materials, (b) the process of manufacturing, and (c) the control of quality.

He now began to put the parts together, deciding that the obvious order would be chronological. He would write a report describing step-by-step the process of manufacturing penicillin. He wrote a rough draft and was dissatisfied with its lack of freshness. As he read over his paper, he decided that what really interested him was the care taken to ensure quality. His research told him that the dependability of penicillin depends upon a meticulous selection of materials and a careful process of manufacture. Curious as to how this state of dependability developed, he decided that the story he wished to tell was that the integrity of the pharmaceutical industry, working within the regulations based on the

Pure Food and Drug Act, was the cause of this success. He now saw that chronology was not necessarily appropriate. He decided to describe the manufacturing process and then work backwards to show how and why the procedure was developed. The student felt that now his thesis was rather significant: he was using the manufacture of penicillin to illustrate how industry, science, and government can work together for the common good.

These three case histories demonstrate how a writer can arrive at the central idea of a paper. By going over their experiences and the results of their research, the writers put together ideas that were new to them. They hurried the creative process by phrasing appropriate questions.

The processes of synthesis illustrated by these three examples vary about as much as other examples of synthesis would vary. On some occasions, almost no synthesis would precede the writing of a paper. A free-lance writer might be commissioned by the editor of a semi-technical magazine to write an article about a new use of a laser. The editor might say frankly, "I'm not asking you to do anything creative. All I want is a straight, factual report." On another occasion the same writer might be asked to do an in-depth study of a new political luminary in the state of Oregon. "See what this guy has to offer," the editor might say. After a great deal of study and thought the writer would come to a conclusion.

Synthesis, which by classical writers was called "invention," can be thought of as the process before organization. When the writer begins to organize his paper he is obviously influenced by the activity that caused him to believe in his own thesis. However, in none of the illustrations of synthesis would the writers cause the reader to follow the paths they took to reach their own conclusions. Each would look at his task and say, "Now what must I do to help my reader understand or accept my thesis?"

All purpose statements and all theses are generative. The reader will look at them and, the writer hopes, want to read on. Because of their nature and the reader's past experiences, he will have some idea of what to expect in content, organization, and language. If the writer announces that he is going to describe a process, the reader will expect a step-by-step treatment. Other purposes, as we shall see, have their own implication of structure.

Insofar as organization is concerned, the thesis or purpose statement has two characteristics: it implies the pattern of development that must follow, and it guarantees the reader that the writer has gone through a synthesizing process that aided him in putting his ideas together. This logical history may be systematic and commendable if the writer has assembled the information and done the thinking himself.

On the other hand, the synthesis may have been completely haphazard, even the product of a coincidence. When a graduate student and his supervisor announced a method to control diabetes, the world was not surprised to learn that the first breakthrough came after the team noticed flies buzzing around dog urine, for advances in all disciplines are sometimes the result of accidents observed by people able to interpret them.

Once the writer begins to organize, synthesis becomes part of the influential past. In organizing, he begins to seek a method of taking an idea apart in order to see how best to present it effectively to his audience.

Division

When a writer knows what his purpose is and begins the analysis that will yield his pattern of organization, he is influenced by his audience and the generative nature of his purpose. When deciding on development and language, he is perhaps more influenced by his audience than when he is thinking about organization. As an oversimplified instance, the writer of a certain type of cookbook may use French terms if he knows that his readers are an educated lot, and he can probably eliminate such basic information as how to beat an egg or knead dough. But no matter how informed or skilled his readers are, the writer will probably give his cooking instructions in chronological order. This is not always true, but it does illustrate how a particular purpose almost inescapably commits a writer to a predictable pattern of organization.

The analysis that determines the organization consists of a series of divisions. First, the writer studies his thesis or purpose for indicators of the major points. Then he analyzes these points as generative sentences and derives his subpoints. These sentences, which are used as topic sentences of paragraphs or as topic headings, are then studied to see what individual patterns they yield.

CHRONOLOGICAL STRUCTURE

Whenever a writer's topic involves the passage of time, he probably will consider using chronological order. He will break his process, or narration, into steps or parts and describe them in the order in which they occur in time. This, one of the simplest forms of division, probably presents the fewest problems.

Whenever one tells someone how to do something, whether it be how to get to a filling station or how to uncover the medieval literature obscured under a double palimpsest, he senses that chronological steps will be most appropriate. Whenever a writer tells what has happened in the past or should happen in the future, he will at least consider the chronological pattern. He may decide to change the order, but he will not let his reader lose sight of how one part follows another.

2. SPATIAL STRUCTURE

Occasionally a writer wishes to describe a visual experience. A drama critic may describe a stage setting, an architect the front of a building, or a football coach may want to show where his team will position itself to be ready for certain offenses. A student may want to describe the layout of his college campus. In such instances, the pattern of organization is almost inevitably spatial. The stage description may be from front to back. The building description may proceed from floor to floor, perhaps starting from the foundation and working upward. The football defenses may move from the left end to the right end of the line and then into the backfield. The student may move from the center of the campus to the outskirts. The writer undoubtedly will further divide his description into parts. The architect may talk about the rooms on each floor, and the football coach about the line and then the backfield. The drama critic might want to describe the background scenery and the foreground scenery; the student may divide the campus into academic, administrative, athletic, and living areas. Whoever the writer, he will see the spatial order that seems most appropriate to the particular scene he wishes to describe.

3. TOPIC STRUCTURE

Other writing problems lend themselves to division into topics. In trying to demonstrate that students work best when motivated, a writer may divide them into men and women; or serious students and playboys; freshmen, sophomores, juniors, and seniors; or even dormitory and commuting students. He divides his subject according to what his message is.

The divisions may be of many kinds; they may be called classes, reasons, objections, objectives, causes, effects, rules, principles, factors, and so on. In contrast to *chronological* and *spatial* organization where division is external to the mind, topics are based on a process of abstraction. A chronological process is divided into its natural steps, and spatial organization is divided into sections suggested by the eye. Some topics are equally obvious. When discussing school personnel, we naturally discuss students, faculty, and administration. When we discuss literature, we recognize certain traditional classes, fiction and nonfiction, or poetry and prose. When we discuss a city, we usually detect such natural divisions as residential and business districts. The following sentences by Donald Hall are from an essay called "The New Poetry," in *New World Writing*, April, 1955.

> Robert Lowell seems to me to be the best of the younger poets of the language. . . .
> A very good poet is Theodore Roethke. . . .
> The Wurlitzer Wits were a school which seems to be closed down. I am speaking of the early verse of John Ciardi, John Frederick Nims, John Malcolm Brinnin, and Karl Shapiro. . . .
> Most of the good poems being written by the youngest poets of today can be considered the products of the School of Elegance. . . . in poetry [American letters have swung] from the austerity of the *vers librists* to the lyrical elegance of Richard Wilbur. . . .

Each sentence begins with an evaluation. Apparently Professor Hall believed that each poet or school should be a topic.

When Jane Jacobs, in *The Death and Life of Great American Cities*, discussed modern city planning, she stated her thesis, "The most influential ideas informing orthodox city planning—and urban architecture—seem by their very nature to predict this awful achievement." Then, one by one she introduced the authors of her "most influential ideas": Ebenezer Howard, Le Corbusier, Daniel Burnham, and so on.

In topical organization, the topics do not necessarily have to be strictly parallel, i.e., either causes, or effects, or problems, or solutions. It may be that to accomplish your purpose, whether it is expository or argumentative, you will need to have *problem and solution,* or *cause and effect.* When Reed Whittemore, in *The Boy from Iowa,* opposed the awarding of the Nobel Prize to Winston Churchill, he wrote, "I think Winston Churchill is 'guilty' of [certain literary faults] and I wish now to discuss briefly some of the results." Two words were generative—his topics were Churchill's literary "faults" and their "results."

To determine the most appropriate topics for an essay, we must determine the innate dynamics of the generative sentence. Often the implied structure is quite obvious, as when a statement that the writer will describe a process is followed by organization based on chronology. Often the structure of a paper is influenced by the grammatical structure of the thesis, as when a writer introduces the two-part body of a paper with, "Although I am aware of the attraction of air travel, when it is time to queue up and buy a ticket almost always I am in a railroad station."

The paper opened with a short section showing that the usual attractions of airline travel did not appeal to the writer, followed by a longer section describing the virtues of travel by rail. The subordinate clause in the thesis sentence necessitated a short preliminary topic; the main clause of the thesis statement obligated the writer to provide a bulkier conclusive section. More often, the structure of the paper is influenced by the nature of the generative sentence—that is, by whether it is an observation, classification, generalization, judgment, or causal relationship.

Sources of issues

It would be convenient if we could reduce the problem of organization to a formula. We would then dispense with the matter by saying that, if your thesis is, say, a generalization, you must have such-and-such a pattern of organization. Unfortunately for those who like life to be simple and fortunately for those who like variety, the matter is not reducible. An understanding of the relationship between organization and generative sentences does, however, provide a checklist of issues that you may or may not decide to use as the basis for your organization. It is imperative that, when you know your purpose or thesis, you analyze your generative sentences to see what questions they suggest.

Suppose you have decided to defend the thesis that Gladstone was a more effective prime minister than Disraeli. In order to prove this contention, you must answer, in your favor, the subquestions implied in your thesis: what do you mean by "effective" and in what ways was Gladstone more effective? These questions are "issues," that is, the crucial questions that must be answered if you are to convince your reader. The various types of generative sentences have their own issues.

THE OBSERVATION

Often an observation does not fall into the class of generative sentences requiring development and organization, but when it does, the structure is usually suggested by the breadth or vagueness of one of the terms. For instance, "James Ryun won the mile run" may require no development, because we agree that the word *won* means "He came in first." Another sentence containing the same verb, "The Americans won the last Olympics," probably does need developing, because few countries agree on what it means to "win" the Olympics. The issues raised are these.

1. What do your terms mean?

2. In what respects are your terms justified?

The Russians prefer to consider every sport, since they usually pile up a number of points in such sports as Graeco-Roman wrestling in which the United States is feeble or does not compete at all. Since their women athletes usually excel, Russia also likes to include results for both men and women. The United States prefers to consider only those track and field sports that characterize an American meet. The writer would have to show what he means by *won,* and then he might show why he thinks the term can be used.

2. CLASSIFICATION

If the thesis is classification, two issues immediately suggest themselves:

1. What are the characteristics of the class?

2. How does the specific instance satisfy the requirement of the class?

If the generative sentence is "Senator Flelps is a right-winger," the issues are "What is a right-winger?" and "In what ways does Senator Flelps act like a right-winger?" What are the issues suggested by the following sentences?

1. Climatically speaking, New England is a disaster area.

2. In 1909, Matisse was a pointillist.

3. Mark Twain was a Romantic.

It does not necessarily follow that every written composition whose thesis is a classification will have two equal main sections. For instance, William Van O'Connor's essay "Why *Huckleberry Finn* Is Not the Great American Novel" does, in a sense, have two parts, but they are unequal parts. Near the beginning of his critique, which appears in *College English*, October, 1955, is a paragraph defining a great novel: "[It] wants to be circumscribed, to live in its own terms, to fulfill itself imaginatively. On the other hand, it speaks to a people and to their beliefs about themselves." This section is quite brief. The bulk of the essay comes after the sentence ". . . there are a number of flaws in *Huckleberry Finn*" as the author shows how the novel does not fit the requirements described in his first part. He charges that the "movement" is contrived and that "there are two sorts of theatricality in the novel, melodrama and claptrap." Thus, the first issue "What are the characteristics of the class 'Great American Novel'?" suggests the topic headings, and the second issue "Does the specific fit the characteristics?" supplies the development of each section.

GENERALIZATION

If the thesis is a generalization, the issues are:

1. What is the meaning of the generalization?

2. What are the instances that yield the generalization?

3. Are there sufficient instances to merit a generalization?

If the thesis is "The French are impolite to tourists," the writer might classify the impoliteness as rudeness by cab drivers, by hotel employees, by pedestrians, by newspapers, and by hosts in general. This would be necessary, because he could not even suggest that he had been exposed to all Frenchmen, but he may have met all "classes" of Frenchmen.

Analyze the following generalizations for their implied structure.

1. Boxer dogs slobber.

2. He has no capacity for business.

3. "All that you miss in Shakespeare you find in John Bunyan." GEORGE BERNARD SHAW, IN *Dramatic Opinions and Essays,* 1907.

Note that each generalization has its own nature insofar as the structure it obligates is concerned. In the first instance, it would be easy to define "slobbering." It would also be easy to describe several examples of slobbering that you have observed. The difficulty would be in proving the third issue, i.e., whether this unlovely habit is characteristic of *all* Boxer dogs. Usually, the more difficult issues to answer, the crucial ones, take up more space. Very often the issues are telescoped, as would be probable of the statement about the Boxer dogs. The writer might describe as many examples as he could to convince his readers that every time he ever saw a Boxer dog, the combined sum of his specific instances, the dog drooled all over the area.

For the second sentence, the writer would first have to define "capacity for business." In contrast to the thesis about Boxer dogs, which would take almost no space for definition, in this case a large share of the paper would have to be used for definition.

The iconoclastic George Bernard Shaw spent about half of his essay demonstrating Shakespeare's deficiencies. Of Shakespeare's heroes he said, "Only one man in them all who believes in life, enjoys life, thinks life worth living, and has a sincere unrhetorical tear dropped over his deathbed." He went on to condemn the "paper origin of his [Shakespeare's] fancies," and spent nearly all of the remaining half of the essay demonstrating that the two requirements of great literature, "energy and elevation of spirit," are missing in Shakespeare, but are found in John Bunyan's *Pilgrim's Progress.* Shaw faced up only briefly to the third issue, "Are there sufficient instances to merit a generalization?," by pointing out that he had studied all "thirty-six big plays" and found that Shakespeare "understood nothing and believed nothing." Later, he commented, "I might multiply these instances by the dozen. . . ." Thus, although he used most of his words on two issues, he did not neglect the third.

JUDGMENT

If the thesis is a judgment, the issues that suggest a framework of organization resemble those for classification and generalization, which might be expected, since the boundary between any two kinds of ideas is often quite indistinct. The issues are:

1. What are the criteria for the judgment?

2. How does my specific instance fit the criteria?

If a writer were to develop the thesis that William Faulkner is a great writer, his organization probably would be suggested by the need for a criterion, perhaps that a "great writer uplifts the human heart" (which was Faulkner's own standard). He then might have to demonstrate that Faulkner, in spite of his preoccupation with lesbianism, sodomy, rape, and other degenerate behavior, demonstrated his faith in the family and in human strength and believed that they could triumph even in a doomed society. For practice, analyze how the following judgments and the issues raised could provide a structure for a theme.

Willie Mays is the greatest of all centerfielders.

"Charles Lamb was at once perhaps the sweetest, sanest, and most human of English prose writers." E. V. LUCAS.

"Freedom of choice in the knowledge of good and evil is the essence of man's humanity and the essence of Christ's teaching." FEODOR DOSTOEVSKY, AS PARAPHRASED BY PHILIP RAHV, IN *Partisan Review,* VOL. XXI, NO. 3.

"Returning to himself, let man consider what he is in comparison with all existence; let him regard himself as lost in his remote corner of nature; and from the little cell in which

he finds himself lodged, I mean the universe, let him estimate
at their true value the earth, kingdoms, cities, and himself.
What is man in the Infinite?" BLAISE PASCAL, *Pensées*.

Judgments are different from generalizations and classifications
in that they are essentially a form of measurement, measuring something
loosely defined as either quantity or quality. The first two judgments listed
above are straightforward in the structure they obligate. If a sportswriter wished to eulogize Willie Mays, the "Say-Hey" kid of the New
York and San Francisco Giants, in terms of the judgment listed above,
he would obviously have to define greatness in a centerfielder. Then
with form-fitting criteria for judgment nicely established, he would show
how "Wondrous Willie" fits all the requirements.

The second judgment has been included to show that skilled
and respected writers occasionally have the temerity to make really
extravagant statements. How do you think E. V. Lucas went about proving
his contention? Whatever information is required, note that at least the
organization of the theme would be clear enough: "sweetest, sanest, and
most human."

The second and third judgments are included to show that a
judgment, which is usually praise or condemnation and thus a value
judgment, is often buried in qualifications. In spite of the grimness of
Dostoevsky's tales, Rahv realizes that the famous Russian novelist regards
life as essentially good; it is good because man can tell the difference between good and evil and can choose between them freely. Thus, Rahv defines
Dostoevsky's standard, and the two points—an explanation of the standard and a description of how the Russian author's characters make their
free choice and are stoically pleased with life—provide the structure
of his essay.

In the fourth judgment, in a statement often cited as the beginning of existential philosophy, Pascal is saying that man is unimportant,
and he suggests a standard by which he proves man's insignificance. The
structure of his chapter on this subject results from his need both to
defend the standard and to demonstrate that man fits the standard.

CAUSAL RELATIONSHIP

Whenever the thesis indicates a causal relationship, the issues are:

1. Was the antecedent present every time the consequent
occurred?

2. When the antecedent was not present, did the consequent
ever happen?

3. Did the consequent happen every time the antecedent was present?

4. Is there a natural explanation why A, the antecedent, causes B, the consequent?

If you were to write a history of the germ theory of disease, its structure might very well be stretched on the framework provided by these four issues. Almost all scientific reports that announce a new discovery are organized around these issues, which, after all, are the heart of the scientific method. Certainly any account of Louis Pasteur's discoveries would reflect his concern for these issues. Pasteur's theory that germs, the antecedent, cause disease, the consequent, was disputed by many of his contemporaries, who thought that disease, mold, and sourness in milk developed spontaneously. Pasteur disproved the theory of spontaneous generation by boiling the milk and killing all the minute mold-producing organisms (or antecedent) and demonstrating that the ailment (or consequent), whether it was a disease or sourness in milk, did not develop when the bacteria were absent. At another point in his demonstrations, he showed that whenever germs entered the human system via, say, the saliva of a hydrophobic dog, the bitten person got the dog's disease. Whenever he found a person suffering from a disease, Pasteur used his microscope to prove that bacteria were present.

STOCK ISSUES *Problem & Solution*

Besides the issues that structure themes based on observation, classification, judgment, and causal relationship, there is another set of issues that are so inevitable they are called "stock issues."

We mentioned in the discussion of "Purpose" that one reason men write is to get an audience to do something. A man whose thesis is "America should intercede in the uprising in Montenegro" is *arguing for action*. Whenever a person argues for action, he has almost no choice but to consider the following four stock issues.

1. Is there a need for a change?

2. What plan shall I suggest?

3. Would this plan correct the need?

4. Is the plan feasible and preferable to another plan?

The thesis of Nancy Walker Alcaro's article "Colleges Don't Make Sense" (in *Woman's Day*, May, 1946) was that colleges should be aimed more at the profession almost everyone will enter, namely, being part of a family. She established her thesis in this fashion:

> The day I graduated from college I believed—modestly, and yet with a nice warm glow of conviction—that I was an educated young woman. I had salted away an impressive supply of miscellaneous information. My mind, after constant limbering up with fancy mental gymnastics, was as supple as a ballerina. I was all set to deal with Life. One year later, at close grips with two very elemental problems of living— marriage and motherhood—I was beginning to suspect that I was poorly equipped to handle either one. Now, after ten years, I know that for a girl who was earmarked for domesticity from the time she diapered her first doll, college was a criminal waste of time.

She then went on to demonstrate a need for a change by showing that although "about 80 per cent of the alumnae in women's colleges marry and raise families" and although admittedly colleges "turn out brilliantly trained teachers, artists, and professional women," the girl "who is destined to be primarily a woman is shortchanged." "Take my own case," she wrote:

> Shortly after graduation I married a young doctor just beginning his internship. Let's take a look at the qualifications of the wife to whom this lucky guy turned over the responsibility for his physical well-being, his house, his bank account, his children, and to a large extent his career itself. I was as informed as all get out when it came to the significance of revolution and romanticism. I could chatter about the minor English poets of the sixteenth century. I had studied Anglo-Saxon grammar. I knew all about the love life of the earthworm. But I couldn't cook a decent meal. I couldn't manage a house. Pregnancy amazed me. Babies scared me. And my knowledge of finance was limited to what-shall-I-do-until-my-allowance-comes?

Having cited examples, testimonials, and statistics to demonstrate the problems of feminine higher education, she presented her plan.

> The preparation of undergraduates for marriage should be a vibrant challenge to the liberal arts colleges. . . . Some standard college courses need only a change of focus. . . . How about a course in the fundamentals of investment, insurance, taxation, and managing a budget? . . . If colleges would offer courses in architecture for home owners and in interior deco-

ration . . . they would earn the gratitude of the husbands of their alumnae. . . . The most progressive step in education for women that has been made in recent years is a course in personal grooming offered by a junior college in the Middle West.

In discussing her plan, she showed how she thought it would correct the worries of many a businesswoman and housewife, and she condemned the established policy of thinking that a woman filled with the "intellectual doodling" of a liberal-arts education has something to apply to practical problems. Thus, Mrs. Alcaro considered each of the four stock issues that are the obligation of a writer arguing for policy.

Similarly, a writer presenting a case for a bond issue to build a new junior high school in his city would undoubtedly cite some statistics or illustrations to show the urgency of the problem of education; at the end of his introduction he would state his thesis that X City should build a new junior high school. His analysis of his task, influenced by his understanding of "stock issues," would probably dictate that he break the body of his presentation into three sections, answering the following questions.

1. Is there a need to increase X City's junior high school facilities?

2. Would a new building solve the problem?

3. Would a new building be better than some other solution, for example, the construction of additions to already existing facilities?

Problem and Solution. Frequently the stock issues are condensed into two major points, *problem* and *solution.* For instance, if an editorial recommends a bond issue to provide money for a new junior high school, it first discusses the need and then the proposed solution. Problem-solution is very often the structure of a paper arguing for an action or policy.

LITERARY CRITICISM AND SCHOLARLY ARTICLES

In some situations, a writer has very little freedom in selecting his structure. In some forms of scholarly discourse the issues are so thoroughly understood that readers frown upon any divergence or meandering. For better or worse, literary criticism and scientific articles are now almost prescribed by precedent and style books. Such rigid structuring guarantees the reader what he needs to know in the shortest number of words. A beginning scholar would ignore such formats only at his peril. Form for literary criticism is outlined by a section from Maurice Beebe's excellent book, *Literary Symbolism* (1960):

> The three essential parts of a critical paper are the introduction, the demonstration, and the conclusion:
>
> A. *Introduction or Proposal.* The opening section of your paper should contain the statement of thesis, a clear indication of your purpose in writing. If your paper is a long one, you may want to describe briefly the plan of what is to follow, outlining for the reader the major steps in your demonstration. In addition to the statement of thesis or purpose, the one essential, your introduction may also include any or all of the following, though not necessarily in this order:
>
> *Survey of Research.* You describe briefly the present position of research on the subject you are discussing and summarize the views held by other critics. Some writers prefer to put such information in a footnote, and some omit it altogether. However, the survey of research often helps to make your subject seem more significant, for you suggest in this way the need for amending the conventional view of the subject. You should avoid setting up a straw-man as opponent; one of the worst sins of critics is a deliberate distortion of current views in order to demolish something which either does not exist or is too weak to need refuting.
>
> *Boost.* You indicate the importance of your discovery or argument. Often the boost may be implied in the survey of research, but if very little or nothing has been said by others on your subject, your boost may consist simply of an expression of wonder at the strange neglect of something which, for reasons you hope your paper will make clear, is actually important for the full understanding of the subject in question. Sometimes the boost consists of the suggestion that your particular thesis opens larger questions concerning the subject in general. For example, in an essay on Hemingway's "The Short Happy Life of Francis Macomber," Warren Beck says in his opening paragraph:
>
> . . . Wilson's assumption that Mrs. Macomber murdered her husband has been rather generally accepted by readers. "Our clue to the full meaning of the act," says one critical discussion in this vein, "is given by the guide." However, one may question not just Wilson's credibility as a witness but his comprehension of Mrs. Macomber and of the Macombers' human situation. And this, in turn, involves larger questions concerning Hemingway's work, as to both its art and its substance. FROM "THE SHORTER HAPPY LIFE OF MRS.

MACOMBER," *Modern Fiction Studies*, I [NOVEMBER, 1955]
28.

Concession. Most arguments are stronger if they concede
something to the other side. You may wish to acknowledge
the existence of other valid critical interpretations or approaches, or you may want to point out that yours is but
one of many ways of viewing a complex subject that will
seem all the richer for the variety of views applied to it.

Capsule Summary. Some teachers ask their students to
include in their introductory section a brief synopsis or description of the work or works being discussed. If you have reason
to believe that your audience may not be well acquainted with
the work or if you want to refresh your reader's memory,
then a capsule summary may be useful.

B. *Demonstration*. This is the orderly presentation of
evidence which supports your thesis. Although it would seem
obvious that the demonstration is the most crucial of the
three parts and ought to be the longest section of the
paper, it is surprising how many critical essays seem to consist entirely of an introduction and a conclusion. In determining the most effective method of demonstration, you may
wish to review the six types of critical approach. . . . You
may use only one, several, or all of the approaches, but it
would perhaps be wise to choose one as the basic approach,
using any of the others to supplement it. If exegesis or explication is your main concern, then you will probably want to
present your evidence chronologically. If you use analysis,
you must organize in terms of selected aspects of your
subject, building up, if possible, to your strongest and most
important point. Comparison is best organized by the basis
of comparison rather than the subjects being compared,
and evaluation by whatever criteria you select. Interpretation has no set method of organization; it usually combines
with explication or analysis.

C. *Conclusion*. Your conclusion may consist of one or all
of the following:

Clincher. Sometimes, particularly in a shorter paper, your
strongest and most convincing evidence provides the only
conclusion necessary. But in such cases the clincher ought
to be something that ties together the several strands of
your subject.

Summary. You summarize briefly what you have attempted
to show, perhaps restating your thesis more exactly and
emphatically. A summary is seldom necessary in very short
papers.

Application of Conclusion. You may wish to suggest the implications of your discovery or argument as it relates to other works by the author or authors you are discussing, a whole period of literature, or a literary concept.

An article submitted for publication in a scientific journal must follow an even more rigid format. Almost every scientific society has a form book or style manual that outlines the exact organization of all reports. An article written by four Birmingham, England, professors, S. A. Barker, Susan M. Bick, J. S. Brimacombe, and P. J. Somers, and published in *Carbohydrate Research*, demonstrates a typical form. To concur with the journal's form book, the authors provided an introduction that explained the purpose of their research: "Purification studies of the type specific polysaccharide of Pneumonococcus Type V and II have revealed the answer to some of these problems, particularly as they concern C-substance and ribonucleic acid." In the next section, which had to be labeled "Experimental," the authors described the exact laboratory processes used. In the third section, "Discussion," the authors fulfilled the requirement of demonstrating "any appropriate reactions in [their] processes, and in the "Summary" they stated their findings: "DEA Sephadex has been shown to afford separation of Type V Pneumonococcus specific polysaccharide, C-substance, and other components, when alcohol fractionation, or detergent precipitation were only partially effective. Dissociable complex formation between Type II polysaccharides and nucleic acid has been demonstrated on the same column. Sephadex G-200 can be used to remove nucleic acid impurities from Type II Pneumonococcus polysaccharide." *Carbohydrate Research* is published in Amsterdam, but its requirements are typical of most scientific journals throughout the world.

Variety in organization

At this point in the discussion of organization, the student may feel that division is a mechanical process, since the selection of major points for a paper seems to depend entirely upon the purpose of the paper. Most writers and readers have been trained in the same thinking habits, and there is great likelihood that many people would organize similar material in the same way; however, there is no incontrovertible law. The following account shows that organization cannot be based purely on the analysis of purpose; it shows why the writer still must have a great deal of flexibility and judgment and why organization must vary with circumstance.

The story concerns the debating team of a small college. The subject of the debate was "Resolved: The United States Should Adopt the Essential Features of the British Broadcasting Corporation." Our team, which had chosen to take the affirmative, prepared for the "stock issues."

1. Is there a need for a change?

2. What plan shall we suggest?

3. Will our plan correct the evils of the present situation?

4. Is it feasible; are there any other factors that are important?

The members of the team prepared a very good case for the first three issues. They were prepared to show that American television has many faults: too many of its programs are based on violence and sentimentality; there is too little serious drama; what good programs there are all too often coincide or overlap during prime time. In preparing for their second and third issues, the debaters described the British Broadcasting Corporation, emphasizing its excellent news coverage, high-grade music, and quality dramatic productions. For the fourth issue, they were prepared only to demonstrate the feasibility of instituting a nationalized broadcasting company, the cost being more than made up by the saving that would result when manufacturers no longer had to sponsor television programs.

When our team met their first opponent, College A, they were amazed that three of their major points were conceded. Yes, there was much to be said against American television; yes, the British system does seem to be working well; and yes, it could be adopted by the United States without prohibitive cost. But—and it was on this point that the team taking the negative view spent all its efforts—such a plan would be dangerous to the American way of life. When Adolf Hitler took over Germany, when Benito Mussolini took over Italy, when Juan Perón took command of Argentina, when Josef Stalin wished to tighten his hold on Russia, and when Fidel Castro started the revolution in Cuba, their first acts were to acquire control of newspapers and broadcasting stations. America must have a free communications system. Our team saw that what they assumed would be issues were not, in this particular debate, *crucial* issues at all. They were not prepared to sort out the real from the imaginary dangers to a democratic way of life, and they lost the debate.

By the time of their second debate, they were ready to show that a governmentally controlled enterprise does not necessarily lead to fascism or to a dictatorship. After all, they were prepared to argue, we already have a federal postal system and a Tennessee Valley Authority that have not infringed upon our civil liberties. College B, however, challenged them on still another issue and proposed a counterplan, which conceded a few of the evils of the American system, but denied there was a need for such a drastic change as nationalizing American television and radio. All that was needed, said the team from College B, was a tightened system of regulation. The Federal Communications Commission had policed radio well, but it was somewhat behind in its job now that television was so important.

Our team was not prepared to debate the relative merits of regulation versus ownership—the issue which became crucial in this debate—and it lost again. The story ends happily, however. For the third debate our team was prepared on every issue presented—and won.

For our purposes in this text, the point is that, whenever there is argumentation for action, the specific organization will depend upon an analysis of the issues, but the writer must decide which issues are likely to be the crucial ones. His organization may therefore vary with the situation and the reader.

A writer may have other reasons to vary the structure of his paper. For instance, if he uses an expression that needs defining, he may insert a paragraph that contains not only the definition but also some examples and a contrast. He may even have to supply some background information that might begin, although in more specific terms, "Before the problem can be understood it is necessary to know a great deal about the history of the situation." A writer must learn to anticipate any questions, uncertainties, opposition, or counterplans that might arise in a discussion of his problem, and he must use this awareness to determine the structure of his paper and the relative importance he assigns to each issue and its consequent development. Organization is not mechanical; it requires a great deal of sensitivity and judgment on the part of the writer.

Order

When the writer has gone through the necessary synthesis and division and he knows his thesis or purpose, his major points, and the information he will use to develop them, he can go on to the next problem of organization. He must decide in which order to present his points, and he may have to decide whether to present his point of view in the introduction as a statement of purpose or thesis, whether to announce his topic, or whether to set up a controlling question.

Here again you, as a writer, should try to anticipate the audience's state of mind. Take the pattern called "problem and solution." In this instance, if you were trying to convince an apathetic audience to adopt a new plan, you would probably have a better chance of success if, instead of presenting your plan at the outset, you first aroused the audience as to the evils of the present situation.

Or take the pattern called "stock issues." Organize your paper by bringing up your points in exactly the order in which you could anticipate objections from your audience.

1. Is there a need for a change? (If not, why all the fuss?)

2. What plan do you propose? (Okay, I am interested now; can you correct the evils you described?)

3. Would the plan work? (Could we pay for it? Is it feasible?)

4. Are there any reasons why we should not adopt the plan? (Your plan sounds fine, but what about other plans? Is yours too liberal? Does it strike at the heart of my cherished rugged individualism?)

Suppose you are writing an expository paper with three main sections. Here are some suggestions that may be appropriate.

1. Try putting your most important or most interesting point first to get your audience's attention. Don't, however, trail off with your least interesting or least significant idea; put it in the middle, thus leaving a stronger attention holder for the end.

2. If one point depends upon another for clarity, you must, of course, delay it until your explanatory point has been covered.

3. Since psychologists believe that the last point is remembered longest, the first point next longest, and the middle point least of all, you may wish to put that point last which you desire your reader to remember best.

4. If you are working on a controversial topic, you will usually be wise to present the points first that will be most readily acceptable to your hostile audience. Get them nodding their heads in agreement; then hit them with the point they will be least likely to accept.

The phrasing of your thesis statement usually will provide clues as to the order of your points. Your order of subtopics must always agree, of course, with the pattern suggested by your actual statement of thesis. If your thesis is "An irritating situation in Egypt is caused by the difficulty of getting trained men to work in the villages," you first answer the question, "What is the irritating situation?" and then turn to the cause, "What is the difficulty of getting trained men to work in the villages?" Your pattern of organization is "effect and cause"; your phrasing provides the clue as to which should be discussed first. Conversely, you might decide to word your topic, "The difficulty of getting trained men to work in the villages has caused a severe problem in Egypt." Here you would discuss the cause before the effect.

Occasionally your thesis will be a compound or a complex sentence. If it is compound, you will probably have to decide which idea is easily acceptable to your audience or which idea is basic; that idea comes first. If the first clause is not controversial but the other is, you may delay the latter. For instance, suppose you have been asked to compare Matthew Arnold and Stéphane Mallarmé as poets and critics. You might come up with the thesis that Mallarmé was the better poet and Arnold the better critic. If the first idea is generally accepted, you may wish to dispose of it first and then lead your audience to your more original and controversial conviction.

Unfortunately, when writing a paper based on a compound sentence, too often you end up with two papers, the parts unrelated and the impact of your ideas lessened. Usually it is better to ask yourself which of the two ideas is more important and cast your thesis into a complex sentence: "Although the critic is right in considering Mallarmé the better poet, he is wrong in thinking Arnold the lesser critic." You will then introduce your first section in a subordinated fashion and devote the larger amount of space to the main clause of the sentence. Very rarely will you develop the subordinated part of the thesis last. If the subordination is a qualification, stating it first may show your audience that you are trying to be fair. If it is a concession to standard opinion, you will avoid sounding like a crackpot taking extreme issue with the world.

One last observation: As you plan your organization you may hit upon a pattern that makes very good sense, but that does not exactly fit your thesis. If you decide that this pattern has greater truth than the original thesis, rephrase your thesis until it exactly fits your preferred plan.

Outlining

A discussion of organization must include the controversial matter of the *outline*. For some reason, many students object to the outline, dismissing the matter with an airy toss of the head. "I always like to just start out and write. An outline cramps my style."

They may be right. Many skilled writers *do* just start out and write. This procedure permits them to take advantage of spontaneous creativity. It permits them to set down a number of words and ideas before the bloom of enthusiasm fades. Once he has sprayed out his blither of words, however, the skilled writer usually condenses the material to a few headings that show him what he has written. He is actually taking notes—making an outline—on what he himself has written. Then he begins to question his material. Does it contain all the points necessary to fulfill its purpose or develop his thesis? Is there some unnecessary material? His brief outline enables him to insert the essential and discard the irrelevant. He studies his first draft for the order of the points. Do they occur in the clearest and most persuasive order possible? He reviews his illustrations and definitions. More easily than if he were looking at his essay as a whole, he can check the material under the subtopics of his outline and make sound judgments.

Some writers use the outline earlier. They painstakingly prepare a full outline and insert each minute point. They argue that this early attention to division, order, proportion, relevance, and completeness actually eliminates many false steps, saves time, and results in a better final product.

Nearly all effective writers have evolved a technique that is somewhere between these two extremes. For that reason the following suggestions are presented.

First and foremost, an outline should have a *thesis statement,* formulating the main idea or message of the paper. This thesis statement should be placed right after the title before the outline begins. As you already know, the thesis statement should consist of a single sentence that states as simply and yet as fully as possible the central point your paper is driving at. It may be a short sentence, or it may be quite long and complex if the idea you are trying to put across is intricate. But whichever it is, it should be an adequate statement of your main point. Incidentally, in your theme itself, the thesis idea need not be fired at the reader in exactly the severe and concise wording of your outline. This is particularly true in those cases where the exact wording of your thesis idea as presented in the outline would be too formal for the general tone of your theme.

Once you have formulated your thesis idea and have a general pattern for the paper in your mind, you can proceed to the outline itself. There are two kinds of formal outlines, *sentence outlines* and *topic outlines.* In a sentence outline, as the term suggests, each item is written out as a complete sentence, while the topic outline consists of a list of topics to be discussed in your paper and should contain no complete sentences (except for the thesis statement, of course).

Each of the sentences in a sentence outline formulates an idea (a subdivision of the thesis idea) that you will explain or defend in the paper. These sentences are arranged in an outline order. Although a sentence outline contains much detail, the topic outline is easier to prepare and is sufficiently clear for most purposes. See, for instance, the sample outlines on pages 80–82.

In the years outline form has been used, writers have developed the following useful conventions.

1. Place the title above the outline. It is not one of the topics within the outline itself.

2. Under the title place the thesis or purpose statement. Like the title, the thesis statement is not one of the topics within the outline itself and therefore should not be numbered.

3. Do not use the terms "Introduction," "Body," and "Conclusion" in the outline. These are merely organizational terms in your own mind.

4. If you follow the most popular system, number main headings with Roman numerals; letter the subtopics under each main heading with capital letters. Divisions of subtopics, in descending order of importance, are given numbers and letters as follows: Arabic numerals, small letters, Arabic numerals in parentheses, small letters in parentheses. Your instructor may recommend a different system.

5. Indent subtopics to place all corresponding numbers or letters under each other in a vertical line, as follows.

    I.

        A.

        B.

            1.

            2.

                a.

                b.

                    (1)

                    (2)

                        (a)

                        (b)

    II.

        A.

        B.

6. Never allow a subtopic or main topic to stand alone; use two or more of each kind or none at all. Subtopics are divisions of the topics

above them (as main points are divisions of the paper), and nothing can be divided into fewer than two parts. The following outline would *not* be conventional.

  C. There are several scholarly journals needed.
   1. *PMLA*
   2. *College Composition and Communication*
   3. *College English*
  D. An international magazine is recommended.
   1. *Pan-America*

The last two items should be combined as follows:

  D. An international magazine, *Pan-America*, is recommended.

 7. Begin each topic and subtopic with a capital letter. In a topic outline, do not follow topics with a period or any other punctuation mark.

 8. (Topic Outline Only): All main topics should be parallel in form; each group of subtopics should be parallel in form. For example, if the first main topic is a noun, the other main topics must also be nouns; if the first subtopic under this main topic is an adjective, the corresponding subtopics must also be adjectives.

 Examples of a sentence outline and a topic outline follow. For comparison, the same subject has been presented first in sentence outline, then in topic outline form. Notice that while even the smallest subtopics in the sentence outline are stated in complete sentences, the only complete sentence in the topic outline is the thesis statement.

SENTENCE OUTLINE: A TOWN IN TRANSITION

Thesis: My home town is part small town and part suburban area in both its physical make-up and major qualities.

 I. Tonford, my home town, has gone through three distinct phases in its history up to today.
  A. By the early nineteenth century, Tonford had established itself well as a small, thriving, attractive, and independent New England town of about 2,500 people with a strong sense of town unity.
  B. By the second decade of this century, it had changed little in size, but with the general movement of young people away from small towns it began to lose its civic spirit and retreated into cantankerousness and pessimistic backwardness.
  C. By the fifties, the migration had turned back to country areas and Tonford became a thriving, slightly urbanized

small town, serving as a suburb for several neighboring sizable cities.

II. Today the town is a blend of the qualities of a small town and an urban society.

    A. Many of Tonford's significant qualities reflect its original small-town nature.

        1. Tonford has the strong conservatism of the New England small town.

            a. It hesitates to appropriate public moneys for anything but the most necessary things and sometimes even balks there.

            b. It fights strongly against any encroachment on its independence by state or federal agencies.

            c. It is polite but a little reserved to strangers and newcomers.

        2. It has also the small-town virtues of strict honesty, fear of God, and sudden and remarkable generosity in a good cause.

    B. The urban group has brought a new civic-mindedness and a strong civic activity, has forced improvements in many areas, and has modified the small-town attitudes in many ways, bad as well as good.

        1. The newer bloc that has moved into Tonford from neighboring cities has revived the original fighting spirit in town affairs.

        2. The same group, marked by an urban consciousness of the importance of planned growth, has forced improvement in town schools, town sanitation and water supply, and in zoning laws to preserve the picturesqueness and attractiveness of the town as a residential area.

        3. This group has given the town the more cosmopolitan flavor and open-mindedness of a primarily professional and business group, as opposed to an agricultural group, although it has a corresponding lack of respect for basic virtues such as honesty and generosity if they happen to combine with a marked and proud illiteracy and close-mindedness.

III. Although these forces are now often in violent conflict, the future will undoubtedly see a modification and reconciliation of both forces to the general benefit of the town.

TOPIC OUTLINE: A TOWN IN TRANSITION

Thesis: My home town is part small town and part suburban area in both its physical make-up and major qualities.

  I. The Past
   A. Early nineteenth century
   B. First part of twentieth century
     1. The Twenties
     2. The Fifties
 II. The Present
   A. Small-town characteristics
     1. New England conservatism
       a. Extreme thrift
       b. Strong sense of independence
       c. Distant attitude to newcomers
     2. Small-town virtues
       a. Honesty
       b. Fear of God
       c. Generosity
   B. Urban characteristics
     1. Competition in town affairs
     2. Improvements in important areas
       a. Schools
       b. Sanitation and water supply
       c. Zoning
     3. Cosmopolitan attitudes
       a. Favorable
       b. Unfavorable
III. The Future

Notice that the sentence outline gives a quite complete résumé of all the ideas presented in the paper. Anyone reading the sentence outline knows what ideas are going to be presented in the paper and can determine the writer's attitude toward each of the specific characteristics of his home town. The topic outline gives no such detailed information, but indicates topics and the basis of organization. Note also that some of the subtopics in the topic outline have been subdivided even further than in the sentence outline (for instance, II-A-2, II-B-2, and II-B-3), primarily because the separate points are indicated in the main subtopic statements of the sentence outline, whereas no such complete statement is possible in the topic outline.

Transitions

When you have decided upon your thesis, the major points, and their order, you will need to consider how to weave them all together. It is the function of *transitions* to provide a smooth flow in meaning, structure, and sound from one sentence to the next. When possible, transitions reinforce the relationship of any unit to the total message of the composition. If the points of your final paper seem to be a series of unrelated essays or paragraphs or if the parts do not stick together, your paper will lack coherence.

In many cases, writers have the logical relationship between paragraphs, ideas, and sentences quite clearly in mind, but, forgetting that their audiences are not mind readers, they fail to insert helpful connections. Note the absence of connectives in the following paragraph.

> Because my grandfather had to help his family, he had to leave school after the sixth grade. He worked every day, read every night and obtained his Bachelor's and Master's degrees from Columbia after he was married.

The student who wrote the paragraph obviously knows all about his grandfather, and the relationships are clear in his own mind, but because of the lack of transitions the reader can only wonder what happened between the time Grandfather left school and the time he obtained his degrees. After the student revised the paragraph, these relationships became clear.

> Because my grandfather had to help his family, he had to leave school after the sixth grade. *He did not want to give up his education entirely, however. From the day he had to leave school and start working,* he read for a couple of hours every night. *As a result,* he covered the whole high school curriculum on his own and, after he was married, was able to enter Columbia University. *In due course, he* obtained his Bachelor's and Master's degrees there.

As you can see, gaps in content and connections can be filled either by necessary information or by transitional devices.

In some cases, whole but brief paragraphs serve as transitions between longer paragraphs, as in this selection entitled "Plot" by E. M. Forster.

I. Let us define a plot. We have defined a story as a narrative of events arranged in their time-sequence. A plot is also a narrative of events, the emphasis falling on causality. "The king died and then the queen died," is a story. "The king died, and then the queen died of grief," is a plot. The time-sequence is preserved, but the sense of causality overshadows it. Or again: "The queen died, no one knew why, until it was discovered that it was through grief at the death of the king." This is a plot with a mystery in it, a form capable of high development. It suspends the time-sequence, it moves as far away from the story as its limitations will allow. Consider the death of the queen. If it is in a story we say "and then?" If it is in a plot we ask "why?" That is the fundamental difference between these two aspects of the novel. A plot cannot be told to a gaping audience of cave men or to a tyrannical sultan or to their modern descendant the movie-public. They can only be kept awake by "and then—and then——." They can only supply curiosity. But a plot demands intelligence and memory also.

II. Curiosity is one of the lowest of the human faculties. You will have noticed in daily life that when people are inquisitive they nearly always have bad memories and are usually stupid at bottom. The man who begins by asking you how many brothers and sisters you have is never a sympathetic character, and if you meet him in a year's time he will probably ask you how many brothers and sisters you have, his mouth again sagging open, his eyes still bulging from his head. It is difficult to be friends with such a man, and for two inquisitive people to be friends must be impossible. Curiosity by itself takes us a very little way, nor does it take us far into the novel—only as far as the story. If we would grasp the plot we must add intelligence and memory.

III. Intelligence first. The intelligent novel-reader, unlike the inquisitive one who just runs his eye over a new fact, mentally picks it up. He sees it from two points of view: isolated, and related to the other facts that he has read on previous pages. Probably he does not understand it, but he does not expect to do so yet awhile. The facts in a highly organized novel (like *The Egoist*) are often of the nature of cross-correspondences and the ideal spectator cannot expect to view them properly until he is sitting up on a hill at the end. This element of surprise or mystery—

the detective element as it is sometimes rather emptily called —is of great importance in a plot. It occurs through a suspension of the time-sequence; a mystery is a pocket in time, and it occurs crudely, as in "Why did the queen die?" and more subtly in half-explained gestures and words, the true meaning of which only dawns pages ahead. Mystery is essential to a plot, and cannot be appreciated without intelligence. To the curious it is just another "and then—". To appreciate a mystery, part of the mind must be left behind, brooding, while the other part goes marching on.

IV. That brings us to our second qualification: memory.

V. Memory and intelligence are closely connected, for unless we remember we cannot understand. If by the time the queen dies we have forgotten the existence of the king we shall never make out what killed her. The plot-maker expects us to remember, we expect him to leave no loose ends. Every action or word ought to count; it ought to be economical and spare; even when complicated it should be organic and free from dead matter. It may be difficult or easy, it may and should contain mysteries, but it ought not to mislead. And over it, as it unfolds, will hover the memory of the reader (that dull glow of the mind of which intelligence is the bright advancing edge) and will constantly rearrange and reconsider, seeing new clues, new chains of cause and effect, and the final sense (if the plot has been a fine one) will not be of clues or chains, but of something aesthetically compact, something which might have been shown by the novelist straight away, only if he had shown it straight away it would never have become beautiful. We come up against beauty here—for the first time in our enquiry: beauty at which a novelist should never aim, though he fails if he does not achieve it. I will conduct beauty to her proper place later on. Meanwhile please accept her as part of a completed plot. She looks a little surprised at being there, but beauty ought to look a little surprised: it is the emotion that best suits her face, as Botticelli knew when he painted her risen from the waves, between the winds and the flowers. The beauty who does not look surprised, who accepts her position as her due—she reminds us too much of a prima donna.
E. M. FORSTER, *Aspects of the Novel,* 1927.

In these paragraphs, the author discusses the qualifications necessary to understand the plot of a novel. Curiosity alone is not enough.

To grasp a good plot, the reader needs intelligence and memory. Paragraph III discusses the need for intelligence. Before shifting to his third point in paragraph V, which, again in considerable detail, treats the need for memory, the author inserts paragraph IV, which, although very brief (only one sentence), supplies the necessary connective idea: "That brings us to our second qualification: memory." The transition between the discussion of intelligence and the discussion of memory is clear. Besides wishing to demonstrate a transitional paragraph, we have included this long passage because we desired to show that one of the best stylists in modern literature is so concerned with keeping his structure clear that he does not reject the most mechanical of all transitions, numbers.

Sometimes transitions between sentences present more trouble than do transitions between paragraphs. In the following selection, for instance, a student described his automobile. These two sentences occurred fairly early in the paper.

> The motor itself is in good condition. Such things as the carburetor, battery, oil filter, brake and radiator are not always up to par, especially at the most inappropriate times.

An instructor—particularly one unfamiliar with the workings of an automobile engine—might write in the margin, "Illogical. Aren't you contradicting yourself?" An inserted transition explains what the student had in mind.

> The motor itself is in good condition, *but* such things as the carburetor, battery, oil filter, brake and radiator are not always up to par, especially at the most inappropriate times.

There are numerous ways to achieve coherence between sentences.

1. In the second sentence repeat a word or phrase that appears in the first sentence.

> A favorite device was to make a *moccasined* person tread in the tracks of the *moccasined* enemy, and thus hide his own trail. Cooper wore out barrels and barrels of *moccasins* in working that trick. MARK TWAIN, "FENIMORE COOPER'S LITERARY OFFENSES," 1894.
>
> The *colors, noise and smells of a football game* hold me spellbound. Not unexpectedly, the *colors, noise and smells of a football game* constitute the earliest recollections of my childhood.

2. In the second sentence use a synonym for a word in the first sentence.

> When I go home for a vacation, *my kid brother* invariably presents the greatest threat to my peace of mind. *The little rascal* thinks nothing of waking me with shouts of glee at six o'clock every morning.

3. In the second sentence use a pronoun whose antecedent is in the first sentence.

> The *engine* will give good service if not abused. *It* will run on gas, castor oil, alcohol or nitro. *It* may be lubricated with many different oil products. *It* may be cooled with water, alcohol, kerosene or methylene. Lastly, an *engine* may be used for almost any purpose.

4. Begin two consecutive sentences with the same grammatical construction.

> *On the right* the visitor sees a dark brown, dismal looking, apparently abandoned cage, with the word "INFORMA-TION" on it. *On the left* is a wooden table, which, at twelve o'clock, is piled high with various student paraphernalia.

5. Draw a logical conclusion in the second sentence from a statement in the first sentence, using logical connectives.

> When I first entered the College of Basic Studies, my study habits were no different from those of most freshmen. As a result, I failed two of my midsemester examinations.

For a demonstration of how a skilled writer uses these internal techniques to guarantee clear organization and coherence, turn back to "Plot" by E. M. Forster and pick out the transitions and the five devices mentioned: repetition of a key word, use of a synonym of a key word, use of a pronoun that has an antecedent in a preceding sentence, repetition of a grammatical construction, and an indication of a logical relationship.

All too often a careless writer uses connectives loosely, forgetting that each one has a specific meaning and special use. Even an experienced writer can profit by occasionally checking over his supply of transitional words and phrases.

1. *To introduce a parallel idea*	and, in addition, moreover, also, and then, secondly, thirdly (etc.), finally

2. *To introduce an example*   for example, for
                                    instance, to illustrate

3. *To demonstrate a contrast*   on the other hand,
                                    nevertheless, however,
                                    still, but

4. *To conclude*   therefore, in conclusion,
                                    consequently,
                                    accordingly, in other
                                    words, as a result

The paragraph below, taken from a student theme about the stereotyped quality of some motion pictures demonstrates the value of transitions. In Variant A, transitions between sentences and ideas have been omitted. In Variant B, they are supplied. Study the difference and determine exactly the relationships between sentences and ideas that are supplied by the italicized parts in Variant B.

A

The "Western" or cowboy movie could use some changes. The cowboy movie opens with two dirty and unshaven cowboys walking along in the desert. They are lost after chasing a no-good outlaw. Their horses are dead, and their canteens are empty. Tex drops to the ground and declares he can't go another step. Idaho drags Tex to some shade and says he'll go for help. He is attacked by Indians, wounded by outlaws and bitten by rattlesnakes. Idaho makes it to town, has a drink, rides all the way back, shoots his gun to scare all the vultures and saves Tex's life. A contented vulture sitting on the bones of old Tex would be a better final scene.

B

Another type of movie that could use some changes is the "Western." The *cowboy movie* opens with two dirty and unshaven cowboys walking along in the desert. *One's name is Tex, and he comes from (of course) Texas; the other one's name is Idaho, and he comes from Massachusetts.* They *had been* chasing a no-good outlaw and are *now* lost *in the desert. As we join the boys,* their horses are dead, and their canteens are empty. Tex drops to the ground and declares he can't go *on* another step. Idaho drags Tex to some shade and says he'll go *on* for help. *On the way* he is attacked by Indians, wounded by outlaws and bitten by a rattlesnake. Idaho, *however*, makes it to town, has a drink, *procures a horse*, rides all the way back, shoots his gun to scare all the vultures and saves Tex's life. *Just once* I would like to see old Idaho not make it back, *and let the final scene be* a contented vulture sitting on the bones of old Tex.

Of all the aspects of writing, probably the process of organization is the one in which the writer shows most effectively the power of his intellect. The aspects of organization—synthesis, division, ordering, and interrelating with transitions—are the essence of the complex idea he wishes to communicate. Organization is to writing what the skeleton is to the human being, the framework to a building or a house. In short, organization is worth a great deal of attention and effort.

Projects

1. Define and illustrate the following terms:

organization	framing sentence
structure	subordinate
chronological	correlative
spatial	issue
implied structure	crucial issue
topical	stock issue
transition	order
cause and effect	standard patterns
problem-solution	

2. Turn back to pp. 80–81, the sentence outline of "A Town in Transition," and analyze how the generative nature of the thesis dictates parts I and II and makes III logical. Analyze sentences I and II to see how they generate the need for A, B, and C. What are the operative words in the sentences? What classes of sentences are they? (Observation, Classification, Generalization, Judgment, Causal Relationship?) Do the issues they generate agree with the analysis on pp. 63–68?

3. Assume that each sentence below appears either in a letter, paragraph, essay, or book. What class of "idea" is it? What issues are likely to be raised? On the basis of the implied structure, deduce the pattern that might be used to analyze and develop the idea. Indicate what transitions would be used to move from point to point.

a. Dear Mother and Father: I want to get married.
b. I have three reasons for acting the way I do—all of them bad.

c. The Fourth of July weekend is the time we commemorate the Declaration of Independence and kill people on the highways.

d. "To renew one's idiom or one's language is to renew one's conception of one's vision of the world." EUGENE IONESCO, *Notes and Counter Notes*, 1964.

e. "The fatigue gets worse up to a certain critical point when gradually or suddenly it passes away, and we are fresher than before." WILLIAM JAMES, DISCUSSING "SECOND WIND," IN *Psychology*, 1892.

f. We should fliggledig the worst foozlepurps.

g. "The tragic disunity of Christians of which contemporaries are so acutely aware is almost as old as Christianity itself." XAVIER RYNNE, *Letters from Vatican City*, 1964.

h. "During the nineteenth century good democrats were primarily concerned with insuring representation in the assemblies and with extending the control of the assemblies over the executive power." WALTER LIPPMANN, *The Public Philosophy*, 1955.

i. "The difficulty in approaching the question of the relations between Religion and Science is that its elucidation requires that we have in our minds some clear idea of what we mean by either of the terms, 'religion' and 'science.'" ALFRED NORTH WHITEHEAD, *Science and the Modern World*, 1925.

j. "The predators—insects that kill and consume other insects—are of many kinds." RACHEL CARSON, *The Silent Spring*, 1962.

4. There is an old saw known by people who are active in civic affairs: "It's disloyal to fight against building a new City Hall, unintellectual to fight against a new high school building, and immoral to fight against a new church building. So you fight against the site they have selected." Can you explain this Machiavellian statement? What does it say about the selection of issues for a debate on such subjects? Do you see how this statement might suggest "good" reasons and "real" reasons for action or thought?

5. Supply the missing transitions and justify each choice by stating the function it performs.

I was accepted and started work. My experience had been derived chiefly from books I was not prepared for the difficult period of adjustment. I soon became discouraged with myself and so dissatisfied with my job that I was on the point of quitting. My employer must have sensed this He called me into his office and talked to me about the duties of my position and the opportunities for advancement. I realized that there was nothing wrong with me or the job, and I decided to stay.

6. The following sentences or sentence groups contain bad transitions, misleading the reader as to the relationship of the ideas expressed. Find the faulty transitions, explain why they are wrong, and replace each one with a correct transition.

a. Susie rarely keeps within the speed limit, whereas she believes she must have the speedometer at a maximum. However, if Susie finds that she is lagging behind another car, she'll honk the horn but ride so close to the other car that she practically goes up his tail pipe!

b. Elevators, escalators, cashiers, shopping carts, and basement bargains are all part of the shopper's world of today, and this world is certainly a far cry from its general-store origin. This, however, shows that the life of a shopper has markedly changed with the growth of the general store into a large-scale shopping plaza.

c. The signal is given, so that the new ship slides on greased rails into the water.

d. Cars became more common, and farmers took their business to the larger towns, in which stores were better and prices were lower.

e. He gave me his skis, but he had no further use for them.

f. The power failed recently in our city, whereas, alarm clocks went forty minutes late. However, most people were late for work that morning.

g. A pilot train always precedes the president's train because of protection from any possible danger.

h. Charles had fallen in the creek because he was on his way home. Moreover, his clothes were all wet.

i. An increase in Federal tax would mean more revenue for the central government. On the other hand, an increase in State tax would mean more money for the local government.

j. Bill had come in from the last school dance well past midnight. Thus his father was very angry.

k. Tardiness is not tolerated in this class. Similarly, if you are late for class, you will be penalized.

l. Tardiness is not tolerated in this class and will be punished. In addition, Mary Ann Roach was late every day last week; thus, I am going to give her a lower grade for the term.

7. In a prose anthology or in a recent edition of a serious magazine, such as *Atlantic Monthly* or *Harper's Magazine*, find the theses of several essays and see whether you can predict the organization that they imply. Outline the essays to see whether you succeeded. Discuss any differences you find and see whether they are based on assumptions about the education and attitude of an audience. Note all transitions and comment on their exact function. Analyze the structure of subsections and paragraphs in the essays.

8. Write a 500–750 word theme based on argument for policy. You must consider all the stock issues, but you may take either side. You may, for instance, argue for reform of your high-school or college curriculum, of the

social structure of your home town or college society, of your church liturgy or prayer book, or of the automobile, television, or steel industries.

Further reading

CLARK, DONALD LEMEN. *Rhetoric in Greco-Roman Education.* (New York: Columbia University Press, 1957). See especially p. 80 on "Order": "The strongest argument should come first."

CHAPTER 4

THE PREDICTED CONTENT: DEVELOPMENT

Recently a woman sent to Saturday Review a manuscript detailing an original and arresting idea. Because the manuscript, interesting as it was, seemed to the editors to be somewhat lacking in detail and documentation, it was returned to the author with the suggestion that she strengthen it where necessary and then resubmit it. In a few days the woman replied in effect: "I don't see why my article needs any supporting facts. It is based on my personal observations. And besides, anybody can see for himself that what I am saying is true."

But the writer is the eyes and ears of his reader, and those eyes and ears must be alert today as never before, in order to show the reader the facts on which he will ultimately base his judgments. JAMES F. FIXX, *Saturday Review,* NOVEMBER 17, 1962.

In this textbook we have directed much attention to the generative sentence. We have learned that the serious messages that intelligent, informed, and responsible people wish to express can usually be summarized in one sentence, but that they cannot really be communicated clearly or convincingly without more information. The generative sentence is occasionally little more than a hint of the total message. Consider this report on a fictitious book called *The Longest Blade*.

> The main reason *The Longest Blade* is such a great book is because it is interesting. Probably the single biggest contribution to this interest is the excellent plot, which covers several generations in its sweep and tells many stories. Another reason that the book is so interesting is that it contains so many excellent characterizations. The central figure is shown from the time he began his worldly life till the time he is near death and, besides the hero, there are many other characters, mostly feminine, that are well developed. It must not be overlooked that *The Longest Blade* also covers an important era in our history. Everyone will be interested in the clothing, manners, morals, and intrigues. Considering these facts, it is easy to see why Clifton Holton was able to say about this book: "It can take its place along with *Gone with the Wind* on any bookshelf."

This brief composition has merit. The fact that the writer liked the plot, characterizations, and setting shows that he raised the proper issues. His generalizations are appropriate in that they add up to a unified thesis. The deficiencies of this report, however, go beyond tautology ("the reason is . . . because"), the excessive use of the weak verb *is*, the flowery diction ("began his worldly life"), and the ambiguity of the "well-developed" women characters. The report, in fact, is really only an outline. To convey a clear message, each elliptical assertion must be illustrated. Each sentence needs to have the prediction of its content fulfilled. We need to know what the "plot" is. What are the "stories" it tells? We need to observe some of the characterization. What "era in our history" is covered? What is meant by "covered"? We must have details before we can accept the writer's conviction that *The Longest Blade* is "such a great book." Without these details, the general and vague assertions fit almost every historical novel ever written.

Effective writing must be a mixture of the general and the specific, a blend of the abstract and the concrete, a tapestry with a texture of foreground ideas and background exposition and evidence. A collection of facts or other specific data can be confusing; they must be given meaning by a generalization. Writing that stays on one level, whether it be a high level of abstraction or generalization—as in the report on *The Longest Blade*—or a lower level of facts and anecdotes, is said to be on a "dead level" of generalization or abstraction.

The "ladder of abstraction"

A simple method of visualizing the complex matter of abstraction levels is provided by S. I. Hayakawa's "ladder of abstraction," a version of which appears below. (This concept was introduced in 1939 in Hayakawa's *Language in Action.*) At the lowest level of abstraction is a specific, named individual, a collection of many attributes, qualities, and characteristics. In the diagram below, "Smoky" is the name of a real, specific, three-year-old gray male housecat. On the second rung of the ladder, Smoky is deprived of the specific qualities of age, color, sex, and name and becomes merely a cat. On the third rung, he is divested even of his cathood: he is seen as a pet—whether cat, dog, or canary is not known. Finally, at the top of the ladder, "matter," the real cat Smoky is merely differentiated from all non-material qualities (like courage or the soul) in the universe. Ladders of abstraction may start from either end—with the specific named individual at the highest level, or with the very abstract name at the highest level. The important point here is that since abstract terms refer to many specifics, they are often vague. They are thus often generative: they need examples and illustrations before they become clear.

matter

living being

animal

pet

cat

Smoky / and all of his qualities and atoms.

The Ladder of Abstraction.

The paragraph

The basic unit of composition that contains the essential blend of the general and the specific is the *paragraph*. The generative sentence, which hints that more should or will be said, is, in this case, the *topic sentence*. The detail that follows or precedes the paragraph's topic sentence is called the *development*.

The following excerpt demonstrates the two parts of a paragraph. The first sentence is the topic sentence. Observe the obligation it generates.

> Behind the urge toward "joining" is the sense of the mysterious and exotic. To belong to a secret order and be initiated into its rites, to be part of a "Temple" with a fancy Oriental name, to parade in the streets of Los Angeles, Chicago, or New York dressed in an Arab fez and burnoose, to have high-sounding titles of potentates of various ranks in a hierarchy: all this has appeal in a non-hierarchical society from which much of the secrecy and mystery of life has been squeezed out. The fraternal groups flourish best in the small towns of the Middle West: the drearier the cultural wasteland of the small town, the greater the appeal of the exotic. Americans have an ambivalent attitude toward secrecy: they want everything out in the open, yet they delight in the secrecy of fraternal groups, as Tom Sawyer's gang of boys in Mark Twain's book did, and as the cellar clubs and the boys' gangs in the big-city slums still do. Much of the appeal of the Ku Klux Klan lies in this mysterious flim-flammery, at once sadistic and grimly prankish. In many ways the American male of adult years is an arrested small boy, playing with dollars and power as he did once with toys or in gangs, and matching the violence of his recreation to the intensity of his loneliness. MAX LERNER, *America As a Civilization*, 1957.

A paragraph *in toto* may be at a high level of generalization, or it may be at a very low level. Contrast these two paragraphs:

(1)

> I am indeed aware that the movement for abolition [of capital punishment] is widespread and articulate, especially in England. It is headed there by my old friend and publisher, Mr. Victor Gollancz, and it numbers such well-known writers as Arthur Koestler, C. H. Rolph, James Avery Joyce, and Sir John Barry. Abroad as at home the profession of

psychiatry tends to support the cure principle, and many liberal newspapers, such as the *Observer,* are committed to abolition. In the United States there are at least twenty-five state leagues working to the same end, plus a national league and several church councils, notably the Quaker and the Episcopal.   JACQUES BARZUN, *The American Scholar,* SPRING, 1962.

(2)

But why kill? I'm ready to believe the statistics tending to show that the prospect of his own death does not stop the murderer. For one thing he is often a blind egotist, who cannot conceive the possibility of his own death. For another, detection would have to be infallible to deter the more imaginative who, although afraid, think they can escape discovery. Lastly, as Shaw long ago pointed out, hanging the wrong man will deter as effectively as hanging the right one. So, once again, why kill? If I agree that moral progress means an increasing respect for human life, how can I oppose abolition? *Ibid.*

Notice that the first paragraph mentions specific people and organizations; it abounds with capital letters and proper nouns. It is low on the ladder of abstraction. The second paragraph is much more abstract. Several of the sentences in the development are themselves generative; they could be the topic sentences for paragraphs lower than themselves on the ladder of abstraction. Both paragraphs, nevertheless, have the essentials of a paragraph: a general topic sentence and a less general development.

Note a second distinction between the two paragraphs. In the first, the topic sentence needs to be clarified or explained. Its development is, therefore, called exposition; the paragraph itself is called "expository." The second topic sentence is controversial. The development required is called evidence or proof; the paragraph itself is called "argumentative."

In addition to being characterized by a topic sentence and its required development, paragraphs are visually identifiable on the page by indentation, an arbitrary use of white space to indicate a change in thought. Furthermore, a page broken into several paragraphs is less oppressive to the average reader, who may be cowed by information so dense it cannot be separated into a progression of ideas.

Many writers seem to indent only when they have an uncontrollable urge to do so. Others arbitrarily break up a paragraph to avoid an overly dense page; they rarely let their paragraphs exceed a half-page in length. Conversely, since a series of short paragraphs conveys the impression of fragmentary, superficial thinking, some writers avoid having more than three or four paragraphs per page. Conversation is treated differently, of course, the transition from one speaker to another being indicated not only by quotation marks, but also by a new paragraph, as in the following dialogue:

> My teacher thought for a while and said, "The two major characteristics of behavior—"
>
> "But I am not asking about behavior," I interrupted. "I want to know what you think."
>
> "Miss Barr," my professor answered severely, "If you keep interrupting, I never will be able to answer your question."

In general, however, writers do tend to assemble thoughts according to the progression of generalization and development, and this relationship results in paragraphs whose bounds are marked by indenting. If we return to the concept of levels of abstraction, we can see that indentations at the beginnings of paragraphs mark the peaks of the vertical play of abstractions. There will be a generative sentence, perhaps a generalization or judgment that is quite abstract, and it will be preceded by an indentation. The next few sentences will be less abstract and will supply the material needed to fulfill the obligatory prescribed content. Then, having stated and developed one idea, the writer will move on to another, which will necessitate another generative sentence and its development and thus another paragraph. It is conceivable and likely that one paragraph might bring up a very broad idea, which will be divided into two or three subordinate ideas, each of which requires a peak of abstraction (a topic sentence) and some lower plateaus of abstraction (development) and thus its own paragraph.

The following paragraph by Howard Mumford Jones illustrates the levels of abstraction.

> We debunked too much. During the iconoclastic period spirited biographers laid about them with a mighty modern hand. They told us that Lincoln was a small-town politician, Washington a land-grabber, Grant a stubborn and conceited mule, and Bryan an amusing idiot. We learned that there was something to be said for Aaron Burr, but not very much for Sam Adams, Longfellow, or Harriet Beecher Stowe. In place of being American vikings, the pioneers turned out to be neurotic, dissatisfied fellows unpopular in their home towns, and Columbia, the gem of the ocean, was described as a sort of kept woman in the pay of millionaires. Apparently the only Americans who ever died to make the world safe

for democracy died in 1917–18, and made a mistake in
doing so. I do not deny either the truth or the necessity of
many of these modern biographies. I am no more comfortable
than the next man in a room full of plaster saints. But, when
the biographers got through, all the heroes had disappeared.
HOWARD MUMFORD JONES, *Atlantic Monthly*, NOVEMBER, 1938.

The first sentence is generative: It creates for Professor Jones
the obligation of demonstrating the concepts set up by the two operative
expressions, "debunked" and "too much." There are really two leading
thoughts.

1. We debunked. (An observation)

2. The debunking went too far. (A judgment)

Professor Jones devotes one paragraph to the first generative thought
and several pages to the second. In the pages that follow this
paragraph, he contrasts the United States to Germany, Italy, and Russia,
which, during this period, were actively and deliberately building up their
heroes. To demonstrate his observation that "we debunked," he uses this
paragraph structure.

We debunked too much.
A. During the iconoclastic period spirited biographers laid about
   them with a mighty modern hand.
   1. They told us that
      a. Lincoln was a small-town politician
      b. Washington a land-grabber
      c. Grant a stubborn and conceited mule, and
      d. Bryan an amusing idiot.
   2. We learned that
      a. There was something to be said for Aaron Burr, but
      b. not very much for Sam Adams,
      c. Longfellow, or
      d. Harriet Beecher Stowe.
   3.
      a. In place of being American vikings, the pioneers turned
         out to be neurotic, dissatisfied fellows unpopular in
         their home town, and
      b. Columbia, the gem of the ocean, was described as a
         sort of kept woman in the pay of millionaires.
      c. Apparently the only Americans who ever died to make
         the world safe for democracy died in 1917–18, and
         made a mistake in doing so.

B. I do not deny either the truth or the necessity of many of these modern biographies. I am no more comfortable than the next man in a room full of plaster saints.

C. But, when the biographers got through, all the heroes had disappeared.

Line C, the final sentence in the paragraph, is really a transition that moves the discussion on to how a country suffers when it has no heroes.

The levels are apparent to the reader. A, B, and C are demonstrated to be parallel by repetition of the word *biographer* or a form of it. Levels 1, 2, and 3 are kept parallel by containing some form of "they wrote." In A3, "they wrote" is omitted, possibly for variety, but it is implied in the subpoints ("turned out to be" and "was described"). The bottom levels—1 and 2, a, b, c, and d—are as concrete as they can be; they are about individual persons. Levels 3a, b, and c are a step above the references to individuals; they are generalizations. We might expect the author to develop these generalizations, low-level though they are, but Professor Jones is writing for an audience that he assumes is familiar with these aspects of American history. He even buttresses this compliment to his readers by throwing in an allusion to a song, "Columbia, the Gem of the Ocean."

The semanticist might show the ladder of abstraction in this fashion:

Top rung	We (all Americans) debunked
Next rung	Biographers talking about Americans debunked
Next rung	We (the debunking Americans) criticized Americans
Next rung	Some Americans (biographers) talked about groups of Americans (heroes)
Bottom rung	Jones lists specific Americans

Now, look back at the book report on *The Longest Blade* (p. 94) and see how flat it is. It gets stuck on the second level (plot, characterizations, history) and is devoid of proof or texture. Let us examine the book report from the same perspective as we examined Professor Jones's passage.

The main reason *The Longest Blade* is such a great book is because it is so interesting.

A. Probably the single biggest contribution to this interest is the excellent plot, which
   1. covers several centuries in its sweep and
   2. tells many stories
B. Another reason that the book is so interesting is that it contains so many excellent characterizations.
   1. The central figure is shown
      (a) from the time he began his worldly life
      (b) till the time he is near death, and
   2. besides the hero, there are many other characters, mostly feminine, that are well developed.
C. It must not be overlooked that *The Longest Blade* covers an important era in our history.
D. Everyone will be interested in the
   1. clothing
   2. manners
   3. morals, and
   4. intrigues
E. Considering these facts, it is easy to see why Clifton Holton was able to say about this book: "It can take its place along with *Gone with the Wind* on any bookshelf."

We see that this review is thin. At no point does it get to the bottom level of abstraction. It is usually only two levels deep. It lacks texture. The contrast between the paragraph by Professor Jones and the book report on *The Longest Blade* illustrates what Wendell Johnson has written:

> If you will observe carefully the speakers you find to be interesting, you are very likely to find that they play, as it were, up and down the levels of abstraction quite as a harpist plays up and down the strings of her harp. . . . the speaker who remains too long on the same general level of abstraction offends our evaluative progress—no matter what his subject may be. WENDELL JOHNSON, *People in Quandaries,* 1946.

Francis Christensen has written that providing the necessary development makes the difference between self-expression and communication. Centuries ago the Greek philosopher Longinus, in praise of the historian Herodotus, wrote, "He takes you along and turns words into sight." Both Christensen and Longinus were emphasizing the value of development.

Which sentence needs development?

Sensitivity about which sentences need development is one of the truly fine arts of writing and speaking. Before making a decision to develop a particular sentence, the writer must analyze his audience.

On March 23, 1775, when Patrick Henry stood up to address the Virginia Convention, he knew the temper of his time and his audience. They were aware, as he said, that this was "no time for ceremony," as aware as he of Britain's "warlike preparations which cover our waters and darken our land," as aware as he that "petitions . . . had been slighted." All such assertions would normally have required a vast amount of evidence, but, as Patrick Henry realized, there is nothing as powerful as an idea in its time. All that was necessary was someone with the courage to express what the audience wanted to hear. A British constitutionalist might have charged that there was not a "shred of evidence" in the speech. Nevertheless, when Henry concluded, "I know not what course others may take; but as for me, give me liberty or give me death!" the audience was so impressed that one man recorded the speech entirely from memory, the only record of it we have.

This situation is rare. Seldom is a point so clear or accepted that it requires no development. If your audience knows what you are about to say or is already convinced that your point is true, there is little reason to take the time or space to express it. Take the assertion, "Centralized government is bad government." If your audience is extremely conservative, it would require almost no development. It is at a very high level of abstraction, but extreme conservatives agree on what it means, and they believe it. You might say, "This is a platitude for my audience. I will cut it out of my speech." On the other hand, you might think, "This is a very vague generalization, and I will not move my speech forward with it, but the assertion is one of our rallying slogans. Therefore, I will use it, not to convince my listeners, but to rally them." Your thinking might be right in either case. If you were confronting a different audience and decided to use the assertion, you would have to cite a great amount of evidence to support it.

In order to determine the kind and amount of development your assertions need, ask yourself the following questions.

1. What is the level of intelligence of my audience and its knowledge about my subject?

2. Is the audience favorable, undecided, or hostile to my thesis?

3. Is the audience familiar with the vocabulary I plan to use, or will I need to explain concepts and define terms?

Besides keeping the knowledge and attitude of your audience in mind, you should be aware that the following types of statements almost always need specific development, no matter who the audience.

1. Any assertion you know to be controversial, original, or new.

2. Any assertion that makes a judgment or an evaluation.

3. Any assertion that suggests a comparison or a contrast.

4. Any assertion that applies an unfavorable "label."

5. Any assertion that contains a vague, general, abstract, technical, jargonistic, or new term.

6. Any assertion that permits an interpretation other than the one intended.

7. Any assertion that contradicts generally held stereotypes.

You might think that the need for development is so obvious that any more discussion would be belaboring the point. If you were a teacher of freshman English, however, you would have seen literally hundreds of the following deficient themes.

1. Reviews of motion pictures that fail to mention film titles or name the stars.

2. Book reports that fail to mention titles, characters, and incidents.

3. Descriptions of a high school that fail to mention the name of the school, where it is located, its size, or any specific teachers or students.

4. Attacks on government policies (toward foreign-aid, deficit-spending, Southeast Asia, cooperation with the U.N.) that fail to refer to specific countries, statesmen, political leaders, sums of money, or actual incidents.

5. Autobiographies that refer to a birthplace but do not tell where it is, to a parent's occupation without identifying it, to a home town without naming it, to sports or hobbies without naming them.

A student put the following sentence in his autobiography: "Before I went to high school, I liked to read." He thought this a simple, straightforward sentence—"I knew what I meant," he said later—but his teacher pointed out that the sentence was loaded with predictive content. Two words were operative, *liked* and *read.* To show that the general sentence had no autobiographic value, the professor recalled that he had received similar sentences in two other student papers. One of these boys, the teacher pointed out, spent many a lazy afternoon reading articles about the Cleveland Browns, the San Francisco Giants, and the Boston Celtics. When he received a subscription to *Sports Illustrated* for Christmas, he enjoyed reading about Jim Brown, Willie Mays, and Bill Russell. This specific information indicated that the *like* was not a strong one and that the interest was perhaps typical of most boys, the only unique aspect being that all the athletes who interested the boy were Negro, a fact significant later when the student became concerned about civil rights.

The other student who "liked to read" was an intense person. When he sat at the breakfast table, he read every word on the cereal box. He read Tolstoy's mammoth *War and Peace,* not once but three times. His real love, though, was science. He read both volumes of Sarton's *A History of Science.* He read biographies of many scientists from Aristotle to Linus Pauling. He read about experiments on phlogiston, heterochromatin, and Mendelism.

"Do you see," the professor asked, "that these details were necessary for the sentence to be meaningful? Both boys 'liked to read,' but they were different boys." The professor went on to point out that, in the sentence, the words *liked* and *read* were generative: they determined what details should be included. The introductory phrase "Before I went to high school" was also predictive. It implied that *after* he went to high school he changed. The boy who was interested in sports demonstrated later in his autobiography that his role changed after high school from that of a spectator to that of an active and successful athlete. The budding scientist became fascinated with laboratory experimentation. He continued to read, but less for pleasure, more for instruction.

The student in conference with his instructor looked again at his sentence and moaned, "I didn't mean anything by 'before I went to high school.' I still like to read," whereupon the instructor pointed out that, in that case, he was guilty of a second defect: in addition to neglecting the predictive content and its obligation, he had permitted the sentence to be ambiguous. He had loaded his sentence with false and unintended predictive content.

The raw material: facts

Often, the greatest difficulty of beginning writers is that they do not get low enough on the ladder of abstraction, i.e., that they are not specific. This deficiency can be remedied in part if the writer tries, whenever possible, to deal in facts.

Very few terms in our vocabulary are used as loosely as the word *fact*. A fact is an idea, but it has qualities of its own. Thus far, we have classified ideas according to the process of abstraction by which they are derived. An observation requires only that you can find the words to describe the action. A classification requires that you abstract certain qualities of a class and ascertain whether your specific has those qualities. A generalization requires that you abstract a commonality, continuation, or reoccurrence. A judgment requires that you abstract a value possessing quantities of more or less or qualities of goodness or badness. A causal relation requires that you abstract the cause set up by an antecedent and its effect on the consequent. Any one of these ideas can be a fact.

A fact is produced by any kind of thought. A statement is called factual because it can be verified; it is called a fact because it has been verified or agreed upon. When there is a method of checking the truth of a statement, there may be general agreement that it is true, and when a statement has been proved true, it is then called a fact. Most people would agree that the following statements are facts.

1. Roger Maris hit 61 home runs in one season. (Observation)

2. A Chevrolet is a product of the General Motors Corporation. (Classification)

3. Most Americans tend to support the President's foreign policies, even though they disagree with his domestic program. (Generalization)

4. An elephant is bigger than an ant. (Judgment)

5. Commercial cetyltrimethyl-ammonium bromide causes some polysaccharides to precipitate. (Causal Relation)

A thought about concrete things and experiences, no matter how it is derived, tends to fall into the category of factual information. These thoughts have a vocabulary that S. I. Hayakawa calls *report lan-*

guage. In his *Language in Thought and Action* (1949), Professor Hayakawa points out that report language is a thought expressed in "such
a way that everyone will agree with the formulation." The language used
at higher levels of abstraction to express judgments and generalizations
that are likely to be controversial or vague Professor Hayakawa calls
inferential language.

You might say, for instance, "Our halfback, Fred Williams, ran
a hundred yards in ten seconds." There is undoubtedly only one Fred
Williams who is your halfback. The word "ran" is relatively specific; its
meaning is quite clear. A hundred yards is a unit of measurement upon
which there is agreement; the same can be said for ten seconds. Chances
are very strong that we could verify the statement. If witnesses other than
yourself cannot be found, very likely Fred could run the distance again
for us. The statement is about a concrete object, Fred Williams, and
relatively specific activity. The phenomenon is *verifiable.* As Aristotle
would have said, the idea corresponds with a reality that is independent
of the mind of the writer; it is, therefore, true.

A true statement, that is, one verifiable by generally accepted
standards and one that can be expressed in report language, is called a
fact. The following would usually be called *facts.*

1. A pound equals sixteen ounces.

2. George Washington was the first President of the United States.

3. A straight line is the shortest distance between two points.

Actually these sentences demonstrate that although a fact is
customarily thought to be a simple idea there is a great deal of argument
about just what is a *fact* and what is not. We could quibble whether
the above sentences are facts. A pound avoirdupois weighs sixteen
ounces, a pound troy weighs twelve ounces, a pound sterling has a varying weight, and who knows what a dog pound weighs? We could also
challenge the second sentence since, before the Constitution was ratified,
the assembly governing the new country elected a presiding officer. He is
forgotten now, but he actually was our first President. The third sentence,
of course, is not true on the earth's surface—as can be demonstrated
by geometry.

The following are *factual* statements. If we agree on the terms
and assume that the truth has been verified, they are *facts.*

1. Her name is Amelia.

2. George Bernard Shaw was a member of the Fabian Society.

3. Potassium hydroxide is used in the manufacture of some soft soap.

4. Roger Bannister ran a mile in less than four minutes.

5. All bodies in the universe have a mutual attraction for each other. (Newton's Law of Gravitation)

6. The clock struck twelve.

7. My shoe has a hole in it.

As you can see, facts can involve vastly different levels of importance and complexity; however, they are alike in that they can be verified by generally accepted standards.

Notice also that "facts" are usually expressed in words about whose meaning people are in almost complete agreement. For instance, we all know or can learn what is meant by the names *Robert Kennedy, sodium chloride, Chicago, West Side Story,* and *Boeing 707.* With lesser certainty we agree on the meanings of the common nouns *ball, man, city, book,* and *game.* We tend to agree on the meaning of certain verbs, for instance, *hit, walk, build,* and *smile.* It is this type of vocabulary that is used to express *facts;* it is "report language."

It is a characteristic also of facts that we can have a high degree of certainty about them. We can justifiably say that we "know" the following.

1. Theodore Roosevelt was President of the United States.

2. My shoe has a hole in it.

3. Chicago, Illinois, is situated on the shore of Lake Michigan.

It is factual material that, very often, is needed to fulfill the obligation of development.

Methods of development

The writer must be able to determine what sentences need development, and he must also be able to select the appropriate kind of development. In general terms, he should use whatever development is needed to make the idea clear and convincing. However, judging by much amateur and professional writing that falls short of its purpose, this truism, in itself, needs development. In order to know just what kinds of development to use, it is necessary to know what tools a writer can have in his kit.

DEFINITION

One of the very common forms of expository development is the definition, an explanation of the meaning of a word or expression. In an article in *Fortune* Magazine, January, 1944, Susanne K. Langer used the word *sign* in a special way not quite covered in a dictionary. She therefore included a definition of her usage of it:

> A sign is anything that announces the existence or the imminence of some event, the presence of a thing or a person, or a change in a state of affairs. There are signs of the weather, signs of danger, signs of future good or evil, signs of what the past has been. In every case a sign is closely bound up with something to be noted or expected in experience. It is always a part of the situation to which it refers, though the reference may be remote in time and space. In so far as we are led to note or expect the signified event we are making correct use of a sign. This is the essence of rational behavior, which animals show in varying degrees. It is entirely realistic, being closely bound up with the actual objective course of history—learned by experience, and cashed in or voided by further experience.

In general, a definition puts a word in a class and then shows how the word differs in meaning from other members of the class. An extended definition often includes examples and shows what happens or can happen because the concept exists. This last aspect is called "operative definition." The following definition of the word *function* is an operative definition from the third edition of the *Columbia Encyclopedia*.

> Function, in mathematics, is a quantity of varying numerical value (a variable) whose value is determined by the value of one or more other such quantities, known as independent variables. For example, the distance a body falls is a function of the time it is allowed to fall; the volume of an expanding sphere is a function of its radius; X^2 is a function of X.

Very often, a definition is inserted briefly as an appositive: "Italic languages, the Indo-European languages that were spoken in ancient Italy, have only one survivor, Latin."

EXAMPLE AND ILLUSTRATION

Another type of expression will require another kind of development. Take an idea that literary critics René Wellek and Austin Warren wished to convey: "At least in England, biography has been one of the earliest and certainly one of the most persistent forms of literary study." The authors evidently decided that definition was unnecessary; a person interested in a book of literary criticism would know what a biography is. The generative words are *earliest* and *most persistent*. The assertion borders on argumentation, and the evidence must be of the kind and amount to be convincing. "Earliest" obligates the authors to provide dates; "most persistent" obligates the writers to list a large number of examples. This is the result:

> At least in England, biography has been one of the earliest and certainly one of the most persistent forms of literary study. Leland and Bale compiled biographical and bibliographical catalogues of authors in the sixteenth century, and a collection of lives was the standard form of English literary history long before Johnson's *Lives of the Poets* and down to Morley's *English Men of Letters*. In the seventeenth century, Walton wrote the lives of Donne and Herbert, treating these poets as Anglican saints. In the eighteenth century, diverse types of literary biography became established. Boswell's *Johnson* is the most famous example of a literary portraiture which tries, by an accumulation of anecdotes, to recreate a moral and intellectual personality. A different type of biography is best represented by Edmond Malone's *Life of Dryden* (1800), the scholarly accumulation, verification, and examination of documents which yield a series of external facts. It was not till the nineteenth century that attempts were first made to write the biography of an author against his social and literary background. William Godwin's much padded *Life of Chaucer* (1803), Scott's *Dryden* (1808—factually derived from Malone), and Nathan Drake's *Shakespeare* (1817) are early examples. The type doubtless culminates in Masson's *Life of Milton* (1859–80), a work which manages to include almost the whole of the political and social history of the time; but many a Victorian *Life and Times* is similar in intent even though it may not equal Masson's performance in bulk or extravagance. RENÉ WELLEK AND AUSTIN WARREN, *Theory of Literature*, 1949.

In exposition, usually only one example is necessary for clarification; in argumentation, the sentence itself dictates how many examples are necessary. Examine the following sentences and determine the number of examples needed to clarify the statement.

1. Most of the girls in my class were bored.

2. Some of the girls in my class were bored.

For generalization, it is often sufficient to cite one or two examples and then present evidence that the sample was typical of the whole class under discussion, as Roul Tunley has done in this passage from an article called "America's Unhealthy Children."

> Despite the protestations of the AMA, lack of money is a formidable barrier to good medical care and it can have tragic consequences. For example, I think of a young mother I know who lives in a large Western city and supports her two children on a secretary's salary. Her eight-year-old daughter came down with a cold and was kept out of school for a week. But, to save money, the mother did not consult a doctor. The child seemed to improve, went back to school on Friday, and the next day was well enough to go to her dancing class. But she came home listless, and seemed tired through the weekend. Around midnight Sunday she became desperately ill, started vomiting and gasping for breath. The panic-stricken mother tried mouth-to-mouth resuscitation. When the child's body went limp, the mother raced across the street to a pay telephone.
>
> Not knowing what doctor to call, she rang the city's medical society, and an answering service responded. After she had explained her desperate need for a doctor, the voice at the other end asked, "Do you have ten dollars?"
>
> "You see," the voice went on, "it's very difficult to get a doctor to make a house call at this hour without a cash payment."
>
> Short of cash and too confused to think of rousing neighbors, the mother slammed down the receiver. Then she looked up and called an ambulance, which arrived in ten minutes. But by this time the little girl was dead. A postmortem was done at the morgue and the cause of death was found to be a virus which attacks the heart. No one knows whether or not a doctor could have saved the child; but no one can doubt that the denial of medical care was a brutal blow to both mother and child.
>
> Uncounted other American children are similarly deprived and billion-dollar research programs will not help them.
> ROUL TUNLEY, *Harper's Magazine*, MAY, 1966.

In the course of this article, the writer provided evidence to demonstrate that the incident was distressingly typical.

Occasionally the examples may be still quite general and

abstract—but only when you are reminding your audience of something already known or accepted. Note this section from Patrick Henry's speech in the Virginia House of Delegates (1775):

> Sir, we have done everything that could be done to avert the storm which is now coming on. We have petitioned, we have remonstrated; we have supplicated; we have prostrated ourselves before the throne, and have implored its interposition to arrest the tyrannical hands of the ministry and Parliament. Our petitions have been slighted; our remonstrances have produced additional violence and insult; our supplications have been disregarded; and we have been spurned with contempt from the foot of the throne! In vain, after these things, may we indulge the fond hope of peace and reconciliation. There is no longer any room for hope.

Had Patrick Henry been talking to King George III instead of to his fellow Virginians, he would have had to present much more evidence. He would have had to analyze each of these charges specifically to show why the colonists deserved to feel abused.

ANALYTICAL EXPANSION

Very often, in both exposition and argumentation, the nature of a generative sentence demands an expansion of the idea itself. In the following three paragraphs, try to determine the operative words in the topic sentences that necessitate the analytical expansion.

(1)

> While these events were occurring at Brussels and Antwerp, a scene of a different nature was enacting at Ghent. The Duke of Aerschot had recently been appointed to the government of Flanders by the State Council, but the choice was exceedingly distasteful to a large number of the inhabitants. Although, since the defeat of Don John's party in Antwerp, Aerschot had again become "the affectionate brother" of Orange, yet he was known to be the head of the cabal which had brought Matthias from Vienna. Flanders, moreover, swarmed with converts to the reformed religion, and the Duke's strict Romanism was well known. The people, therefore, who hated the Pope and adored the Prince, were furious at the appointment of the new Governor, but by dint of profuse promises regarding the instant restoration of privileges and charters which had long lain dormant, the friends of Aerschot succeeded in preparing the way for the installation.
> JOHN L. MOTLEY, The Rise of the Dutch Republic, 1856.

(2)

After two years of inconclusive fighting in North America
the enemy, triumphant over Napoleon in Europe, began in
1814 a vigorous prosecution of the conflict west of the Atlantic. The British navy tightened and extended its blockade
of American ports. A detachment of troops began what was
expected to be the permanent occupation of Maine. Britain
hoped to rectify the boundary between the United States and
Canada. Another landing party in August marched into Washington, from whence the harried and discredited Madison
had fled, and put the torch to the Capital. Two British armies
of invasion were formed, one to take New Orleans and the
other, under General Prevost, to advance into the Hudson
Valley by Burgoyne's old route along the west shore of Lake
Champlain. The attack upon New Orleans was slow in getting
under way, with the result that the decisive operations were
initiated by Prevost. Before he began his southward march the
American high command, with an ineptitude which amounted
almost to genius, removed to Sackett's Harbor on Lake On-
tario most of the force which would have opposed the invader.
When Prevost faced the earthworks at Plattsburg, the decisive
moment in the history of the Republic had come. RALPH
HENRY GABRIEL, *The Course of American Democratic Thought*,
1956.

(3)

What caused the boy most disappointment was the little he
got from his mates. Speaking exactly, he got less than nothing,
a result common enough in education. Yet the College Catalogue for the years 1854 to 1861 shows a list of names rather
distinguished in their time. Alexander Agassiz and Phillips
Brooks led it; H. H. Richardson and O. W. Holmes helped to
close it. As a rule the most promising of all die early, and never
get their names into a Dictionary of Contemporaries, which
seems to be the only popular standard of success. Many died in
the war. Adams knew them all, more or less; he felt as much regard, and quite as much respect for them then, as he did after
they won great names and were objects of a vastly wider respect; but, as help towards education, he got nothing whatever
from them or they from him until long after they had left college. Possibly the fault was his, but one would like to know how
many others shared it. Accident accounts for much in com-
panionship as in marriage. Life offers perhaps only a score
of possible companions, and it is mere chance whether they
meet as early as school or college, but it is more than a chance

that boys brought up together under like conditions have nothing to give each other. The Class of 1858, to which Henry Adams belonged, was a typical collection of young New Englanders, quietly penetrating and aggressively commonplace; free from meannesses, jealousies, intrigues, enthusiasms, and passions; not exceptionally quick; not consciously sceptical; singularly indifferent to display, artifice, florid expression, but not hostile to it when it amused them; distrustful of themselves, but little disposed to trust any one else; with not much humor of their own, but full of readiness to enjoy the humor of others; negative to a degree that in the long run became positive and triumphant. Not harsh in manners or judgment, rather liberal and open-minded, they were still as a body the most formidable critics one would care to meet, in a long life exposed to criticism. They never flattered, seldom praised; free from vanity, they were not intolerant of it; but they were objectiveness itself; their attitude was a law of nature; their judgment beyond appeal, not an act either of intellect or emotion or of will, but a sort of gravitation. HENRY ADAMS, *The Education of Henry Adams*, 1918.

COMPARISON

Often a point can be made by comparing it to something else. In an essay, E. M. Forster wished to show how modern India is different from pre-1947 India. To emphasize that the change is political and educational, he wished to show that

Externally the place has not changed. . . . Outside the carriage windows it unrolls as before—monotonous, enigmatic, and at moments sinister. And in some long motor drives which I took through the Deccan there was the same combination of hill, rock, bushes, ruins, dusty people and occasional yellow flowers which I encountered when I walked on the soil in my youth. There is still poverty, and, since I am older today and more thoughtful, it is the poverty, the malnutrition, which persists like a ground-swell beneath the pleasant froth of my immediate experience. I do not know what political solution is correct. But I do know that people ought not to be so poor and to look so ill, and that rats ought not to run about them as I saw them doing in a labour camp at Bombay. Industrialism has increased, though it does not dominate the landscape yet as it does in the west. You can see the chimneys of the cotton mills at Ahmedabad, but you can see its mosques too. You can see little factories near Calcutta,

but they are tucked away amongst bananas and palms, and
the one I have in mind has an enormous tree overhanging it,
in whose branches a witch is said to sit, and from whose
branches huge fruit occasionally fall and hit the corrugated iron
roofs with a bang, so that the factory hands jump. No—externally India has not changed.   E. M. FORSTER, *Two Cheers
for Democracy*, 1951.

The word *externally* was the operative word. By comparing similarities between what he sees now and what he saw before India became
independent, Mr. Forster accentuated the differences he described later.

ANALOGY

There is a famous story told about Ambassador Joseph Kennedy
when he found his sons fighting. He gave Joe, Jack, Bob, and Ted each
a small stick and asked them to break their sticks. They did so easily.
He then put four sticks together and asked one of the boys to try to
break all four of them. To his disappointment, the first boy who tried
it succeeded. The Ambassador had read of the idea in a book somewhere,
and it had worked. To console his father, Jack spoke up, "It's okay, Dad.
We get your point."

The father could have said something platitudinous like, "If
you boys stick together, you will be more likely to succeed." Instead, to
dramatize his point, he turned to an *analogy*, which is another form
of development.

As the next example shows, analogy is a variation of comparison.
During a debate in Congress, about a highway bill, a U.S. Representative
from an eastern state objected to the arguments of his colleagues from
the Middle West, saying that they were strictly negative. "You are always
against everything."

"You have us wrong," a tall Representative from Michigan said.
"You do not understand us. If you come out to Michigan I would show
you acres of corn. You would see our farmers spraying the fields. But
we are not against corn borers, grasshoppers, and chinch bugs. We are
for corn! Here in Congress we Middle Westerners are not merely *against*
federal intervention; we are *for* good highways—so we want them built
by the people in the states which will use them."

An analogy is a form of comparison, but it compares objects and
concepts that are basically dissimilar except for a certain pertinent
abstract quality. Words and clothing have little resemblance, but Walter
Lippmann noted a similarity between them which helped him make his
point that we must not use words carelessly.

Words like *liberty, equality, fraternity, justice,* have various meanings which reflect the variability of the flux of things. The different meanings are rather like different clothes, each good for a season, for certain weather and for a time of day, none good for all times. In the infinite change and diversity of the actual world, our conceptual definitions are never exactly and finally the whole truth. For, as James said, while "the essence of life is its continually changing character . . . our concepts are all discontinuous and fixed." Like a winter overcoat, none can be worn with equal comfort in January and in July. Yet the summer will end, it too being subject to change. There will come a season and a time for wearing the warmer coat. So it is a mistake to think that we could wear the same coat all the time, and a mistake to throw it away, supposing in the summer that it will never be winter again.   WALTER LIPP-MANN, *The Public Philosophy,* 1956.

The next paragraph is a famous analogy from Edward Bellamy's *Looking Backward:*

By way of attempting to give the reader some general impression of the way people lived together in those days, and especially of the relations of the rich and poor to one another, perhaps I cannot do better than to compare society as it then was to a prodigious coach which the masses of humanity were harnessed to and dragged toilsomely along a very hilly and sandy road. The driver was hunger, and permitted no lagging, though the pace was necessarily very slow. Despite the difficulty of drawing the coach at all along so hard a road, the top was covered with passengers who never got down, even at the steepest ascents. These seats on top were very breezy and comfortable. Well up out of the dust, their occupants could enjoy the scenery at their leisure, or critically discuss the merits of the straining team. Naturally such places were in great demand and the competition for them was keen, every one seeking as the first end in life to secure a seat on the coach for himself and to leave it to his child after him. By the rule of the coach a man could leave his seat to whom he wished, but on the other hand there were many accidents by which it might at any time be wholly lost. For all that they were so easy, the seats were very insecure, and at every sudden jolt of the coach persons were slipping out of them and falling to the ground, where they were instantly compelled to take hold of the rope and help to drag the coach on which they had before ridden so pleasantly. It was naturally

> regarded as a terrible misfortune to lose one's seat, and the apprehension that this might happen to them or their friends was a constant cloud upon the happiness of those who rode. EDWARD BELLAMY, *Looking Backward,* 1888.

Having established this analogy, the author goes on at some length to develop it, explaining the attitude of those who rode on the coach toward each other (they felt "that they were not exactly like their brothers and sisters who pulled at the rope, but of finer clay, in some way belonging to a higher order of beings") and toward those whose fate it was to pull ("Had they no compassion . . . ? Oh, yes; commiseration was frequently expressed by those who rode"). The analogy serves not only to clarify the author's attitude but also to persuade the reader that existing social arrangements must undergo radical change.

Analogies are often used to clarify a religious or theoretical concept, as in this eighteenth-century sermon by Jonathan Edwards:

> The God that holds you over the pit of hell much as one holds a spider or some loathsome insect over the fire, abhors you, and is dreadfully provoked; his wrath towards you burns like fire; he looks upon you as worthy of nothing else but to be cast into the fire; he is of purer eyes than to bear to have you in his sight; you are ten thousand times so abominable in his eyes as the most hateful and venomous serpent is in ours. You have offended him infinitely more than ever a stubborn rebel did his prince: and yet it is nothing but his hand that holds you from falling into the fire every moment. Tis ascribed to nothing else, that you did not go to hell the last night; that you was [sic] suffered to awake again in this world after you closed your eyes to sleep; and there is no other reason to be given why you have not dropped into hell since you arose in the morning, but that God's hand has held you up. There is no other reason to be given why you have not gone to hell since you have sat here in the house of God, provoking his pure eyes by your sinful wicked manner of attending his solemn worship. Yea, there is nothing else that is to be given as a reason why you do not this very moment drop down into hell. JONATHAN EDWARDS, "SINNERS IN THE HANDS OF AN ANGRY GOD," 1741.

CONTRAST

In the following passage, Martin Luther King uses the technique called *contrast* to differentiate between a just law and an unjust law.

Now what is the difference between the two? How does one determine when a law is just or unjust? A just law is a man-made code that squares with the moral law or the law of God. An unjust law is a code that is out of harmony with the moral law. To put it in the terms of Saint Thomas Aquinas, an unjust law is a human law that is not rooted in eternal and natural law. Any law that uplifts human personality is just. Any law that degrades human personality is unjust. All segregation statutes are unjust because segregation distorts the soul and damages the personality. It gives the segregator a false sense of superiority and the segregated a false sense of inferiority. To use the words of Martin Buber, the great Jewish philosopher, segregation substitutes an "I-it" relationship for the "I-thou" relationship, and ends up relegating persons to the status of things. So segregation is not only politically, economically, and sociologically unsound, but it is morally wrong and sinful. Paul Tillich has said that sin is separation. Isn't segregation an existential expression of man's tragic separation, an expression of his awful estrangement, his terrible sinfulness? So I can urge men to obey the 1954 decision of the Supreme Court because it is morally right, and I can urge them to disobey segregation ordinances because they are morally wrong.

Let us turn to a more concrete example of just and unjust laws. An unjust law is a code that a majority inflicts on a minority that is not binding on itself. This is *difference* made legal. On the other hand a just law is a code that a majority compels a minority to follow that it is willing to follow itself. This is *sameness* made legal.

Let me give another explanation. An unjust law is a code inflicted upon a minority which that minority had no part in enacting or creating because they did not have the unhampered right to vote. Who can say the legislature of Alabama which set up the segregation laws was democratically elected? Throughout the state of Alabama all types of conniving methods are used to prevent Negroes from becoming registered voters and there are some counties without a single Negro registered to vote despite the fact that the Negro constitutes a majority of the population. Can any law set up in such a state be considered democratically structured?

These are just a few examples of unjust and just laws. There are some instances when a law is just on its face but unjust in its application. For instance, I was arrested Friday on a charge of parading without a permit. Now there is nothing wrong with an ordinance which requires a permit for a parade, but when the ordinance is used to preserve segregation and to deny citizens the First Amendment privilege of peaceful assembly and peaceful protest, then it becomes unjust.   MARTIN LUTHER KING, *Why We Can't Wait*, 1963.

STATISTICS

Frequently, development takes the form of *statistics*.

But that Iowa football team's ground game was staggering. Iowa's 528 net yards gained was a new Rose Bowl record. Its 441 yards on the ground was the best the Bowl had ever seen. And its total of 24 first downs matched the previous record. Although they don't keep track of such things, Iowa's average gain per ground play was almost eight yards, a fantastic average against a major opponent.   AL GRADY, IOWA CITY *Press-Citizen*, January 2, 1959.

The following paragraph from Hans Zinsser's *Rats, Lice, and History* uses a great number of statistics:

A rat census is obviously impossible. It is quite certain, however, that they breed more rapidly than they are destroyed in many places in the world. We can appraise the rat population only by the numbers that are killed in organized rat campaigns and by the amount of destruction they cause. In about 1860, Shipley tells us, there was a slaughterhouse for horses on Montfaucon, which it was planned to remove farther away from Paris. The carcasses of horses amounted to sometimes thirty-five a day, and were regularly cleaned up completely by rats in the following night. Dusaussois engaged in this gruesome traffic. He set horse-meat bait in enclosures from which the exit of rats could be prevented, and in the course of the first night killed 2,650. By the end of a month, he had killed over 16,000. Shipley estimates that there are about forty million rats in England at one time. In 1881 there was a rat plague in certain districts of India. The crops of the preceding two years were below average and a large part of them had been destroyed by rats. Rewards offered for rat destruction led to a killing of over 12,000,000 rats. Shipley estimates that a single rat does about 7s. 6d. worth of damage in a year, which makes a charge of £15,000,000 upon Great Britain and Ireland. It costs about sixty cents to two dollars a year to feed a rat on grain. Every rat on a farm costs about fifty cents a year. Lantz adds to this that hotel managers estimate five dollars a year as a low estimate of the loss inflicted by a rat.

He thinks that in the thickly populated parts of the country an estimate of one rat per acre is not excessive, and that in most of our cities there are as many rats as people. He investigated, in 1909, the approximate total damage by rats in the cities of Washington and Baltimore. From the data he obtained, he calculated the annual damage in the two cities as amounting to $400,000 and $700,000 respectively—which, considering the populations, amounted to an average loss of $1.27 a year per person. On the same basis, the urban population of the United States, at that time 28,000,000 people, sustained an annual direct injury of $35,000,000 a year. In Denmark, the estimated rat cost is about $1.20 a person; in Germany, eighty-five cents a person; in France, a little over a dollar. Add to this the inestimable depreciation of property and the costs of protection. HANS ZINSSER, *Rats, Lice, and History,* 1935.

HYPOTHESIS

Occasionally it is useful to invent some development, a procedure called hypothesizing. To test his belief that history must be true, Vilhjalmur Stefansson wrote:

Supposing, just for argument, that the biographers of Lincoln could prove, as some of them have tried to do, that he was of illegitimate descent, would you then want that taught in the schools? The conclusive arguments against are: (1) Such teaching would attack the Home, the most precious of all our institutions; for Lincoln is our greatest national hero, and having him illegitimate, even if only back in his parents' or grandparents' generation, would be a destructive influence. (2) That teaching would also attack the institution of National Heroes. Lincoln is our greatest hero; nothing is more beneficial than to have heroes to look up to; we would not look up to Lincoln quite so much if he were in any degree illegitimate; therefore, we ought to hide the fact, if it were a fact. (3) Nothing could be gained by encouraging children to attach scandal to the names of great men. (4) It would be in bad taste to teach in school about the illegitimacy of anyone. On the basis of these and many similar reasons, all decent people will agree that the question of whether Lincoln was illegitimate should never be mentioned in the schools. VILHJALMUR STEFANSSON, *Adventures in Error,* 1936.

Note that Stefansson does not hypothesize completely ridiculous arguments to overturn later. However, it is in his interest that the hypothetical arguments should not be *too* strong. When you utilize hypothetical development, then, be certain that you can support the hypothesis with sufficient strength to carry your reader's opinion in the direction you desire.

With all these possibilities—definition, example, illustration, comparison, analogy, contrast, statistics, and hypothesis—at his command, the writer can effectively provide the exposition or evidence required by his generative sentences.

How much development is necessary?

Some beginning writers have the misconception that writing has just two levels of abstraction, the topic sentence and concrete development. A good writer, however, demonstrates his virtuosity by providing a texture of many levels. Within a sentence he may perceive that an abstract word needs a concrete appositive. A sentence in the middle of a paragraph may need two or three subsentences to clarify its contention. Another sentence may need three paragraphs, one to clarify and two to prove. The broadest generalization will need a book.

The writer must decide every time he sets down a sentence what amount of exposition or evidence he needs. He has three principles to follow.

1. Let the nature of the generative sentence determine the type and amount of development.

2. Don't be afraid of having too much development.

3. Avoid irrelevancy.

1. *Let the nature of the generative sentence determine the type and amount of development.* The key to the development of a sentence is once again found in its predictive content. In general terms we could almost formulize this relationship. For instance, an assertion that is a classification would need a routine series of steps. Suppose the assertion is "Mistletoe is a parasite." Your mental analysis might go something like this: "The assertion is a classification. Since it is one generally accepted by scientists, it is not argumentation, but exposition. The operative words are *mistletoe* and *parasite*. Since my audience probably knows what mistletoe is, I will define only the word *parasite*, because I want to use a special scientific class. To clarify the definition of the class, I will use some examples of other plants that are parasites. Having established the meaning of parasite, I will show by analytical expansion that *mistletoe* has the characteristics of the plant group called 'parasites.' To wrap up the

development, I can turn to testimony and cite an authority who has called mistletoe a parasite. When, in my research, I come across the enchanting fact that Indians chewed on mistletoe to stop a toothache, a sign in my head will flash 'Irrelevant!,' and I will resist the impulse to smuggle the information into my paragraph."

This illustration demonstrates the use of the routine questions that we can add to those discussed under "Which Sentences Need To Be Developed?," pp. 102–104. The routine questions are:

1. What kind of an assertion is the sentence? Is it observation, classification, generalization, judgment, or causal relation?

2. Is it expository or argumentative?

3. What are the operative words?

4. What kind of development is required—definition, example, illustration, comparison, contrast, statistics, analogy, or hypothesis?

2. *Don't be afraid of having too much development.* Usually in discussions of writing, brevity is labeled a virtue. In view of this, you may be surprised that we are telling you not to worry about length. The sin of wordiness and the virtue of minute detail are vastly different. The ratio of words in a first draft to those in the final draft is often something like seven to five. A student writing a 500-word theme probably should have a first draft of 700 words. However, the 200 words that are cut out during revision hardly ever are details; almost always they are overblown generalizations and useless words. Very likely 300 unnecessary words will be removed, and 100 words, details, will be added.

Another consideration at this point is that, in and of themselves, details and specifics often have charm. A series of vague generalizations will bore the reader, but a series of anecdotes, incidents, or even statistics may be entertaining or meaningful to the reader. They provide life and color, as in these paragraphs by Nancy Hale:

> We, the youngest children in the school, had as our classroom a large room on the south side of the ground floor. The school had been a private mansion in which a few changes had been made. We sat on little, chunky, green-painted chairs around long, narrow tables to do our reading lesson or to sing:
>
> > All things bright and beautiful
> > All creatures great and small
> > All things wise and wonderful
> > The Lord God made them all.

In the middle of the morning, we went into an adjoining pantry, where we were served either cold milk or hot cocoa. The cocoa was served in tall, narrow, white china mugs with a blue pattern; I remember how the scum on top of the cocoa clung to the bowl of the spoon as one lifted it carefully off, for I had learned, listening to the others squealing or groaning, that scum is disgusting. With the drinks went Huntley & Palmer's biscuits called *Petits Beurres*. The winter sun streaked through the southern windows to the right; the window at the left was partly blocked by the end of Miss Cavendish's conservatory.   NANCY HALE, *The New Yorker,* 1955.

By choosing her detail with care, the writer takes us into a classroom where we can see and hear the children. Had she merely referred to the customary furniture of an elementary classroom, we would never have been able to visualize "chunky, green-painted chairs." As we read the words of the song she quotes, we can almost hear the children singing "All Things Bright and Beautiful." How much less communicative she would have been had she said "Singing frequently occurred"! The scum on the cocoa is lifted out of the "tall, narrow, white china mugs" so graphically that we smile at the child's accomplishment.

In the following paragraph, the writer David Lang uses detail to dramatize his impressions of the then new aircraft:

The men at Otis differ from their comrades at propeller-plane bases in that they breezily employ a vocabulary that is special even in the Air Force—"lighting up" is jetese for "starting the engine," "leaping off" means "taking off," and so on. But what really sets a jet-fighter base such as Otis apart is, of course, the nature of the planes themselves. Just coming upon a flock of them parked on the ground is likely to give one a feeling of awe. Propellerless, with their cavernous air ducts blackened and gaping, their two-seater bodies of unpainted aluminum glittering brightly, and their wings swept back in nervous lines, the machines convey a sense of miraculous power. This is almost excruciatingly intensified when a jet leaps off, rushing forward with an earsplitting angry scream and with seemingly irresistible force, a six-foot ball of flame shooting out from its tail. A moment later, the jet has been lost in the sky, so far up that while the ear can detect its still angry whine, the eye perceives only a wispy trail of smoke as its pilot streaks through the upper atmosphere—a skywriter with a message never really comprehensible to the earthbound. Standing on the ground, one finds it hard to believe that way up there, invisible in their invisible plane and hurtling along at an inconceivable speed, just this side of the sound barrier, are the two ordinary-looking young men who almost no time ago were climbing into their cockpits on the field. DAVID LANG, *The New Yorker*, 1954.

Lack of detail is a disease of most writers; in college writing it is epidemic. It is a malady of such proportions that it has, at least facetiously, a name: "specific anemia." For most writers, the advice of Rudolf Flesch in *How To Make Sense* is completely appropriate: "Learn to be specific; concentrate on details; give names, dates, places, facts, and figures; focus on the visible, audible, measurable; pass on your direct experience—rather than your thoughts, opinions, general ideas." RUDOLF FLESCH, *How To Make Sense*, 1954.

3. *Avoid irrelevancy.* The assurance that a writer has little to fear from using too much detail does not, however, give him license to use detail that is not appropriate or purposeful. Do you find any details in the following student theme that should be omitted?

> *Tom Sawyer* is my favorite book. Partly this is because it is a boy's book with plenty of action in it. The boys play and fight, they run away, they get involved in a murder, and they search for hidden treasure. In short, they do what all boys would like to do and all grown-ups wish they had done. More importantly, however, *Tom Sawyer* is my favorite book because it is laid in my home town. I was born and brought up in Hannibal, Missouri, and almost as soon as I learned anything I learned the names of Tom Sawyer, Huck Finn, and Becky Thatcher. (I was at least ten before I knew the real people were Sam Clemens, Tom Blankenship, and Laura Hawkins.) As I grew a little older, I visited Tom's house and imagined myself crawling out his bedroom window and sliding down the waterspout. A little later I took the guided tour through Tom Sawyer's cave and saw first-hand the spot where he and Becky were supposed to have eaten their cake and the place where Tom was supposed to have seen Injun Joe. For days afterward Becky was my dream girl and Injun Joe the chief character in nightmares that used to bring me out of bed howling. By the time I was ten or twelve I was allowed to row over to Jackson's Island to swim and fish just as Tom and Huck did. Once I even waited out a thunderstorm there—under the tree that I was sure Tom and Huck and Joe Harper had used for cover years before. I doubt that any book will ever replace *Tom Sawyer* in my affections, for

it's not only a book to me; it's a story that I have relived in
Hannibal many times.

Of the hundreds of ideas and details the author had available
about *Tom Sawyer* he selected only certain ones. Why? The answer is
obvious enough, but it is often forgotten. He selected only those details
that were relevant, that would serve best to clarify or prove the topic sentence. He cited only those bits of information that showed why *Tom
Sawyer* was his favorite book. Contrasting this theme to the book report
on *The Longest Blade* on p. 94 is instructive.

Do you find any irrelevancies in the following paragraph from
an essay called "Sherlock Holmes to Mike Hammer" by Dwight Macdonald?

> The role of science in Mass Culture has similarly changed
> from the rational and the purposive to the passive, accidental,
> even the catastrophic. Consider the evolution of the detective
> story, a genre which can be traced back to the memoirs of
> Vidocq, the master-detective of the Napoleonic era. Poe, who
> was peculiarly fascinated by scientific method, wrote the first
> and still best detective stories: *The Purloined Letter, The
> Gold Bug, The Mystery of Marie Roget, The Murders in the
> Rue Morgue.* Conan Doyle created the great folk hero, Sher-
> lock Holmes, like Poe's Dupin, a sage whose wizard's wand
> was scientific deduction (Poe's "ratiocination"). Such stories
> could only appeal to—in fact, only be comprehensible to—an
> audience accustomed to think in scientific terms: to survey the
> data, set up a hypothesis, test it by seeing whether it
> caught the murderer. The very idea of an art genre cast in the
> form of a problem to be solved by purely intellectual means
> could only have arisen in a scientific age. Other art genres
> include, of course, sculpture and painting. This kind of de-
> tective fiction, which might be called the "classic" style, is still
> widely practiced (well by Agatha Christie and John Dickson
> Carr, badly by the more popular Erle Stanley Gardner) but of
> late it has been overshadowed by the rank, noxious growth
> of works in the "sensational" style. This was inaugurated by
> Dashiell Hammett (whom André Gide was foolish enough to
> admire) and has recently been enormously stepped up in
> voltage by Mickey Spillane, whose six books to date have sold
> thirteen million copies. The sensationalists use what for the
> classicists was the point—the uncovering of the criminal—as
> a mere excuse for the minute description of scenes of blood-
> shed, brutality, lust, and alcoholism. At the time he wrote
> these novels, Spillane was about thirty-five years old. The cool,

astute, subtle Dupin-Holmes is replaced by the crude man of action whose prowess is measured not by intellectual mastery but by his capacity for liquor, women, and mayhem (he can "take it" as well as "dish it out"—Hammett's *The Glass Key* is largely a chronicle of the epic beatings absorbed by the hero before he finally staggers to the solution). Mike Hammer, Spillane's aptly named hero, is such a monumental blunderer that even Dr. Watson would have seen through him. According to Richard W. Johnson, "Mike has one bizarre and memorable characteristic that sets him apart from all other fictional detectives: sheer incompetence. In the five Hammer cases, 48 people have been killed, and there is reason to believe if Mike had kept out of the way, 34 of them —all innocent of the original crime—would have survived." A decade ago, the late George Orwell, apropos a "sensationalist" detective story of the time, *No Orchids for Miss Blandish*, showed how the brutalization of this genre mirrors the general degeneration in ethics from nineteenth-century standards. What he would have written had Mickey Spillane's works been then in existence I find it hard to imagine. DWIGHT MACDONALD, *Diogenes*, SUMMER, 1953.

The purpose of the paragraph is clear enough. The author carries on from the topic sentence and demonstrates that "The role of science . . . has changed from the rational and purposive to the passive, accidental, even the catastrophic." All information contained in the paragraph should be concerned only with that purpose. Most of the sentences live up to that obligation. However, with apologies to the writer, we have added two sentences that were related, but not relevant. Before reading on, look back and try to find them. As you look back at the paragraph, you can see that the statement, "Other art genres include, of course, sculpture and painting" has little to do with the change in mass culture being discussed. Likewise, the age of Mickey Spillane is irrelevant. Those two sentences were not in the writer's printed version.

By rephrasing your main thesis into a controlling question, you can make sure that every word in your writing contributes to the answer. Omit whatever goes off on a tangent. The cardinal rule is to include all the necessary information, but nothing that is unnecessary.

To repeat, very likely you will need to develop the following types of assertions in your writing.

1. Any assertion you know to be controversial, original, or new.

2. Any assertion that makes a judgment or an evaluation.

3. Any assertion that suggests a comparison or a contrast.

4. Any assertion that applies a "label."

5. Any assertion that contains a vague, general, abstract, technical, jargonistic, or new term.

6. Any assertion that permits an interpretation other than the one you intend.

7. Any assertion that contradicts generally held stereotypes.

You will also need to take your audience's level of intelligence, information, and its state of mind about your thesis or subject into consideration. Ask yourself the following questions.

1. What kind of an assertion is the sentence? (Observation, classification, generalization, judgment, or causal relationship?)

2. Is it expository or argumentative?

3. What are the operative words?

4. What kind of development is required: definition, example, illustration, comparison, analogy, contrast, or hypothesis?

Five italicized sentences that follow have been discussed on the basis of all of the considerations discussed above.

1. *I was always jealous of my brother.* This sentence starts a number of different mental motion pictures rolling. As the sentence is expressed, the brother could be older and a famous athlete, or he could be younger and so cute or brainy that he outshines the writer. We need to know the sex of the writer. We need to know the ages of the two. We need to know whether the brother was superior to the writer in some way, or whether the writer simply imagined that he was. To say, "He was a good athlete" would not suffice; instead, the writer should supply some such information as, "He made the Illinois all-state football team in his junior and senior years and received offers of thirty-eight scholarships." If his superiority was scholastic, we need to know if he made the National Honor Society or if he received C's and B's (in which case, we could infer that the writer received something lower). We need to know how the writer felt. Why was he jealous instead of proud of his brother? What, exactly, did the brother *do* to antagonize the writer? Maybe the writer could cite examples of cutting remarks made by the brother or a parent, remarks that hurt deeply and could not be forgotten.

2. *I always enjoyed my summers.* This sentence communicates

very little. Each year approximately 25 million young people enjoy their summers. This observation, therefore, is hardly worth making, but if the sentence could be developed to show the character and interests of the writer, it might be worthwhile. The writer might show that he played American Legion baseball almost every night, even describing several notable triumphs. He might describe the jobs he had—jobs, perhaps, that left him still fresh for his first love, baseball. If he worked as a forest-fire fighter, he could describe some of his experiences. If the writer is a girl, she could write about the summers she spent teaching underprivileged children at Boston's Columbia Point Housing Project. In each case, the details supplied will create a vivid picture of the speaker in the mind's eye of his audience.

3. *People complain when we talk about using buses to take Negro children from the Roxbury schools to other districts; actually, transporting children from one area to another is a common American practice.* Here the writer would need to cite example after example to prove his point, to show that in New York City superior students are transported to special schools such as the Bronx High School of Science and the High School of Art and Design and in Boston to the Boston Latin School. In many cities mentally and physically handicapped students are transported to opportunity schools that the writer might name and describe.

4. *"The difference between an American cookbook and a French one is that the former is very accurate and the latter exceedingly vague."* RAOUL DE ROUSSY DE SALES, *Atlantic Monthly*, MAY, 1938. This sentence needs development, because any generalization, judgment, or comparison involving two countries is bound to be controversial—this one especially so, since it gives the French a label for vagueness which is unflattering. This generalization is aimed at readers of the *Atlantic Monthy* who, presumably, would be relatively neutral on this issue but reasonably well-educated and informed. The form of development needed here is a series of illustrations, not the carefully documented large number needed if the audience were hostile, but some rather general reminders. The expressions *"very accurate"* and *"exceedingly vague"* are especially generative and must not be ignored. This is what De Sales wrote:

> A French recipe seldom tells you how many ounces of butter to use to make *crepes Suzette*, or how many spoonfuls of oil should go into a salad dressing. French cookbooks are full of esoteric measurements such as a *pinch* of pepper, a *suspicion* of garlic, or a *generous sprinkling* of brandy. There are constant references to seasoning *to taste*, as if the recipe were

merely intended to give a general direction, relying on the
experience and innate art of the cook to make the dish turn
out right. American recipes look like doctors' prescriptions.
Perfect cooking seems to depend on perfect dosage. Some
of these books give you a table of calories and vitamins—as
if that had anything to do with the problem of eating well!

De Sales brought up his last point, for the sake of *comparison*,
to demonstrate that Americans think of love and cooking in the same way.
He concluded:

> In the same way, there is now flourishing in America a
> great crop of books which offer precise recipes for the things
> you should do, or avoid doing, in order to achieve happiness
> and keep the fires of love at a constant temperature. In a
> recent issue of *Time* magazine, four such books were reviewed
> together. Their titles are descriptive enough of the purpose of
> the authors as well as the state of mind of the readers: *Love
> and Happiness, So You're Going to Get Married, Marriages
> Are Made at Home, Getting Along Together.*
>
> I have not read all these books, but, according to the re-
> viewer, they all tend to give practical answers to the same
> mysterious problem of living with someone of the opposite
> sex. They try to establish sets of little rules and little tricks
> which will guarantee marital bliss if carefully followed, in the
> same way that cookbooks guarantee that you will obtain
> pumpkin pie if you use the proper ingredients properly
> measured.

5. *"Whether you like it or not, anyone who chooses to do so can
know everything—both true and false—that it is possible to know about
you, in fact, more than you know about yourself."* ASHLEY MONTAGU,
Saturday Review, MARCH 31, 1956. The development for this generalization
must be in the form of evidence, since the infringement of privacy is now
a controversial topic. The expressions "anyone" and "whether you like it
or not" are especially generative; a substantial amount of real proof will be
needed. It must be in the form of factual information that can be verified.
This is what the author wrote:

> In this our Government sets the example, for the Federal
> Bureau of Investigation has millions of such records on file in
> Washington. The files of the Congressional Committee on
> Un-American Activities are open to anyone who cares to use
> them. Then there are the manpower lists, the biographical
> reference works, specialty lists, credit ratings, telephone books,

Black Books, Red Books, Who Knows What Books, the scandal-mongering yellow press, private eyes, public eyes, FBI's, wiretapping, TV and radio brainwashing, and so on. Privacy has gone with the waves. "Big Brother" of George Orwell's powerful and prophetic novel, "Nineteen Eighty-Four," is already watching you. A life of one's own is already well-nigh impossible, and the paradox is observed that in a world in which the private life of the individual daily shrinks, and his social life with his fellow human beings is reduced to the narrowest dimensions, his life should become increasingly more public.

Small-town gossip was at one time the only medium through which such publicity could be achieved—or rather thrust upon one. But that was a very primitive medium compared with the devices at our disposal in the modern age. Today we have gossip sheets with huge circulations which specialize in the exposure of the most intimate details of the individual's life—whether such details are true or false matters not one bit. Duly elected members of the Congress use their positions for political and private purposes to institute public Congressional Inquisitions during which the reputations of those whom they wish to destroy are nakedly exposed to the public gaze. If the Government sets the example for such antinomian indecencies, it is not surprising that innumerable individuals have set themselves up in everything ranging from one-man vigilante committees to group organizations dedicated to the investigation of the private life of any and every individual whom they choose to pillory. These individuals and organizations are more than willing, they are anxious, to supply anyone who asks for it with such information. And if it isn't asked for they will supply it whenever they can. As a consequence of such publicity many persons have been deprived of the right to earn a living.

Projects

1. Analyze the sentences below to determine how you might develop them. Estimate the number of words you would need to develop them. Where appropriate, indicate the audience to whom they are addressed. Your estimates may be only educated guesses, but they will be meaningful when you compare them with those of your classmates.

    a. Dear Mother and Father: I want to leave college.
    b. Her boyfriend is really flaky.

   c. The United States exhibits the same symptoms of decadence that led to the fall of the Roman Empire.

   d. LSD can have devastating effects on its users.

   e. Skleakerness is a quarkingly micked flizz.

   f. In women, philogyny is called homosexuality and society condemns it; in men it's called virility and society hails it as an attribute of its heroes.

   g. William Faulkner is more important in American literature than Ernest Hemingway.

   h. Baptists differ fundamentally from Episcopalians.

   i. Willie Mays is the best baseball player of all time.

   j. Religious institutions have historically been the enemy of science.

   k. Toads do not cause warts.

   l. The followers of Juan Perón in Argentina were much more obligated than the feudal *arrière-ban*; his vassals owed him their very souls.

   m. Messalina is conventionally regarded as the worst of Roman women.

2. A game played in intellectual circles sharpens the process of abstraction and use of analogy. It is called "Who Am I?" The person who is "It" decides what person he will be. He can be any historic figure, modern celebrity, or a member of any other class agreed upon. He decides to be, say, Julius Caesar, and announces his category as "historic figure." The other players then ask questions phrased in this pattern: "If you were a _____ what would you be?" "Julius Caesar" responds with one word. The dialogue might go like this:

"If you were an animal, which would you be?" "A lion." (Because lions are warlike, as was Caesar.)

"If you were a corporation, which would you be?" "General Motors." (Because General Motors, like Caesar, is one of the most important members of its particular classification.)

"If you were a book, which one would you be?" (Here "Julius Caesar" thinks to himself, "I would not be *The Decline and Fall of the Roman Empire* because that would give me away, but he cannot think of any book about leaders or warrior-writers. Then he rather weakly says *"Advise and Consent,"* because it is about a plot to undo a leader.)

Eventually a member of the group puts together all the abstract qualities they have discovered and shouts out "You must be Julius Caesar!" Try the game some time, perhaps in a meeting of your English class.

3. Go back over all your themes and analyze them for "specific anemia." Which sentences had predictive content that you failed to provide? Which sentences had unintended predictive content? Make a chart showing what types of development you tend to rely on—i.e., Theme #1, examples used eight times, analogy once, and so on. Write a 500-word report based on your analysis.

4. Paying special attention to development, write a 500-word theme

on one of the following or similar subjects. Insert enough evidence to prove all your assertions and cite many examples to illustrate your key ideas.

    a. Teen-age slang
    b. The importance of the automobile to young Americans
    c. Literature's contribution to my life
    d. The attraction of minority causes
    e. Religion in modern suburbia
    f. Confidence as a basic attribute of the modern economy
    g. Legal problems that really trouble society (or a segment of society)

CHAPTER 5

PROPER WORDS,
PROPER PLACES: STYLE

It is not enough to know what we ought to say; we must also say it as we ought. ARISTOTLE

When you write, you are influenced by three forces. Aristotle, when defining style, alluded to these influences. "Style", he wrote, "is the selection of words which has the desired effect on the reader and gives the expression a distinctive air." The first influence on your writing style is yourself. Your verbal habits, vocabulary, personality, knowledge, patience, and energy will direct your fingers as you write. Since the other influences, the writing situation and the reader, are filtered through your mind, in the final analysis you yourself are the greatest force upon your writing style. This circumstance caused a French critic to comment, "Style is the man." The more you write, and the more demanding are the occasions for which you write, the more your writing will come to have an entity of its own from which you can afterwards detach yourself. You either will take pride in what you have written, or you will not. If you do, it will be because you have considered all the forces which should influence your writing and feel that the result has a character and quality all its own, a certain grace that may be strength, beauty, vitality, or effectiveness—whatever the goal you sought as you wrote.

As the second influence, you have the demands and limitations of the writing situation. In college and afterward, many of your responsibilities will be prescribed. Someone else may have indicated your assignment, its topic, and its length. As you write, you will be dealing in generative ideas whose imperatives you must fulfill. These imperatives demand a content and structure—and they may also demand, or at least suggest, certain patterns of sentences and words. If your purpose is serious, your tone must be serious. If your subject is complex, you may need a technical vocabulary and involved sentences.

In the third place, you obviously are influenced by your desire that your reader understand or be convinced. This desire causes you to pry into your reader's mind for a hint as to the most effective expression. As you look beyond your typewriter and into the heart and mind of your prospective reader, you can make a number of accurate assumptions about him. You assume, for instance, that he will be unable to read your mind and that you must therefore express your ideas in the clearest way possible. You know also that he will have limited patience. As Mark Twain put it, few sinners are saved after the first twenty minutes of a sermon. You may assume also that your reader's interest will lag if your expression is commonplace and monotonous. Your writing must therefore have variety. Since your reader is a total person rather than a disembodied mind, he will react to your writing with every sense he has. He will react to the sound of your writing, whether he reads it aloud or not. Finally, your reader will have a sense of the fitness of things. Some of your expressions may amuse him, and some may offend him. In summary, when you let your perception of your reader influence your writing style, you will seek the goals of clarity, brevity, variety, euphony, and good taste.

Clarity

Professor Francis Christensen of the University of Southern California has written that clarity is the difference between self-expression and communication. There are writers, to be sure, who are content with self-expression. Some writers deliberately leave their prose obscure in the belief that, when a reader does not find something, he will put it in. Some poets, particularly between 1920 and 1950, exploited suggestive obscurity. They believed that, since life is chaotic and meaningless, poetry should be equally so. This "cult of significant darkness," led by Ezra Pound and T. S. Eliot, became very fashionable, but even during the fad, such critics as Yvor Winters, Karl Shapiro, and David Lambuth demanded clarity. "Obscurity," wrote Professor Lambuth of Dartmouth, "is not profundity. Neither is it art."

There are two aspects of the problem. You must remove all the barriers that cause obscurity, and you must exploit all possible devices to achieve clarity.

* BARRIERS TO CLARITY

Amphiboly. English is a code. If your reader has been trained in the use of this particular language, you should not write in the Swahili or Khmer languages. In other words, you should not ignore the symbols that your audience expects and will understand. The conventional Standard American sentence is a grouping of words that approximates most nearly what an American reader has been trained to expect. A misuse of the standard patterns may erect a barrier to your reader's understanding. A sign that appeared in a U.S. Officers' Mess in London delighted everyone and informed no one for months before it was removed. The sign read, "Let all those who are going out first." Fortunately, such sentences, which do not communicate at all, occur rarely. Of more frequent occurrence are those sentences that confuse *momentarily*, because of a deficiency on the part of the author in phrasing, spelling, or punctuation.

> Momentarily confusing: I like Bob and Betty likes Bill.
> Instantly clear: I like Bob, and Betty likes Bill.

When we read, "The man told John he had to go," we are not sure whether it was John who had to go, or the man.

So-called grammar errors offend either because they break "rules" of grammar or because they confuse the meaning. Whatever we think of grammar rules, we are probably agreed that we should avoid grammatical patterns that are confusing. Grammatical constructions that permit confusion of meaning are called *amphibolies* (am-FIB-O-Leez). The barrier may be confusing or only amusing, but the ludicrous construction may actually stop the chain of thought longer than the confusing one. A famous example, which Lionel Ruby included in his *Logic: An Introduction* (1960), is supposed to have appeared in a newspaper description of the departure of a dirigible: "The Graf Zeppelin was leaving the Lakehurst airport. Among the last to enter was Mrs. Smith, the lone woman passenger. Slowly her huge nose was turned into the wind. Then, like some huge beast, she crawled along the grass. . . ."

Another famous amphiboly is "The king yet lives that Henry shall depose." Who will depose whom? Some amphiboly is deliberate, as was the Delphic Oracle's answer when Croesus asked her if he should go to war against Cyrus of Persia: "If Croesus goes to war with Cyrus, he will destroy a mighty empire." Croesus heard what he wanted to hear, went to war, and destroyed an empire: his own. The prudent oracle would have been right, no matter who had lost the battle. More frequently, however, amphiboly is unintentional. It may be caused by dangling modifiers.

1. Before signing a contract, the small print should be read. (Sounds as though the small print will do the signing.)

2. To understand youth, they have to be viewed from many angles. (Sounds as though youth is trying to understand youth.)

3. While trying to understand the book, the long words confused him completely. (The long words were trying to understand the book?)

4. The plan, hopefully, will succeed. (Sounds as though the plan is hoping.)

The misplaced modifier is another source of amphiboly.

Confusing: The design was approved by the committee which was most exciting.

Clear: The design which was most exciting was approved by the committee.

Still another source of amphiboly is the grammatical deficiency referred to as faulty parallelism, as in this sentence: "In their plays, Capek and Shaw speak out against loss of identity and automation." The ambiguity can be shown diagrammatically. Where does the parallelism begin?

```
                                    ⎯ loss of identity
    . . . speak out against  <          and
                                    ⎯ automation
```

or

```
                                       ⎯ identity
    . . . speak out against loss of  <    and
                                       ⎯ automation
```

The careful writer would rephrase the sentence: ". . . speak out against automation and loss of identity."

If he is to write clearly and effectively, the skilled writer does not fight grammatical conventions. No matter how unorthodox he is in his thinking, he puts his adjectives and adverbs close to the words they modify, avoids split constructions, and makes sure that every pronoun clearly has a word, phrase, or clause as an antecedent; in general, he relies on conventional, reasonable patterns for his word choice and sentence structure.

Thorstein Veblen, Charles Darwin, and Albert Einstein, no matter how revolutionary their thoughts, clothed them in conventional English. Karl Marx, no matter how radical his theories, wrote in prose so conventional that he could supplement his earnings by writing for a conservative New York newspaper.

Ambiguity. Technically, amphiboly is ambiguity caused by unclear grammatical constructions. Rhetorical ambiguity is a confusion set up when one word has two meanings:

> She is in *fast* company.
> Some 300-*odd* students have just entered the auditorium.

Care and frequent reference to the dictionary are the required antidotes.

Faulty punctuation. Faulty punctuation often will cause ambiguity. An eminent historian once complained bitterly to a printer about a sentence that appeared in the scholar's book:

> The American Indians, who took delight in torturing their captives, deserve to be called savages.

The commas were the contributions of the printer; the author had written:

> The American Indians who took delight in torturing their captives deserve to be called savages.

"What's the difference?" the printer asked. "All you have done," the author responded, "is to make me guilty of over-generalizing about American Indians and condemning all Indians when actually some tribes were very peaceable and helpful to the white encroachers."

Do you see why the author was disturbed? Would you have been able to use the punctuation necessary to convey the three ideas expressed below?

1. That student thinks his teacher is the best in the school.

2. That student, thinks his teacher, is the best in the school.

3. That student thinks; his teacher is the best in the school.

If you could not, and if you do not understand why the historian saw that a different idea was conveyed by the printer's version, you should consult the section in this textbook on "Punctuation," pp. 422–430.

Esoteric words. Although there is an understandable temptation to parade a large vocabulary, to do so is to place an unnecessary responsibility on the reader and interrupt his thought. A writer may write, "The caitiff osculated the pulchritudinous damsel," but he will communicate better if he says, "The rascal kissed the pretty girl." You should certainly use exact words, and you need not avoid technical words—though you would define them if necessary—but it is inadvisable to use the *esoteric word,* the word known only to a select few, which is trotted out for pretension and display. When you have a choice of two equally exact words, select the shorter, more familiar one every time.

AIDS TO CLARITY

Images. Almost 2,500 years ago a Chinese philosopher is supposed to have said, "A picture is worth a thousand words." The advice is sound. You should not "write writing"; you should write pictures. Imagine that you are preparing a scenario for a film about the Emperor Nero. When you are done, the photographer must have scenes to shoot. If you have written, "The Emperor was cruel," he has nothing at which to aim his camera. On the other hand, if you had written the following paragraph, you would have supplied him with a wealth of vivid details.

> Nero poisoned his rival Brittanicus, and deserted his wife Octavia, and sentenced her to death. At first he kept the slave-woman Acte as the head of his domestic revels, but he soon strangled her in favor of Poppaea. After the burning of Rome—which he, surprisingly, did not cause himself—he almost bankrupted the citizens by heavy taxes. Those who would not or could not pay the taxes he put to death by running chariots over them. After kicking Poppaea to death in a fit of rage, Nero secured the affection of Statilia Messalina by stabbing her husband. During his courtship of Statilia Messalina, Nero killed his own stepdaughter Astonia because she resisted his clumsy attempt at seduction.

Remembering the "thing-word-idea" relationship described on pp. 7–10, attempt to describe the "thing." Try to recreate dramatically what you want to communicate by describing particular incidents in dramatic and vivid words. In the description of Nero, for instance, to say he "killed" Acte is not so expressive as to say he "strangled" her.

Herbert Spencer, in *Philosophy of Style,* demonstrated this lesson by citing two passages, one using general words.

> In proportion as the manners, customs, and amusements of a nation are cruel and barbarous, the regulations of their penal code will be severe.

MISS PEACH **By MELL**

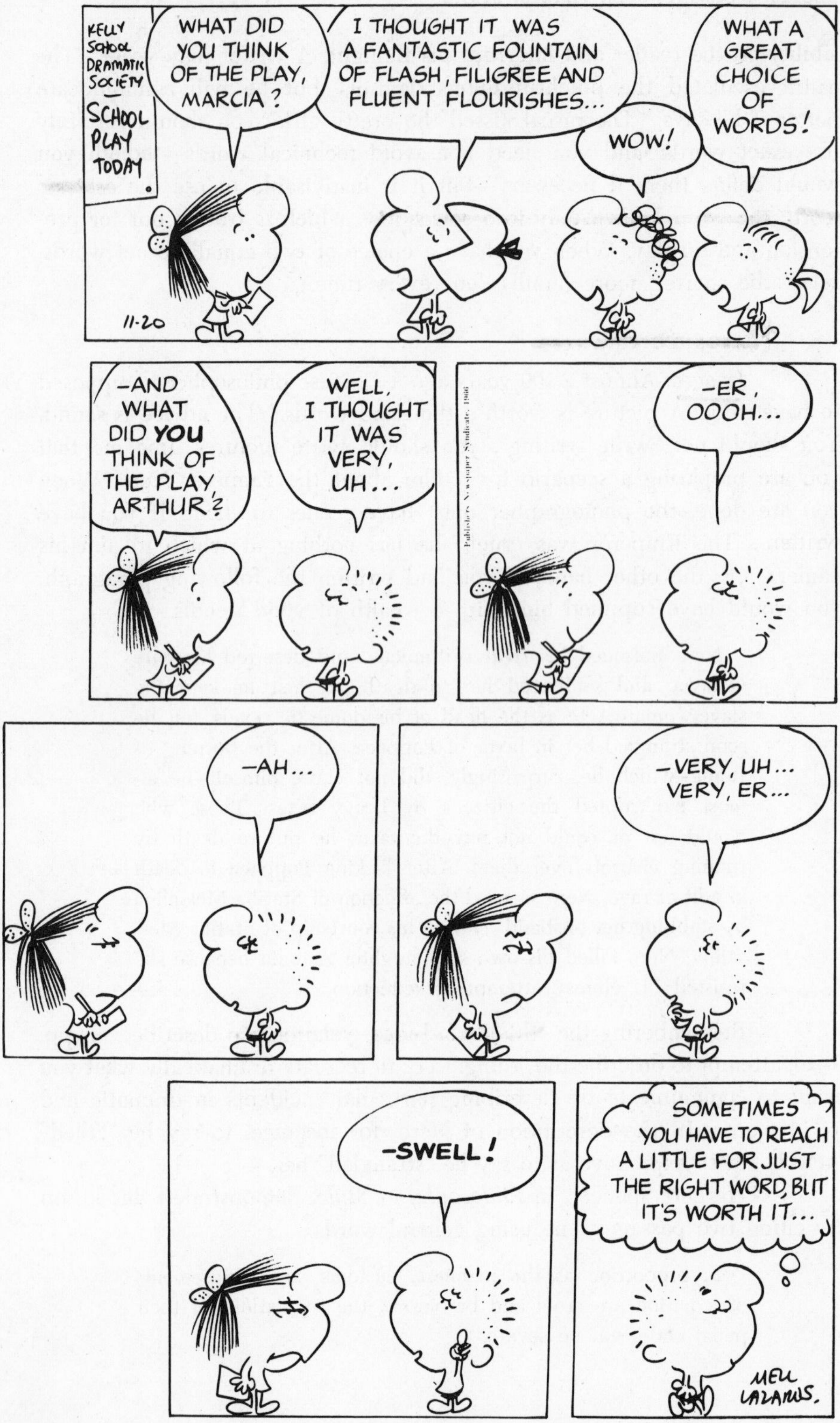

The other conveys images.

> In proportion as men delight in battles, bullfights, and com-
> bats of gladiators, will they punish by hanging, burning,
> and the rack.

The sensitivity of the reader to pictures provides the first rule for achieving vividness: *write in pictures*. Writing teachers constantly tell their students to be specific, which is good advice. Specifics create images, and a reader can react to things, to incidents, better than he can to symbols and labels. Television influences an audience more than radio does; likewise, writing that abounds in sense images influences more than does less pictorial language. To create images, cite exact names and places. If you are describing a date at a football game, tell what game, what quarter, and what girl. Bring your pictures to life. Don't say "a local eating establishment," say "Ho-Jo's." If you are writing your autobiography, tell what town you live in, what high school you attended, what church you belonged to, what sports and/or instrument you played. You are right: your writing *will* abound in capital letters. It is no matter that your reader will not know who "Mette Hansen" is; putting that exact a handle on a character will make the writing more authentic and vastly more interesting.

There's more to this technique than thinking in pictures and describing the pictures. You must habitually use words that, by their nature, *draw* pictures. Take the word *walk*, for instance. Its deficiency is simply that it does not communicate an exact image. It describes, rather vaguely, a means of locomotion that all animals use. On the other hand, some near-synonyms of *walk* conjure up lively and picturesque images:

saunter The walker is in no hurry; he is probably in a park; the weather is balmy. He has time to smell the leaves and listen to the play of children.

stroll Somewhat the same picture as *saunter*, but our walker has exercise in mind, or he is more interested in the scenery.

stride Now he is in a hurry; his pace is purposeful; he is probably a big man, and masterful.

lunge He is a big man, he is probably angry or in some state of high emotion; the "walk" is only a few steps.

skip Now the walker is a child, in a playground, lighthearted.

At the end of many entries in your dictionary you will find a synonymy, a collection of words that are similar in meaning to the entry word but have shades of difference. Under "diplomatic" in *Webster's*

Seventh New Collegiate Dictionary, you note, "syn see SUAVE." Under "suave," you find

> syn SUAVE, URBANE, DIPLOMATIC, BLAND, SMOOTH, POLITIC mean ingratiatingly tactful and well-mannered. SUAVE suggests a specific ability to encourage easy and frictionless dealings with others; URBANE implies high cultivation and poise coming from wide social experience; DIPLOMATIC stresses an ability to deal with ticklish situations tactfully; BLAND emphasizes mildness of manner and absence of irritating qualities; SMOOTH suggests often a deliberately assumed suavity; POLITIC implies shrewd as well as tactful and suave handling of people

Even though you are already familiar with the synonyms, you can profit by a checklist and thus sharpen or confirm your perception of their meanings. A few synonyms for some general, familiar words will show how helpful such a review can be:

kill	slay, murder, assassinate, dispatch, execute
grand	magnificent, imposing, stately, majestic, august, noble, grandiose
frown	scowl, glower, lower
tight	taut, tense
erase	expunge, cancel, efface, obliterate, blot out

When you have conditioned yourself not to use general, vague words, you will rarely write a sentence like, "He looked at the girl." *Gaped, stared, peered, glowered,* and *leered* all do much more for your picture.

The goal the good writer tries to achieve is an image that depicts the message he wishes to convey. When he transmits the right code word, his reader will convert the word, or symbol, into an image, and his message will then be transmitted as vividly as possible. The following selections from modern writers will demonstrate skilled control of imagery and connotation.

> The mob did not cross the ghetto lines. It would have been easy, for example, to have gone over to Morningside Park on the west side or to have crossed the Grand Central railroad tracks at 125th Street on the east side, to wreak havoc in white neighborhoods. The mob seems to have been mainly interested in something more potent and real than the white face, that is, in white power, and the principal damage done

during the riot of the summer of 1943 was to white business
establishments in Harlem.   JAMES BALDWIN, *Notes of a Native
Son*, 1955.

But I should be the first to point out that we must not
let engines and bombs monopolize our imaginations of disaster.
Let us turn rather to the opposite quarter and consider some
of the cultural effects of science, beginning with the lesser
ones. I spoke of mumbo jumbo. I had in mind the invasion of
every language by hundreds of empty noises like Bab-O,
Duco, Rinso, Kodak, Kotex, Kleenex, Vapex. Why is X so impressive and O so reassuring? It is the echo of science. With
this goes the would-be technical compounding of names
(Hydramatic, Hooperating), and all the verbs in -ize suggesting that some secret process has transformed the commonplace
into the miraculous. Do not suppose that you wash your hands
with powdered soap; not at all: it's "a specially formulated
skin cleanser." And you dry them on an "Aqualized" paper
towel, made by the "wet-strength process."   JACQUES BARZUN,
God's Country and Mine, 1959.

In the next example note how Mary McCarthy has used exact
words to create pictures: instead of merely saying she was "unhappy," her
reference to suicide makes us recall, perhaps with a gentle smile, the self-
pity of misunderstood adolescence.

I myself was an ardent literary little girl in an Episcopal
boarding school on the West Coast, getting up at four in the
morning to write a seventeen-page medieval romance before
breakfast, smoking on the fire-escape, and thinking of suicide,
meeting a crippled boy in the woods by the cindery athletic
field, composing a novelette in study hall about the life of a
middle-aged prostitute ("Her eyes were turgid as dishwater")
when the name *Vassar* entered my consciousness through the
person of an English teacher. She symbolized to me the critical spirit, wit, cool learning, detachment—everything I suddenly wished for, from the moment I first heard her light,
precise, cutting voice score some pretentious, slatternly phrase
or construction on the part of her pupils. With blond buns
over her ears, gold-rimmed glasses and a teacher's taste for
dress, Miss A .... was severe and formidable, yet smoked,
as I knew, on the side, read *The American Mercury* and was
shocked by nothing. She advised me to send my novelette
to H. L. Mencken for criticism. The idea of going to Vassar
and becoming like Miss A .... immediately dominated my

imagination. I gave up a snap course in domestic science and registered for Latin. I tutored in Caesar during the summer and coaxed my family. To go east to college was quite a step in Seattle. MARY MCCARTHY, "THE VASSAR GIRL," IN *On the Contrary*, 1961.

Idiomatic usage. The literal meaning of many English expressions is puzzling. Think about these sentences. What, exactly, do they say? What, idiomatically, do they mean?

Did you carry out my command?

Now, then, what shall we do?

He made good.

Take it from me; I know I'm right.

Go to the foot of the class.

The airplane took off.

His advice turned out to be a bum steer.

He was named after his uncle.

An expression that is characteristic of a language but whose meaning comes from agreement and custom rather than from the exact meaning of the words is called an *idiom.* You can imagine the trouble idioms give a foreigner—but they give native Americans difficulty too. At a Massachusetts supermarket, groceries are put into a paper "bag"; in Iowa they go into a "sack"; and in Georgia they go into a "tote," all three words referring to the same paper container. There are a number of idioms that differentiate American from British English. We say "go to the hospital"; the British say "go to hospital." Americans get *on* or *off* a train; the English get *in* or *out* of it. Americans are "on time" but the British would be "up to time."

The sensitive writer must learn the idioms appropriate to his situation almost by osmosis. Since there are so many of them no one has ever prepared a comprehensive list. The following idioms are representative:

1. Divide the cake *among* the three boys. (Not *between*. Use *between* for two.)

2. I wonder *whether* he is coming. (Not *if*)

3. We request adherence *to* our policy.

4. He is careful *with* idioms.

5. Worry is conducive *to* sleeplessness. (Not *of*)

6. I agree *to* an idea, but I agree *with* a person.

7. He was embarrassed *by* his sister. (Not *at* her)

8. The movie was inferior *to* the book.

9. Her pie was different *from* the one in the picture. (Not *than*)

10. He seemed oblivious *of* the snarling dog. (Not *to*)

11. We were receptive *to* the idea.

Obviously, if you wish to get your meaning across to your reader, you must use idioms with which he is probably familiar.

Denotation and connotation. Besides "writing in pictures," you can guarantee clarity by exploiting all the levels of meanings common to some words. Many words have only an exact meaning or *denotation.* Such a word points specifically to its referent, whether it be a thing, concept, or action. Most words have a broader significance, perhaps based on the experiences or emotions of the writer or reader. The word *house,* for instance, has a limited, strict meaning, but the word *home* may suggest memories of Mother, Wife, and Child, of fireplaces, toy closets, and the dining table. To some readers, the pictures are warm, pleasant, appealing, or *meliorative.* For the person who hates his father, left home eagerly at the first opportunity, and dreads the thought of returning, the echoes are unpleasant, or *pejorative.* However, through long usage, certain words have come to have, in addition to denotations, some emotional or dramatic overtones that are relatively similar in the minds of all speakers of the language. The extra dimension of these words is called *connotation.*

Connotation can be pleasant or unpleasant. *Womanly* is a pleasant term, but *womanish* is unpleasant. With only a few exceptions, any recently coined adjective with the suffix *-istic* is pejorative: *fadistic, simplistic, sadistic, masochistic. Premeditated,* a synonym of *deliberate,* has so long been associated with crime that it is pejorative, having overtones of evil design.

There are other kinds of connotation besides the meliorative or pejorative. Between *impending doom* and *imminent doom* the former has less sugestion of immediacy. We can expect an *imminent* flood at once, but we may speak of a rebellion that has been *impending* for some time. *Dissolve, fuse,* and *thaw* all have different connotations, *dissolve* suggesting that a solid melts into a liquid, *fuse* suggesting a substance subjected to high heat with a consequent mixing together, and *thaw* suggesting a cold solid becoming a warmer liquid. In another synonymy, *practical* implies a rather ordinary ability to accomplish everyday tasks; *judicious* refers to the use of discretion in accomplishing a task; and *sensible* is perhaps less concerned with discretion and more concerned with shrewd common sense.

Connotations often change. *Fat* formerly suggested a jolly, Santa Claus type; now it is pejorative, conjuring up images of overeating, bulges above the belt, and potential heart conditions. The skillful writer keeps abreast of such changes in the language and uses the term with the connotation he seeks. When you write, be aware of all the denotations and connotations of your words. Only then can you achieve real clarity.

✱   *Rhetorical devices: metaphor, synecdoche, metonymy, allusion.* About a doctor a student once wrote,

> His hands held the saucer and cigarette as if they were surgical instruments. The wrinkles of his brow were the worries of yesteryear and today and tomorrow, and the sleepless nights of coronaries and obstetrics, the pains and sufferings that he felt as acutely as did his patients.

These sentences transmit an idea vividly through the use of what are called figures of speech. By a skilled use of such figures a writer can create prose that is full of life and fresh in spirit. He writes with pictures, and he writes clearly.

The class name for figures of speech is *metaphor,* a term that suggests an idea by an implied comparison. Technically, a *simile* is also a metaphor, but the comparison of a simile is expressly indicated by the word *as* or *like,* whereas in a metaphor the comparison is only suggested. "He was a tiger in the fight" is a metaphor, but "He fought like a tiger" is a simile. In the sentence, "He wolfed his food," the verb is a metaphor that could be expressly stated in a simile: "He ate like a wolf." In *Prometheus Unbound,* Shelley writes of "multitudes of white fleecy clouds . . . wandering along the mountains, shepherded by the slow, unwilling wind." The comparison of clouds to sheep is an obvious metaphor. In an interview, a Dartmouth quarterback, when asked if he were in shape for the season, replied, "No, I am as soft as a sneaker full of marshmallows." That was a simile.

Two other figures of speech, *synecdoche* and *metonymy,* give drama to prose. A *synedoche* is an expression which, by mentioning a part, indicates a whole, or, by mentioning a whole, represents a part. "Hollywood" is used to represent the entire film industry; "Madison

Avenue" symbolizes all advertisers. A student may ask, "Have you gotten the word yet?" when he means an entire message. Speaking of an employee as a *hired hand* is synecdoche. *Wings over Britain* referring to German bombers is synecdoche, as are *campus life, Foggy Bottom* (the location of State Department headquarters), and "Nebraska won." This last uses the state name to represent not the state, or even the university thereof, but an athletic team of the University of Nebraska. (In passing, we should point out that "synecdoche" is pronounced sin-EK-doe-key and should not be confused with the city in New York called Schenectady.)

Metonymy, on the other hand, is the use of an aspect or attribute of a concept to stand for the concept itself. For example, a sportswriter may say that the Baltimore Orioles have a strong "bench," which is metonymy meaning that the Orioles have many good substitute players, for in baseball as in many other games, substitutes sit on a bench until they are called upon to play. Shakespeare's "A plague on both your *houses*" is metonymy. In Genesis, we read "In the sweat of thy face shalt thou eat bread;" "sweat" is a metonym because it is vividly associated with "hard work." In our daily newspapers we often read, "The White House announced today that . . . ," which is a metonymic way of referring to the President of the United States. The distinction in government circles between "hawks" and "doves" is a reference to the general stereotype of the nature of two birds, one seeking battle and the other avoiding it. By objectifying certain concepts that provide mental images, these two figures contribute to a vivid literary style.

Another device that contributes vividness to writing is the *allusion* —a reference to history, literature, or legends. For instance, according to Greek mythology, after Prometheus offended the gods by stealing fire from heaven, the deities resolved to punish Man by creating Woman. The gods all bestowed gifts upon this first mortal female, Pandora, and Zeus gave her a box with instructions not to open it. The curious Pandora immediately opened the box, and, like the winds, out rushed all the evils that were to beset man forevermore. In another version of the legend, the box contained all human virtues, which escaped when she opened it, leaving her with just one, hope. The story sets up a picture of a bewildered woman, almost blown over by the outpouring winds, a dramatic scene. Once, when a group of legislators were talking about what to do with the farm surplus, they discussed the possibility of sending the surplus to impoverished countries as foreign aid. "No," said one of them. "That would be opening Pandora's box. It would start a lot of questions we can't answer and start some battles we could not win." He was using allusion to make his point.

When a Negro leader is called an "Uncle Tom," the allusion is to the central character of the abolitionist novel *Uncle Tom's Cabin* by Harriet Beecher Stowe. In the eyes of today's militant Negro leaders, Uncle Tom was too content with his servitude. Calling someone a "Uriah Heep" labels him with the hypocritical humility of a character in Charles Dickens' novel *David Copperfield*. A "pyrrhic victory" is one gained at too great a cost, as that of Pyrrhus over the Romans in 279 B.C. Using such an allusion takes advantage of the drama of a whole chapter in history.

Not every writer naturally and easily creates metaphors; not everyone thinks in figures of speech. Somerset Maugham, for one, lamented that metaphors just never occurred to him. Other people seem to think in figurative language, and expressions like these flow:

"This is a spooky house; it's like a Charles Addams cartoon."

"I do not like to talk with him. I feel dirty when I am through, like walking out of oily sludge."

"If I drove like that in Wichita, I would get a bushel basketful of traffic tickets."

"Yes, it's a fairly neat little lash-up." (Response of an electronic engineer to a compliment about a computer he has just devised.)

"A mystic is a man who has his own telephone connection with God."

"Nobody is interested in following a man who, with his eyes fixed on the ground, spends his life looking for a pocketbook. . . . When I paint, my object is to show what I have found, not what I am looking for." PABLO PICASSO.

"Youth is the time to go flashing from one end of the world to the other . . . to hear the chimes at midnight . . . to see sunrise in town and country; to be converted at a revival; to write halting verse, run a mile to see a fire." ROBERT LOUIS STEVENSON.

"She would rather light a candle than curse the darkness." ADLAI STEVENSON, ABOUT ELEANOR ROOSEVELT.

The impulse can, of course, go too far. If figures are stretched, they become obtrusive and halt the reader momentarily, blocking the flow of thought. If they are obscure, they block communication completely, if only for an instant. Occasionally metaphors may inadvertently be mixed, that is, present two contardictory pictures, and the result is ludicrous.

"The hand that rocked the cradle has paved the way for America's youth."

"It is a time of uneasy peace; forged on the anvil of many dreams the ship of state has sprung a leak."

"You must salt away a nest egg for a rainy day."

These metaphors create a confused picture. The writers would have been better off to stick to straightforward, simple prose.

Sentences structured for emphasis. Some writers become so skilled that they can use sentence patterns to suggest meaning that goes beyond the content of the words. In diction and grammar, these two sentences are equivalent:

1. The boy is unhappy.

2. Unhappy is the boy.

Though the same four words are used in both sentences, the word order is different, and, subtly, so is the meaning. The word *unhappy* gets more emphasis in the second sentence because of its placement at the beginning. Since the syntax is strange, the structure could be used on an occasion where the subject or the locale is unusual, as in "Unhappy is the despot," or "Uneasy lies the head that wears the crown." In the sentence "Unhappy is the despot" the writer wishes to attach the most meaning to the adjective, which normally would come later in the sentence. In the following paragraph by C. M. Doughty, the author inverts the first sentence, apparently to stress the pleasantness that pervades the whole paragraph. The sentences are rather strange in pattern, but the scene is Arabia, and the sentences are meant to convey a sense of exotic foreignness.

> Pleasant, as the fiery heat of the desert daylight is done, is our homey evening fire. The sun gone down upon a highland steppe of Arabia, whose common altitude is above three thousand feet, the thin dry air is presently refreshed, the sand is soon cold; wherein yet at three fingers' depth is left a sunny warmth of the past day's heat until the new sunrise. After a half hour it is the blue night, and clear, hoary starlight in which there shines the girdle of the milky way, with a marvellous clarity. As the sun is setting, the nomad housewife brings in a truss of sticks and dry bushes, which she has pulled or hoed with a mattock (a tool they have seldom) in the wilderness; she casts down this provision by our hearthside, for the sweet-smelling evening fire. But to Hirfa, his

sheykhly young wife, Zeyd had given a little Bedouin maid
to help her. The housewife has upon her woman's side a
hearth apart, which is the cooking-fire for the stranger: Zeyd,
her husband, who is miserable, or for other cause, eats not
yet, but only near midnight, as he is come again from the
mejlis and would go in sleep.   C. M. DOUGHTY, PASSAGES FROM
Arabia Deserta, 1931.

In general, words at either end of the sentence seem to influence
the reader most. A word that might lose its effect if buried in the middle
of a sentence can be more meaningful if placed at the beginning of the
sentence.

> The mob suddenly headed for the Italian embassy, as though
> it realized too late that the film had not been made in the
> United States.

> Suddenly the mob headed for the Italian embassy, as though
> it realized too late that the film was not made in the United
> States.

The second version, with its emphasis on "suddenly," suggests that the
author is planning to discuss why attention was no longer on the United
States. If the writer plans to tell what the mob did at the Italian embassy,
the sentence might better be stated:

> Suddenly, as though it realized too late that the film was not
> made in America, the mob surged toward the Italian embassy.

Attention is now clearly turned toward what will happen at the Italian
embassy. The three versions demonstrate how a subtle change in the
position of a word, phrase, or clause influences meaning.

Structurally speaking, modifiers and subordinate clauses are relatively unimportant in a sentence. Sentences that tend to have these
weaker, less important units at the end are said to be *loose sentences* in
contrast to *periodic sentences*, which have the stronger, more meaningful structures at the end. A style that is habitually loose in sentence structure gives off an air of weakness, as though the point is made, and then
qualified, another made, and then weakened. This can be done deliberately,
as, for instance, when Charles Lamb wished to describe his timid and dependent poor relations. Note that his sentences are loose:

> He entereth smiling and—embarrassed. He holdeth out his
> hand to you to shake and—draweth it back again. He casually
> looketh in about dinner time—when the table is full.   CHARLES
> LAMB, "POOR RELATIONS."

The looseness is, in fact, exaggerated by his use of the dashes, which emphasize the lateness of the structurally unimportant member of the sentence. Even the verbs with their -*eth* suffixes, anachronistic even in Lamb's time, emphasize the falling rhythm of the sentence. In general, effective writers avoid loose sentences and prefer the periodic, which cause the reader to rush on to get at the meaning at the end of the sentence. The stimulation of this speed emphasizes the meaning of the final parts of the sentence. Compare these two sentences:

1. There will soon be another riot if no improvement is made.

2. If no improvement is made, there will soon be another riot.

Both sentences are grammatically sound, but the former being a "loose sentence" is an unemotional statement of fact. It is an observation. The second sentence, the periodic one, is stronger. It is a threat.

You can emphasize an imbalance of meaning by repositioning an important word, or you can use periodic structures to heighten the idea you wish to emphasize. When you wish to show balanced or parallel ideas, you can point up their evenness by carefully equal structures. Arthur Miller once wrote, "I left Ann Arbor in the spring of 1938 and in two months I was on relief." The two thoughts are almost tonelessly equivalent; apparently he wanted to show the measured passage of time and action. Benjamin Disraeli's pronouncement, "Youth is a blunder; manhood a struggle; old age a regret," uses similarity of structure to emphasize the flatness of the meaning. Balanced ideas can be extended to a series. The following paragraph by Robert Lindner shows how parallel ideas may be accentuated by a series of structurally similar sentences:

> The human race, at this juncture in its history, is increasingly exhibiting all of the symptoms shown by the most profoundly disturbed psychopathic personality. Like him, we are as a species becoming conscienceless and violent. Like him, we are becoming predatory and selfish. Like him, we are slaves of impulse and baser instincts. ROBERT LINDNER, *Must You Conform?*, 1956.

The parallelism may sometimes be emphasized all the more by letting the anticipation of the reader carry part of the structure of the sentence, as in "Youth is a delight, old age a joy," and "I loved her, and she me." Omitting part of the sentence in this way is called *ellipsis*, one of the most famous examples being Francis Bacon's "Reading maketh a full man; conference a ready man; and writing an exact man." The reader can feel the parallelism so strongly that he supplies the missing verbs. In a long series, the unit omitted may be the conjunction, in which case it is called *asyndeton.* It is usually appropriate when each unit of the series is to be considered singly and perhaps solemnly, as in "I came, I saw, I conquered." Occasionally if the rhythm desired is strong and the sense simple or jolly, asyndeton can be used to pile up the units quickly, as in the barroom ballad, "They ripped, they tore, they fell upon the floor." On another occasion the writer may use asyndeton to play a trick on the reader. He gets the series going and then surprises the reader. Since there is no conjunction, the reader rushes on to the final unit, and gets a mild shock: "The duke played the violin, gaily, loudly, badly."

Much of the effect of balance and parallelism is achieved by building up the expectation of the reader. The writer may wish to jolt his reader into an especially acute awareness of the opposition of two ideas. Just as the balancing of equal structures emphasizes the similarity of ideas, so does a slight deviation emphasize contrast. The result is called *antithesis.* The sentence "Man proposes; God disposes" is semantically in antithesis but structurally in parallel. The next two examples were used by two presidents:

> The world will little note nor long remember what we say here, but it can never forget what they did here.   ABRAHAM LINCOLN.

> Ask not what your country can do for you; ask what you can do for your country.   JOHN F. KENNEDY.

Violating the expectancy of his reader is an effective way for a writer to achieve a vigorous expression of an idea.

Still another violation of expectancy is the sudden use of a short sentence, or a very long one. Inevitably, some ideas will take more or fewer words for their expression. As a reader moves along, he becomes accustomed to the rhythmic pulse of long, medium, and short sentences, but they fall into a pattern. For instance, in an *Atlantic Monthly* article, "But What's a Dictionary For?" by Bergen Evans, the first sentences average twenty-four words and range, except for three sentences, between twenty-one and twenty-eight. Near the end of the page there is a thirteen-word sentence, then one with thirty-two words, and, finally, one with just seven words. In the next section of the article, Professor Evans gets back into the long rhythms again with a sentence having fifty-eight words. For several paragraphs the sentences are approximately the same length, about twelve words, with few variations, and then, he hits the reader with a sentence only four words long.

As might be expected, the two short sentences are the most important ones in the entire passage. The first, in addition to being short, is inverted into a question, and it indicates what the whole article is about. The second, in addition to being short, is alliterative ("Yet wild wails arose") and introduces a major section of the article. The longest sentence in the essay comes immediately after the seven-word question, and it amplifies the question that will be answered by the entire article. Professor Evans is doing what many writers do. He sets up a pattern of expectancy, and then by violating it intensifies the meaning of the atypical sentences.

A single famous sentence illustrates some of the devices a writer can exploit. In the marriage ceremony when the bridegroom says, "With this ring I thee wed," the situation is formal and solemn; a rather atypical sentence structure is thus acceptable and even advisable. The six one-syllable words give an air of simple dignity. The substitution of *thee* for *you* is appropriate for a serious religious occasion. *Thee* has two connotations— the "affectionate familiar" of its old use (like the Latin *tu*) and antiquity, adding to the ritualistic solemnity of the ceremony. The phrase "with this ring" is put at the beginning; it is important and it is chronologically first. These three words have short vowel sounds; in contrast, the next two have long vowel sounds, slowing them down. The unity symbolized by marriage is emphasized by juxtaposing *I* and *thee*. The last word is, like *thee*, archaic. It is also blunt and final. It is the end of the sentence; except for prayers and benedictions, it is the end of the rite.

Brevity

Most people have only so much patience. When a person goes into a store, he is annoyed if the clerk approaches with a languid air to wait on him. He expects a brisk, "businesslike" manner. Occasionally, a customer may himself be slow-moving, willing to take time and be entertained, but usually he has something on his mind. He has a problem, a need, an interest, and he wants quick satisfaction. Speed and efficiency, which are ideals of the American character, are reflected in our language. Americans once rode in omnibuses, taximeters, motor cabriolets, automobiles, aeroplanes; now they ride in buses, cars, taxis or cabs, and planes or jets. We seldom speak of television, stereophonic radios, examinations, the United Nations, or international society. We have TV, stereos, exams, the U.N., and the jet set.

The reader does not demand that the writer use one-syllable words, the shortest possible sentences, or brief paragraphs. He may like or dislike a writing style that is terse, even clipped, just as he may like or dislike writing that is fluid, rhythmic, and smooth. As a rule, the reader will gladly endure an extra detail or illustration if it has a point, but he will not tolerate an unnecessary extra word. He says only, "Get the job done without wasting my time."

BARRIERS TO BREVITY

✓ *Truisms and platitudes.* You can attain brevity by avoiding the unnecessary or the obvious. If you ask yourself, "Is this something my reader already knows?," you will ensure against boring him, and he will reward you by paying greater attention to what you do say. President Calvin Coolidge was guilty of a *truism,* an idea so obvious that it need not be uttered, when he commented soberly, "When men lose their jobs, unemployment results." Often a speaker will deliver a truism in such a pretentious way that it is called a *platitude,* a self-evident statement expressed as though it is important and original, for instance,

1. We ought to do our duty.

2. All of us, some day, will die.

3. Paris is, indeed, a city.

There are many other words to describe unnecessary expressions, among them *commonplace, banal, hackneyed, stereotyped,* and *trite. Commonplace* means dull and uninteresting; *banal* means the same, but it adds a dimension of hollow pretension. *Hackneyed* means worn out and jaded from acceptance and overuse. *Stereotyped* suggests an automatic response, the expected, totally devoid of any originality. *Trite* labels an expression that once may have been profound or appropriate, but now, through repetition, has lost all freshness.

✓ *Redundancy.* Besides avoiding useless and trivial ideas, you can tighten your sentences by avoiding unnecessary words. In some writers, wordiness is a disease. Some people write not for communication, but because they like to read their own words; they write, "Such are the vicissitudes of this our sublunary existence," instead of "Such is life." The name of the disease is *redundancy,* which is defined as "the use of more words than are necessary." The disease has many forms, only one of them excusable. Occasionally, an extra word may be inserted deliberately to emphasize a meaning, as "to dare boldly," in which case it is called a *pleonasm* and can be an effective expression. *Verbosity* is an extreme form of the disease and is completely inexcusable; words are thrown in so profusely that the writing cannot be remedied merely by cutting out offending expressions. *Verbiage* (or "verbal garbage") is nearly fatal to meaning; so many words are used that the meaning disappears almost completely. *Prolixity* is the result, often, of stuffiness; the writer calls unnecessary attention to his writing by prolonging it with synonyms or other words. *Diffuseness* is used to refer generally to a style; when a composition tends to be written loosely, it is said to be *diffuse*, which is the opposite of concise. *Circumlocution* refers to an expression that is stated in a roundabout, indirect, or euphemistic way; it often is an attempt to avoid using an unpleasant term. *Tautology* is a wordiness caused by a near-exact duplication of meanings. The sentence, "The English language is one-half redundant," seems concise enough, but the sentence, "English is half redundant," uses only half the words and conveys the same information. The sentence, "He walked the entire distance *on foot*," is tautological. Delete the last two words. Other examples of tautology are:

"The reason I am doing this is because . . ."	Condense to "I am doing this because . . ."
mental telepathy	Telepathy is always mental; the first word is unnecessary.
general consensus of opinion	The word *consensus* means "general opinion." Omit three words.
"According to the ACD, *mystic* is defined as . . ."	Better: "The ACD defines *mystic* as . . ."
elfin-like	Elfin means "like an elf."
many new innovations	If it weren't new, it wouldn't be an innovation. Omit "new."

AIDS TO BREVITY

Economical modes of expression. Besides avoiding unnecessary ideas and words, you can achieve brevity by using those standard forms of English that are most economical. You can express any idea in ten or twenty different ways; often the shortest is the best. These are some of the most common principles.

1. *Cancel double negatives.* You have seen the politician on television who huffs, "This charge was not unexpected." Mouthing the two extra syllables may have given him time to think, but they did not im-

prove his expression. He might better have said, "This charge was expected," or "We expected this charge."

  2. *Write with nouns and verbs.* The editor of a New York newspaper once told a cub reporter that he should choose adjectives and adverbs the way he would choose a mistress. To be frank, we do not know exactly what the editor meant. Certainly he was suggesting care, and we *think* he was suggesting that the young man avoid having too many mistresses, adjectives, and adverbs. The real power of the English language is in its nouns and verbs. The hack reporter writes, "The drunken man walked awkwardly," but the copy editor changes it to "The drunk staggered." "He made the room dark" becomes "He darkened the room." "I move that we lay it on the table," becomes "I move that we table it."

OVERLY ADVERBIAL OR ADJECTIVAL	NOUNS AND VERBS
I feel unhappy about	I resent
He will watch over me	He will protect me
He ruled over	He ruled
give out in small quantities	dole
feeling of uncertainty	doubt
He made an unpleasant face	He frowned

  3. *Tend to use active, transitive verbs.* It has long been fashionable to condemn the passive voice—and to use it. In 1837, according to Bergen and Cornelia Evans in *A Dictionary of Contemporary American Usage*, a critic called it "philological coxcombry" and "an outrage upon English idiom, to be detested, abhorred, execrated and given over to six thousand penny-paper editors." Since then, writers of grammar and rhetoric textbooks have almost universally insisted that the passive voice be strictly avoided.

  The stigma on the passive voice is ironic when we realize that it is often a mark of sophistication. Writers in scholarly journals use it more often than do writers in tabloids. At times we can scarcely avoid it. When the writer wishes to conceal the agent of an action, he must use the passive, as "unkind things were said," or when the agent is irrelevant or unknown, as "the message was sent," or conversely, when special attention is desired for the agent. For instance, "A boy broke the window" calls no special attention to the agent, but "The window was broken by a boy" does.

  There are, nevertheless, three legitimate objections to the passive voice. In the first place, it fosters a momentary ambiguity. When a sentence begins, "The dog was given . . ." we do not know whether the dog is the recipient of the action ("The dog was given a brushing") or whether he is acted upon ("The dog was given to the girl"). This ambiguity lasts only for an instant, but it demonstrates that the passive is a rather fuzzy construction.

In the second place, the passive is not dramatic. It puts the attention on the thing that is not performing the action. In "The child was given a spanking," our attention is focused on the spanked, rather than the spanker. In this particular sentence, it may be preferable to focus on the child, but the passive voice often results in many changes of focus:

> His clarinet was taken from its case and music was placed
> on the rack. His lungs were expanded and many notes were
> blown. Before the piece was completed, much beautiful music
> was played.

This is an exaggerated example, but it illustrates the change in point of view and the lack of action that is characteristic of the passive voice. In the following passage the prose is still something less than deathless, but it shows how the active voice keeps a focus that the passive often loses:

> He took the clarinet from its case and put his music on the
> rack. He expanded his lungs and blew many notes. Before
> he finished the piece, he played much beautiful music.

Finally, passive voice requires more space than does active. Contrast these two pairs of sentences.

1. The dog was given a brushing by the man. (9 words)

2. The man brushed the dog. (5 words)

1. A dog was given to the girl by him. (9 words)

2. He gave the girl a dog. (6 words)

Active voice thus not only gives an illusion of brevity; it actually is briefer than the passive. It requires fewer words and, because it often is less ambiguous and causes fewer changes in point of view, the reader can read active-voice prose more rapidly than passive; active prose thus seems shorter, even when it is not.

Variety

In his attempt to develop a style, the writer soon realizes that he must have nothing to do with someone else's tired old personality. He realizes that using the words of another writer might tempt him to use the ideas of another, and that real style grows out of original thinking.

Then, too, he knows that his readers like freshness. They do not want to travel the old roads.

BARRIERS TO VARIETY

✔ *Institutionalized style*. If you wish, you can get a whole, ready-made style cheaply, as though from a mail-order house. Having it handy, you will be able to express wonderfully banal ideas without doing any thinking at all. If you order the businessman's style, you will receive packages of sports-page clichés.

> He can hit singles and doubles, but he's no good on the home runs. He's bush league.

Or you will get a beautiful conglomeration of mixed metaphors.

> Let's throw this idea into the mixer to see whether it grows or not. If they shoot it down, we'll know it has too many gremlins in it.

In no time at all you'll be able to master this branch of English, called "Madison Avenue."

If you want to enter the military-political world, you can easily order gobbledegook. Defense Department officials are never pessimistic; they have a "low confidence factor." They do not start or end anything; they "initiate" or "finalize" it. Politicians will supply you with grand models of gobbledegook. You'll learn to say "In my opinion it is not an unjustifiable assumption," instead of "I agree." Some other choice expressions are:

GOBBLEDEGOOK	TRANSLATION
give consideration to	consider
make inquiry regarding	inquire
is of the opinion	believes
comes into conflict with	conflicts
information which is of a	confidential information
confidential nature	

You will learn to give your ideas an undeserved grandeur by expressing them in such terms as *phenomenon, element, objective, exploit, utilize, epic, inevitable, veritable, clarion, expedite, extraneous, humane, patriotic, realistic,* and *just*.

If you want to become a teacher you can learn "pedaguese." An "underachiever" is a pupil who is "producing minimally or below his peer group." His "grade achievement under the multiple-track plan reflects his predisposition to those factors frequently associated with late bloomers lacking the developmental key of meaningful motivation and without the

felt need to effectuate the tasks involved in the learning process." In other
words, he "is doing rather poorly compared with others in his age group,
not because he's stupid, but apparently because he just is not interested
in learning." Later, he does not merely graduate; he "achieves baccalau-
reate status."

the small society   **by Brickman**

HE'S A WELL-MOTIVATED
ACHIEVER WITH AN ADEQUATE
PLACEMENT RATING IN THE
COLLEGE-LEVEL PERCENTILES —   WHAT?   HE
                                              PASSED —

$2 \times 2 = 4$

CAT $\begin{array}{r} 4 \\ +2 \\ \hline 6 \end{array}$

1-17

Washington Star Syndicate. Inc.   BRICKMAN

We must have some sympathy for the writers who use these
institutionalized languages. Men of high position occasionally cannot commit themselves; they need a courteous way to say nothing. We can appreciate also the lure of in-group expressions, with their connotations of
friendship and togetherness. Many of the expressions we now ridicule
once had specific, needed meanings: "initiate" and "finalize" meant to
begin and end operations with which the person probably had no other
connection. The expression "cease and desist" is essential in legal documents; lawyers must be sure that an operation is not merely stopped, but
that it will stay stopped, i.e., "desist."

the small society   **by Brickman**

WHAT YOU
DON'T KNOW   WHATEVER HAPPENED
WON'T HURT   TO 'NO COMMENT'?
YOU...

12-9

Washington Star Syndicate. Inc.   BRICKMAN

The jargon of the astronaut in its proper place is exact and dramatic. The voice of Gemini Control announces, "The countdown has
started. The malfunction of the retrorockets has been corrected. It is now
three minutes to blast-off here at the launching pad. All systems are A-

OK." This language, even though strange to the layman, is appropriate and adds to the excitement of the moment. The same jargon in the mouth of a professional fund-raiser giving his tired talk to jaded citizen volunteers sounds like this: "Fellows, the countdown has begun. The rocket we are raising is $11 million. We are shooting for the moon. We must be sure that all systems are A-OK. We do not need any retrorockets; we must have no malfunctions. We are going to have a tremendous blast-off from the launching pad at Brae Burn Country Club at eighteen hundred hours next Tuesday." Obviously the humor is forced and the message inexact.

Clichés. Besides ordering a ready-made style, you may also acquire a pack of expressions, available for instant replay, called clichés. The cliché may once have been a vivid, even witty expression, but the world is now tired of it. Its origin is so remote that it is meaningless. What, for instance, is the meaning of "dead as a doornail?" Fatigued expressions become part of the language and are trotted out with no thought at all. It always rains cats and dogs. The weather report may be trite but true, or it may be as dull as dishwater. A girl is as pretty as a picture, as innocent as a new-born babe, or as slow as molasses in January. An old man who marries a young girl is old enough to be her father. Twins are as similar as two peas in a pod. A boy who takes too much food has eyes bigger than his stomach; a girl may look like something the cat dragged in. If it all comes out in the wash, it is a blessing in disguise.

Many clichés are similes: *sober as a judge, skinny as a rail, old as Methuselah, nutty as a fruitcake, cold as a statue, honest as the day is long, fine as silk, busy as a beaver, strong as an ox.* Others are dead metaphors or forgotten allusions: *cut-and-dried issue, toe the line, ride rough-shod over, stand shoulder to shoulder, play into the hands of, an axe to grind, Achilles' heel, swan song, hotbed of intrigue.* Other clichés have developed because one man succeeds, he thinks, in selecting an impressive or colorful way to express an idea and others delightedly follow him, and follow him, and follow him. Such expressions are often pretentious and wordy, like *render inoperative* for *stop* or *break; militate against* for *oppose; make contact with* for *meet;* and *come through with flying colors* for *succeed.* They are thus institutionalized style. Other expressions wear out as the newspapers drum them into our consciousness. The most overworked word in journalism is "hailed." Other tired terms are *violence flowed, flatly denied, kick-off, oil-rich nation, gutted by fire,* and *riot-torn.* These expressions have the virtue of brevity for headlines and they arouse the excitement that sells newspapers, but when they occur in serious writing they often strike a maudlin and falsely dramatic note.

Clichés become a problem because not everyone reads enough

to identify them. Frequently an instructor will mark "trite" or "cliché" in the margins of a theme, to the dismay of the student to whom the idea or expression was new. The writer must watch his own sentences carefully and demand that every expression be appropriate not only for the writing occasion but, more importantly, for himself. Emily Dickinson, when describing the sea, wrote "Laces reveal the surge," indicating that she was a woman and that she had seen the sea. If a student writes, "It exploded like an atomic bomb" he should have seen such an explosion. The first person who wrote "cute as a speckled puppy" probably had seen such an animal. Today, however, a student describing a girl he dated last night should find a simile that fits the girl, his experiences, the time and place. He would not say that she has an "hourglass figure" or even that she is "cute as the Boop-boop-a-doop Girl," because the expression would be meaningful to his grandfather but not to his friend. Whatever expression he uses will be dated, but the date must be now, and his writing must have its own personality, not that of some earlier writer and period.

If you seek variety, you will not find it in institutionalized language or the cliché. You should use someone else's moldy old expressions just about as frequently as you use his toothbrush.

Repetition. In addition to achieving individuality by avoiding clichés and institutional mannerisms, the skilled writer seeks variety within his own writing. Variety begins with an avoidance of obtrusive repetition of words and expression patterns. This desire can be carried too far, as when the author of the *Tom Swift* series of boys' books tried so hard to avoid repeating "he said" that his series of "he ejaculated . . . lamented . . . exclaimed . . . complained . . . gesticulated . . . queried" and the like made him the laughingstock of readers for five decades. But, within limits, a writer should try to avoid using the same word too frequently. He should select a synonym that will give a more exact cast to the idea being developed. He probably will avoid having his sentences all the same length, or the same structure, but he will usually work within an average range—say, from twelve to sixteen words in length and then occasionally throw in a very short or very long sentence. He will use a blend of simple, compound, and complex sentences. This range of language, coupled with the inevitable variety of levels of abstraction when a writer plays up and down the spectrum between abstract or general thoughts and the specific details and words that are thus necessitated, will tend to provide the variety that is a quality of good style.

AIDS TO VARIETY

The original twist. Once you learn to trust yourself, your personality will introduce variety and freshness into your writing. You show your personality first when you decide on your point of view. Will you be consistently critical, favorable, or "objective"? Will you be the remote, omniscient observer or will you be physically and emotionally involved? Will you treat the matter seriously, or will you find it amusing?

A word might be said here about humor. Some humor takes the form of gentle irony, as when a writer announcing a serious political meeting writes, "The revels will begin this evening at eight," or when he refers to an important international document as a "conversation piece." By using cool words in times of passion, using words of praise to imply blame, or using diminutives to label important concepts, the writer creates an air of restraint and detachment.

The following excerpt from the "Talk of the Town" column in *The New Yorker* Magazine on March 19, 1966, used irony frequently.

> Custom and continuity are so lacking in these quick times that it was downright heartwarming last week to hear Richard M. Nixon warning us once again about the creepy, infinitely devious ways of the Communist Party. Prolonged absence from the national fireside has not diminished Mr. Nixon's fondness for an old-fashioned, heavily plotted mystery, and the other day when he took down his old Red Story Book, opened it to a new chapter, turned the lights low, and began to read aloud in that deep, chilling voice, we instantly threw ourself down in front of the hearth in our old listening position, belly to the floor and chin cupped in hands, and scanned the embers for devil faces and F.B.I. men.

The result is an air of urbanity and poise that makes the subject of the article seem like a boy playing C.I.A.

A play on words, an amusing anecdote, or a current joke perhaps rephrased slightly to fit the occasion serve to remind the reader that the writer is present, a human being viewing and thinking about his subject and his audience. When the writer points up his observations with *paradox* or *oxymoron,* he makes his presence, a thinking presence, known.

A *paradox* is a statement that at first seems absurd, obviously untrue, or contradictory, but that, upon reflection, may actually be sound and true. A paradox recently noted is that the so-called beatnik of the 1960s is one of society's most slavish conformists. At first, he seems to rebel against the standards of society, but when we think of his "uniform," the beard, long hair, dirty jeans and feet, and his disorderly "pad," we see that he has only selected a different set of standards to conform to. Other examples of the paradox are the following.

Television spends more money on worse programs each year.

The voices which complained when the United States did not intervene in support of the uprising in Hungary or did not defend Israel in 1967 objected when we intervened in Korea and Vietnam. The voices which cry loudest that church and state should be kept separate were most vociferous that the Buddhists should have a part in the Vietnam government.

The paradox of the Affluent Society is that although we have more opportunity to do good, we have more time to get into trouble.

Oxymoron (ox-ee-MOR-on) is a brief paradox, expressed in two opposite terms, that conveys a total vivid concept. A writer may find a woman "nasty-nice," or he may be intrigued by the "sweet-sour" taste of chicken cooked by the Chinese, or he may find a poem "bitter-sweet." He may write of a "wise fool" or a "thunderous silence." He may call gossip "delicious dirt." A jet pilot, describing his escape from an airplane, wrote, "Then, for a *brief eternity*, my seat pack snagged on the cockpit ledge."

Two other devices that mark a thinking writer are *hyperbole* and *litotes*. Hyperbole is exaggeration, and litotes (lie-TOE-teez) is either understatement or a statement that is actually in opposition to the idea it conveys. An example of *hyperbole* is, "He is a giant of a man," or "For eons, the prime minister kept his constituents in doubt." The British are much given to *litotes*, as when the Royal Air Force pilots coming home from a dangerous World War II mission over Germany referred to it as a "piece of cake." A rather clumsy example of litotes is "He does not think cheese is too good," if the person doesn't think it is good at all.

These then are the barriers to variety: institutionalized style, the cliché, and repetition. For variety, search for your own original expression.

Euphony

Even when he reads silently, a person has a tendency to be affected by the sounds in each sentence. The subject of the sentence usually gets more stress than other elements. Some words have a cadence that falls away, like *TWEN-ty, HAP-py, de-PEN-da-ble*. Some words or phrases require distinct separation (juncture) between them, like *great-great-grandfather, conscious artistry*. Some sentences end on a high pitch; some have a falling pitch: I will *not* go! Will *you* go? I will go, if *necessary*.

A blend of stress, pitch, and juncture can be pleasant or not. Contrast "great, gushing gargoyle" with "the ethics of my profession." The former requires obtrusive juncture and unpleasant sound and hence is difficult to say. The second has equally unpleasant sounds, particularly the consonants in *ethics* or *profession*, but it has a rolling rhythm. Americans generally think of such words as *moment* and *murmur* as pleasing, in contrast to words like *gosh, sissy, fish,* and *pluck.* All other considerations being equal, a skilled writer usually avoids unpleasant sounds. Pleasant sounding prose is said to have *euphony*; if grating, rasping, or harsh, it is *cacophonous.*

It is not the purpose of all prose to be pleasant to the ear. Some prose is supposed to irritate or arouse, and cacophony can contribute to this end. Prior to the American Revolution, Thomas Paine wanted his readers to march, not sleep. In the crisis he put together a series of different sounds, slowed measures, and marching rhythms: "These are the times that try men's souls. The summer soldier and the sunshine patriot will, in this crisis, shrink from the service of their country; but he that stands by it *now*, deserves the love and thanks of man and woman."

In short, prose is heightened in style when its sound conforms to and emphasizes its meaning. Some words, by their very sounds, suggest their meanings, such as *hiss, slam, buzz, whirr, sizzle, murmur,* and *snort.* The pairing of sound and meaning is called *onomatopoeia.* A preponderance of matching sounds, called *assonance,* can enhance meaning. Assonance is related to rhyme (*date, mate*) but requires only similar vowel sounds as in *lake, fame,* and *tape.* Assonance calls attention to itself and may make its words more important in the sentence. Note the contrast of the short and long *i* sounds in Sherwood Anderson's "It has itched and squirmed with life and now it is night and the life has all gone away." The assonant words are important in the sentence; had the unimportant words been too similar in vowel sound, the effect would have been destroyed. A series of words beginning with the same sounds is called *alliteration,* for instance, Lord Conesford's "The wooly word betrays the muddled mind," or an unknown writer's "When fortitude has lost its fire, and freezes into fear."

The devices of sound can be effective, or, if not used with great care, obtrusive and inappropriate. Warren G. Harding was fascinated by alliteration, and some of his sentences were abominations; for instance, when nominating the cautious President Taft for a second term in 1912 he declared:

> Progression is not proclamation nor palaver. It is not pretense nor play on prejudice. It is not of personal pronouns,

nor perennial pronouncement. It is not the perturbation of a
people passion-wrought, nor a promise proposed.

Henry Wadsworth Longfellow may currently be returning to favor,
but his apologists are embarrassed by his frequently defective ear. In one
line of his poetry, for example, "A poet there was whose verse was tender,
musical, and terse," the prominent rhyming sounds of *verse* and *terse* are
neither "tender" nor "musical." In this case, sound contradicts meaning. In
his "Psalm of Life," Longfellow is trying to convey a serious point, but he
unfortunately uses a rhythm that sounds like the ditty, "Row, Row, Row
Your Boat." The words go one way and the rhythm another:

> Tell me not, in mournful numbers,
> Life is but an empty dream!
> For the soul is dead that slumbers,
> And things are not what they seem.

The same error can be made in prose, and the skilled writer, of course,
avoids it. Sound must enhance sense; when it does, style is much more
effective and attractive.

Good taste

As much as we would like to think of ourselves as a race of individuals, we often are a race of sheep. We frequently do what others do
because others do it. Sometimes this is bad, prejudice about race, religion,
and color being examples. Sometimes this is good. We have social customs,
or manners, for convenience and courtesy and to prevent confusion; life is
smoother and more pleasant when we follow them. More often, following
the crowd is neither good nor bad. If you go along with the majority, the
only advantage is that you avoid being unnecessarily conspicuous.

SOCIAL LEVELS OF WORDS

Like clothing, words have social position. In the sentence, "The
speaker feels *it is a must* for him to *size up* his audience," there is nothing
really "wrong" about the two italicized expressions, but in some situations
they would be too informal. They are called *colloquial* which means "appropriate for familiar conversation." They would not ordinarily be used in
a term paper, business letter, or military report.

The converse is true also. A drill sergeant talking to a platoon of
Marines would not use the language of this textbook; he would use a more

colorful vernacular. A corporation vice-president presenting a resolution to the members of the board of directors might use language more formal than we have in this paragraph.

Effective modern writers try to select the right word for the right audience on the right occasion. This is the relationship Jonathan Swift was talking about two hundred and fifty years ago when he urged, "Proper words in proper places." Choosing the proper word is based upon a psychological perception of one's audience. Suppose a man has been asked to give a talk to a meeting of the local Parent-Teachers Association. He would think briefly about what clothes to wear. Should he wear a tuxedo? A business suit? A sport shirt? His secretary may make a discreet telephone call to inquire, "What's dress?" In a real sense he is equally concerned with the dress of his own speech. Should he use slang? Should he use colloquial expressions? Or should he adhere to formal and precise grammar-book usage? If he is too casual in either his dress or his speech, he may offend his audience, who may feel he downgraded and misjudged the importance of the occasion and their education or intelligence.

/ EUPHEMISMS

Death, taxes, war, governmental control, financial difficulty, and many physiological details are unpleasant, but they must be discussed. The writer, therefore, occasionally turns to *euphemisms*, expressions that will convey his idea but spare the feelings of his readers. Although such terms have been lampooned for being overly delicate, the minister who speaks at a funeral of one who is "no longer with us" is being tactful, and the "dear departed's" relatives are understandably appreciative. It is not hard to understand that men who spend all their lives cleaning sewers might choose to refer to themselves as "sanitation engineers" or that the "rat catcher" prefers to be known as an "extermination engineer."

It has become great sport to poke fun at euphemisms such as these, for many of them are pretentious and overly delicate, conceal mushy thinking, and all too often result in hazy, sentimental, and flaccid writing. Once again we are in the area of good taste. Try to avoid the maudlin, the hypocritical, and the prissy. However, it is perfectly justifiable to use certain euphemistic expressions to avoid offending the legitimate sensibilities of your readers, who will appreciate your concern and be more receptive to your writing.

CONCERN FOR THE FEELING OF OTHERS

Much good taste in writing is a matter of good manners rather pragmatic case for courtesy and kindness. A writer is more likely to be effective if he does not joke about a sensitive subject, if he avoids profanity or obscenity. He certainly does not avoid controversial subjects; in fact, he is able to face up to them more effectively and courageously because he incurs no emotional rejection due to a lapse in manners.

Learning from others

In spite of our suggestion that in developing style you should be influenced by the needs of your reader, when you become interested in style you become most individual and creative. Your writing becomes dialogue. The You-Reader relationship becomes heightened: you become aware of his interests and feelings, and he becomes aware of your personality, tastes, and judgment.

There are ways to improve your style other than the ones surveyed in this chapter. Robert Louis Stevenson, for instance, recommended that a young writer imitate writers he admires—"play the sedulous ape," Stevenson called it. Benjamin Franklin and Abraham Lincoln, rather than imitating, paraphrased the writing of others and then compared the results.

There is a value to studying the style of good writers, and, fortunately, there is an abundance of good models. The editors of a number of magazines demand that, in addition to having worthwhile information, their articles be written in distinctive and even distinguished style. Such magazines include the *Atlantic Monthly, Harper's Magazine, The New Yorker, Saturday Review, Horizon,* and *Holiday.* Articles written in excellent style are found in *Daedalus, The Yale Review, The American Scholar, Foreign Affairs,* and *Scientific American.* The prose of the following recent or contemporary writers is usually distinguished and worth studying: Joseph Wood Krutch, Lionel Trilling, Herbert Read, James Baldwin, H. L. Mencken, Marya Mannes, Edmund Wilson, Jacques Barzun, Rachel Carson, George Santayana, Paul Gallico, Wallace Stegner, Adlai Stevenson, George L. Kennan, E. M. Forster, Winston Churchill, Somerset Maugham, Santha Rama Rau, Richard Rovere, Mary McCarthy, Martin Luther King, and Anne Morrow Lindbergh.

Although there is no standard by which one can judge that any given author is the best English-language stylist, the prose of E. B. White is certainly among the most respected. About White's style James Thurber wrote, "Those silver and crystal sentences have a ring like nobody else's in the world." Leonard Bacon wrote, "His most successful moments are due . . . to a high sense of nobility of the ridiculous tempered with an ingenious kindness." *Time* magazine called his writing a "kind of precocious offhand humming." Obviously his writing has "style."

Mr. White, born in 1899, commutes between New York City and his farm in Maine, which makes it possible for him to write with equal insight about city and rural life. For years he has written for *The New Yorker*, and he has published many collections of essays.

One of his best essays appeared first in *Holiday* Magazine and since then has been anthologized innumerable times. Titled "This Is New York," it begins:

> On any person who desires such queer gifts, New York will bestow the gift of loneliness and the gift of privacy. It is this largesse that accounts for the presence within the city's wall of a considerable section of the population; for the residents of Manhattan are to a large extent strangers who have pulled up stakes somewhere and come to town, seeking sanctuary or fulfillment or some greater or lesser grail. The capacity to make such dubious gifts is a mysterious quality of New York. It can destroy an individual, or it can fulfill him, depending a good deal on luck. No one should come to New York to live unless he is willing to be lucky.

After this introduction, White continues his eulogy with this sentence:

> . . . New York is the concentrate of art and commerce and sport and religion and entertainment and finance, bringing to a single compact arena the gladiator, the evangelist, the promotor, the actor, the trader, and the merchant.

After exemplifying these various types, he goes on with his description of the city:

> New York blends the gift of privacy with the excitement of participation; and better than most dense communities it succeeds in insulating the individual (if he wants it, and almost everybody wants or needs it) against all enormous and violent and wonderful events that are taking place every minute. . . .
>
> There are roughly three New Yorks. . . . The commuter is the queerest bird of all. . . . A poem compresses much in small space and adds music, thus heightening its meaning. The city is like poetry: it compresses all life, all races and breeds, into a small island and adds music and accompaniment of internal engines. The island of Manhattan is without any doubt the greatest human concentrate on earth, the poem whose magic is comprehensible to millions of permanent residents but whose full meaning will always remain

illusive. . . . At the feet of the tallest and plushiest office buildings lie the crummiest slums. . . . It is a miracle that New
York works at all. . . .

Storekeepers are particularly conscious of neighborhood
boundary lines. A woman friend of mine moved recently from
one apartment to another, a distance of three blocks. When
she turned up, the day after the move, at the same grocer's
she had patronized for years, the proprietor was in ecstasy,
almost in tears—at seeing her. "I was afraid," he said, "now
that you've moved away I wouldn't be seeing you any more."
To him *away* meant three blocks, or about seven hundred and
fifty feet. E. B. WHITE, *Holiday* MAGAZINE, APRIL, 1949.

The two outstanding qualities of White's prose probably are texture
and virtuosity. His lines abound with capital letters, indicating the name
of a street, broken-down prize fighter, orchestra conductor, or brand. By
illustrating almost every point, he gives his paragraphs a texture of four or
five levels. He generalizes about New Yorkers, then backs up his generalizations with concrete examples. He dips into one-block neighborhoods and
describes the customs of Negroes, journalists, commuters from Westchester.
He cites specific persons who write or play for a living, mansions that have
been torn down, buildings that have gone up.

Only a single sentence separates "The music stops and a beautiful
Italian girl takes a brush from her handbag and stands under the street
lamp brushing her long blue-black hair till it shines" and "The Consolidated
Edison Company says there are eight million people in the five boroughs
of New York, and the company is in a position to know"—a jump from one
person to eight million. White's generalizations provide a pattern; underneath, the riot of illustration, the coloration, and the metaphor give depth
to his highly textured tapestry.

By White's virtuosity we mean that he uses every tool in the
writer's kit. In "This Is New York," there are allusions to Roman antiquity
("gladiators"), to medieval literature ("grail"), to British history ("mud-
dling through"), and to children's literature (the "Wizard of Oz"). There
is explicit symbolism ("Harlem symbolizes segregation") and a wealth of
metaphor: "The whole city is honeycombed with abandoned cells. . . .
Broadway is a custard street. . . . batteries and batteries of offices. . . . Standing sentinel at each sleeper's head is an empty bottle from which he received his release." Note the alliteration of "Standing sentinel at . . sleeper's" and "received his release." There is joking reference to tired metaphors:
"It should have been touched in the head by August heat and gone off its
rocker." There is analogy: "It is to the nation what the white church spire

is to the village—the visible symbol of aspiration and faith." "Visible symbol" is, of course, from the *Book of Common Prayer*. There is hyperbole: "I heard the Queen Mary, and its sound carried the whole history of departure and longing and loss." There is antithesis: "lofty housing projects —high in stature, high in purpose, low in rent," and varying degrees of synecdoche and metonymy: "No one feeds the hungry IN-baskets"; "New York, the capital of memoranda, in touch with Calcutta, in touch with Reykjavik, and always fooling with something." In fact, there is no device that is not represented. There is oxymoron: "dubious gifts" and "all is cheerful and filthy and crowded."

There is an appeal to every sense: "Street noises fill the bedroom"; "slapped down by a bus driver"; "massive doses of supplementary vitamins"; "voodoo charms of Harlem"; "white plume, a love message blown through a pneumatic tube—pfft—just like that"; "burned with a low steady fever"; "casually dressed—slacks, seersucker jacket, a book showing in his pocket"; "Coins rattle to the street"; "the mounted cop, clumping along on his nag"; "cool salvation"; "green salad with a little taste of garlic"; "skirts of girls approaching on the Mall are ballooned by the breeze." There is contrast— harsh sounds and soothing sounds, long sentences and short sentences, simple expressions and long piled-up structures. There is an amusing description of a "young intellectual . . . trying to persuade a girl to come live with him and be his love," a literary allusion to Christopher Marlowe's poem "A Passionate Shepherd to His Love." "She has her guard up, but he is extremely reasonable, careful not to overplay his hand." In somber contrast there is subdued understatement, a reference to a young couple who have "failed to catch the miracle. The place has been too much for them; they sit languishing in a cheap restaurant over a speechless meal."

Just how much style can a college student expect to achieve? Certainly few of you are or will become E. B. Whites. Nevertheless, some of you already have a fineness of writing and an exactness of expression, perhaps even a conscious style that reflects your personality. Very likely you come from homes where good books are always available and where you are encouraged to develop an ear and an eye for language. But even you and certainly all other college students can take great strides toward a better writing style and all that can be accomplished with it.

What you must do, of course, is gradually work out your own procedure. To help, George Orwell has suggested that you answer the following questions as you write.

1. What am I trying to say?

2. What words will express it?

3. What image or idiom will make it clearer?

4. Is this image fresh enough to have an effect?

5. Could I express the idea in fewer words?

6. Have I said anything that is avoidably ugly?   GEORGE ORWELL, *Shooting an Elephant and Other Essays*, 1950.

In *The Summing Up*, Somerset Maugham, on the other hand, listed clarity, simplicity, and euphony as his goals. You will want to prepare your own aims to fit the nature of your audience, as you perceive it, and your own strengths and weaknesses, as you see them. Ernest Hemingway, if it consoles you, gave up trying to make his sentences sound smooth. As you refine your list of desired qualities, you will need to know a great deal about the tools available to you to achieve those goals. The historical background of the basic tools in language and logic is discussed in Chapters 7 and 8.

No writer at any one time uses all the devices available to give his writing clarity, effectiveness, vividness, vigor, and variety—in other words, that extra something called style. The devices that he chooses to use tend to fall into a pattern that is individual with him.

With constant effort, you will get results, and your writing will come to have a happy blend of rhythm, precision, originality, vibrancy, color, and a prevailing harmony; it will have that state of muscular tension, the fat gone and the sinews working together, which make up your own style. When exposed to such writing, the reader will not consider himself the target of lifeless words; instead he will feel he is taking part in a dialogue with an intelligent, informed person.

Projects

1. Define and illustrate the following terms:

abstract word	cacophony	idiom
active voice	concrete word	inversion
alliteration	connotation	irony
allusion	coordination	jargon
ambiguity	denotation	litotes
analogy	emphasis	loose sentence
antithesis	euphemism	melioration
assonance	figure of speech	metaphor
balance	gobbledegook	metonymy
barbarism	hyperbole	onomatopoeia

oxymoron	pleonasm	synecdoche
paradox	redundant	synonymy
parallelism	repetition	tautology
passive voice	rhetorical question	tone
pedaguese	simile	trite
pejoration	specificity	truism
platitude	style	verbiage
	subordination	

2. In your out-of-school leisure reading, you encounter newspapers and magazines, each of which attempts to develop and reflect its own style. Examine several of the periodicals with which you are already familiar and identify both the kinds of style represented and the specific methods of achieving them. You may discover that everything you read is written in the same style, perhaps "subway journalese," or "sophomore collegiate." If you do make such a discovery, examine critically some of the following individual periodicals, which are *not* offered as models:

The New York Times	*Partisan Review*
The Christian Science Monitor	*McCall's*
Time	*Ladies' Home Journal*
Newsweek	*Playboy*
The Reporter	*Mad*
Ramparts	Any Hearst newspaper or magazine

3. Style is a subject so vast that only an introduction to it can be presented in this textbook. The following rhetorical terms are not covered in this chapter, and you may therefore want to check their meaning in any unabridged dictionary, Thrall, Hibbard, and Holman's *A Handbook to Literature*, and/or Sheridan Baker's *The Complete Stylist*.

anacoluthon	dilemma	hypothesis
anaphora	dithyramb	isocolon
antonomasia	elision	malapropism
aphorism	epigram	parataxis
apophasis	epistrophe	parody
aposiopesis	exigesis	personification
apostrophe		

4. Using either your course anthology or some articles in a serious magazine, analyze a prose style you like or dislike. Count the number of words in each sentence; contrast the frequency of simple, compound, and complex sentences. Read aloud and describe the sound patterns, including alliteration, assonance, and rhythm. Locate and label all figures of speech. If present, single out such sins as redundancy, mixed metaphors, cacophony, gobbledegook, and stilted diction. You may wish to compare the writing of two authors. Write a

500–750 word theme about the results of your research. Besides the writers mentioned in the chapter, the authors listed below should provide provocative models:

Kenneth Burke   William Faulkner
George Santayana   James Gould Cozzens
Thorstein Veblen   Dwight Eisenhower
Paul Tillich   Warren G. Harding
Richard Nixon   Paul Goodman
Barry Goldwater   Marshall McLuhan
Ernest Hemingway

5. React to the metaphors given below. Are they fresh, unstilted, generally appropriate for any audience? Are they ambiguous, mixed? Could you devise better ones to demonstrate the same concept?

a. Effective as a blind lifeguard
b. Hysterical as a coop full of chickens
c. Awkward as a bull in a china shop
d. Thin as the homeopathic soup made by boiling the shadow of a pigeon that had starved to death
e. Unplanned as a hiccup
f. Restless as a windshield wiper
g. Helpful as throwing a drowning man both ends of a rope
h. Welcome as a monthly bill
i. Graceful as a fawn
j. Silly as a loon
k. Her eyes were bluer than the feet of a Sicilian wine-crusher.
l. Her face was as expressionless as a smoked herring

6. The following words are grouped by approximately similar meanings. After referring to your dictionary, indicate the shades of differences among the meanings, paying particular attention to connotations, melioration, and pejoration. Use each word appropriately in a sentence.

abandon, relinquish, renounce
answer, reply, response, retort
assign, allocate, allot
contempt, disdain, scorn
continual, constant, continuous, incessant, perpetual, perennial
dark, obscure, dim, vague
defender, guardian, custodian, keeper
direct, order, command, demand
lead, guide, conduct, escort, pilot, influence
progressive, forward, enterprising, liberal
release, free, dismiss, discharge
see, perceive, witness, inspect, interview, discern, regard, deem, look, behold, gaze, scan, skim

7. Listed below are some expressions that are often quoted, quite out of their original context. We can assume, therefore, that they have been judged to be particularly effective ways of expressing thought. What do you think is their appeal? Is it the message itself, or the way it is expressed? What are other expressions that have caught your fancy for one reason or another?

"Burning with a gem-like flame" Walter Pater (paraphrased)
"Hail to thee, blithe Spirit!" Percy Bysshe Shelley
"Pronounce it trippingly on the tongue." William Shakespeare
"The balance of power" Sir Robert Walpole
"Sea of upturned faces" Daniel Webster
"Hitch your wagon to a star." Ralph Waldo Emerson
"Heaven will protect the Working Girl." Edgar Smith
"When you call me that, smile!" Owen Wister
"There is no cure for birth and death save to enjoy the interval."
    George Santayana
"The moral climate of America" Franklin Delano Roosevelt
"Let there be spaces in your togetherness." Kahlil Gibran
"The moral obligation to be intelligent" John Erskine
"A separate peace" Ernest Hemingway
"Sour grapes" Aesop
"Deeds live longer than words." Pindar
"The ship of state" Sophocles
"Love conquers all." Virgil
"Man is a reasoning animal." Seneca
"Words are but the shadows of action." Democritus

8a. Many skilled professional writers have translated famous passages of prose into gobbledegook. Here are some examples:

I returned, and saw under the sun, that the race is not to the swift, nor the battle to the strong, neither yet bread to the wise, nor yet riches to men of understanding, nor yet favor to men of skill; but time and chance happeneth to them all. Ecclesiastes 9:11.

Objective consideration of contemporary phenomena compels the conclusion that success or failure in competitive activities exhibits no tendency to be commensurate with innate capacity, but that a considerable element of the unpredictable must invariably be taken into account. GEORGE ORWELL'S TRANSLATION INTO "MODERN ENGLISH," IN *Shooting an Elephant and Other Essays*, 1950.

A sentence of Franklin D. Roosevelt, "I see one-third of a nation ill-housed, ill-clad, ill-nourished," has been translated by Stuart Chase into "standard bureaucratic prose":

It is evident that a substantial number of persons within the Continental limits of the United States have inadequate financial resources with which to purchase the products of agricultural communities and industrial establishments. It would appear that for a considerable segment of the population, possibly as much as 33.3333 per cent of the total, there are inadequate housing facilities, and an equally significant proportion is deprived of the proper types of clothing and nutriment. STUART CHASE, *Power of Words*, 1954.

8b. To sharpen your perception of what to avoid in your own style, translate the following quotations into gobbledegook:

I think the true discovery of America is before us. I think the true fulfillment of our spirit, of our people, of our mighty and immortal land, is yet to come. THOMAS WOLFE, IN *You Can't Go Home Again.*

We must act, and act quickly. FRANKLIN D. ROOSEVELT, *First Inaugural Address.*

The frontier is the outer edge of the wave—the *meeting point* between savagery and civilization. FREDERICK JACKSON TURNER, "THE SIGNIFICANCE OF THE FRONTIER IN AMERICAN HISTORY," 1893.

Four score and seven years ago our fathers brought forth on this continent, a new nation, conceived in liberty, and dedicated to the proposition that all men are created equal. ABRAHAM LINCOLN, GETTYSBURG ADDRESS.

The writer's duty is to . . . help man endure by lifting his heart, by reminding him of the courage and honor and hope and pride and compassion and pity and sacrifice which have been the glory of his past. WILLIAM FAULKNER, ON ACCEPTING THE NOBEL AWARD, STOCKHOLM, SWEDEN, 1950.

8c. Some time when you and your friends have nothing to do, suggest that they assemble a list of specialized American group nouns, that is, words used to indicate certain collections. One speaks of a *team* of horses, but of a *span* of mules. When the game flags, you can move it along by suggesting a pride of lions, a brace of pistols, a gaggle of geese, a yoke of oxen, a bevy of girls, and an anthology of prose.

9. Rewrite one of the following selections. The results should be the best possible example of your style. Use Orwell's six suggestions listed at the end of the chapter. Your instructor may suggest or permit paragraphs by other authors.

The Americans, and especially the Americans who live in the open, have always been storytellers—one need recall only the rivermen, the lumberjacks, the cowmen, or in fact the loafers round any stove at a rural crossroads—but there have been no stories beyond those told by the map-minded breakers of trails, hunters of beavers, and exterminators of Indians. Most of their yarning has been lost to history, but it was a chronicle of every watercourse, peak, park, danger, violent mirth, of Indians whose thought was not commensurate with white thinking and therefore inexhaustibly fascinating, fantasy of mythological beavers or grizzlies, of Welsch Indians or Munchies of the Fair God, of supernatural beings and spectral visitants and startling medicine and heroes who were cousin to Paul Bunyan. It was a shop-talk, trapping, hunting, trailing, fighting and always the lay of the land and old fields revisited and new fields to be found, water and starvation and trickery and feasts. BERNARD DE VOTO, *Across the Wide Missouri,* 1947.

The prosperity of America is legendary. Our standards of living are beyond the dreams of avarice of most of the world. We are a kind of paradise of domestic security and wealth. But we face the ironic situation that the same technical efficiency which provided our comforts has also placed us at the center of the tragic developments in world limits. There are evidently limits to the achievement of science; and there are irresolvable contradictions both between prosperity and virtue, and between happiness and the "good life" which had not been anticipated in our philosophy. REINHOLD NIEBUHR, *The Irony of American History,* 1952.

10. Assume you are an adviser for one of the new countries in Africa, and you have been asked to write a Declaration of Independence suggested by the American one. Write the first paragraph, which may be influenced by the paragraph below from the U.S. Declaration, but must be in your own best style.

When, in the course of human events, it becomes necessary for one people to dissolve the political bands which have connected them with another, and to assume among the powers of the earth the separate and equal station to which the Laws of Nature and of Nature's God entitle them, a decent respect to the opinions of mankind requires that they should declare the causes which impel them to the separation.

11. The passage given below appeared on an English Advanced Placement Program examination and is reprinted by permission of the College Entrance Examination Board. Students were asked to locate the rhetorical devices and write a careful analysis (not a paraphrase) of the passage with special attention to the choice of words, phrasing, sentence structure, figurative expressions, tone, and whatever else they considered pertinent. In a 500-word theme, demonstrate how you would have handled this assignment. "COURSE AND EXAMINATION DESCRIPTION," COLLEGE ENTRANCE EXAMINATION BOARD, 1966.

Meantime our society has lost its own soul. The landscape of Christendom is being covered with lava; a great eruption and inundation of brute humanity threatens to overwhelm all the treasures that artful humanity has created. Brute humanity has the power to destroy polite humanity, because it retains the material equipment of modern industry which has recently grown upon man like fresh hide, horns, and claws. Armed with this prodigious mechanism, any hand at headquarters can spread death and ruin over the earth. But whose hand shall this be? Anybody's: the first man's who jumps at the lever, touches the button, and takes possession of the radio.

Yes, but this is so easy, so alluring, that more than one man may attempt it at once. Then the really great war, in the modern sense of greatness, would begin. The whole mechanism in one hand would clash with the whole mechanism in another hand. Will they simply blow each other up, and perish together? Or at the last moment will they agree to pool their machinery and draw lots as to who shall be boss?

Or will one of the explosions miss fire, so that only one party survives, and makes an appeal to chance unnecessary? In any case, it will be a war of extermination establishing an absolute power. There will be no consideration of rights or liberties, no talk of honour, and no nonsensical chivalry. GEORGE SANTAYANA.

12. The Inaugural Address of President John F. Kennedy was a conscious orchestration of stylistic devices. In the speech, which appears below, locate all examples of connotation, alliteration, epigram, paradox, allusion, analogy, repetition, balance, parallelism, antithesis, metaphor, inverted sentences, and other devices. Then replace them with other expressions the President might have used, and by contrast, try to analyze the particular effect he sought. If, after you have completed your work, you wish to know how a professional rhetorician accomplished such an analysis, see "President Kennedy's Inaugural Address," by Burnham Carter, Jr., *College Composition and Communication*, February, 1963.

Mr. Chief Justice, President Eisenhower, Vice President Nixon, President Truman, reverend clergy, fellow citizens, we observe today not a victory of party, but a celebration of freedom—symbolizing an end, as well as a beginning—signifying renewal, as well as change. For I have sworn before you and Almighty God the same solemn oath our forebears prescribed nearly a century and three-quarters ago.

The world is very different now. For man holds in his mortal hands the power to abolish all forms of human poverty and all forms of human life. And yet the same revolutionary beliefs for which our forebears fought are still at issue around the globe—the belief that the rights of man come not from the generosity of the state, but from the hand of God.

We dare not forget today that we are the heirs of that first revolution. Let the word go forth from this time and place, to friend and foe alike, that the torch has been passed to a new generation of Americans—born in this century, tempered by war, disciplined by a hard and bitter peace, proud of our ancient heritage—and unwilling to witness or permit the slow undoing of those human rights to which this nation has always been committed, and to which we are committed today at home and around the world.

Let every nation know, whether it wishes us well or ill, that we shall pay any price, bear any burden, meet any hardship, support any friend, oppose any foe, in order to assure the survival and the success of liberty.

This much we pledge—and more.

To those old allies whose cultural and spiritual origins we share, we pledge the loyalty of faithful friends. United, there is little we cannot do in a host of cooperative ventures. Divided, there is little we can do—for we dare not meet a powerful challenge at odds and split asunder.

To those new states whom we welcome to the ranks of the free, we pledge our word that one form of colonial control shall not have passed away merely to be replaced by a far greater iron tyranny. We shall not always expect to find them supporting our view. But we shall always hope to find them strongly supporting their own freedom—and to remember that, in the past, those who foolishly sought power by riding the back of the tiger ended up inside.

To those peoples in the huts and villages across the globe struggling to break the bonds of mass misery, we pledge our best efforts to help them help themselves, for whatever period is required—not because the Communists may be doing it, not because we seek their votes, but because it is right. If a free society cannot help the many who are poor, it cannot save the few who are rich.

To our sister republics south of our border, we offer a special pledge—to convert our good words into good deeds, in a new alliance for progress, to assist free men and free governments in casting off the chains of poverty. But this peaceful revolution of hope cannot become the prey of hostile powers. Let all our neighbors know that we shall join with them to oppose aggression or subversion anywhere in the Americas. And let every other power know that this hemisphere intends to remain the master of its own house.

To that world assembly of sovereign states, the United Nations, our last best hope in an age where the instruments of war have far outpaced the instruments of peace, we renew our pledge of support—to prevent it from becoming merely a forum for invective—to strengthen its shield of the new and the weak—and to enlarge the area in which its writ may run.

Finally, to those nations who would make themselves our adversary, we offer not a pledge but a request: that both sides begin anew the quest for peace, before the dark powers of destruction unleashed by science engulf all humanity in planned or accidental self-destruction.

We dare not tempt them with weakness. For only when our arms are sufficient beyond doubt can we be certain beyond doubt that they will never be employed. But neither can two great and powerful groups of nations take comfort from our present course—both sides overburdened by the cost of modern weapons, both rightly alarmed by the steady spread of the deadly atom, yet both racing to alter that uncertain balance of terror that stays the hand of mankind's final war.

So let us begin anew—remembering on both sides that civility is not a sign of weakness, and sincerity is always subject to proof. Let us never negotiate out of fear. But let us never fear to negotiate.

Let both sides explore what problems unite us instead of laboring those problems which divide us.

Let both sides, for the first time, formulate serious and precise proposals for the inspection and control of arms—and bring the absolute power to destroy other nations under the absolute control of all nations.

Let both sides seek to invoke the wonders of science instead of its terrors. Together let us explore the stars, conquer the deserts, eradicate disease, tap the ocean depths, and encourage the arts and commerce.

Let both sides unite to heed in all corners of the earth the command of Isaiah—to "undo the heavy burdens and let the oppressed go free."

And if a beachhead of cooperation may push back the jungle of suspicion, let both sides join in creating a new endeavor, not a new balance of power, but a new world of law, where the strong are just and the weak secure, and the peace preserved.

All this will not be finished in the first hundred days. Nor will it be finished in the first thousand days, nor in the life of this Administration, nor even perhaps in our lifetime on this planet. But let us begin.

In your hands, my fellow citizens, more than in mine, will rest the final success or failure of our course. Since this country was founded, each generation of Americans has been summoned to give testimony to its national loyalty. The graves of young Americans who answered the call to service are found around the globe.

Now the trumpet summons us again—not as a call to bear arms, though arms we need; not as a call to battle, though embattled we are; but a call to bear the burden of a long twilight struggle, year in, and year out, "rejoicing in hope, patient in tribulation"—a struggle against the common enemies of man: tyranny, poverty, disease, and war itself.

Can we forge against these enemies a grand and global alliance, north and south, east and west, that can assure a more fruitful life for all mankind? Will you join in that historic effort?

In the long history of the world, only a few generations have been granted the role of defending freedom in its hour of maximum danger. I do not shrink from this responsibility—I welcome it. I do not believe that any of us would exchange places with any other people or any other generation. The energy, the faith, the devotion which we bring to this endeavor will light our country and all who serve it—and the glow from that fire can truly light the world.

And so, my fellow Americans, ask not what your country can do for you: ask what you can do for your country.

My fellow citizens of the world: ask not what America will do for you, but what together we can do for the freedom of man.

Finally, whether you are citizens of America or citizens of the world, ask of us the same high standards of strength and sacrifice which we ask of you. With a good conscience our only sure reward, with history the final judge of our deeds, let us go forth to lead the land we love, asking His blessing and His help, but knowing that here on earth God's work must truly be our own.   JOHN F. KENNEDY, *Inaugural Addresses of the Presidents of the United States*, 1961.

13. Divide the class into committees of four or five students and have each committee make a study of the writing that appears in a number of periodicals, reporting its findings orally to the class. Assign different tasks to each student, for instance, devices for vividness, vigor, and variety. Possible categories for study are headline rhetoric, sports-page lingo, the language of the advertising man, preacher prose, and academese.

14. It is agreed that the King James Version of the Bible has had an influence on English writing style, but there is disagreement whether the influence has been beneficial. Select a magazine article or an essay by an author whose style you admire and, by comparing it to a section in the King James Version, decide whether your author seems to be influenced by Biblical style, and whether you think he should be influenced. Suggested technique: Contrast sentence length, ratio of compound-complex-simple sentences, use of tenses and voice; list figures of speech and other rhetorical devices for both writers; and contrast their euphony, cacophony, alliteration, and assonance. You may

wish to refer to a translation of the Bible into modern English, the Revised Standard Version. Write a 500–750 word theme in which you analyze both styles, state your conviction, and support it.

15. Write a theme on a very abstract subject and, using your very best style—with perhaps an emphasis on rhetorical devices—attempt to clarify your ideas and persuade your reader. (Do not let the abstractness of the topic, however, keep you from being specific.)

Suggested topics:

Americanism	Nonviolence
Democracy	Freedom
Pacificism	Urban life
God (or "godliness")	Conservatism
Existentialism	Enlightened self-interest

Further reading

1. One of the recent phenomena of education publications is the anthology of essays about rhetoric. In each of these valuable but inexpensive paperback collections a student will find work by such writers as Aristotle, Cicero, Quintilian, Herbert Spencer, John Stuart Mill, and more modern stylists. Examples include:

BAILEY, DUDLEY (ed.). *Essays on Rhetoric*. New York and London: Oxford University Press, 1965.

CONNER, JACK E., and KRAFCHICK, MARCELLINE (eds.). *Speaking of Rhetoric*. Boston: Houghton Mifflin, 1966.

CORDER, JIM W. (ed.). *Rhetoric: A Text-Reader on Language and Its Uses*. New York: Random House, 1965.

TEMPLEMAN, WILLIAM D. (ed.). *On Writing Well*. New York: Odyssey Press, 1965.

WATKINS, FLOYD C. and KNIGHT, KARL F. (eds.). *Writer to Writer*. Boston: Houghton Mifflin, 1966.

WERMUTH, PAUL C. (ed.). *Modern Essays on Writing and Style*. New York: Holt, Rinehart and Winston, 1964.

2. Standard works to which students can go to settle questions of usage and style include, besides standard dictionaries:

BRYANT, MARGARET M. *Current American Usage*. New York: Funk & Wagnalls, 1962.

EVANS, BERGEN and CORNELIA. *A Dictionary of Contemporary American Usage*. New York: Random House, 1957.

FOWLER, H. W. *Dictionary of Modern English Usage*. 2d rev. ed. London and New York: Oxford University Press, 1965.

NICHOLSON, MARGARET. *Dictionary of American English Usage.* 2d ed. London and New York: Oxford University Press, 1957.

PARTRIDGE, ERIC. *Usage and Abusage.* London: Hamish Hamilton, 1957.

PERRIN, PORTER. *Writer's Guide and Index to English.* rev. ed., Chicago: Scott, Foresman, 1965.

CHAPTER 6

"HARD WRITING": REVISION

Easy writing makes damned hard reading. GEORGE GORDON, LORD BYRON. *I write. I write again. I write again.... Then I take the third; I literally fill the paper with corrections. I then write it out fair for the printer. I put it by; I take it up; I begin to correct again; it will not do. Alterations multiply; pages are rewritten; little lines sneak in and crawl out. The whole page is disfigured; I write again; I cannot count how many times the process is repeated.* JOHN HENRY CARDINAL NEWMAN.

Almost every enterprise of man has its weakest point. In the newspaper industry, for instance, thousands of men cooperate, work for hours, and spend thousands of dollars to get a paper into the hands of a newsboy—and then the thirteen-year-old lad throws it into the snowbank outside the door and the subscriber never sees it. All too often, the writing process is analogous to this disrupted chain of events. A student will do extensive research, take copious notes, scratch his head, worry, create, and prepare the first draft of a potentially superb paper, and then—overcome by the understandable urge to have done with it—he will turn the paper in without the extra effort and polish that would have brought about the fruition of its potentiality. Every writer, novice and expert, must have the discipline to move past the early creative steps, past the first draft, and

180

through the essential revision, the lack of which, too often, is the flaw—like the newsboy's bad aim—that prevents final excellence in the paper, article, essay, or report.

Insofar as the first draft of any written composition is concerned, a writer tries to determine the natural dynamics of the situation, his purpose, and the standard conventions of usage. The almost routine nature of the early steps of the writing process has led to the development of what are called the principles or rules of writing. These rules can be summarized briefly as follows:

1. Every written composition should have a central purpose or thesis, which is made clear in the introduction and referred to in the conclusion.

2. The body of the paper must fulfill the purpose by proceeding in orderly steps or subtopics.

3. There must be sufficient detailed material or specifics to clarify or prove all generalizations or other generative sentences.

4. Ideas must be expressed conventionally, exactly, and vividly—and as briefly as possible.

Whole books can be and have been written on these four basic points. Such books introduce the reader to many situations and help him to become sensitive to many other situations whose dynamics have been observed and codified. For instance, a student of composition can memorize the fact that argument for action almost invariably demands a consideration of the stock issues. But, as was pointed out by the first-century Roman rhetorician Dionysius of Halicarnassus and has been learned an infinite number of times since, no rules contained in a manual will guarantee good writing if the writer is not willing to do the hard work of revision.

The "principles" of rhetoric decrease in importance in the process of revision, and the personality, ability, and information of the writer influence the writing. During the revision process, a writer learns what he can do. An applicant for a Rhodes Scholarship, required to submit an essay as part of his application, stopped at the home of his adviser and asked for advice. The adviser, a writing teacher, insisted that the student rewrite the application; in fact, he made the student rewrite the essay seven times. The applicant, now a successful lawyer in San Francisco, has said, "I got the scholarship all right, but I learned more about writing that night than during the rest of my life. At three o'clock in the morning his wife got up and made us some coffee. At eight o'clock we had breakfast, and for the first time in my life I saw what I could do with words. I had written something I was proud of."

In the revision process, the writer demonstrates his creativity, taste, energy, and sensitivity—his artistry. At first, revision may be sheer drudgery, but as the ultimate and desired form begins to emerge, revision becomes exciting and exhilarating. When John F. Kennedy was a student at Harvard, he was, at first, "far from diligent," but in his senior year he was so stimulated by his honors thesis that he did, as he said, "more work than I've ever done in my life." According to the President's father, at this point his son learned to appreciate the lure of excellence. For the rest of his life, he took delight and care in revision. His secretary commented once that she could not remember how many times his Inaugural Address had been written and rewritten.

Some basic principles

Most writers, we suspect, hurry through their first drafts. Rather than one total composition, they prepare a series of small essays laid out in some order on yellow sheets of paper. If a particular essay does not satisfy them, they rush on, perhaps even leaving some blank stretches or pages in their manuscript. Later they go back over the weak sections, strengthen them, perhaps with the help of some extra research, and then tighten up the transitions. When they reach this point, they have a workable first draft.

During revision, what you must be seeking is the ultimate development of your thought and expression. You are plumbing your talent. Only as you experiment with your own ideas and language will you be able to develop your own technique. Our instruction during this phase of writing can only take the form of suggestions of alternatives among which you must choose. Try out the suggestions—even though they may be foreign to you. Having tried them—and only then—you can see what works for you and what does not.

There is an important distinction between *proofreading* and *revision*. When you proofread you are looking for possible improvements in grammar, diction, spelling, and punctuation. Almost every time you look at your paper you proofread. Almost unconsciously you may pencil in a comma or take out an exclamation point. In this chapter we discuss *revision*, which is a series of conscious steps taken to bring your paper to the peak of its potentiality. Each step must be taken separately. Different writers may take the steps in different order, but all revise with the goal and unity of their work in mind. In revising, be sure that your introduction looks forward properly to the rest of the paper and that the conclusion looks backward to the preceding parts. In a separate step, make sure that the body of your paper fulfills what your introduction obligates. In another step, stand back and look at your subtopics and review their order, proportion, and relationship. In yet another step, evaluate the content of your paragraphs. Have you supplied the detail that your internal generative sentences require? Look at the language and, finally, at the mechanics of spelling, grammar, punctuation, and manuscript conventions. *Re-vision* requires that you "look again," as the word itself says.

As you take these steps, you will vary your thinking and your actions. You may even use different tools. To check organization you may make an outline—or you may use scissors and paste. When you proofread, your lips should move; you may even mispronounce words to stress spellings, for example, *soph-O-more, pic-nic-KING, vac-U-UM, at-ten-DANCE,* and *in-dis-pen-SABLE.* If you are to succeed with your revision, you must keep the steps *se-PAR-ate.*

A sample problem

In order to demonstrate how the step-by-step process of revision can work, assume that you have been asked to look at a theme written by a high-school drop-out who has just returned to school. It is your job to criticize the paper, encourage the writer, and direct him through the thinking that will help him prepare a worthwhile end product. Here is his first draft.

SADDER BUT WISER

After searching intensely during a break I took during my high school education, I found that in order for survival in this complex world, an education must be attained. I base this theory on my many experiences after quitting school and leaving home at the age of sixteen. Many people think getting a job without an education is very difficult, but this is false. Getting a job, any job, is easy, but finding one you enjoy is hard. Without the necessary education you cannot compete for anything worth while. You have but one quest in life, to fill your belly. So, after months of deliberation, I came to the conclusion that in order to live and not just exist, an education must be secured.

Now read the theme again and try for some second thoughts. If you concentrate on the grammar, spelling, and punctuation, you may miss the opportunity to make this a really important paper. Forget the mechanics. Is any idea in the paper worth saying? We would answer affirmatively. There is in this student theme a considerable amount of wisdom. Although any sixteen-year-old *knows* that an education is necessary, every year discontented students leave school. They also know they can get a job. Jim over on the other side of town got a neat job working in Bill's foreign-car garage. What a deal, nine to five, nothing to do nights but run around, no work on Saturdays, just go to hot-rod races. Mom makes the bed and cooks the meals; Pop pays the rent and furnishes the family car. What a deal! But the writer of this paper has gone beyond this limited perception. He makes a fine distinction, and an important one. He balances two ideas against each other: what the drop-out expects, and what he gets. The paper has sufficient merit to make revision worthwhile. We are not speaking of merely technical proofreading; the student must *revise*.

First he must dig out his central thesis. His purpose seems to be to attempt to settle an unsettling problem for the potential drop-out. His parents and the guidance counselor say he won't be able to get a job, but he *knows* he can. Who is right? The writer must dramatize what happens to a young man freshly departed from his junior year in high school. If the purpose of the paper is fairly clear in our minds, we can move on to the development, the lack of which is the worst deficiency in the paper, for there are many generative expressions that have done no generating.

"searching intensely"	He should describe his efforts. Let us see two kinds of action, head-scratching thought and pounding the pavements.
"a break"	How long? From what high school? In a city, suburb, or small community? Let us *see* this young man in dreary, disconsolate action; first confident, and then increasingly despondent.
"survival in this complex world"	What is meant by "survival"? Since he says "getting a job is easy," we would think that the "filling his belly" type of "survival" would be easy. Apparently the student is speaking of another type. He will need to delay this phrase or make it clear by showing in detail what it is that the drop-out cannot achieve.
"many experiences"	Dramatize these. We need to *see* this action. Think of preparing a documentary television show about this. What would your camera have to watch? Details!

"Getting a job . . . is easy."	Show this. List the "opportunities" and how they are available. Want ads? Word of mouth from the "fellows"?
"one you enjoy . . . anything worthwhile"	These two expressions set up two perhaps contrary distinctions. We need some examples to show a job that the drop-out might find both enjoyable and worthwhile.

The student must now rewrite the paper putting in the required details. At this time we can suggest to him that his paper already has a three-part organization. The first sentence is the introduction; the last is the conclusion. The student will refine them later, but he should separate them now from the rest of the paper to emphasize the fact that he is working on the body of the paper. We can explain that, although the theme has a three-part organization, its body does not have internal organization. After looking at the key ideas we plan to develop, we can see that a combination chronological and topical structure makes sense. We could start out with the "getting a job is easy" concept. Describe the young man who had odd jobs while in school; he was confident—in spite of his parents' warning. Perhaps he even beats the game before leaving school by getting a job—at a drugstore? garage? pool hall? men's club? construction crew? The money begins to roll in. (How much? $1.75 an hour? An astronomical $3.00 per hour?) Then the first big disillusionment: the building job is completed, and he has to buy a jalopy to get to a new site. Wow! Extra expenses! He has to get up two hours earlier? And work on Saturdays? Or business gets slack, and our hero is the first to be laid off? Let us *see* the situation. Make us weep.

In the next paragraph our hero trudges the pavement. There are still plenty of jobs, but after his previous dismissal he knows what to expect from most of them. List the jobs he turns down: Traveling with a magazine crew made up of a sharpie and a bunch of other drop-outs? Making phone calls for a shady outfit selling chances on a Cadillac? A construction job for which he must pay a hundred-dollar union-initiation fee? Big deal! Exact details will pay off here. Did our hero cool his heels in an employment office while a college graduate walked right in ahead of him? A similar observation would be priceless to demonstrate the central point.

So far our structure has been: Part One, Happy Anticipation, and Part Two, Gradual Disillusionment. In Part Three, he can take a step backward to enlarge his perspective of the scene. He begins to think. He sees what the drop-out can expect; he can look into the future and cite hypothetical details or, better, he can describe the lot of some of the men he has encountered during his own jobs. What do they do? What did they, his fellow workers, advise him to do? What did he learn about himself? What kind of a job will it take to satisfy him? Be specific. Would he like a job in which he does something for humanity? What, exactly? How much money per year does he decide he needs? What kind of a neighborhood does he like? What kind of a car does he want? What hobbies does he wish to pursue? What vacations would he like to take? End of Part Three.

Soberly, our hero describes his return to school. In his conclusion, he must be honest: School is no more fun than it was, but it is not as bad as the last job he had. And it is nice to be back with the winners; the losers are still out looking for jobs.

With this kind of thinking and planning, our student can write a draft that is worth working on. After this draft is written, he can refine the organization. At first, the chronology will get the stress; it all happens in order. The topical structure will emerge soon. Part Two of the body can be pointed up with an introductory comment: "Slowly I began to see the light." This is a cliché, but we can doctor that later. Part Three can be started with a comment like, "Finally, I began to look around, not just at myself, but at people who had done what I was doing. The picture was not encouraging."

To get past the purpose, organization, and development stages may take two or three drafts. When they have been written, focus on more minute aspects of the paper. Probably much of the grammar and diction will have been refined in the process of telling a better story, but we will assume for illustration that all of the sentences in the first version still exist. We scrutinize them one by one—and immediately see that loose thinking has resulted in two glaring grammatical errors.

". . . in order for survival in this complex world, an education must be attained. . . ."

Notice that it sounds as though it is the education that wants to survive. Change to "In order to survive in this complex world, *we* (or I, or a person) need(s) an education." Now look down in the final sentence. Find the same trouble? This time the writer seems to be saying that an education wants to "live and not just exist." Rephrase as ". . . I had better get an education" or something less colloquial.

"this is false"	Strictly speaking, the word *this* should have an antecedent, but grammar rules aside, do you agree that either of these choices is a better sentence: "Many people think . . . but they are wrong" or ". . . but this belief is false."
"a job without an education"	The rule is that you should put modifiers close to what they modify. This sentence sounds as though the job is the one without the education. How would you rephrase it?

The next step is to look at the diction. First, cull questionable usages.

"in order for survival"	Better: "in order to survive"
"one that you enjoy doing"	Tautology. "one that you enjoy" is sufficient.
"I came to the conclusion"	"I concluded."

Normally at this level of revision we would experiment with alternate word choices to find ones that are exact or vivid; the version with the greater detail would have more exact ideas and thus more exact and dramatic diction. Even in the first form, some changes suggest themselves.

"After searching intensely"	Not an exact statement of what happened. Something like this would be better: "After a distressing but highly profitable experience after I quit high school and left home at the age of sixteen. . . ." Better still, put in a brief description of what actually happened: "After weeks of walking the pavement looking for a decent job . . . ," or whatever applies.

After working over the body, the student should return to the introduction. Perhaps the key to a good appeal step is suggested by the phrase "Many people believe. . . ." If he could quote some dire threats from newspapers or magazines about the difficulty drop-outs have in finding work, he could then catch the reader's attention by having the temerity to say, "Dr. So-and-So is a nationally known authority, and I am only a high school senior, but I know he is wrong."

A last step in revision is to take another look at the title. "Sadder but Wiser" is a bit trite and, since the student seems to feel he has profited by the experience, "sadder" hardly seems appropriate. It is perhaps less specific a reference to the actual incidents than it should be; this title would fit hundreds of student themes about "a lesson learned." Since the introduction makes a reference to a subject of timely interest, perhaps the word *drop-out* should be included in the title. Maybe just "Drop-Out" would do. Could we make something out of "The Return of the Drop-Out"? The title can only be phrased, of course, after we have seen the final draft, but it must encapsulate the entire message.

First objective: significance

As we have just shown in the analysis above, the first task in revision is to find whether you have said anything at all. One kind of writer reads what he thought he wrote; the other reads like an audience. In other words, he reads what he did write, as it will appear to his reader. One sees his intended meaning; the other sees his expressed meaning. You should try to be the latter type of writer, and face the possibility that what you have written amounts to precisely zero. During the first reading of your draft, however, you can be the first type of writer and dwell on your dreams of your product as well as on the product itself. There is no need to chill the high excitement that often accompanies the first stages of writing. Think big. Try to see something important in what you write. However, try to learn to recognize when you have said something important and when you have not. The following paragraphs were written by a student who became almost too fluent a writer; his words and sentences always sounded so eloquent that he never quite developed a critical sense to turn on his own ideas. All through his college career he was plagued by getting either A's or F's. At one point a professor wrote on his paper, "This is the most beautiful job of saying nothing I have ever seen."

EDUCATION THROUGH REALITY

A person enters a new world through realization; a spark ignites a fire of thought and the fantasy of the past is devoured by the present reality.

This person enters college, not by choice, but due to the needs of present day society. Previously he had gone to a small boarding school of little acclaim and yet after five

weeks of college, he realizes that the college consists of
definite individuals, but mostly toys played with by a child-
like society. If the individual is broken, replace him, don't
mend him. To the other school, each person worked as a part;
without one of the parts, the school could not produce. If a
new part took its position, the old would have to adjust in
time.

What of the people? What is different about them? People?
Are they really people? One is afraid of speaking honestly;
one is afraid of being seen as he really is. People you say?
What has happened to their individual beliefs, their ideals,
their concepts of truth, honesty, and justice? Hushed, hushed
by fear, uncertainty, and confusion. And what of the few who
do speak? A "conference in confidence," only to be put before
a class in the form of a question, and to be chewed, digested
and given back far from its original form. Who would want
to speak? Play with your toys, humanity, for as you break,
you destroy what is good in an individual. In five weeks he
has learned more from people than college could ever teach
him.

The paper expresses the germ of the idea that society somehow
blights a sensitive individual, which is, of course, sometimes true. The idea,
if we are to accept it without qualification, is probably not true. If we
are to accept it with the qualification that society *can* or *sometimes*
does thwart an individual, it becomes almost platitudinous and banal. On
the basis of what the student has written, a person who believes the thesis
will continue to do so, but one who disagrees, especially one who is enthusiastic about the beauty and value of the college experience or who
is oriented to think that society helps the individual, will not even understand what the writer is talking about.

At first, this student was hurt by his instructor's criticism. "You
are saying it in nice words, but what you are really saying is that I should
junk it." "Yes," the instructor replied, and then he read the student an essay
by a Negro athlete who explained why he had enrolled at a Big Ten
university:

> I was all-state in three sports, and I had over 550 in my col-
> lege boards. I could have gone almost anywhere to school.
> My town is a manufacturing town, and there is always a
> cloud of factory smoke in the sky. I got on a train and headed
> west by northwest. I kept looking out at the sky as I passed
> through the cities and towns. I had gone quite a distance be-
> fore the sky became clear. . . . I am not sure I even knew

it but I was trying to get out from another cloud. In my hometown there is a street which I hate more than any other place in the world. That street marks the boundary between White land and Black land. Many times I have had to run till I was out of breath to get past that street because there is the rule in the town that no Negro can be north of that street after the sun goes down. Now that I am at school, I have not found such a street. I have been rushed by fraternities, I have danced with white girls—no, I still do not want to marry a white man's daughter—and my roommates are both white.

The student who had written the first paper went back to his dormitory and started all over. He called the result "Culture Shock," and he described how it felt to go from a small private Episcopal prep school, where he had a half-hour conference each week with the headmaster, to a large urban university. He described how he had arrived too late to be admitted officially to his university dormitory and how he had spent the first night in his room, but with no blanket, mattress, or pillow, just cold metal springs. "Welcome to the U," he had thought just before he dropped off to a fitful sleep. As he wrote, he recalled other incidents that demonstrated his thesis about the difficult adjustments he had to make —and he worked them into his ultimately very successful paper.

As you think of your purpose you must ask yourself, "What am I trying to say? What question am I answering? Is the question worth asking—or answering?" You expect, of course, to find the answer focused in the introduction or conclusion.

CASE HISTORY 1. "MY FAMILY TRIPS"—IN WHICH A STUDENT GETS LOST

A student wrote a paper discussing the many trips his family had taken during his boyhood. The final sentence of his introduction read, "In a panorama of personalities, situations, and settings, by coming in closer contact with people different from those I had known I had become aware of the distinctions and distinctNESS of my own personality." His draft ended with, "Traveling has accomplished what my parents intended it to: it has broadened my horizons physically, mentally, and emotionally, and also has made me aware of my position in the world."

There is no question about the value of this thesis. That "travel is broadening" may seem a truism or a platitude until we remember how often tales of what happened when the writer was very young become popular best sellers or important literature. Harry Golden's *For Two Cents Plain* and Sam Levenson's *Everything but Money* are recent examples.

Anne Morrow Lindbergh has written beautifully on the value of a vacation in *Gift from the Sea*.

  The question about the student's paper was therefore not a matter of whether his thesis was worthwhile, but whether he stuck to it. According to the paper the family traveled from Teaneck, New Jersey, to the Civil War South, to the rolling prairies and billowing skies of the Middle West, and to the national parks in the Far West. The paper was a travelogue —the sun even "set slowly in the west"—but when the student looked at his thesis during his revision he realized he was off the track. Although his paper was supposed to be about how travel had affected him, he had talked only about the travel itself, not about its effect. In the revised version he related the journey to his resolution to major in both history and law before going into politics, his thought being that a legislator should understand the background and traditions of his country.

CASE HISTORY 2. "THREE STORIES"—IN WHICH A STUDENT DISCOVERS SHE HAS SOMETHING TO SAY

  In an essay she titled "Rituals in Reality," a student discussed three short stories, Isaac Babel's "The Story of My Dovecot," Shirley Jackson's "The Lottery," and Lionel Trilling's "Of This Time, Of That Place." She was satisfied with the unity she had achieved. She had analyzed the three stories to show that modern man has not yet learned to overcome his willingness to live in concordance with legend and myth. In the first story, a young Jewish boy adjusts to the religious fanaticism of his father and to the prejudice of the Russian peasantry. In the second story, a town adjusts to the ritual of drawing by chance the name of a person who must be sacrificed. In the third story, a teacher dares not jeopardize his own career to defend a bright but nonconformist student; instead an admitted fake triumphs because he follows the myths and traditions of the school.

  In reconsidering her theme, the student-writer was momentarily nonplused. Is this enough? she asked herself. All I am really doing is retelling the stories. The student finally decided she was *not* merely retelling the stories; she was, indeed, interpreting them. *Exegesis* is sufficient to make a worthwhile paper. Carlos Baker of Princeton has written many articles about Ernest Hemingway's stories, and Cleanth Brooks of Yale has published many articles about the message of William Faulkner. The student realized that in her paper she was discussing a comment that three artists had made about society. The stories were credible, and it was important that the common theme be identified. The student decided that her paper had passed the test, insofar as significance of purpose was concerned.

CASE HISTORY 3. "THE DEATH OF A GOD THAT
NEVER WAS"—IN WHICH A STUDENT COMMENTS
ON A TIMELY SUBJECT

A student reread her introduction and subjected it to the double
test: (1) Does it set up a thesis? (2) Is the point significant?

> "God is dead!" This is the creed of a new movement which
> took roots in the philosophy of Nietzsche. The movement pro-
> claims that the masses no longer are able to believe in God.
> It is known as a movement of atheism. But is God—not the
> King with the white beard, but the belief in the essence of
> life—is this God really dead? Is this death not of God, but
> rather the institution called the Church?

Since serious theological questions are always important, the student decided that her point was significant enough to merit a paper in
defense of it. The subject had an extra justification in that it was written
at the height of the "God Is Dead" controversy—and articles on the subject had appeared in *The New York Times,* the *Atlantic Monthly, The New
Yorker,* and a host of other periodicals.

CASE HISTORY 4. "A COLLEGE FRESHMAN VERSUS
PLATO"—IN WHICH A STUDENT DEVELOPS
CONFIDENCE

A student in a Western Civilization class had read that Plato condemned literature because it excited the reader to false imitation and thus
interfered with intellectual and moral development. The student reasoned
that, although he could accept Plato's belief that literature cannot imitate
"eternal Forms or Ideas which are entirely spiritual," he still believed that
literature has value. The student boggled as he reread his essay and
realized that he was contradicting Plato. He decided, however, that he
could be bold, because he had some insight that Plato had lacked, namely
Freud's perception that "vicarious emotional outlets are necessary as defense mechanism for mental soundness." In the writings of John Dewey,
he found further support for his ideas. He felt justified in opposing Plato
also because of a recent personal experience with literature. He had read
Chekhov's *The Cherry Orchard* and had found in it a clear comment on
his own society. In his paper, the student wrote:

> The decayed élite, the faded gentry in my own home town,
> like Chekhov's Russian landowners on their country estates,

failed to see what they must do to keep up with history. . . .
Chekhov's semi-feudal landowners refused to cut up their
"Cherry Orchard"; the old rich in my home town fought to
save their sycamores. . . . Plato may be right that literature
cannot be true, but it is not inherently "deceptive and misleading". . . . I *know* that Christopher Marlowe's *Doctor Faust-
us* and Chekhov's *The Cherry Orchard* are not true, but almost because they are not true I can look at them with a
special feeling of disinterest. I am involved, but I am not
involved, and I can now judge a series of incidents so close to
what happened to my town, but not really true, that I have
learned more, I think, than if the story were true. . . . Something which increases a person's knowledge should not be
censored. Poets should be encouraged, not banned.

The student decided that an argument over a value is always important. Instead of dodging a fight with Plato, he decided he would give
his challenge more focus; his introduction began:

As a dutiful Episcopalian I have frequently sung a hymn
written in 1668 by Peter Sohren. When I came to one sentence I think I knew that the poetry was probably rather bad,
but I assumed that I should believe what the words said:

Sing praise . . .
For Socrates who, phrase by phrase
Talked men to truth unshrinking,
And left for Plato's grace
To mold our ways of thinking.

After thinking about these lines I am sure the poetry is not
for me—I do not think *grace* rhymes with *phrase*—and I do
not agree with the words. I do not feel that I am less an
Episcopalian when I believe that Plato should not be permitted to "mold our ways of thinking."

The preceding illustrations of this part of the revision process have,
we hope, shown that as you work through your first revision you must question whether, dimly or clearly, you have centered on a purpose. Ask yourself whether the purpose is worthwhile. Look around you to see whether
important writers or established authorities have faced the same question.
Relying on your own sensitivity, which has been sharpened because you
have asked the question, determine whether, as a result of your thinking,
reading, or personal experience, you could possibly have something to say
to an informed unkown reader on the subject.

Second objective: coherence

The next step in the revision process is to review your organization, both the basic skeleton and the internal structure of your paragraphs. The body of your paper is most important, for the introduction and conclusion are dependent upon it. As the body of your paper changes, so will the beginning and end. It is wise, therefore, to ignore your introduction and conclusion for the time being, except to make sure that they contain, perhaps stated very mechanically at this point, either your thesis statement or your purpose statement. To provide the stern discipline you may need, you probably should write out your thesis or purpose statement and prop it in front of you as you write. You may wish to phrase it as a question. Do not worry about transitions until rather late in your total revision process.

A few suggestions now about how to revise your organization. Probably the most frequently used technique at this step is to make an outline of your paper. Keep it simple; include only your major points. To be sure that these points stick out obtrusively in this draft, you may wish to underline the sentences that introduce these major sections. If they are evident, you will be able now not only to check them for their appropriateness and order, but also for proportion. If one of them obviously takes little space, you will notice this at once, and you may decide either to eliminate it because it is unimportant, or to expand it to balance with other sections.

At this time you may need special tools: scissors and paper clips, perhaps a pencil with heavy lead, and some paste. To focus your attention, make the structure as obvious as possible. The thesis may be circled, the topic headings may be underlined, and the topic sentences may be indicated by stars in the margins. When you delete a section, delete it lightly, because you may want to put it back in. You may want to cut the paper into sections and ink in a topic heading at the top of each section. Rearrange the parts according to what your analysis tells you is appropriate, but also consider alternative orders. If you have your paper cut into, say, four sections, try shuffling them around by chance. What is the effect? Does any new order have merit? Do not let yourself be caught in rigid patterns. Experiment to see what happens when you make a change.

Probably the first question you ask yourself after you have created a brief outline is, "Does the order of my points build toward my thesis, or toward a resolution of the reader's questions stimulated by my thesis?"

CASE HISTORY 1. "THE SALEM WITCH TRIALS"—IN
WHICH A STUDENT DISCOVERS A THESIS

When studying an outline of his own work, a writer may find that
if he organizes his paper in a certain way an unexpected and significant
thesis may emerge. For example, a student writing a theme about the Salem
witch trials dealt with his major points in chronological order:

1. The first hints

2. The accusations

3. The trials

4. The deaths

As the writer reviewed his organization, he thought, "Most of my
readers will know, at least in general terms, that there was a witchcraft
scare and that some women were persecuted. What does my outline tell
that they do *not* know? Really not very much, I guess. I had better look
again. Let's see; under each point are the facts of the case, dates, places,
names, and incidents. What is there besides these facts that makes it possible for me to infer anything of significance? What will my reader want to
know? I begin to see a paradox here: The colonists came over to avoid
persecution and yet, here they are, involved in persecuting other people.
Why? Maybe a discussion of this point will make my report worthwhile.
I will refine my purpose; instead of writing a chronological report of what
happened, I will try to explain why it happened. In my introduction or in
the first part of the body I will briefly relate *what* happened; then in the
second and largest part of the body I will try to show the insecurity of
the time. It was a time of misfortune. The Bay Company had just lost its
charter, and property ownership was in jeopardy. It looked as though the
Devil was getting the upper hand. The colonists were in a state of particular tension. The bewitched children were nearly all the pupils of the
especially zealous preacher, the Reverend Samuel Parris, who encouraged
them to tell their wild stories. At the time of the trials, if the accused confessed, she was freed; if she did not confess, she was burned. The purpose
of my paper will be to ferret out the information to explain the events, as I
see them. I will subordinate the factual history and organize the body of my
paper into three sections dealing with the following three topics:

1. The special tension of the times

2. The stimulated imagination of the children

3. The nature of the trials: those who confessed were freed, those who did not were put to death.

Now the paper gives me a chance to do something creative; I am hazarding an explanation that I have not seen before.

CASE HISTORY 2. "WHICH COMES FIRST?"—IN WHICH A STUDENT DISCOVERS MISSING POINTS

Occasionally, a scrutiny of one's major points will indicate that an important point has been ignored. A student was asked to provide an answer to the question, "Who comes first, the artist or the scientist?" Earlier the instructor had reported that a critic believed that the artist, using some kind of a special sense, sees a truth and writes about it. Then the scientist comes along and "proves" what the artist has suggested. After thinking it over, the student decided that the critic was right, and he dashed off his case. He was very proud of his draft, in which he discussed Sigmund Freud's theories in relation to Henrik Ibsen's play *Hedda Gabler*. The student showed that, about twenty years before Freud formulated his theory of the Oedipus complex, the Norwegian playwright had created a character, Hedda Gabler, who acted the way Freud was later to predict that a woman with a severe Oedipus complex would act. Hedda had overloved her father and wanted to be like him, but could not. She wore boots and was preoccupied with horses. She refused to recognize that she was pregnant. She dominated her husband and tried to dominate her lover. In other words, she tried to play the man's role in all her relationships. When she was frustrated in this attempt, she subconsciously took vengeance on her enemies. For example, she burned her lover's "baby"—that is, the manuscript he wrote with Hedda's rival—and she maliciously destroyed the hat of an aunt who represented everything she, Hedda, hated.

When the student reread the paper, he realized that he had not told his audience enough about Freud's theories. He therefore had to insert a whole new section discussing the Oedipus complex, sublimation, phallic symbols, role identity refusal, and misplaced aggression. He indicated that Freud had advanced these theories between about 1900 and 1910. Then, after pointing out that Ibsen had created a character in 1890 afflicted with all the same symptoms, he had a convincing argument that Ibsen had presupposed Freud. Actually, there was sufficient question about Freud's dates to raise doubts about the student's case, but the weakness was in his research, not his organization.

CASE HISTORY 3. "COLLEGE DROPPED-INS"—IN
WHICH A STUDENT SEEKS PROPORTION

A student who started to write a paper about "drop-outs" soon
realized that there had already been a great deal spoken and written about
them. As she read, she began to be aware that there is also a type of
student who might be called a "dropped-in" and about whom nothing had
been written. She changed her thesis to "The college 'dropped-in' is a
serious problem." Her first outline was:

1. Definition of a "dropped-in"

2. "Dropped-ins" unfairly take college seats that students with
   better motivation should have

3. The fate of the rejected student whose place is taken by the
   "dropped-in"

4. Situation not the fault of the college admissions officers

The writer quickly decided that Point 4 could be omitted by showing in the definition section that a dropped-in cannot be identified by tests
and admissions porcedures. Point 3 remained from the writer's earlier intention to write about "drop-outs," but it was relevant to the new topic. Under
Point 1, the student defined the dropped-in as a person who goes to college
for the wrong reasons: because his parents force him to, because society
dictates that everyone must have a college degree, and because society believes that college is the best place to find a spouse. The dropped-in has no
personal motivation that makes college worthwhile or makes him worth
the while of the college and its faculty. As her thoughts took shape in her
mind, the student saw that the body of her paper would have a three-part
structure that would show why the dropped-in is a problem:

1. Without motivation, he tends to do poorly and flunk out.

2. Having no direction he selects courses irresponsibly.

3. He takes the place of a student who might have better motivation.

She could develop these points fully, because she knew several students
who exemplified poor motivation. She read an article that described how
the nondirective guidance in some colleges permitted students to plan their
curricula around such whimsical requirements as no courses before 10 A.M.
or after 3 P.M., none on Friday, no laboratory courses, no heavy reading

courses, no writing. She talked to some dropped-in seniors and jotted down the subjects they had taken. Their curricula were fragmentary, with courses in Russian foreign policy, but none in Russian government or history; courses about foreign policy from 1810 to 1900, but none covering the periods before or after; courses in subjects like astronomy in which the student had had no interest and whose content he had quickly forgotten. To develop Point 3 about displaced candidates, the student decided to describe how several friends, who had not been admitted to any accredited college but had done well when they took correspondence courses in the army, could have done as well in college because they were motivated.

The student was still not satisfied with her analysis of the problem. She kept thinking, "What if my reader says 'So what?' after he reads my paper?" She resolved to condense her paper as much as possible and add still another section. The section already written would present the "Problem," and the new section would advance a "Solution." She suggested that poorly motivated students be permitted to take a year off from their studies. She began to read on the subject and found that the "year-off" idea has a history. The Church of the Latter-day Saints customarily lets its young men travel for a year to do missionary work. The system is valuable because the tour provides a chance for the young men to decide what they want to do. In the 1880s in the United States, select Eastern society let its sons and daughters take a *"Wanderjahr"*; frequently the young people would audit lectures in the universities of Europe to see what would excite their intellects. Our student came across some statistics showing how well World War II veterans did when they returned, with the help of the G.I. Bill, to complete their education. Now the whole structure of the paper appeared to the student. Her purpose would be to recommend a solution for one of today's educational problems, the poor academic performance of the "dropped-in." In the first section, she would show the difficulties at least partially attributable to poor motivation; in the second part, she would show how a year off for travel, military service, or work could save such students. Almost organically this paper grew before the eyes of the writer.

CASE HISTORY 4. "MARTIN LUTHER"—IN WHICH A STUDENT REINTERPRETS HIS RESEARCH

In contrast to the previous examples in which a section of a theme was either incomplete or missing altogether, occasionally a section mushrooms completely out of proportion and leads nowhere or in a misleading direction.

A student, who happened to be a Lutheran, was writing a theme about Martin Luther. He had written a first draft, which he thought was a straightforward factual report. As he revised, he tied in his account of Luther's break with the Church to the current ecumenical movement, stating that before the Protestant and Catholic churches could merge again, the causes of the original separation had to be understood. All well and good, he thought. He saw three reasons for Luther's secession from the Catholic Church:

1. He objected to the corruption of the Church, especially the selling of indulgences.

2. He questioned the infallibility of the Pope.

3. He believed that only two of the seven sacraments were vaild.

However, as he surveyed his paper, he saw that the first point occupied three-fourths of it, and he began to suspect that, as a twentieth-century student who was somewhat anti-Catholic, he had run his information through the filter of his own bias. In his research, he encountered the sentence, "Whereupon he [Luther] rose from his knees and slowly and sadly walked away," and he realized that it was at this point that Protestantism began. The symbolic walking away came while Luther was "climbing the Sacred Stairs at the Lateran," when "the thought arose in Luther's mind that justification came by faith alone, and that physical acts availed nothing. This was the first of several doubts Luther had about the Church, and it resulted in his revolution against it."

The student began to see that he had misinterpreted his own notes. He had overexpanded the section on the selling of indulgences and had neglected the basic cause for the split, which was, he realized, that Luther had come to believe that only God can save man. Neither man nor any other earthly power, including the Church, can in any way help. Thus the Church was a minor part of spiritual life. Luther's objection to the selling of indulgences was not so much a question of morality as it was a question of theology. The error was not that the Church sold indulgences to the rich; it was that the Church granted them at all. This put the Roman Church in a new light for the student. In a subsequent draft, he described the basic conflict Luther had with the Church, his belief that it must play a minor role, that it cannot grant indulgences, that the Pope is not infallible, that sacraments are symbolic rather than literal acts, and so on. The student recast his entire paper to show that Luther broke with the Church not because (as the student had originally believed) it was a haven for embezzlers, but because it was the proponent of a theological view different from his own.

CASE HISTORY 5. "THE LIFE OF ITALO BALBO"—IN
WHICH A STUDENT IMPROVES HIS TOPICAL ORDER

A student, writing on the life of Italo Balbo, Mussolini's Air Chief
of Staff, derived the following outline:

1. Early education and flying experience

2. Association with Mussolini

3. Mass flight from Italy to America

4. Experiences in World War II

5. Mysterious death

Looking at his outline, the student thought, "There were dozens
of high officers in World War II. What is so important about Balbo that I
should write about him instead of about Göring, Zhukov, Montgomery,
or Pétain?" The writer's attention fixed on his Point 3, and he continued,
"Because Marshal Balbo was the first to make a formation flight across the
ocean with all the planes arriving at their destination, people all over the
world came to have a confidence in air travel, and Balbo has been called
the 'father of commercial aviation.' I will put this point first and lead up to
my purpose statement, something about how it is ironic that the father of
commercial aviation is now almost forgotten; his biography is not even
included in most encyclopedias. I will use Point 3 to show why he is important, and I will use Points 4 and 5 to show why he is now forgotten:
He was on the losing side during the war, and he was so popular with
Italians that Mussolini became jealous and had his plane shot down. In
the outline above, Point 1 is unimportant; every air-force officer goes to
school, learns to fly, and goes through the junior ranks. I will cut it out
completely; any details I need about his early life, including the fact that
his family's social status was higher than that of Mussolini's family, I can
slip in at the appropriate place."

These five case histories illustrate the kind of thinking you must
do during the organizational aspect of your revision. You will need to make
sure that your body fits your thesis and vice versa, and that you have the
proper points in the proper balance and order. Having achieved this stage,
you will need to look again at your conclusion and introduction.

RETOUCHING INTRODUCTIONS AND CONCLUSIONS

Usually at this point you will find your introduction dull, general,
and inappropriate. An example is the following.

Every age and every society has its fill of social problems, and this year is no different. Right now we are faced with teen-agers drinking and taking LSD, and having automobile accidents. The problem I would like to discuss is the voting age—should it be lowered from twenty-one to eighteen years?

This student knew that his subject was something of a chestnut: probably 10,000 freshmen themes have been written demanding that the voting age be lowered. He resolved to try for a fresh introduction. He knew that most of his readers had heard the maxim, "If you are old enough to fight, you are old enough to vote." He decided to test this proverb in reverse.

In the years 1941–1945, the United States fought its most extensive war. At one time over eleven million people were in uniform. Over twenty years have passed, and those men are no longer young enough to fight. We should now have a referendum; those men should be deprived of their voting franchise. If they are too old to fight they are too old to vote. Is this position logical? It is if we accept some of the thinking we hear every day about lowering the voting age. Every year the subject comes up and every year we hear a lot of sound and fury with little of it signifying anything.

The student knew that most of his audience were for lowering the voting age, and he hoped he could start a good fight with this introduction. He actually planned to argue for lowering the voting age, but first he wanted to attack the usual silly arguments and then give his own serious ones.

During the process of revising your introduction, keep the following edicts in mind.

1. The introduction must funnel into your thesis or purpose statement. You can start with a specific, catchy illustration of part of your point and broaden out to the whole thesis, or with a reference to a general, important, timely problem and narrow to your specific thesis.

2. Try to involve the audience. Your reader is not a captive audience; you must grasp his attention by showing that your subject is very much a part of his life, something of significance to him. He is the Unknown Reader, but you know that he is human—and you must appeal to his human interests.

When you revise your conclusion, again put yourself in the place of the reader. Ask, "What would be the state of mind of my reader? Would he be convinced? Still hostile? Maybe a little tired of my hammering at him?" One student wrote a very good paper about the apathy of modern college students. Incident after incident, illustration after illustration, he piled up evidence to prove that his peers were unconcerned with the problems of society. He compared college-student response to World War I, World War II, and the Korean War to the response of his classmates to the war in Vietnam. He had his case so well established that he was even a little wearied himself. He resolved to try for some detachment, to let his readers off the hook a bit, to give them some perspective on the subject. This was his revised conclusion.

> A story is told about a man who, while walking through the fields in the country, came upon a stallion tied to a post. The man saw the beauty of the animal—its slim lines, its luminous black coat—and was awed by the perfection of the animal. He spied a farmer standing near the horse and the man expressed the desire to see the horse run. The farmer untied it, slapped it on the rump and the horse galloped through the field. As it ran, it seemed even more beautiful than before, and the man was even more enchanted. But suddenly the horse ran straight into a tree.
>
> "Why," the man exclaimed, "that horse must be blind!"
>
> "Not blind," the farmer calmly replied, "He just don't give a damn."
>
> Modern students are not blind to the problems of our time; they are not blind to where their conduct is taking them. They have been beaten across the rump with so much pressure, so many crises, and so many false values that now they just don't give a damn.

A humorous story is not always advisable. Often it may blur your focus or damage the tone of your essay by seeming frivolous. Once again your originality, based on your imagination, taste, and sensitivity, must guide you.

Relentlessly the focus of your paper tightens. First, the purpose; then the organization; now the development. During the organization step, we were primarily concerned with larger elements: whether the major points in the body added up to the thesis you phrased, whether the appropriate points had been established, whether one point got too little attention or another too much, and whether they were in the most effective order. Finally we looked again at the thesis, then at the introduction, and then at the conclusion. Now it is time to scrutinize the individual paragraphs and their details.

Third objective: completeness

After you are reasonably satisfied with your purpose and rudimentary structure, focus on your paragraphs. Scrutinize each sentence to see what generative sentences you have left vague and undeveloped. Look for barren assertions like "Herbert is dominated by his wife." The phrase "dominated by his wife" is generative; alone it gives no true picture of the relationship of the couple, but expanded it tells the reader a great deal.

> Herbert is dominated by his wife. When he was invited to his friend's wedding, he arrived in the family car. Enthroned in the back seat, all frilly and bouffant, sat his wife and teenage daughter. Alone in front, like a chauffeur, was Herbert. No wonder he spends evenings alone in his study classifying stamps.

Hypothetical information does not pass as development. The next paragraphs are from a student theme about the difficulty a man faces when he reaches retirement.

> The average middle-class man of today started work early in his life. This work was often necessary to supplement the income of his parents who often had families much too large for their income. Starting with a paper route at ten, he worked his way up to a venerable "soda-jerk" at a neighborhood ice-cream parlor. If he was conscientious, he made it through high school. College was for the rich. The war came, the World War or the Korean conflict, and John Doe found himself behind a rifle. He shot and was shot at. Wars end and he found himself a job with a local manufacturing concern. Marriage and family followed. Unionization gave the man a constant salary growth and an enviable living condition. Promotions came with time and the man saw his offspring doing much that he could not do when he was their age.
>
> With the growth and eventual independence of his children, John Doe's mind turned towards himself. "Why should I work when I can live off retirement benefits?" With a tear in his eye and a gold watch in his pocket, John Doe retires. He has doomed himself to death.
>
> After working steadily for forty years John has forgotten how to live.

Essentially this paper is argumentative. The author begins it with the sentence, "To the average man, retirement is a paradise ahead," and then goes on to show how Mr. Average Man, when he does retire, is disabused of this fantasy. Retired, with time hanging heavily on his hands, he becomes restless and bored. "His children detest his meddling in their affairs," the student writes. When the purpose of an author is to change the beliefs of his reader, however, hypothetical examples such as this will not do, for the reader knows that anyone can make up such examples, and he will not be convinced by them. This paper needs hard, concrete *evidence*. To show that our senior citizens are not content with retirement, the student must dig up statistics to show how many men come out of retirement not because they need money, but because they are bored. He will need to talk to his grandfather, and quote him. He will need to describe the frantic efforts of some of his aged friends to keep busy and to feel useful.

In this paper the student calls his hypothetical example "John Doe." If he had, instead, described the retirement dilemma of an actual person, perhaps his grandfather, he would have demonstrated his familiarity with what is called the "psychology of securing confidence." Whenever pertinent, the writer should cite facts, exact dates, and correct professional terms to indicate to his readers that he knows what he is talking about. For example, in the paper about Ibsen and Freud discussed on page 196, the student reported that Freud lived till 1939, but that Ibsen died in 1906; that Ibsen wrote *Hedda Gabler* in 1890; that Ibsen's first name was *Henrik*, not *Henry*. In discussing Freud, he used Freud's terminology. All this attention to detail created an aura of authenticity. In contrast, citing a hypothetical character is psychologically unsound, for the account does not sound real.

The writer will be in a constant dilemma as to how much detail to supply. He knows he should write as though his Unknown Reader is the whole educated community. And, though he applies the test: "Can a trained mind, not expert in my subject, understand what I am saying?" his answer cannot be exact, and he worries lest he bore his audience with an excess of information. Fortunately, the danger of supplying too much detail can be averted, at least in part, by being sure that the details, the examples, and the illustrations are in themselves interesting. The writer may put in more details than necessary to clarify or even to convince, but, if his details are vivid and entertaining, his reader will not complain. When Dale Carnegie wrote *How To Win Friends and Influence People*, his thesis was simple; it could have been developed in a paragraph. However, he inserted chatty little anecdotes about celebrities—and a million people bought the book.

An excerpt from a student theme illustrates the problem we are now discussing.

> By means of certain techniques an author can introduce deeper meanings than his simple plot suggests. He may use symbols to emphasize his theme or to generalize the message he wishes to convey.

Undoubtedly some readers would have a rather clear understanding of what these sentences mean, but some—perhaps many—would not. The problem is how to clarify the message for the uninformed reader without boring the knowledgeable one. The student reasoned that even the informed reader would be interested to know how certain highly respected writers used symbols. He turned to a short story by Katherine Mansfield, a play by Edward Albee, and a novel by William Faulkner in the belief that both levels of readers would find the explanation profitable and interesting.

> In the short story, "Bliss," Katherine Mansfield accentuates the immaturity of her protagonist by giving her the name "Bertha Young," which hints that she is as young as at birth. When Bertha's rival is mentioned, the reference is often juxtaposed to the ripening of a pear tree. To make sure that the reader catches the relationship of the second girl and the mature tree, her name is Pearl (Pear + l). In the story, a black cat continually chases a gray cat. Bertha pointedly ignores the two cats, just as she remains ignorant that her husband is chasing her rival.
>
> In Edward Albee's *Who's Afraid of Virginia Woolf?*, the two leading characters, George and Martha, have created a son in their imagination. The game they play of talking about him shuts out their insufferable actual life. Their question whether they should cease the fiction by having the son die points up the author's belief that man must hold certain beliefs, true or not, if he is to endure real life. The similarity of their pretense to the life of Jesus Christ suggests that religion is one of the fictions that man creates for support. When they "kill" their son, they are forced to face up to their problems—perhaps Albee is suggesting that man is better off with the crutch of imaginative (or religious) support. We must not forget that it is hardly coincidental that their names are the same as George and Martha Washington. Is Albee telling

us that Americans are strong only because of myths they maintain?

In William Faulkner's *Light in August,* there is no place on earth where Joe Christmas can go, and he is finally murdered. This is a gruesome story, we think? It can't happen here, we say? Perhaps Faulkner thinks differently. Joe Christmas has the same initials as Jesus Christ. The parentage of both is very unusual. They were both thirty-three years old when put to death; the story has frequent references to the cross and to crucifixion. Is Faulkner telling us that mankind had the same fate for Jesus, the founder of Christianity?

In this way, authors can suggest subtly a great deal more than the observable action and characters do on the first level of perception.

The development of this example must be involved because the concept is complex. Significant ideas take considerable development. The writer has the choice, however, of avoiding such provocative assertions, or of giving them the full treatment they require. In the paper above, the student found that he needed so much space to develop the two generative sentences quoted on page 205 that they became the thesis of his entire theme. In his first draft, these sentences had been buried in a paragraph with a series of equally undeveloped thoughts.

You too will have to make similar decisions. You will have to make certain that you have either developed or removed all generative sentences, and that the ones you have developed have been developed in the most effective manner. When you revise, review Chapter 4 to ensure that you have exploited as fully as possible the various methods of development suggested there. Eventually, of course, sufficient practice will permit you to recall these methods automatically, but until that time, you will find review most useful.

Fourth objective: artistry

When you reach this stage of revision, your manuscript is probably very rough. In fact, it is probably a mess of scratched-out phrases and insertions. You can profitably use your time by retyping the whole theme. You may prefer to triple space to leave room for the insertions that you will now begin to make.

The previous steps in revision have inevitably resulted in expansion. You have added details, definitions, statistics, and illustrations to the body of your theme, and your introduction and conclusion are considerably longer than they were when you started out. Your present step *must* primarily be condensation. You must cut and cut and cut, stopping only when the prose bleeds. Second, you must seek exactness. Verify every name, every date, every detail. George Bernard Shaw wrote in *Advice to a Young Critic*, "Get your facts right first; that is the foundation of all style." After you have read your paper enough times, you will believe everything you have written, so you must therefore verify, verify, and verify. A student once entered an essay contest and was given a superior rating by two of the three judges. The third judge gave the paper a very low rating, explaining later that the student had reported that three life boats were sent to rescue a trawler, whereas the judge remembered reading that there were two life boats. One erroneous fact had counterbalanced all the merits of the paper.

As you carry out this aspect of revision, consider alternatives, especially alternative verbs. Look for synonyms in either your dictionary or in a thesaurus. Reject none of them without trying them. Write them in one by one and decide what each does to the message of the sentence. Random, even haphazard experiment may refine one of your thoughts and add a great deal to your paper. The author of the previously discussed Freud-Ibsen paper started out with the following sentence: "The ideas in the play are the same as in Freud." He then tried out "The ideas . . . illustrate. . . ." and "The ideas . . . foreshadow. . . ." The sentence that finally emerged from this experiment was, "In *Hedda Gabler*, Henrik Ibsen anticipated Freud's analysis of the dynamics of human behavior," a vast improvement over the original statement.

The same student wrote the following two sentences, which could have profited by condensation:

1. Hedda had to return back to the estate.

2. Brack alone had the power to dominate over her.

Do you see words that can be eliminated? Try leaving out *back* in the first sentence and *over* in the second.

In the following practice theme, draw a line through every word you can omit and put brackets around every phrase you can condense, inserting a word to replace the longer expression.

A FATHER'S PROBLEM

Not long ago a man walked slowly along the walks of a small and very select Eastern institution of higher education. He was caught in the horns of a dilemma, the reason being because his son was studying along the lines of chemistry, and he was not succeeding. Before the father came to the campus he had received a highly personalized letter from his son. The son reported that his inferior high school background had been a factor in his failure. The father was very puzzled because he knew his son was a boy who was very ambitious. Either from mental telepathy or from reading, he knew it was the general consensus of opinion of most educators that failure was usually the fault of the student. Personally he thought his son should have been able to triumph over his educational deficiencies and develop the necessary essentials of a good study technique. Irregardless of what were the contributory causes, his son was in trouble. It looked very much as though he would soon no longer be a member of the student body at good old Hamilgate. As the man sauntered slowly along, trying to decide what he should do, he referred back to his son's interest in higher education. At first, the father had thought he had gotten a son who was lazy, unmotivated, ignorant, and etc. Later, due to the fact that the boy saw that a graduate of higher learning could get a financially more remunerative position he began to endeavor more strenuously, and he managed to be admitted by a good school.

Your result should be something like this:

      Recently   strolled
[Not long ago] a man [walked slowly] along the walks
                                 college.
of a small, and ~~very~~ select Eastern [institution of higher educa-
                   distressed
tion.] He was [caught in the horns of a dilemma, the reason
                   failing
being] because his son was [studying along the lines of]
chemistry, ~~and he was not succeeding.~~ Before the father
came to the campus, he had received a ~~highly personalized~~
               who   he was failing
letter from his son, [The son] reported that [his inferior high
       because of his poor high school background.
school background had been a factor in his failure.] The

father was ~~very~~ puzzled because he knew his son was a ~~boy~~

~~who was~~ very ambitious. ~~Either~~ From ~~mental~~ telepathy or
~~from~~ reading, he knew ~~it was the general consensus of opinion~~

that   believe   is
~~of~~ most educators ~~that~~ failure ~~was~~ usually the fault of the student. ~~Personally~~ He thought his son should have been able to

    correct
[triumph over] his educational deficiencies and develop ~~the~~

~~necessary essentials of~~ a good study technique. Regardless of

~~what were~~ the ~~contributory~~ causes, his son was in trouble. [It
    Apparently
looked very much as though] he would soon ~~no longer~~ be [a
    expelled from
member of the student body at] good old Hamilgate. As the

man sauntered ~~slowly~~ along, ~~trying to decide what he should~~

    reflected about   early   college.
~~do~~, he [referred back to] his son's interest in [higher edu-

cation.] At first, the father had thought he had ~~gotten~~ a ~~son~~
    son;
~~who was~~ lazy, unmotivated, and ignorant [, and etc.] later,

    since
[due to the fact that] the boy saw that [a graduate of higher

    college was necessary for a good job,
learning could get a financially more remunerative position]

    work harder,
he began to [endeavor more strenuously] and he managed to

be admitted to a good school.

A Father's Problem (Condensed Version)

Recently a man strolled along the walks of a small and
select Eastern college. He was distressed because his son
was failing chemistry. Before the father came to the
campus, he had received a letter from his son, who reported
that he was failing because of his poor high school background. The father was puzzled because he knew his son
was very ambitious. From telepathy or reading, he knew that
most educators believe that failure is usually the fault of
the student. He thought his son should have been able to correct his educational deficiencies and develop a good study technique. Regardless of the causes, his son was in trouble.
Apparently he would soon be expelled from good old Hamilgate.

As the man sauntered along, he reflected about his son's

early interest in college. At first, the father had thought he had a lazy, unmotivated, and ignorant son; later, since the boy saw that college was necessary for a good job, he began to work harder, and he managed to be admitted to a good school.

The result of this condensation is hardly deathless prose, but most of the sludge is gone, and the writer can now take other steps to improve the narrative.

The ruthless yet profitable art of condensation is one that most students reject at first—until they have gone through the experience of cutting a fifth of the words in an essay and found that their thoughts were not only left intact but actually made clearer. Try the experience by covering the right-hand column below while you condense the sentences in the left-hand column. To cut properly, focus on small units of expression.

He insisted that the word should be removed.	Delete *should*.
Most of the students eventually achieve baccalaureate status.	Delete the last three words; substitute *graduate*.
I got a job working in a factory.	Delete *working*.
Today's businessman wants to acquire as many sales as possible.	Condense to "Today's businessman wants to increase his sales."

To understand how a writer's mind should function during revision, study the columns below. The italicized expressions in the left-hand column should give rise to the reactions in the right-hand column.

Many *modern* elementary school *systems are providing* an advanced program *of education* . . .	This section is wordy. Whether the school is modern or not is irrelevant; I can tell it is happening today. *Systems* is unnecessary; all I need is "Many elementary schools." "Are providing" can be shortened to "provide." "An advanced program of education" is wordy; I know it is education, and I know it should not be

for some of their students,
most commonly *centering*
around the fields of math
and languages.

"advanced *program*," because
it seems to be limited to
math and language.

The qualification "for some
of their students" can probably be assumed and thus deleted.
"Centering around the fields of" is
pure pedaguese and is
better omitted entirely.
If I simply write: "Many
elementary schools now
offer advanced courses in math and
languages," all I need is
there, and I have eliminated
over half the words.

In order for this program
to be beneficial to *these*
and future students, careful consideration of the
participants must be given.
. . . Before a student is selected for this advanced
study, *tests of both academic*
and psychological stability
should be *administered and*
corrected.

Redundant; I need only
"for this program to benefit
students" and once
again I have removed well
over half the section.

Wordy. Why not just
"academic and psychological
tests"?
Unnecessary. Correcting
is part of the administration.

As it now stands, pupils are
chosen to participate solely
on *the basis of* their previous academic record. . . .
Obviously this might result
in serious psychological
problems *on the child's*
part. . . .

Wordy, a cliché. "Pupils
are now chosen" is all I
need.

Idiom and brevity here
suggest "problems for the
child."

A battery of tests should be
administered to all children
that would predict their
aptitude and whether or not
they have been working
to their fullest capacity.

This is a cliché, and wordy. Just
say, "Tests should be . . ." Difficulty
with misplaced modifier here. Sounds
as though the children will be
expected to do the predicting.
Put modifier closer to noun: "Tests
. . . which diagnose aptitudes

and determine whether student has been working up to capacity." Not "fullest capacity." Who ever does?

After the results of these tests have *verified the fact that* the child is *totally* capable of advanced study, then, *and only then,* should the student be selected.

This whole section is wordy and repetitious. Substitute: "Only when the child has demonstrated his capability for advanced study should the school consider him for the program."

This point being reached, *the child and his parents should be confronted.* If teachers, parents, and child agree *on the helpfulness of the program,* then the child should be admitted.

Recast the entire passage to reduce duplication: "At this point, the child, his parents, and his teachers should determine whether he ought to be admitted."

After condensing the passage, the writer still has a great deal of work to do on the paper, which at present would get zero for development. Presumably the school authorities have some reason for their present policy, and the writer must show that they are wrong by citing cases where students have been really upset and frustrated by a load of school work beyond their capability. Then he must show, in detail, that tests exist or can be developed that will determine mental and emotional capacity. If possible, the exact tests should be named and described. It is possible that the writer may realize, as ne probes into the situation, that the school authorities are right, in which case he will either change to another topic or do some significant research. At any rate, his paper has profited from the revision process called "condensing." Even if he has as yet said little, the reader is better off for having less of his time taken. The passage at this stage of the revision would read, after some rephrasing, something like this:

> Many elementary schools provide advanced courses in math and language. . . . For these courses to benefit students, school authorities should exercise great care in the selection of participants. . . . They should give academic and psychological tests to determine whether students have been working near their capacity and whether they have aptitude. Pupils now are chosen solely by their academic record. . . . Only when the child has demonstrated his capability for advanced study should the school consider him for the program.

> At this point the child, his parents, and his teachers should determine whether he ought to be admitted.

This is still not perfect prose, but it has the virtue of greater brevity and clarity than the previous version.

As you polish your writing, strive for exactness, vividness, and variety. Make sure you have used your key words properly. A student once received a low mark on a term paper about Ernest Hemingway because she misused the word "spiritual." She thought it meant "basically interested in religion"; using it thus, she caused her reader to think that she believed Hemingway constantly expected a mystical revelation. Another student mentioned in his conclusion to a paper on Thoreau that he had written the "definitive" paper on Thoreau's concept of art. What the student *expressed* was a boast that his effort was the final and complete paper on the subject; what the student *thought* he was saying was that he had "defined" Thoreau's concept of art.

Ambiguities, either structural or verbal, must be detected and removed. When you reread your paper, try to perceive every possible meaning of the words and expressions you have used. Cover the right-hand column below while you try to catch the double meanings in the left-hand column.

She had outlived her ambition without realizing it.	We can't tell whether her ambition had not been realized or whether she does not realize that she has outlived her ambition.
I was originally born in South Dakota, but I've spent most of my mortal life in Nebraska.	How else were you born besides "originally"? Where have you spent your *immortal* life?
Have you spent all your life in Vermont?	Not yet.
Loosely wrapped in a newspaper, she carried three dresses.	She may get cold.
When I called his roommate, he said he'd be out of town for a few days.	I'm doubly confused: I don't know who did the saying or who will be out of town.
The military A-3 bag is light and empty you can pack it easily in another bag.	The bag is "light and empty"? or do you mean that when it is empty you can pack it?

One frequent ambiguity occurs in attempting to end a paper: "In conclusion, Descartes must be considered the father of. . . ." The writer probably means that he is concluding, but it sounds as though Descartes is concluding.

While you are removing deficiencies, seek opportunities to improve your diction. If possible, strengthen your verbs. The best tool for this process is one of the felt-tipped pens with yellow see-through ink, but you can use any heavy pencil, preferably with colored lead. Read through the entire paper again and mark heavily every verb that either is a form of the verb *to be* or is in the passive voice. If you do not find your paper filled with marks, breathe gratefully. The more writing you have done, the more likely it is that you will be slave to these weak verb forms. To prove our point the editors of this textbook deliberately did not revise our own last few sentences. Look at the verbs. So pernicious is the habit of using weak verbs that at the very time we were telling you what *not* to do, we were doing it ourselves. Almost every verb we used was weak. In the following draft of a student's paper about witchcraft in early New England, we have screened the weak verbs.

> After many trials and many hangings came an event which was responsible for causing public sentiment to stir. The event was the death of Giles Corey. He was a man over eighty years old and had been "carried away by the delusion for a time." His testimony was to be used for the conviction of his wife; the old man, however, refused to plead one way or the other. After three such scenes were demonstrated, he was taken into an open field, stripped, and thrown on his back; a heavy weight was placed upon his body until he was pressed to death. It took this unfortunate incident to stimulate the residents of Salem to think seriously about the way they had been acting.
>
> Could events like this continue? The answer was no, for the force of public sentiment became so powerful that even Stoughton, the chief justice, retired from the bench. What actually broke the spell, what actually caused the downfall, however, was that the accusers began to strike too high. They aimed at the ruling class, at relatives of the magistrates, at the President of Harvard, at the wife of the governor, and at Mr. Willard, the godliest minister in Boston. Accusation of Mrs. Hale, wife of the minister of the First Church, "hit the nail on the head." Although Rev. Hale had been one of the leaders of the witchcraft delusion, things looked quite different when they came directly to him. His eyes opened;

the whole community under his influence became convinced
that the "afflicted" children had "perjured themselves" and
from that moment their power was gone. The awful delusion
began passing away and Salem began returning to her senses.

A shift in viewpoint can convert the weak verbs to active, strong
expressions. The writer should have the townspeople doing the action:

. . . the townspeople tried so many suspects and hanged so
many witches that they became aghast at their brutality.
When they tried Giles Corey, an eighty-year-old man who
acted as though he were deluded, they knew they had gone
too far. He was supposed to testify against his wife, but
when he refused, they took him into an open field, stripped
him, and threw him on his back. They then placed a heavy
weight on his chest until he was pressed to death. This especially unfortunate incident caused them to think—to realize
with horror what they had done.

Indicate the weak verbs in the following student theme and decide how they can be strengthened.

Each spring high school students all over the country are
confronted with various college entrance examinations; the
most often taken of these exams are the Scholastic Aptitude
Tests. Of all the tests given to college students, I believe
these are the least indicative of a student's ability.

Now you may ask, "How can she say these things?" and
I'll say, "Easily!" The psychological effect that college board
exams have on high school students is unbelievable. All of the
students who are about to take these exams are well aware
of the ultimate effect their scores will have on their immediate
future. They are so nervous and so tense that they are just
not able to function in their normal capacity. Speaking for
myself, when the day came for me to take my final set of
boards, I was so nervous, that I was ill, and naturally didn't
do as well as I should have.

I'm not using myself as an only example, because I'm not.
What happened to me happened to thousands of others all
over the country.

One way to improve your diction is to consult *Roget's Thesaurus*
for exact words. To illustrate how this technique works, replace the italicized words in the left-hand column below with words from the right-
hand column. Compare your effort with the version on page 217, which
was written by E. M. Forster. Read the entire left-hand column first to see

the continuity. Be able to explain why you reject any word in the right-hand column.

	From *Roget's Thesaurus*
The people I *like*	admire, respect, revere, enjoy, love, relish, favor, desire, fancy, crave, choose, take delight in, revel in, gloat over, appreciate, acknowledge, relate to, regard, esteem, venerate, idolize, honor
most are those who are *sharp,*	sensible, discriminating, touchy, subtle, refined, responsive, sensitive, receptive, sympathetic, delicate, demonstrative
and want to *make*	grow, generate, produce, create, breed, work, cause, form, manufacture, fashion, forge, build, construct
something or *find*	learn, discover, master, bring to light, encounter, ascertain, absorb
something, and do not see life in terms of power, and such people get more of an *opportunity*	more time, more chance, occasion, room, scope
under a democracy than elsewhere. They *start*	begin, invent, establish, create, set up, found, form, forge, build, concoct
religions, great or small, or they *write* literature	create, perform, produce, manufacture, originate, devise, hatch, contrive
and art, or they do disinterested scientific research, or they may be what is called "ordinary" people who are *constructive*	productive, prolific, creative, contriving, inventive, blastogenetic, epigenetic, incubational, fruitful
in their *own* lives,	personal, secluded, private, confidential, individual, intimate

rear their	bring up, produce, raise, grow, garden, share crop
children decently, for instance, or *aid* their	succor, assist, help, remedy, benefit, subsidize, befriend, give a leg up for, defend
neighbours. All these people need to *talk;*	speak, express themselves, chatter, converse, gab
they cannot do so unless society *permits*	allows, lets, sanctions, tolerates, suffers, enables, authorizes
them to do so, and the society which allows them most liberty is a democracy.	

E. M. Forster in *Two Cheers for Democracy,* from which this passage is taken, almost always selected the simplest synonyms, avoiding any expressions that were jocose or frivolous. He is speaking seriously. His version:

> The people I admire most are those who are sensitive and want to create something or discover something, and do not see life in terms of power, and such people get more of a chance under a democracy than elsewhere. They found religions, great or small, or they produce literature and art, or they do disinterested scientific research, or they may be what is called "ordinary people," who are creative in their private lives, bring up their children decently, for instance, or help their neighbours. All these people need to express themselves; they cannot do so unless society allows them to do so, and the society which allows them most liberty is a democracy.   E. M. FORSTER, *Two Cheers for Democracy,* 1951.

The word you seek must be exact; occasionally you can draw the clearest thought with a metaphor. Avoid an inappropriate selection.

Her speech was *interlarded* with compliments . . .	A compliment must not be compared to lard. Try: ". . . was flowered with compliments," "decorated with compliments," or "interspersed with compliments."
At the *ripe old age of* thirty-two, Captain Billy Mitchell became the *spearhead* forcing the army . . .	Ugh! A cliché. Steady! A spearhead goes ahead.

See what you can do with this: "Columbus was a man of the Renaissance." Paul Horgan, in *The Conquistadores*, wrote, "Columbus was the son of his time, the dawning Renaissance, when the spirit of discovery of man's arts and sciences was breaking across the western world." Mr. Horgan is impressed with Columbus, and he took a chance on being extravagant. Working to express the basic thought, "Jessamyn West usually writes light fiction; this time she has gone into more sombre work," Webster Schott, in a review of *A Matter of Times*, a book about terminal cancer, wrote, "Jessamyn West is a nice lady who writes nice fiction. Lately she has been having midnight thoughts." Good?

According to Samuel Taylor Coleridge, there is in the sentences of the greatest writers a "reason assignable not only for every word, but for the position of every word." When you are fairly comfortable with the words you have selected, look again at your sentences and arrange each element in them properly. Writers addressing a reader who is reasonably well educated tend to compact their sentences and give them "texture." A sentence may be particularly interesting because it has many ideas compressed in it.

1. There Ruth sits.

2. There Ruth sits, quietly.

3. There Ruth sits, quietly, and in slow decay.

Make your prose as compact as possible, being careful, however, to avoid a howler like, "Coming from St. Louis' rain and slush, Palo Alto's climate is heaven sent."

The selection below contains one idea per sentence.

All societies are governed by laws. The laws are really hidden. These hidden laws are not spoken. They are profound. They are assumptions. The assumptions are by the people. Our society is like all societies. A writer has a job. An American writer has a special job. His job is to find out the laws and assumptions. Our society has a special quality. The quality is that we smash taboos. We still have to pay attention to the taboos. American writers will have a hard time finding our laws. They will also have a hard time finding our assumptions.

The staccato effect is monotonous and amateurish. Note how James Baldwin conveyed the same ideas:

Every society is really governed by hidden laws, by unspoken but profound assumptions on the part of the people, and

ours is no exception. It is up to the American writer to find
out what these laws and assumptions are. In a society much
given to smashing taboos without thereby managing to be
liberated from them, it will be no easy matter.
JAMES BALDWIN, *Nobody Knows My Name*, 1960.

Earlier in this chapter we had an illustrative paragraph about
poor henpecked Herbert. Now look at another version of the account:

Herbert's wife dominates him. When they attended his
friend's wedding, his wife and daughter sat in the back seat.
They were dressed in frilly, bouffant dresses. Herbert sat in
the front seat. He collects stamps for a hobby.

Compare the draft above to this one.

Herbert is dominated by his wife. When he was invited to
his friend's wedding, he arrived in the family car. Enthroned in the back seat were his wife and daughter, all
frilly and bouffant. Alone in front, like a chauffeur, was Herbert. No wonder he spends his evenings in his study classifying stamps.

The second draft is almost exclusively in the passive voice to point
up Herbert's docile nature. Two sentences are reversed (the two beginning
with *enthroned* and *alone*) to emphasize the status of the wife and daughter in relation to Herbert's status. The simile of Herbert as chauffeur is
contrasted to the metaphor of his family "enthroned." Only the last sentence, in which the one positive act of Herbert is mentioned, is in the
active voice.

As you revise the structure of your sentences, seek variety. In the
margins of your draft, jot down the number of words in each sentence.
If your sentences are all long, unload some of them. An abrupt, terse
sentence can be effective. It can catch attention. Try it. Indicate also in
the margins whether your sentences are simple, compound, or complex—
and make any changes necessary to correct an overabundance of any one
type. Observe what patterns your modifiers follow, and try for other patterns. Here are some unusual structures, collected by Francis Christensen:

He shook hands, a quick shake, fingers down, like a
pianist. SINCLAIR LEWIS.

The jockeys sat bowed and relaxed, moving a little at the
waist with the movement of their horses. KATHERINE ANNE
PORTER.

Calico-coated, small bodied, with delicate legs and pink

faces in which their mismatched eyes rolled wild and subdued, they huddled, gaudy, motionless and alert, wild as deer,
deadly as rattlesnakes, quiet as doves. WILLIAM FAULKNER.

Joad's lips stretched tight over his long teeth for a moment,
and he licked his lips, like a dog, two licks, one in each direction from the middle. JOHN STEINBECK.

All this chiseling, carpentering, and experimenting, all this con-
triving, all this chopping, condensing, and pictorializing will form a product
which, at this moment, may not be *you*. The English language has a huge
collection of patterns and word choices, but each writer must select what
suits him most. Read your prose aloud. Is this you talking? If it is not,
polish it to satisfy yourself. Which sounds better to you?

1. Luther rose from his knees and walked slowly away.

2. Luther rose from his knees and slowly walked away.

Both sentences are effective, logical, grammatical, clear, and exact,
but you may feel more comfortable with one version than with the other.
Somerset Maugham once complained that "Many writers without distress
will put two rhyming words together, join a monstrous long adjective to
a monstrous long noun, or between the end of one word and at the beginning of another have a conjunction of consonants that almost break
your jaw." If you are to avoid such troubles, you must experiment and
select, rearrange, and polish till you have what satisfies you.

Fifth objective: perfection in grammar, spelling, and punctuation

Glory of glories, you have finally gotten through all the steps of
the revision process. At this point, you probably have an almost overwhelming urge to submit your paper to your instructor without looking
at it once more. But remember the sad fate of the newspaper: all that
work is wasted if the newsboy throws it into the snowbank. You must,
once again, reread your work to be sure that the grammar, spelling, and
punctuation are conventional and effective.

There is no point in our pretending that you can learn all you
need to know at this time about proofreading, but we can give some
suggestions. In the first place, go through the process a single step at a
time. First of all, check the grammar. Look back at your previous compositions to see what types of barbarisms you have committed before: comma
splice? misplaced modifier? singular subject and plural verb? Fortunately,
since there are only so many mistakes you can make, you can prepare a
checklist of those *you* usually make—and then set out to avoid them. Read

the paper aloud, thinking about sentence structure. Do you find any howlers your instructor will put on the bulletin board?

Then shift to punctuation. Here it is very important that you read aloud. Drop your voice and pause with each comma; pause longer for each period. Read interpretively, as though you are talking to a small child. Pause here; put stress there. Does your punctuation, insofar as it can, reflect the voice effects so important to meaning? Don't use too many commas. If too many are needed, recast your sentences in shorter forms. If necessary, just before you read your manuscript for punctuation, read over the examples for punctuation in the handbook section of this textbook. (Pages 422–430) Read the examples aloud, inflecting them more heavily than you ordinarily would. Emphasize stresses, pauses, and accents to dramatize the need for punctuation. As you proofread, watch for mistakes you've made in previous papers. Where you have an incomplete word at the end of the line, divide correctly at a syllable break.

And now for spelling. Take your pencil and put the point on every syllable. Read aloud. Think what the word is. The troublemakers are such pairs as *then/than, whose/who's, their/they're*, and *its/it's* rather than long words, but look up any words of which you are uncertain. If you customarily misspell three words per page, search for four or five.

Conclusion

At last the job is done. William James once complained that "everything comes out wrong with me at first, but I torture and poke and scrape and pat it until it offends me no more." When you go through this long process and see bad writing become the good writing you perhaps saw glimmering up there ahead of you all through the ordeal, you feel a tremendous satisfaction and have a sense of real accomplishment. This feeling, and the knowledge and skill in writing that you have gained, will encourage you to revise your next paper with the same careful attention to detail—and the next, and the next. Each time you will learn, and each time you will be impressed with the results.

Project

Go back over your old themes and completely revise the best one. Perhaps your instructor will help you in your selection. Carry out every step described in this chapter. Turn in all of your work, including your original version, two intermediate drafts, and the final version. Number each draft to help your instructor perceive the growth of your paper. Your instructor may make other suggestions for this assignment.

PERSPECTIVES

II

If we are to understand any problem completely, we must look at it three ways. We must look directly at the problem—that is "particle perspective." We must look at it historically to see how our present situation has developed—and what may happen in the future—that is "wave perspective." We need to look at its environment to see what is presently related to the problem—that is "field perspective." A. L. BECKER AND KENNETH L. PIKE.

CHAPTER 7

LANGUAGE: PAST, PRESENT, AND FUTURE

Once upon a time author *was pronounced with a t-sound (autor), and everybody was quite happy about it; now, everybody says it with a th-sound and is equally happy about it, but nothing has been gained by the change, and there was no need of the uncertainty that prevailed during the period of transition.* ROBERT A. HALL, JR., *Leave Your Language Alone!,* 1950.

A student who has been assigned this chapter may say, "A carpenter does not necessarily know about the kind of wood and steel in his hammer. Why do I have to know so much about words? Are all good writers students of language?"

The answer is no, not all, but most. Some writers have developed a command of expression without formal study. More often, however, able writers *are* students of language. Napoleon, Disraeli, Julius Caesar, Thomas Hobbes, Harry Truman, John Kennedy, Henry Ford, and Knute Rockne were fascinated by language study. John Quincy Adams, Thomas Jefferson, and Henry Adams wrote important commentaries on aspects of communication.

Certainly language is important to man. Although in its broadest sense, it is not limited to man, in its most usual sense language is the faculty that clearly distinguishes man from the "lower" animals. It is basic to all of man's relationships with his environment and with other men. It is a factor in most of his triumphs and the cause of many of his failures. Almost every civilization has considered an understanding of language the basis of education. Ancient Greece, which fostered Homer, Socrates, Plato, Aristotle, Demosthenes, Pericles, and Sophocles, thought of the trivium— grammar, rhetoric, and logic—as all there was to higher education. Under the Roman Empire, during the Middle Ages, and during the Renaissance, training in the use of language was the most important aspect of education. The great teachers Quintilian, Petrus Ramus, Roger Ascham, Thomas Aquinas, and Peter Abelard were, at least in part, teachers of rhetoric.

Regrettably, many students, by the time they reach college, are somewhat less than enchanted by the study of "English." Since third grade, they have gone over and over the grammatical precepts that have become popularly identified as language study. Such students may need the advice of Matthew Arnold, who once said that a person should do what he knows he should do; habit and acquired skill will make it pleasant. If you are one of the students who chafe under the disciplines of language, we ask you to suspend your irritation and give this study a good college try. When you study language and develop the habit of watching it grow and change, you join a select group of intellectuals. When you master its use, you join a real élite, one whose pleasure and power are out of all proportion to their numbers.

The origin of language

No one authority has been able to convince everyone that he has discovered how language began. To reflect their dissatisfaction with extant theories, linguists have given them many silly names. There is the "bow-wow theory," the notion that words originated in imitation of natural sounds, like those of birds, dogs, and thunder. According to this theory, in a primitive language words resemble baby-talk: a dog might be a "bow-wow"; thunder might be "boom-boom." There is also the "pooh-pooh theory," the theory that words originated from exclamations. Baby might call a pain an "ouch," and Mother might report to Father, "Baby got an ouch today." The third theory is called the "ding-dong theory." Its defenders believe that language comes from expression induced from sensory impressions—that is, the sound that springs to mind when a sensation is first experienced. Baby might think of candy as a "yum-yum." "Ding-dong" applies because, in English, this is a bell's response when it is struck by the clapper.

The nature of language

Whatever its origin, historical linguists have described certain characteristics of language. *Language is an arbitrary and constantly changing set of symbols which, when arranged in a certain order and expressed either orally, physically, or graphically according to certain conventions, makes possible the communication of an idea, emotion, or desire.**

This definition includes, of course, "sign language," an important part of communication. The report of the fall of Troy, for instance, is said to have been relayed from Asia Minor to Greece by a series of signal fires. American Indians communicated intertribally by gestures and smoke signals. African natives communicate by drum beat. Sign language is used by football referees, traffic policemen, the man who guides an airplane onto the landing deck of an aircraft carrier, and many others. Sign language may not always communicate effectively, however. The same gesture that looks like a farewell wave to an American, for instance, actually means "Come here" to a Pakistani. In Russia, a gesture that looks like applauding with closed fists actually signifies counting by tens. When a Tamil in southern India seems to nod affirmatively, he is actually saying "No." Signs, of course, are not used only by man; a bee communicates its discovery of nectar by a ritualistic dance.

The definition of language given above admits of communication by many different written symbols, and such forms of communication are important today. Traffic experts have discovered that pictorial traffic signs communicate more forcefully than words. As a result, on road signs we see crosses, wiggly lines, and silhouettes of children.

Although our language is not, strictly speaking, a sign language, it is more than a series of words. Oral communication relies heavily upon gestures and other physical activity. A speaker smiles, raises his voice, or an eyebrow. He clenches his fist. In addition, he uses his voice mechanisms in a number of ways. Take, for instance, a sentence that would be written:

The dog bit a man.

This sentence correctly conveys a certain bit of information. The

* This definition is partially derived from Edward Sapir's *Language: An Introduction to the Study of Speech* (New York: Harcourt, Brace & World, 1949).

position of the words indicates that it is the dog who has done the biting. The meaning would be changed if the noun order were reversed. The form of the words indicates there are one dog and one man; otherwise, the sentence would read *dogs* and *men*. The form *bit* indicates that the action happened in the past. All this the written transcription communicates.

Suppose, however, that the speaker had put stronger emphasis on the word *dog*. The sentence might then have meant, "The dog—not the tiger—bit the man." Suppose the speaker had put emphasis on the verb; then he might have meant, "The dog *bit* the man; he didn't merely growl at him." Emphasis on the final word might have meant, "The dog bit the *man*, not the boy." This additional or changed meaning is made possible by intonation, pauses, emphasis, pitch, stress, and other tricks of the voice, which are often, as in this illustration, basic to its meaning. Every language has a set of special sounds—stresses, emphases, changes in pitch, rising and falling inflections—and these special sounds must be mastered before exact meaning can be transmitted orally.

Written language, which is an attempt to transcribe oral language, also must be more than a collection of words. Punctuation is an important part of written language; it must convey, if possible, the changes in pitch, inflection, intonation, and the stops in sound that are necessary if men are to communicate effectively with one another. In English, at least, neither the words nor the punctuation marks are *signs*; they are not an attempt to record ideas pictorially, nor are they visually related to what they represent. They are *symbols* that were derived arbitrarily in dim history—symbols upon whose meaning men have agreed, if not by contract, at least by custom and convention. Finally, although written language is an attempt to transcribe oral language, they are different languages, or dialects, because men usually do not write the same as they talk.

The relationship of languages

Although linguists do not agree upon how man first developed language, most admit the "splash-wave" theory of historical development. They believe that at certain places on the earth several basic languages began. The phenomenon that caused the original splash is not known, but the waves by which it spread have been quite accurately traced. Some time before 3000–2000 B.C., probably somewhere in eastern Europe or western Asia, the ancestor of the English oral language, or a cluster of ancestral dialects, formed. Waves of languages developing from this parent language spread to northern India and western Europe, and so the original language of our linguistic family is called "Indo-European." By comparing related words, linguists have made intelligent guesses about this original language. These assumed forms appear in dictionaries to show the very early etymologies of some words. A word in the dictionary marked with an asterisk (for example, *sororinus*) is a hypothetical Indo-European word. The descendant languages of the Indo-European language tend to have similarities in the numerals from one to ten and in the words for close family relationships (*father, mother, sister,* and *brother*).

The technique of the comparative linguist needs to be explained in more detail. Even an elementary study of a foreign language has shown most of us that English has many words that resemble words in other languages; for instance, *paternal* resembles the Latin *pater*. These similar words are called *cognates*. Advanced students have observed that the separation between the German *v* and the English *p* is indistinct. Thus, the German *vater* and the English *paternal* are related, as are *father* and *pater*. The Scottish *k* sound is related to the English *ch*. Thus we find *church* in English poetry, and *kirk* in Robert Burns. The linguist plots similar words on a map and observes what languages are related. The very similar are brothers and sisters; the less related are cousins, to keep up the metaphor. He learns that French and Spanish are closely related, as are English and German. He learns that all four are related, but less intimately so.

The linguist has learned to look backward. When he sees that from the shores of England to the borders of Hindustani India, the word for *sister* is much like the Latin word *soror*, he postulates that the parent of all the languages, Indo-European, must have had a similar word. Thus, *sororinus*, from which English distantly derives *sorority*, is assumed to have been an Indo-European word.

Approximately one billion people now speak languages that descended from Indo-European. The main branches of the ancestral language are Indo-Iranian, Balto-Slavic, Hellenic or Greek, Italic, Celtic, and Germanic or Teutonic.

An important descendant of the Indo-Iranian language is Sanskrit (*c.* 1500 B.C.–1500 A.D.), as important as Latin and Greek in the perpetuation of great literature. The Old Persian of Darius and Xerxes is a derivative. Languages spoken in modern Iran, Afghanistan, Pakistan, and India are descendants. Modern derivatives of Balto-Slavic include Lithuanian, Serbian, Croatian, Russian, Polish, and Czech. Modern Greek is a descendant of the epic Greek of Homer, which became the Attic Greek of the great literature and culture. Because of the wealth of literature and religious liturgy retained by it and because of the political and economic importance of the Roman Empire, Latin, an early form of the Italic group, is the most

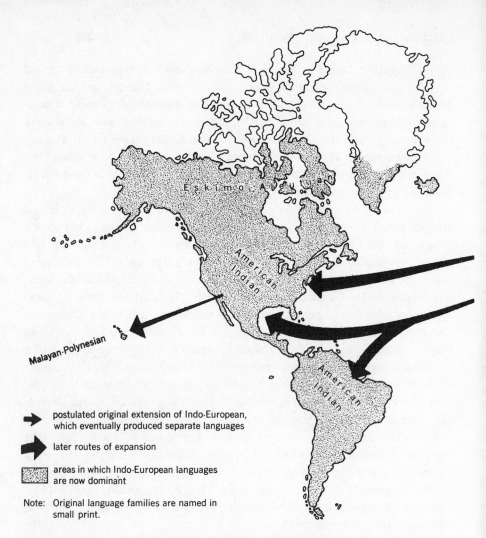

important pre-modern Indo-European language. Today's Italian, Rumanian, French, Portuguese, and Spanish are derivatives. The ancient language of Ireland, the Gaelic of the Scottish Highlands, Welsh, and Cornish are the offspring of Celtic. Forms of the Germanic or Teutonic language existed as early as the fourth century A.D. in the language spoken at that time by the Goths on the Lower Danube. Branches include Norse or Scandinavian, modern Danish, Swedish, and Norwegian. A branch called West Germanic is the language of southern Germany. The Nibelungen epics and the lyric poetry of the minnesingers were written in this language. New High German is the language of Luther's Bible and of most German literature since the Reformation. Low German is the source of the English language, as well as of Frisian, Dutch, and Flemish. Low German gave rise to Anglo-Saxon, or Old English, which is the grandparent of our own English.

Three minor branches of Indo-European have almost no modern

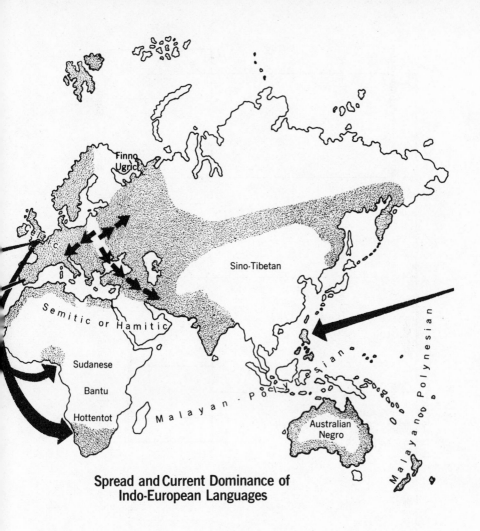

**Spread and Current Dominance of
Indo-European Languages**

descendants. Thraco-Illyrian may be the parent of modern Albanian. Thraco-Phrygian once existed in what is now eastern Europe, but Armenian is the only derivative. For many centuries, the Tokharian language was lost completely, but in recent years manuscripts have been discovered in Chinese Turkestan. Tokharian has very little resemblance to Indo-Iranian, which is geographically nearest to it. Instead, it has closer cognates with Italic and Celtic. When comparative linguists can go to work on these Chinese manuscripts, they will undoubtedly open to us a whole new chapter of history.

One way to find out what will happen to a language is to see what has already happened to it. Our main emphasis therefore is to demonstrate that every class of change in the English language—no matter whether first noted in the time of King Arthur, Shakespeare, Abraham Lincoln, or Robert Kennedy—is happening now.

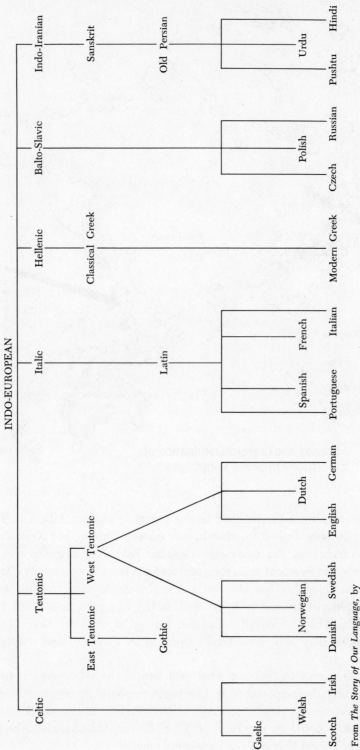

INDO-EUROPEAN

Celtic

Gaelic
Scotch   Welsh   Irish

Teutonic

East Teutonic   West Teutonic

Gothic

Danish   Norwegian   Swedish

English   Dutch   German

Italic

Latin

Portuguese   Spanish   French   Italian

Hellenic

Classical Greek

Modern Greek

Balto-Slavic

Czech   Polish   Russian

Indo-Iranian

Sanskrit

Old Persian

Pushtu   Urdu   Hindi

From *The Story of Our Language*, by
Henry Alexander. (Thomas Nelson
and Son, Ltd., 1940.)

Background of the English language

ANGLO-SAXON, CA. 449–CA. 1066

The language we call English was not, strictly speaking, the native language of England. Prior to recorded history, there were several dialects spoken by the Celts, Picts, and other tribes who inhabited the British islands before 55 B.C., the year Julius Caesar invaded the islands. In 43 A.D., the Emperor Claudius conquered the tribes of central and southeastern Britain and thus began the Romanizing of the language, a process that is still going on. Celtic words still remain, mostly in place names, the words *Kent*, *London*, and *Thames* being of Celtic origin. By the time the Roman legions departed in 410 A.D. to help protect the Empire at home, many Latin words had been absorbed into the language, including *camp, wall, street, cheap, wine, bishop, flask, kettle, cup*, and *dish*.

In the latter half of the fifth century, three northwest European tribes, the Angles, the Saxons, and the Jutes, invaded and conquered the entire island. The amalgamation of the Angle, Saxon, and Jute languages was the basis of English. We call it Anglo-Saxon, or Old English. Anglo-Saxon is a half-way language, partly like its Germanic origins and partly like Modern English. Our first written records of Old English are relics from the eighth and ninth centuries that closely resemble the records of continental Germanic speech of the same time. You can recognize this partial Anglo-Saxon prayer as the ancestor of the Lord's Prayer:

> Fæder ure
> þu þe eart on heofonum
> si þin nama gehalgod
> Tobecume þin rice.
> Gewor þe ðin willa on eor ð an swa swa on heofonum.

From Old English, modern English inherits basic inflections, syntax, and vocabulary. Inflections are the changes in word forms that indicate plurals, tenses, possessives, and other grammatical variations; syntax refers to word order and sentence structure. In the prayer above, as in modern English, a past tense is made with a *d* sound, prepositional phrases are used to modify nouns, and word order is much the same as today.

The vocabulary of Old English has many resemblances to that of other members of the Indo-European family, some of them apparent and some of them recognizable only by linguists. The Latin words for *foot* and *fish* (*pes* and *piscis*) do not seem to be related to their English equivalents until we discover that, according to a phenomenon called Grimm's Law, the Indo-European *p*, retained in Greek and Latin, became *f* in the Germanic languages. Further, the Indo-European *t*, retained in Greek and Latin, became *th* in English; thus the Latin *tres* is related to (or a cognate of) the English *three*. Notice how the word *Fædur* in the prayer above is affected by Grimm's Law.

DEVELOPMENT OF THE ALPHABET

No one knows the origin of the runic alphabets of the old German tribes; the runes appeared in the third century among the East Goths and seemed to be a variation of Greek cursive writing. Runes consisted mostly of perpendicular and oblique lines, possibly because they had to be carved on wood. They were used primarily in England and Scandinavia, being used in Sweden as late as the fourteenth century.

The origin of the English alphabet is as uncertain as that of the runes. As Anglo-Saxon developed, it was recorded in a form of the Latin alphabet. We know that at first men could communicate only by sounds and gestures, and when records and messages became necessary, pictures were used. One picture represented a man, another a house, and another a ship. These pictographs came eventually to be used for syllable sounds; a joined picture of a bee and a leaf, for instance, might have the obvious meaning, "belief." The pictures were eventually simplified and came to represent only their initial sounds.

Our own alphabet probably developed among the Seirites, a people living on the Sinai peninsula between what are now Egypt and Israel. The Seirites took part of the older Egyptian cuneiform system, which as early as 3000 B.C. used complicated characters to represent ideas, words, and sounds, and used the symbols only to represent sounds, as we do today, a simplification that possibly accounts for its triumph over other alphabets.

In the second millennium before Christ, the Phoenicians, a seafaring and trading people, absorbed the Seirite alphabet, and six centuries later the Greeks absorbed the Phoenician alphabet. When the Greeks found the Phoenician alphabet, it was without vowels, as are many Semitic and Asian alphabets today. *Building* would have been spelled much as we abbreviate it, *bldg*. The Greeks adapted the Phoenician alphabet to their own sound system, using the left-over consonants to signify their vowel sounds. The *V*, for instance, became a vowel sound. The alphabet of the Etruscans, the most highly civilized people on the Italic peninsula before the rise of Rome, bears close affinities to the alphabets of the Greeks and the Phoenicians, and it is this alphabet that the Romans later adopted and changed into nearly its present form.

The history of a few letters shows the gradual progression from picture to letter. The Egyptian sign for "ox" became first the Phoenician *aleph*, then the Greek *alpha*, and finally our own A. This diagram shows the development of our letter B:

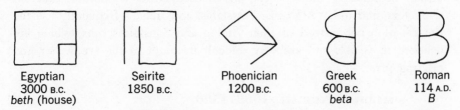

Egyptian	Seirite	Phoenician	Greek	Roman
3000 B.C.	1850 B.C.	1200 B.C.	600 B.C.	114 A.D.
beth (house)			*beta*	B

The Development of the Letter B.

As late as during its Phoenician use, the letter still looked something like a floor plan with an open door. The Greeks curved the lines, added a second loop, and turned the character around. The Romans turned it back again. The Egyptian *door* (*daleth*) ultimately became the Greek *delta* (Δ) and our D. Originally E came from the symbol for man, S from mountain. In the Middle Ages, Latin used the *v*-sound, but made it by a double-*u* or a double-*v*. English kept the double-*v* but called it the double-*u*. This confusion is reflected in cognate variations from language to language. Germans pronounce "Wagner" as though it begins with a V; Pakistanis fly an airplane that was sold to them as the "Harvard," but they call it the "Harward." They call a "vicious virus" a "wicious wirus." It makes you "womit."

The Anglo-Saxon alphabet was much like the Latin of the time, including two signs for *th*—the thorn, þ and the eth, ð —and the Latin digraph, æ. The Z was known as *izzard,* and today in England and Canada is called *zed.*

The modern English alphabet is not perfect. To represent about 45 English sounds, we have only 26 characters, and some of them must do double duty. A stands for six sounds, U for four, E for five or six, and G for two. Several sounds are made with many different combinations of letters. It nevertheless has the advantage of being a phonic alphabet, in which characters represent sounds. Like the Russian and other Slavic alphabets, which came from the Greek, and like the Arabic and Sanskrit, which came from the Aramaic via the Phoenicians, our alphabet can be used to spell new words as they are formed. In contrast, the Assyrian, Babylonian, Mayan, and Aztec alphabets, which were pictographic and thus not flexible enough to change and grow with the times, have all died out. Japan and China have recently changed from pictographic to phonic systems. In

China, using the old characters, a scholar had to know well over a thousand symbols to represent abstractions, sounds, and words. Because of its effective phonics, flexibility, simplicity, adaptability to the typewriter and printing press, the Latin alphabet is still making new converts. In 1928, Turkey abandoned Arabic script, which used nearly a hundred different characters, and today Afghanis, Pakistanis, and Indians frequently use the English alphabet instead of their Arabic and Sanskrit scripts, which are deficient in vowels and are very difficult to adapt to the typewriter and printing press.

MIDDLE ENGLISH, 1066–1500

The subjugation of England by the Normans under William the Conqueror after 1066 drastically changed the English language. By 1075, eighteen of the twenty-one bishops of England were French; by 1076, all twelve earls of England were French. In other words, the ruling classes of England were almost all French-speaking. The users of English were, in general, uneducated servants and farmers, and although they kept English alive, they simplified it during the years of French political domination. In grammar, the result was a gradual loss of inflections. Anglo-Saxon nouns and adjectives had different endings to show changes in number, case, and gender; in Middle English, many of these endings were either simplified or lost. Separate pronoun forms were retained to show gender (*him, her*), number (*she, they*), and case (*he, him; they, them*), but almost all other parts of speech lost complicated forms. English serfs and yeomen had little time or concern for the niceties of complicated inflections, just as today less fastidious speakers are impatient with the distinctions between *who* and *whom, shall* and *will.*

Besides losing inflections and other grammatical distinctions, English absorbed a great number of words from the French. By 1250, the English vocabulary included some 900 French words, most of them the type of words lower classes might learn from their nobility (*baron, noble, servant,* and *messenger*), and from their governmental and ecclesiastical leaders (*government, crown, reign, court, allegiance, rebel, manor, homage, peasant, justice, equity, felon, proof, forfeit, theology, sermon, prayer, lesson, passion, image, chapter,* and *sanctuary*). As might be expected, many military terms were absorbed also (*army, navy, battle, combat, skirmish,* and *sergeant*). Since the French set social customs, there was also an abundance of words suggesting entertainment, culture, and fine living (*apparel, garment, ermine, tawny, jewel, dinner, supper, appetite, oyster, beef, mutton, biscuit, salad, curtain, screen, chandelier, towel, falcon,* and *stable*). The cultural and intellectual interests of the ruling classes show in words relating to architecture, literature, and science, particularly medicine (*painting, sculpture, music, title, logic, physician, anatomy,* and *stomach*). The peak of this absorption occurred in the fourteenth century; by 1400 borrowing began to taper off.

Spoken English dialects differed almost from county to county, until the fifteenth century when the language absorbed from the farmlands north of London became the language of the city itself. Influenced possibly by the writing of Geoffrey Chaucer and by the scholars of Oxford and Cambridge universities, and certainly by the printing press introduced in 1476 by William Caxton, who wrote in London English, this language became the most widespread English dialect. Here is an example of William Caxton's prose:

> Our language now used varyeth ferre from that whiche was used and spoken when I was borne. For we englysshe men ben borne under the domynacyon of the mone, which is never stedfaste, but ever waverynge, wexynge one season, and waneth & dyscreaseth another season. And that comyn englysshe that is spoken in one shyre varyeth from a nother. . . . And thus bytwene playn, rude, & curyous, I stande abasshed. But in my judgements the comyn termes that be dayli used ben lyghter to be understonde than the olde and auncyent englysshe. And for as moche as this present booke is not for a rude uplondyssh man to laboure therein, ne rede it, but onely for a clerke & a noble gentylman that feleth and understondeth in faytes of armes, in love, & in noble chyvalrye, therfor in a meane bytwene bothe I have reduced & translated this sayd booke in to our englysshe, not ouer rude ne curyous, but in suche termes as shall be understanden, by goddys grace, accordynge to my copye.   FROM THE PROLOGUE TO CAXTON'S EDITION OF THE *Aeneid.*

The fifteenth-century prose of Caxton, when compared to the Anglo-Saxon prayer on page 233, illustrates how a language grows to fit its time and people. It acquires a larger vocabulary—if necessary, by borrowing. It may exhibit regional variations, but common exchange will eventually develop a common currency. It may be structured according to education, the language of the ruder people coming into conflict with that of the more educated. The student observing the phenomena of borrowing, inflection and syntax simplification, and conflict of dialects can look to his own time and try to see how these changes are taking place now. By doing so, he may be able to anticipate much of what he will now study about the modern English language.

Modern English, 1500–today

Since 1500 (the approximate date when the printing press became influential and therefore the date usually associated with the beginning of Modern English), the English language has continued to change with history. Besides the extension of printing, the changes resulted from the spread of popular education, the development of new inventions and industries, the increase in travel, the expansion of the British Empire in the nineteenth century, and the increasing influence of the United States.

SPELLING, 1500–YESTERDAY

Prior to the sixteenth century, there was little uniformity in spelling. Words were usually spelled the way they sounded. However, in some cases letters that were not pronounced were inserted in words simply because the corresponding word in Latin was so spelled (*debt, debitum; doubt, dubitare*); in other cases, letters were inserted by analogy to words similarly pronounced. On the model of *night*, for instance, a *gh* was inserted into *delight*, which in Old French and Middle English had been spelled *delit*. This *gh* once represented a sound, but when the sound was dropped the spelling was unrelated to the new pronunciation.

There was little desire for standardization. In 1592, Robert Greene spelled the word *coney* nine different ways. In Shakespeare's early manuscripts his name is spelled at least four different ways. The first generation of printers, sensitive about comparison of their work with hand-written pages, felt more impelled to have their right margins straight than they did to have words spelled consistently; consequently they inserted just enough letters to use up the right number of spaces. If *Shakespeare* was too long, they simply shortened it to *Shaxpere*.

The first attempt to standardize spelling, *An ABC for Children* (1558), was puny, only a few pages in length. In a more ambitious effort, Thomas Smith in 1568 wrestled with an alphabet of thirty-four letters. John Hart, in 1570, tried to popularize special letters for *ch, sh, th*, and other sounds. In 1580, William Bulloker used accent marks, apostrophes, and hooks to reflect sounds, with special attention to varying vowel sounds.

The first success in standardizing spelling was Richard Mulcaster's in 1582. Mulcaster recommended the elimination of unnecessary letters (as in *put* for *putt*, and *led* for *ledd*), but he retained double consonants if they occurred in separate syllables, as in *sitting*. He used a final *e* to indicate a previous long vowel, as in *stripe, made,* and *rope*. He used analogy extensively. Since we write *hear*, he argued, we should therefore write *fear* and *dear*. He was more concerned with standardization than phonetics, and he sought always to find the most common spelling of a particular word. Although his spellings are not always the ones we now use, his "General Table" of 7,000 words was very influential.

In spite of the popular belief that English spelling was fixed by Dr. Samuel Johnson's dictionary of 1755, English spelling in its modern form existed a century before. Since 1650, the Latin *prae* has changed in favor of *pre*, more final *e*'s have been dropped (as from *kinde*), and such words as *gratefull*, *harshnesse*, and *logick* have been simplified. Other than these few changes, spelling has been remarkably static.

The inconsistencies of English spelling are, of course, still under attack by those who charge that we should not expect a child or a foreigner to master *through*, *cough*, *thought*, *though*, *hiccough*, and *drought*. Attempts at reform based on pronunciation all too often flounder on the different pronunciations found in different regions of the country. Melvil Dewey, who devised the Dewey Decimal System used for library cataloguing, tried to phoneticize English spelling but succeeded only in simplifying his own first name. Colonel Robert McCormick, using the platform of his widely distributed *Chicago Tribune*, tried for years to simplify spellings (*nite*, *lite*, *telegraf*, and *thru*), but none of his innovations are listed as accepted spellings in modern dictionaries.

The most powerful modern effort toward standardization was that of the British and American Philological Societies in 1893; in 1906 the Simplified Spelling Boards of England and America reinforced the earlier efforts, and *Webster's New International Dictionary, Second Edition* (1947), deferred in almost all cases to their edicts.

SPELLING TODAY

With the exception of advertising copy writers and the authors of road signs, who come up with such words as *Vu-Lite*, *waterpruf*, *hiway*, *thorofare*, and *thru street*, the impulse for spelling reform is dead. It is a pity. Spelling is one of the major drawbacks to using English as an international language, only French being more difficult. Spanish spelling, in contrast, is much more closely related to its sounds. Ironically, in view of the difficulty of English spelling, the ability to spell is often considered the surest indicator of education. Several years ago, when a Stanford professor asked a number of prospective employers what they considered the essential aspects of education, the ability to spell led all other choices. Any number of college-admissions officers have said that a letter of application containing misspellings has almost no chance of a favorable response. Many employment officers say that they almost invariably ignore letters of application containing poor spelling. This reaction is superficial and unfair, but it is a fact of life.

Students of the language, especially students in freshman English, therefore, are faced with a paradox: the impulse to simplify spelling has declined, but the demand for correct spelling is almost unanimous. We continue to spell English words with French spellings, and we still have many words with silent letters (*pneumonia, psychology*). We even spell some English words differently from the way Englishmen do (curb/kerb, labor/labour). And, too, new words enter the vocabulary every year, posing yet another spelling problem. We accept *sputnik* from the Russians and, by analogy, invent *beatnick*—or do we spell it, like Russian, *beatnik*? We devise something called *programed* learning, or do we spell it *programmed*? We have not yet decided, and we feel unsure of ourselves whichever we use.

The growth of the English vocabulary

The really important development of Modern English, the one that makes English almost more useful as a tool of civilization than any other language, is the proliferation of its vocabulary.

The most obvious explanation for the growth of the English vocabulary is that it has had to keep pace with new interests, ideas, and inventions. The growth of science is reflected in the expansion of our scientific vocabulary. Medicine has contributed *appendicitis, aspirin, iodine, insulin, adenoids, metabolism, proteins, anesthetic,* and hundreds more. Chemistry has contributed *alkali, creosote, radium,* and *cyanide;* physics has provided *calorie, electron,* and *relativity.* Psychology has popularized *egocentric, extrovert, behaviorism, inferiority complex,* and *psychoanalysis.* The automobile, radio, television, and motion-picture industries have made their numerous contributions.

SOURCES OF NEW WORDS: BORROWING

English speakers have not always been hospitable to foreign words, but early in the Renaissance scholars consciously began to enrich the relatively impoverished English vocabulary. The discovery of America, the reform of the Church, the Copernican theory, the spread of education, a burst of literary productivity unequaled before and hardly since, and many scientific developments placed prodigious stress on the language. The period was also marked by a new interest in Latin and Greek, and these classical languages were the sources of many new words. However, with the development of nationalism in the late Renaissance, critics objected to anything foreign, especially long Latin words, the so-called inkhorn terms. Again in the eighteenth century, a period with a strong desire for order and regulation, many people, including John Dryden, Jonathan Swift, Alexander Pope, and Thomas Sheridan, charged that English was being corrupted; they urged that it be restored to a polished, rational, and permanent form. This zeal for a "settled rule; an established standard," was one of the reasons Dr. Samuel Johnson began to prepare his dictionary.

In time the need for new words became so intense that the gates could not be kept closed. In spite of serious efforts, led by Jonathan Swift, to form an Academy that would attempt to preserve the purity of English, and although James Boswell credited Dr. Johnson's *A Dictionary of the English Language* (1755) with having conferred "stability on the language of his country," English has increasingly absorbed "loan words," as words from other languages are called. Contact with American Indians yielded *hickory, moccasin, toboggan,* and *papoose.* From the Spanish and Mexican came *chili, chocolate, canoe, hurricane, potato,* and *tobacco;* from Peru, *alpaca, jerky,* and *quinine;* from Brazil, *buccaneer, petunia,* and *tapioca.* When English speakers went to India, they came back with *bandana, bangle, bungalow, dinghy, jungle, loot, khaki, thug,* and *verandah.* From Africa came *banana, boorish, palaver,* and *zebra. Boomerang* and *kangaroo* came from Australia. *Camouflage* came from the French in World War I, *blitzkrieg* from the Germans in World War II, and *sputnik* from Russia in the Cold War. *Goulash* comes from Hungarian, *hacienda* from Spanish, *pajamas* from Urdu, and *robot* from Czech. As a result of American enthusiasm for Italian food and *la dolce vita,* we have *spaghetti, pizza, lasagna,* and *confetti;* from other impulses, but the same language, come *mafia* and *vendetta.*

SOURCES OF NEW WORDS: COINAGE

Through the years, new concepts have necessitated the invention of completely new words, for even other languages were unable to supply them. Some *neologisms* (new words) were made by adding familiar prefixes and suffixes to familiar roots, as in *transoceanic, postimpressionism, superman, submarine,* and *stardom.* Latin and Greek were tapped to make *orthodontia, bacteriology, immunology, endocrine,* and *ionization*—words that Caesar or Homer could have interpreted roughly but would not have understood.

Another source is called the *portmanteau word,* a word created by combining parts of two other words, as in *smog,* from *smoke* and *fog.* The word *gerrymander,* meaning to divide a voting area in a way that gives an unfair advantage to one political party, originated when such an attempt by Elbridge Gerry, a governor of Massachusetts, to redistrict Essex County was observed to look (on a map) like a salamander, thus "gerry-mander." From *Alice in Wonderland* came *chortle*, a blending of *chuckle* and *snort*. The *Oxford English Dictionary* first reported *brunch* in 1900, and it seems to be here for good. Other innovations, predominantly by *Time* and Walter Winchell (*alcoholiday, blessedeventing,* and *cinemactress*) seem less likely to endure.

Another group of words are proper names that have become common expressions. In 1759, Étienne de Silhouette, the French Minister of Finance, levied taxes so demanding that Frenchmen claimed only a shadow of their income was left; perhaps as a consequence the word *silhouette* has come to mean an outline drawing resembling a shadow. In 1880, Captain Charles Boycott was shunned by his servants, tenants, and neighbors for refusing to accept rents at the fixed figure; since then, *boycott* has come to mean to force someone to do something by preventing anyone from having dealings with him. During World War II, Vidkun Quisling, a Norwegian politician, betrayed his country and became its puppet ruler during the Nazi occupation; since then, a local leader who serves for an invading power is called a *quisling*. The term *McCarthyism* is used to label the use of indiscriminate and often unfounded accusations, sensationalism, and inquisitorial investigative methods, in "honor" of Senator Joseph McCarthy, to whom such practices were attributed. *Sandwich, paisley, sadism, lynch law, mackintosh,* and *raglan* have come into common usage via this route.

Some words were formed by *analogy,* that is on the same pattern as other words in existence; *addressograph* is made on the pattern of *phonograph* and *autograph, travelogue* on *dialogue. Bureaucrat* and *plutocrat* are formed by analogy to *aristocrat* and *autocrat.*

Another method of word formation is the *acronym.* In 1670 a plot against England supported by the unpopular Charles II was encouraged by a group of the King's advisers called the "Cabal," the title being made up of the first letters of the names of its members. Since then, *cabal* has come to mean a small group of persons joined in a secret design or scheme. Acronyms are now quite common, as demonstrated by *radar* (from "radio detection and ranging"), *loran* (from "long range"), and *laser* (from light amplification by stimulated emission of radiation).

Changes in English Studies Since 1500

Modern English grammar has been relatively stable over the centuries, although some simplification has taken place. Many pronouns have been dropped (*thou, thee*), and some verb endings have been changed (*hath* and *saith* have become *has* and *says*). Many other distinctions are being lost. Perhaps to avoid the choice between *whom* or *who*, for instance, many writers now use *that* to refer to people; until recently *that* would have been used only for things. Even language purists ignore the difference between *shall* and *will*, and not one college graduate in fifty can explain the "sequence of tenses"—formerly a preoccupation of English teachers.

Since today's nouns and pronouns have so few inflectional endings, their use in the sentence must be shown by their position. In Latin, no matter where a noun occurred, its use was clear because of its ending. In English, if we reverse the order of the nouns in the sentence "Dog bites man" we reverse the meaning. Adjectives must come very close to the words they modify or confusion results. Syntax is thus less flexible.

THE NEW LOOK IN LINGUISTICS

Although changes in grammar have been slight, the change in the way one looks at it has been very great. Grammar is defined as that branch of language study that classifies words and describes the changes in form, treatment, and position in the sentence that indicate the relationships and function of words. It is a very old discipline. Some of the earliest manuscripts extant are parts of a Sanskrit grammar by Panini, who lived some time between 400 and 200 B.C. Knowledge of grammar occupied a very high place in early scholarship, and it has continued to do so up to the present, ranking with knowledge of history and literature as one of the attributes of an educated man. The Greeks gave extensive attention to grammar; in their system of thought, it closely accompanied logic, since grammar was held to be logic in its most evident form.

Greek learning exerted a great effect on Latin learning, and the two together had a tremendous influence on education all over Europe. Grammar continued to be one of the most important parts of education, particularly since the only formal education available in the Western world (until perhaps 200 years ago) began with Latin and Greek and in many cases stopped with Latin and Greek.

Consequently, since scholars of the Middle Ages and the Renaissance were so completely convinced that the only true learning came from the classical languages and literature, the general view was that these languages were the most perfect, beautiful, and expressive that the world had ever known. Any other language, including English, was at best a poor rival and at worst a bastard, uncouth jargon that had no place in the mouths of educated men. The low repute of English continued through the sixteenth and seventeenth centuries and then, ironically, scholars in the eighteenth century tried to "purify" or "fix" the language, by which they meant to keep it the way it had always been. According to Albert C. Baugh in *History of the English Language*, grammarians in the eighteenth century attempted (1) to "codify the principles of the language and reduce it to rule; (2) to settle disputed points and decide cases of divided usage; and (3) to point out common errors or what were supposed to be errors, and thus correct and improve the language." These authorities were not content merely to be scholars; they wished to become law-givers. Robert Lowth (1762) wrote that the "plain way" to learn "propriety" in language was "to lay down rules, and to illustrate them by examples." The "law-givers" made pronouncements about such points of grammar as *older than I/older than me, shall/will, different from/different than, lie/lay,* and *it is I/it is me;* they condemned *this here* and *that there;* they condemned comparing an incomparable (they would have censured "in order to form a *more perfect* union"); and they denounced the double negative.

Not everyone accepted prescriptive rules. Possibly remembering Horace, who had written that "use is the sole arbiter and norm of speech," John Hughes, in 1698, wrote that general acceptance is the "only standard of speech." Dr. Johnson and Lord Chesterfield in the eighteenth century wrote to the same thesis. Chesterfield wrote, "Every language has its peculiarities; they are established by usage, and whether right or wrong, they must be complied with." Joseph Priestley wrote in 1761 that the "custom of speaking is the original and only just standard of any language." George Campbell, in his *Philosophy of Rhetoric* (1776) wrote: "Language is purely a species of fashion. . . . It is not the business of grammar, as some critics seem preposterously to imagine, to give law to the fashions which regulate our speech."

The clamor for "purity" prevailed, however, and during the next century and a half, hundreds of grammar books were written, most of them attacking various forms of "incorrectness." About 1915, influenced by the publication of Leonard Bloomfield's *Introduction to the Study of Language,* grammarians began to point out that a language kept in check by rules can only be artificial, bookish, and pedantic. This attack on a rule-based grammar was stimulated by the development of a new kind of language scholar, the structural linguist. These new linguists looked at English grammar and pointed out its inadequacy. Grammar during the Renaissance and eighteenth century, with its reliance on Latin and Greek, may have been meaningful to Ben Jonson and other scholars learned in the classical languages, but it had become decreasingly so. The linguists pointed out that great writers in English, from Chaucer, Shakespeare, and the translators of the King James *Bible* (1611) to the best modern writers, leaned more heavily upon the spoken, colloquial vernacular than they did on the language demanded by the "rules." Thus, the linguists contended, a student of writing can profit more from studying how the language is used than from learning the "rules."

They pointed out that the traditional system was inadequate. The definition of the adverb, for instance, is circular: "a word which modifies a verb, adjective, or another adverb." The traditional definition of a noun, "the name of a person, place, or thing," leaves unclassified such concepts as the first and last words in "Misery loves company." Traditional grammar is absolutely silent on some of the most significant aspects of the language, especially intonation. The sound of an utterance is very important to its meaning and to its analysis. That *stress*, the emphasis that is put on a syllable, is important is shown by the illustration, "I think that man is honest." This sentence, if pronounced with the stress on *that* means that a certain person is honest. If the stress is on *man*, we are speaking of man in general. The importance of *pitch*, the elevation or lowering of the voice, is shown by the response we might get to the statement, "The Giants are going to get a new manager." If a person says, "Who?" with rising pitch, the first speaker will answer, "The Giants." If the question is "Who?" with falling pitch, the first speaker will return with the name of the new manager. *Juncture*, the pause that occurs between words, is significant, as shown by the fact that the following expressions have quite different meanings: "see Mabel" and "seem able"; "cease taking" and "ceased aching"; "What's that up there on the road ahead?" and "What's that up there on the road? A head?"

About still another important aspect of language, *syntax*, or word order, traditional grammar is not helpful. Obviously, "awful pretty" differs in meaning from "pretty awful," but how do traditional grammar rules dictate the placement of modifiers?

Linguists' distress about traditional grammar reached a peak when American English assumed new status as an international language. Students of English as a second language were puzzled when they realized that "light house keeper" can have three different meanings, depending upon how it is pronounced: (1) a housekeeper who is not fat, (2) the keeper of a lighthouse, or (3) a lady who is employed to dust and iron, who, as the idiom goes, does "light housekeeping." Foreigners learning English were overwhelmed by the inconsistencies of the language, and prescriptive grammar rules were of little help. When engineers began to develop computers for translation, the traditional system was of little help to them. A computer cannot yet differentiate between such expressions as we have just been discussing. It would need pitch, stress, and juncture programmed into it.

The new linguists have attempted a scientific approach to language, their study being based on three principles: (1) Language consists of a set of behavior patterns common to the members of a given community. (2) Each language or dialect has its own unique system of behavior patterns, and thus, there is no "universal language." (3) Any linguistic science must have the essentials of any scientific theory: simplicity, consistency, completeness, and usefulness. The new linguists widened the field of interest assumed by the old grammar, believing that *spoken* language is the basis of language development, that dialect is an important aspect of language, and that spoken and written language are distinctly different dialects.

The structural linguist began his study by turning from the old emphasis on meaning. In a historically important observation, while discussing the traditional definition of a sentence—"a group of words containing a subject and predicate which express a complete thought"—Professor C. C. Fries reminded scholars that words that have no meaning could have all the attributes of a sentence. The words of Lewis Carroll, "The slithy toves did gyre and gimble in the wabe" have no meaning, but they obviously make up a sentence, with its parts easily identified. Its subject is *toves*; *wabe* is the object of a preposition; *slithy* is an adjective. Perhaps, the structural linguists said, a sentence should be analyzed by word form and position rather than by the meaning of its parts.

To analyze the form of words, the linguist begins by breaking up the flow of speech into basic sound-units, or *phones*. He selects phones used in the language he is analyzing and calls them *phonemes*, which, though used by the language, have no meaning by themselves. For instance, *mb* (at the beginning of a word as in *Mboya*) is not a phoneme of the English language; in Swahili, it is. In Urdu, *kh* as in *Khyber* is a phoneme; in English, it is not. According to one analysis, American English has forty-five phonemes. These phonemes are grouped into units that have meaning, called *morphemes*, for intance $[p/\epsilon/t]$ (pet). There are free morphemes, which by themselves are "words." There are also "bound morphemes" such as *un* and *pre*, which have meanings, but which must be tied to other morphemes. Initial *s* is a phoneme because of its ability to convert *lice* into *slice*, but it has no meaning exclusively its own. The terminal *s*, on the other hand, is a phoneme *and* a bound morpheme; it definitely has a meaning: added to almost any noun it forms a plural. The linguist surveys all possible combinations of morphemes and determines which of them belong on the word list of a language. He also studies how words are grouped into meaningful utterances, which is the content of grammar.

There are many new linguistic theories, the varieties being based on preoccupation with signals, slots, or "kernels." The "signals" linguist pays particular attention to special characteristic warnings. The word *the* means "noun coming." At the end of a word, *ed* probably means "past tense verb." A rise in pitch at the end of an utterance converts it to a question. A very hard stress on a word near the beginning of the utterance may mean "this is the subject."

The "slots" linguist will point out that if a word can be moved about in the sentence, "John ate," it is probably an adverb. (Slowly John ate; John slowly ate; and John ate slowly.) A subject is what fits into the slots before the verb, as in: "——————— ran," or "——————— exists." Slot and substitution theories are now refined to a study of "tagmemes," defined as "slots in a system where substitution is possible."

A more complicated linguistic theory has been developed to overcome the deficiency of these linguistic analyses—i.e., that they are based only on "immediate constituents." Signals and slots are understandable in a sentence where the complete subject is found at one spot and the complete predicate at another, but in the sentence, "Did you go home?," the slots and signals are confused; in this case, the verb is not an immediate constituent but is found in two different places in the sentence. This linguist therefore classifies all sentences into *kernel sentences* and *transformed sentences*. "Mary loves John" is a kernel sentence from which the following and many other transformed sentences are possible:

Did Mary love John?	*Who loves John?*
Mary doesn't love John.	*Whom did Mary love?*
Mary did love John.	*When did Mary love John?*

The transformation linguist, who is also called a "generative linguist" because the kernel sentences "generate" subsequent sentences, is attempting to analyze all kernel structures and to determine the possible structures into which they can be transformed and still be meaningful English utterances. In contrast to descriptive grammars, which only inventory, transformational or generative grammar attempts to predict the acceptable possibilities.

The new grammar is not yet what its proponents hope it will be, a solid science. In a gentlemanly way, the tagmemists joust with the transformationalists, and they both disdain the signalists. But there is already much profit from the "New Look" linguists. They have pointed out the importance of going beyond "meaning" into word order, function words, and inflections. They provide hints of understandings that will facilitate the teaching of English, especially as a foreign language. The new look has replaced much vague and sloppy thinking and terminology by more clear and precise analysis. What used to be known as an "ungrammatical sentence," a violation of good breeding, is now recognized as a breakdown between form and meaning that only needs to be rephrased to convey the proper meaning and secure the appropriate response—not a laugh, a question, or an uplifted eyebrow, but "I understand."

Along with this change in attitude toward the language came a subsequent new look at punctuation. As long as there has been written communication there has been some kind of marking for clarification or additional meaning, but the practices have been arbitrary and they have changed. In ancient Greece, the semicolon was used where we use a question mark; in modern Spain, the question mark and exclamation point are put both before and after the sentence. For centuries, writers and printers inserted punctuation for a myriad of reasons, but in Venice (*ca.* 1490) the publisher Aldus Manutius began putting out such beautiful editions of the classics under his Anchor and Dolphin imprint that he has influenced printers ever since. Two of his innovations were the *italics* font of print and standardized punctuation. He is called, justifiably, the father of modern punctuation, his system being close to the conventions of today.

In the eighteenth century, writers became as obsessed with rules for punctuation as they were for grammar, and the matter was reduced to a formula. More concerned with meter than they were with intonation, juncture, or pitch, the rules were: use the comma for a pause of one time count, the semicolon for a pause of two time counts, the colon for a count of three, and the period for a count of four.

A different phrasing of the edict, one-fourth of a stop for a comma, and so on, explains why in England the period is still called a "full stop." In the nineteenth century, punctuation was often used so profusely, to follow the rambling, spontaneous thoughts of Romantic novelists and essayists, that it hindered rather than helped. Excesses became so common that H. W. Fowler felt constrained to warn that "Anyone who finds himself putting down several commas close together should reflect that he is making himself disagreeable, and question his conscience, as severely as we ought to do about disagreeable conduct in real life."

The new look at punctuation has been as much conditioned by the modern American character as it has by the new linguists. The national desire for speed and efficiency has resulted in sentences so short and clipped, especially in newspapers, that little internal punctuation is necessary. Many linguists, influenced by the rediscovery that oral speech is the natural speech, now insist that punctuation is what you hear; it should reflect pitch, intonation, and juncture. Other authorities accept its relation to sound, but go on to point out that the sound contains meaning, and punctuation should reflect that meaning. The colon means "something coming." The semicolon says, "I am joining related balanced ideas." Paired and raised commas say, "We are enclosing an expression to separate it from other ideas on both sides of us."

THE STORM OVER THE DICTIONARY

As important as all these developments have been, of at least equal importance has been a change in attitude toward the dictionary. Probably the most dramatic evidence of this change—and the opposition to it—was the publication of a certain dictionary in 1961. The events leading up to it are instructive.

The growth and evolution of the English language has made necessary a series of new dictionaries. The English vocabulary of 50,000–60,000 words in Anglo-Saxon expanded to 100,000–125,000 words in Middle English and to about 650,000 words in Modern English.

The English dictionary began with the *glosses* that appeared either between the lines or in the margins of early medieval Latin manuscripts. English words were inked in to show the meaning of difficult Latin words. The first wordbooks were simply lists of these Latin terms with their meanings expressed in simpler, more familiar Latin, and later in the native English of the time. These Latin-English glosses were expanded throughout the Middle English period, with a 1499 version finally placing the English term before the Latin equivalent. During the Renaissance, interest in trade and travel made further foreign-language dictionaries necessary, examples being Welsh-English, English-Spanish, and perhaps the best known, Florio's Italian-English dictionary of 1599. During the early Renaissance (*ca.* 1560), interest in Latin and Greek brought a flood of esoteric words into English. The deluge became so great that no one could read scholarly or literary writing without a good background in Latin and Greek —or a glossary such as Cockeram's *The English Dictionary: An Interpreter of Hard Words* (1623).

In the eighteenth century, hard-word dictionaries were replaced by dictionaries whose editors were sure that English was then ideal for any literary effort. They believed that its purity must be protected from vulgar innovations. Dr. Samuel Johnson began his work with this purpose in mind. As he proceeded with his "arduous post," Dr. Johnson realized that he had made a mistake. He lamented to his friend Boswell that he could not determine the best pronunciations from "the best company because they differ so much among themselves." When the book finally appeared in 1755, Dr. Johnson wrote that he had dreamed of permanently purifying and regulating the language, but that he finally found it impossible to embalm something that was living and changing. "Words are the daughters of the earth," he concluded, and they could not be completely "brought to book."

Thus began the conflict between two traditions, one contending that the function of a dictionary is to be the "supreme authority" of the language and the other that it is the function of the lexicographer to be an objective historian, a recorder of the language. The two traditions came to be called, respectively, *prescriptive* and *descriptive*.

In America, the *prescriptive* responsibility was first assumed in 1828 by Noah Webster under the title *An American Dictionary of the English Language*. Webster insisted on American spellings and on keying his definitions to American history and events. His work had a historical-descriptive aura, but in temperament and technique Webster was an eighteenth-century purist, a stance that subsequent publications adopted when they claimed in their advertising to be the "supreme authority" of the American language. In 1934, *Webster's New International Dictionary of the English Language* (second edition) was so well received that it did almost become the final authority.

In England, the most distinguished proponent of the *descriptive* tradition has been the *New English Dictionary* (1836, 1858, 1888, 1928, 1933), also called the *Oxford English Dictionary*, and therefore abbreviated either *NED* or *OED*. The *OED*'s manifesto contained the pronouncement that it "embraces not only the standard language of literature and conversation, whether current at the moment or obsolete, or archaic, but also the main technical vocabulary, and a large measure of dialectal usage."

After the *OED*, American lexicographers, setting out to chronicle the development of the American language, published the *Dictionary of American English on Historical Principles* in 1944. Its rejection of authoritarian principles brought it scholarly approval and popular attack. "Limey Dopes Yank Talk" headlined the *Chicago Tribune*, offended by the fact that it was edited by an Englishman, Sir William Craigie. Since then, a *Dictionary of Americanisms on Historical Principles*, edited by Mitford M. Mathews and published in 1951, has continued the descriptive-usage tradition. These two publications were relatively obscure and purchased mostly by scholars. In September, 1961, the *Webster's Third New International Dictionary* brought on the storm.

The publication of a dictionary is not ordinarily an event to upset a nation, but Webster's 3, as it is called, caused what one newspaper termed a "furore greater than nuclear fallout." (*Berkshire Eagle*, March 8, 1962). The *Toronto Globe and Mail* (September 8, 1961) complained that some entries "will comfort the ignorant, confer approval upon the mediocre, and subtly imply that proper English is the tool only of the snob." The *Washington*

Sunday Star (September 10, 1961) fussed that the dictionary "tolerated the debasement of its language." The *Saturday Review* (September 30, 1961) commented that "permissiveness, now on the wane 'n child-rearing, has caught up with the dictionary-makers," a development *The New York Times* (October 12, 1961) found disastrous because "it serves to reinforce the notion that good English is whatever is popular." *Time* (October 6, 1961) noted that the dictionary had vacated its place as "a Supreme Court of language" and become "a Social Register of words." Several publications officially rejected the *W3*. Saying "it is no more snobbish to insist that words be used correctly than it is finicky to insist that chisels be sharp," *The Nation* announced (March 10, 1962), that "this magazine will continue to cite the Second Edition of the *Webster's International* as its authority." On its staff bulletin board, *The New York Times* decreed, "Editors representing the news, Sunday, and editorial departments have decided without dissent to continue to follow Webster's Second Edition for spelling and usage." *Life* (October 27, 1961) wrote, "We're not opposed to progress, but we'll just keep Webster's Second Edition around awhile for little matters of style, good English, winning at Scrabble, and suchwise." The *Washington Post* (January 17, 1962) advised its readers, "If you love truth, accuracy, and a little grammar to improve your speech or writing, you had better 'hang on' to your battered and dog-eared second edition."

Much of the opposition was good-natured, with Sydney J. Harris using words "approved" by the dictionary to comment, "wordwise it's a gasser," and lampooning it for relying on "such authorities as Art Linkletter, Polly Adler, Willie Mays, and Mickey Spillane." (Chicago *Daily News*, October 20, 1961). Several editors entertained at least themselves by writing paragraphs with words supposedly approved by the *W3*.

> A passel of double-domes at the G. C. Merriam Company joint in Springfield, Mass., have been confabbing and yakking twenty-seven years—which is not intended to infer that they have not been doing plenty of work—and now they have finalized *Webster's Third New International Dictionary, Unabridged*, a new edition of that swell and esteemed word book. *The New York Times*, October 12, 1961.

> Irregardless of the enormity of the upsurge, none of us are able, governmentwise, in a time of normalcy, to act like we can ignore it; we don't mean to infer otherwise in saying so. *Life*, October 27, 1961.

Some of the criticism was irrelevant, and some was downright unfair and erroneous—including the charge that the *W3* had given a "blanket endorsement" to such words as *ain't* and *irregardless*—but the following comments illustrate what was really at issue in the controversy. Varying from sober to violent in reaction, *The New York Times,* the *Washington Post,* the *Saturday Review*—at least in the person of John Ciardi—*Life,* the *American Bar Association Journal,* and the *Library Journal* took exception to what they regarded as a serious lowering of standards. *The Nation* (March 10, 1962) lamented that the editors [of the dictionary] had defected from their "duty to defend the niceties of the language against the erosion of vulgar usage." In the *Detroit News* (February 10, 1962) the Rt. Rev. Richard S. Emrich complained that "the greatest language on earth has lost its guardian." In defense of the book on this particular issue the editors of the *St. Louis Post-Dispatch* (December 17, 1961) wrote, "The critical reaction to *Webster's Third New International Dictionary* has revealed a cultural lag in unexpected places . . . a misconception of the purpose of a dictionary." Recognizing the issue and taking his stand, Dwight Macdonald wrote,

> [Since the Second Edition] a revolution has taken place in the study of grammar and usage, a revolution that probably represents an advance in scientific method but that certainly has had an unfortunate effect on such unscientific activities as the teaching of English and the making of dictionaries—at least on the making of this particular dictionary. The scientific revolution has meshed gears with a trend toward permissiveness, in the name of democracy, that is debasing our language by rendering it less precise and thus less effective as literature and less efficient as communication. It is felt that it is snobbish to insist on making discrimination—the very word has acquired a Jim Crow flavor—about usage. And it assumed that true democracy means that the majority is right. This feeling seems to me sentimental and this assumption unfounded. *The New Yorker,* March 10, 1962.

To be sure, W3 had its vigorous defenders. An editor of the *Christian Science Monitor* (November 29, 1961) called it an "intensely interesting and distinguished scholarly work, an important milestone in the history of a particularly living, flexible, and beautiful language." The *Louisville Times* (October 18, 1961) called it "a staggering accomplishment; no language watcher can fail to be awed by its virtues." Randolph Quirk called it "this magnificent and meticulously complete register of English vocabulary . . . a large and noble book." Moray McLaren (*The Scotsman,* March 10, 1962) labeled it "the most staggeringly erudite work I have ever seen." As a rule, the more a writer knew about the language the less he complained about W3. In the *Atlantic Monthly* (May, 1962) Bergen Evans concluded that "anyone who solemnly announces in the year 1962 that he will be guided by a dictionary published in 1934 is talking ignorant and pretentious nonsense."

By now the criticism has nearly ceased and the considered judgment of professional linguists is that W3 is an impressive and commendable addition to the history of lexicography.

English as an international language

Frequently, as American businessmen, educators, and military and government personnel are stationed abroad, they are denied the opportunity to learn and use the native language. Idealistically desiring not to be "Ugly Americans," they resolutely set out to use nothing but the language of their host country. Instead, their hosts insist on using English. In many countries, the knowledge of English is a status symbol. Whether they like Americans or not, many people are insulted to be thought so uneducated as not to know English. This is not to suggest that Americans should not learn other languages, but it does suggest the possibility that English is becoming an international language. Is this so, or is it likely to become so?

Few will deny that there is a need for an international language. Historically, for trade, literature, diplomacy, invention, science, and travel, men have needed to talk to each other across national and linguistic borders.

Linguistically, English has serious deficiencies as an international language. Its flexibility often turns out to be a trap for the foreigner, who would prefer a set of simple, learnable patterns to the idiomatic variations of English. Its spelling is more whimsical than that of most other languages. There are too many irregular verb forms, some of them very illogical. Foreigners are confused by the dialects of different areas, by slang, and by the rapidly changing vocabulary. The vocabulary has an eclectic quality that makes some words easy and familiar, but there is equal certainty that every learner will find some very difficult words, especially when they are homonyms. Think of the meanings of the word *fast*, for instance.

If an international language were to be selected purely on linguistic considerations, it is possible that Spanish would be the most likely choice. There are no hidden sounds; every letter is sounded, and sounded consistently. As for simplicity of spelling, Spanish (or Italian, Finnish, or

Hungarian) would be more satisfactory than English. In addition, Spanish grammatical forms are relatively consistent, and its vocabulary reasonably extensive. Certainly among American students, Spanish is usually considered the easiest foreign language to master, and speakers of many other tongues agree. One Punjabi, for instance, found Russian easier to learn than English, and Spanish easiest of the three.

It is not likely, however, that if there is ever a universal language, it will be adopted on purely linguistic considerations. People react to the cultural consciousness that comes with language. Indonesians, when they drove out the Dutch, militantly obliterated most traces of the Dutch language, even though they set their country back immeasurably in education and military efficiency. China and Russia oppose the spread of English, for obvious reasons.

Attempts have been made to construct an absolutely neutral language, but so far none of the three most important, Interlingua, Esperanto, or Basic English, has been successful. Any natural language starts with a great number of speakers, but a constructed language has none. Actually, the constructed languages tend to be zonal rather than international. A speaker with a knowledge of French, Italian, Latin, Spanish or even English has a much faster start learning Interlingua than a Chinese, for instance. Basic English has not been met enthusiastically even by the English-speaking peoples. The 850 words in the basic vocabulary provide a rather unlovely flow of sound, *endure* becoming *put up with* and Winston Churchill's famous "blood, sweat, and tears," an eloquent and earthy phrase, becoming "blood, body-water, and eye-wash." Then too, critics complain that it is just as difficult to unlearn their own vocabulary and limit themselves to so few expressions as it is to learn, say, Spanish.

Communist countries, perhaps consciously, fight the cultural accompaniment of English by developing zonal languages, a combination of Slavic and Russian sufficing for the Russian sphere and a blend of Cantonese, Peking, and Mandarin Chinese being supported by the People's Republic of China. But even Russian scientists and sociologists admit that they need to keep up on international research, and all over the world, humanity gropes toward a satisfactory single universal language.

During the medieval period and early Renaissance in Europe, Latin, the language of the Roman Empire and Catholic Church, was the logical choice. In the twelfth century, a language originating near Calcutta and now most closely represented by Urdu and Hindi, began to be a *lingua franca* from Spain south along the Mediterranean coast and east to what is now East Pakistan. A polyglot language, its present name comes from the Turkish word for "camp" or "army" and is related to *horde* via the German and perhaps *order* and *ordnance* via Latin and French. Its vocabulary is largely Arabic and Persian, but it contains many Spanish words including *mesa* (table), *peon* (peasant), and *padre* (father, or priest). It was spread by Islamic missionaries, warriors, and traders, especially the Moors, who spread their language, like their religion, by the sword. *Urdu*, written in Arabic script by Muslims and in Sanskrit by Hindus (and called *Hindi*) is still spoken by at least a hundred million people.

In the nineteenth century, French, because of its great literature, the conquests of Napoleon, and the "snob appeal" of the language left from when the French were the upper class of England, was the international language at least of diplomats.

In the twentieth century, English has almost become an international tongue. There is no denying its wide usage. At the United Nations the official languages on translation channels are English, Russian, French, Chinese, and Spanish—but English is used most often. In Oslo, Moscow, Beirut, Paris, Zurich, Hong Kong, and Tokyo, internationally important scientific papers are most often read in English. American films, without native-language subtitles, play in Rawalpindi,   New Delhi, Bangkok, and Saigon. As far as numbers of native speakers are concerned, English is probably second only to North Chinese. In geographic distribution and as a second language, in commerce, education, literary scholarship, industry, economics, and diplomacy, English is unquestionably first. It is spoken by approximately 270 million people as a native language and approximately another 30 million as a second tongue. It is now the first foreign language taught in almost all countries, including France, Holland, Norway, India, and Pakistan. Americans visiting Russia are often amused when their interpreters switch easily from Bronx English to Texas English —amused and then startled at the thought of what good spies the interpreters would make.

The spread of English has resulted from many circumstances. One is what might be called "situational English." Throughout the western Pacific a form of very simple English, called "Sandalwood," was developed by American missionaries and traders, as was Pidgin English in China, Japan, and some Pacific islands, the latter with a big assist from American G.I.'s in World War II. From Kabul to Bombay, beginning in the eighteenth century, the British talked to their servants in a tongue called "Babu English." Like Sandalwood and Pidgin, Babu is an impressionistic mixture. The sentence, "He esspilt chae (tea) all ovah my veddy best cupra (coat)," demonstrates its eclectic nature, the pronunciation for "spilled" reflecting the difficulty the Babu has with an initial *s* sound, the pronunciation of *over* and *very* demonstrating the British contribution, and the words for *tea* and *coat* coming from Pushtu and Hindi.

In the twentieth century two other forms of situational English are developing, one by tacit agreement among scientists and the other as a result of a formal international agreement of airline pilots. Scholarly scientific periodicals, even though published in Geneva, Amsterdam, and Berlin, are more and more being set in English. The language is basic, its vocabulary deliberately limited and synonyms arbitrarily ruled out. There are only two tenses, experiments being described in the past passive voice, and conclusions stated in the present tense. The second new language, International Pilots' English, is really only a jargon. The vocabulary is limited to about 800 words, and words are pronounced in such a way as to give them the highest possible "survival value," *five* being pronounced *fife* because that form can be heard better over radio background noise. A purist would disdain the grammar: "I read you loud and clear, Five by Five" for "I hear you as loudly as the capabilities of my equipment permit." Pilots' English demonstrates, once again, the ability of one language to absorb words from other languages. When a pilot uses the international air distress signal, "Mayday! Mayday!" he is not speaking English at all. He is speaking fractured French, for the word comes from "*M'aidez*," a form of *aider*, meaning "Help me."

Having learned one of the situational forms of English, whether it be Pidgin or Pilots', its user almost inevitably goes on to increase his vocabulary and perhaps to adopt the more complex grammatical forms. He is, willy-nilly, soon a speaker of English.

A second reason for the international use of English stems from certain circumstances in the newly emergent countries of Asia and Africa. When the British Empire began to fragment, the new countries that emerged hoped to jettison English and use a native language—only to find that a universal native language was not in existence or was too limited in vocabulary. In Pakistan, natives of the east province speak Bengali and those from the west speak Urdu, Pushtu, Punjabi, Sindi, or one of several other languages or dialects. At the height of the recent pro-Red China, anti-American feeling, the Pakistan National Assembly was being conducted in English, the Urdu speakers being more fearful of losing out to the Bengali speakers than they were of being influenced by English. India has at least 385 different dialects whose users frequently cannot communicate with each other. In many new countries the users of native tongues prefer being unified by the language of their former "oppressors" rather than giving up their own dialect for that of a near neighbor, whom they distrust even more than they do the departed colonials. Equally important, the native tongues tend to be deficient in the new scientific and technical terminology. Thus, the new countries have often been forced to use English in self-defense.

A third factor in the spread of English is the ubiquitous nature of its users. When the Bengali *babu* wanted to work for the British, he had to learn English. When Pacific Islanders wanted to sell their aromatic sandalwood, they had to learn at least a form of English. It is just as true today; economic, educational, scientific, and cultural power still are forces for language distribution, and a foreign diplomat, industrialist, educator, or soldier ignores English at the peril of his own professional advancement. In a very real sense, the spread of American tourists, diplomats, soldiers, advisers, and dollars to foreign shores has created a market and a source of information that can be tapped only by those who understand English. By the same token, the educational opportunities that exist in America and England make English a key to opportunity too valuable to be ignored by any ambitious student.

The name of a thing tends to come from the language of the country where it was developed, which is why the Danes go to a "swimming pool" and the French eat "le hot dog." An English-speaking physicist invented a jar to hold liquid oxygen, which is primarily manufactured in England and America; now, all over the world, *lox* is kept in *dewars*, the former word being a portmanteau word made from *l*iquid *ox*ygen, and the vessel being named for the scientist, Sir James Dewar. If only because they have so much more money than their counterparts in other countries, American industry, universities, and government are developing many new products and concepts. When these go to the rest of the world, they arrive with English names.

Conclusion

There is much value in a writer's being sensitive to the fact that in its fifteen hundred years of existence the English language has demonstrated its suitability for great dramatic, poetic, and prose literature, stirring oratory, and exact scientific prose. It has reflected the nature of its people in each era, the inventiveness and creativity of the Renaissance, the order of the Augustan age, the spontaneity of the nineteenth century, and the scientific materialism of the twentieth century. Perhaps perceiving its dynamic nature is the single most important lesson that can come from a study of its history. The writer who is sensitive to what is happening to his language is the one who can use it most effectively.

All around him he perceives the excitement of a living, developing language. He watches *astronaut* being coined from a classical language and *maser* being made as an acronym (from *m*icrowave *a*mplification by *s*timulated *e*mission of *r*adiation). He observes the gradual extinction of the old regional differences in American speech under the influence of radio, television, the mobility of American life, and popular education; he watches Standard American becoming the general American dialect just as surely as London English became the general and literary tongue of England. He watches with amusement when some prescriptivists try to preserve customs that never existed. He watches overly careful speakers pronounce *either* as *eye-ther,* even though it has no historical justification and even though the speakers succeed only in sounding affected.

He does not become careless or slovenly. As fine a tool as English deserves the most discriminating use. Using English expertly, he can achieve goals absolutely shut off from him otherwise. In many other pursuits, the best tools are often too expensive to use. English, free to all, is a fine tool that it is expensive *not* to use.

Projects

1. In order to understand the history and nature of language, you should be able to define and illustrate the concepts listed below. If necessary, refine your definitions and perceptions by referring to a good dictionary.

acronym	Indo-European	pitch
Anglo-Saxon	inflection	"pooh-pooh" theory
basic vocabulary	international language	prefix
borrowings	intonation	prescriptive
"bow-wow" theory	kernel sentence	Romance languages
cognate	language	scientific tradition
coinage	lexicography	sign language
descriptive	lexicon	"splash-wave" theory
dialect	linguistics	stress
dictionary	loan words	structural linguistics
"ding-dong" theory	London Standard	suffix
etymology	loss of inflection	syntax
Germanic languages	Middle English	tagmemes
glossary	morphemes	transformational
grammar	neologism	grammar
grammatical slots	OED/NED	usage
Grimm's Law	phonemes	W3
hypothetical word	pictograph	zonal language

2. In order to contribute to class discussion, prepare lists of the following:

a. acronyms

b. words to replace lost positives, the words being derived from existing negatives. Examples: *ane (from inane), *cessant, *couth, *sipid, *imical, *scrutable, *peachable, *consolate
c. blends (or portmanteau words)
d. inconsistent or illogical constructions
e. possible false analogical patterns for verbs (know-knowed, bring-brang-brung)

3. Invent one word that you think the language needs. Be able to explain how you derived the word, why it is needed, and how it would be conjugated if a verb or compared if an adjective or adverb. Some thoughts: What is a better word than *pedestrian?* What is a verb to describe becoming a delinquent? To *delink?* What do you call a person who does not belong to a fraternity or sorority? Some campuses contrast the Greeks to the Barbarians. Can you do better? The old division of conservative and liberal seems to be confused. Can you think up a better pair of words to cover habitual splits in arguments about politics?

4. To fill in your knowledge of the whole phenomenon of communication, prepare a short paper or a report for the class on any one of the following subjects:

a. The History of the Alphabet
b. The Speech Mechanism
c. The History of "Capitalism" (or any other abstract word)
d. Examples of Extension, Restriction, Pejoration, and Amelioration
e. The Communication Theory of Shannon and Weaver

5. Collecting illogical English idioms is an interesting pastime, and it is often amusing to analyze them. Considering them grammatically and literally, what do you think of the ones listed below? You may want to start a collection of puzzlers.

to put up with	to tinker with
Now, then . . .	He is on time.
to come in handy	in fact
to see one off	free and easy
to catch fire	fair and square
strike a bargain	to be given a bum steer
takes after her father	to set a table
hard put to it	to run for office
to tamper with	

6. *Fractured formations.* Newspaper advertising has announced the availability of "paper table linen," "plastic dining silver," "aluminum drinking glasses," a "monokini bathing suit," "topless waitresses," and a refrigerator that makes "round ice cubes." Comment on the contradictions in these expressions and explain their origin.

7a. One of the points we have wanted to make in this chapter has been that, except for the relatively few cases of onomatopoeia in the English lexicon, there is no necessary relationship between the sound and meaning of English words. The next time you are in the company of some foreigners or world travelers, you can demonstrate this by asking them how various sounds are shown in different languages. In America, a rooster, we think, says "cock-a-doodle-doo," but in Germany he wakes up the farm by saying "kikeriki." A French rooster says "coquerico." In Germany, instead of pealing "ding-dong," a bell says "bim-bam." Foreigners seem to be quite confused about what dogs say. We know that they say "bow-wow," but the Germans think they say "wau-wau." The French are completely mistaken; they think that Fido says "gnaf-gnaf." Ask your foreign friends how animals and bells talk in their languages.

7b. Another interesting topic of conversation with foreigners is the subject of syntax or word order. Ask your foreign friends how they would translate this sentence (which is a direct translation into English from the strictly ordered Persian): "Abdul for a visit in the morning on the bus to Kabul went." Americans will have several possible versions, but some speakers, for instance a German, may have only one possible plan for some units in the sentence. Another sentence for contrast is "I am hungry." The Spanish say, "I have hunger."

8. Select a short poem written before 1900. Using the *OED*, check all the words to see whether the poet might have intended meanings that are not evident today. Make a report to the class about any appropriate observations. Even if you have found no changes or cleared up no confusions, your negative report will be valuable; for instance, you might report that all the words in Andrew Marvell's "To His Coy Mistress" can be interpreted according to today's dictionary.

9. Write a 500-word theme called "Names on the Land." You will need a detailed map, a good atlas, and a history of the region. After some preliminary observations, classify the names of towns, cities, counties, and states. You may wish to have such classifications as Indian names, hero names, names from foreign countries, humorous names, and virtue names. In your theme correlate the names with the history of the area. Some suggestions:

a. The Influence of Spain and Mexico in the Settling of the Southwest.
b. German Influence in Pennsylvania.
c. French Influence in the Mississippi Valley and Louisiana.
d. Indian Names.
e. The Decreasing Influence of England with the Westward Movement of Settlers.
f. The Pairing of the Names Jasper and Newton.
g. Western Humor as Demonstrated by Place Names.
h. An American Atlas of Place Names.
i. "The Thin Red Line": British names in Asia (or China, or Africa).

10. From some documents prepared during the Renaissance, for instance the King James Bible (1611) or some plays of Shakespeare, make a list of words and grammatical structures that are used today. You may, in particular, look for expressions that today would be called "bad grammar." If necessary, check their meanings at the time of writing by referring to the *OED*. You may also want to refer to *A Shakespearian Grammar* by Edwin A. Abbott. Write a 500-word theme classifying the obsolete expressions and attempting to explain the movement of English away from them. What general development in English do the losses parallel?

11. Make a list of all the slang expressions, jargon, speech variants, and other characteristics you can find in the speech of your friends. Then classify your findings and write a theme in which you analyze the influences upon their speech.

12. Write a 500-word theme evaluating the three most popular college desk dictionaries, *Webster's New Collegiate Dictionary*, the *American College Dictionary*, and *Webster's New World Dictionary*. You might select a hundred words classified according to some basis you think important, for instance, scientific, slang, literary, everyday, new, and difficult. The classes may overlap, Then make a decision as to which dictionary you prefer and try to justify your decision. You may decide that you find them equally helpful, or you may find one superior in some respects but deficient in others; in all cases, defend your decision.

Further reading

ALLEN, HAROLD B. *Readings in Applied English Linguistics*. New York: Appleton-Century-Crofts, 1958.

ANDERSON, WALLACE L., and STAGEBERG, NORMAN C. *Introductory Readings on Language*. Rev. ed. New York: Holt, Rinehart and Winston, 1962.

DEAN, LEONARD F., and WILSON, KENNETH G. *Essays on Language and Usage*. 2d ed. New York and London: Oxford University Press, 1963.

EVANS, BERGEN and CORNELIA. *A Dictionary of Contemporary American Usage*. New York: Random House, 1957.

PARTRIDGE, ERIC. *Usage and Abusage*. 5th ed. New York: London House & Maxwell, 1957.

PYLES, THOMAS. *Words and Ways of American English*. New York: Random House, 1952.

English. 2d ed. Englewood Cliffs, N.J.: Prentice-Hall, 1954.
ROBERTSON, STUART, and CASSIDY, FREDERIC G. *The Development of Modern*

SLEDD, JAMES, and EBBITT, WILMA R. *Dictionaries and That Dictionary*. Chicago: Scott, Foresman, 1962.

CHAPTER 8

EPISTEMOLOGY AND LOGIC

Nothing is so dull as logic, and nothing is so important. WILL DURANT. *The lack of instruction in logic is one of the most serious blemishes in modern education. Certainly a rhetoric which fails to make the fullest use of logic is a shadowy thing.* DONALD L. CLARK, *Rhetoric in Greco-Roman Education,* 1957.

According to some learning theorists, any problem has three perspectives. When we look directly at a problem by itself we get only what is called *particle perspective.* For instance, if a traffic commissioner trying to prevent congestion at any one corner has only particle perspective, he might try to solve the problem by the way he times his traffic light. If he widens his view and observes that traffic runs parallel along certain streets and then intersects, and that the traffic is worse at some hours than at others, he is attempting to achieve *field perspective.* If the traffic engineer looks at the problem historically, both to the past and to the future, he is seeking *wave perspective.* For instance, he may profit by the information that there was no problem at this point until a new turnpike opened and poured cars into the intersection. He may learn that since a huge defense plant in the area is soon to be closed there will be no problem in the future.

Looking at the problem exclusively gives particle perspective;

looking at it in its surroundings gives field perspective; looking at it historically with special attention to its causes and effects gives wave perspective. A group of community leaders trying to settle some problem of race tensions might say, "We do not care how the problem started, and we do not care what the situation is in Alabama or Chicago; we want to face up to our own problem now." They would deliberately be seeking particle perspective. On the other hand, a West German industrialist interested in introducing credit cards to Germany suspects that credit cards may not work in Germany, and thus he decides to compare the American and German economic systems, banking procedures, advertising, and the state of the market. He needs field perspective. A statistician for the U.S. Public Health Service specializes in the history of certain diseases. Observing that the incidence of venereal disease increases in wartime, he recommends certain precautions during such periods. He has wave perspective.

For a complete understanding of any given problem we need all three perspectives, but there may be times when any one perspective is more relevant and necessary. In our study of writing in Part I of this book, we keep our attention on particle perspective, the immediate writing situation at an immediate time. In Part II, we are seeking other perspectives. In Chapter 7, "Language: Past, Present, and Future," we sought field and wave perspective. In this chapter, we continue to expand our view.

To write well, we obviously need to be able to think well. To think well, we need to understand the process of effective thought, which is a useful definition of logic. To understand logic, we must have particle, field, and wave perspective. Twentieth-century logicians focus their efforts on an attempt to go beyond the limitations of Aristotelian logic. In the seventeenth century, Francis Bacon tried to develop induction as a potentially creative alternative to logical processes based solely on form. The directions Bacon took for his reform anticipated the channels of modern contemplation, a concern for language, for fallacies (Bacon called them

Idols), and for information theory. All this is wave perspective. To understand logic, we need as a base an understanding of the nature and source of knowledge, which is a workable definition of epistemology. Such a study will give us our field perspective. Putting this study of epistemology and logic into the context established by our study of language should give us aid in solving some of the problems of writing. The study of logic begins with Aristotle.

Aristotle and syllogistic reasoning

For a scholar and intellectual, Aristotle (384–322 B.C.) was born in an ideal world. The son of the court physician for Philip II of Macedonia, he had every opportunity to learn. At the age of eighteen he went to Athens to study at Plato's Academy and remained there for the next two decades. During the twenty years he spent in Athens he was introduced to the world of the mind, particularly Plato's concept that true reality subsists in universal Ideas, external to any individual mind, but he was permitted to differ, and he emerged much more interested than were Plato and *his* teacher, Socrates, in the world as it is knowable through the senses.

In 343 B.C., Aristotle returned to Macedonia to tutor Alexander, the young son of Philip II. Alexander succeeded his father in 336, subdued the restive cities of Greece, and set out to conquer Persia. Few scholars in history have had so useful a patron as Alexander became for Aristotle. Alexander wished to further Greek learning and culture, and when he sacked Thebes the only home he left standing belonged to Pindar the poet. We are told that, wherever he slept, whether on the battlefields of Persia, northern Africa, or Central Asia, he kept a copy of Homer's *Iliad* under his pillow. After conquering almost all of the world known at the time, he built Greek cities after the model of Athens, beginning with temples and libraries.

Until the latter years of their lives, Alexander's support of Aristotle was complete. The young king subsidized Aristotle's grand dream of a center of all knowledge in Athens, and for thirteen years students were attracted from all parts of the empire to Aristotle's Lyceum.

The essence of man is man thinking, and to understand thought one must understand Aristotle. Fifteen hundred years after his death, he greatly influenced the Renaissance. Eighteen hundred years after he died, scientists studying anatomy had to start with Aristotle's concepts. After twenty-two centuries, a group of mathematicians trying to refine logic started with Aristotle. His influence on art and literature has been as pervasive as on logic and science: Leonardo da Vinci and Michelangelo worked within Aristotle's concept of the human figure; even today, many literary and art critics use Aristotle's system of analysis.

As Aristotle talked and taught, it was his habit to walk with students among the groves of the Lyceum; as a result his school of thought or philosophy came to be known as peripatetic. Since the days of Socrates, philosophy had meant "all knowledge," but to Aristotle it meant something more limited. For him, philosophy was the study of the method of thought. In contrast to the method of Plato and Socrates in which answers were often achieved by disputation and reflection, Aristotle emphasized observation. To expand his research, he persuaded Alexander to let him hire over a thousand research assistants, who went to all corners of the known earth to record observations and send back data and specimens of vegetation, birds, animals, fish, and rocks. The assistants recorded measurements of ocean coastlines and kept a record of weather. They looked into the heavens and contrasted the positions of the planets and the stars.

Much of all this has been forgotten, and we do not now think of Aristotle so much as the scientist, but as the literary critic, the rhetorician, and the logician. Ironically, the logic that he is credited with inventing came as a by-product of his other studies. Aristotle wrote somewhere between four hundred and a thousand books, only six of them about logic. We are not even sure that the six books were collected by Aristotle himself into the one work now called the *Organon*.

The study of the origin and nature of knowledge is called *epistemology*, and Aristotle's system of logic grew out of the epistemological findings of his assistants. As his assistants began to send their observations to him, he had to classify them as to whether they were factual or inferential. Realizing that many of the observations were either *definitions* or a form of *predication*, Aristotle devised a set of rules about what he considered legitimate definition and predication. A definition, he wrote, must first put the object to be defined into a class and then show how the object or phenomenon differs from other members of its class. Once this system was established, when an observation came back that such was a certain species of fish, both the assistant and Aristotle knew what was meant.

Aristotle's second concern was predication. When field workers sent him messages such as "the warriors are fierce," or "the mountain is high," it was Aristotle's task to make those assertions meaningful, and it was to this end that he classified the types of legitimate predication and stated how each should be verified and expressed. Although much of what he wrote is relevant only to Greek grammar, what he said about classification is important today, because it is the basis of the deductive syllogism.

A deductive syllogism is a trio of statements, as in the standard example below. These statements should be read: "All (things in the class) men are (things in the class) mortal. (All of the class) Socrates is a (thing in the class) man. (Therefore, all of the class) Socrates is (a thing in the class) mortal."

Major premise: All men are mortal.

Minor premise: Socrates is a man.

Conclusion: Socrates is mortal.

Aristotle's formal syllogism has been subject to much controversy. On one hand, following the rules for formal syllogistic reasoning, the conclusion follows from the premises, as it must, for the argument is tautological. On the other hand, the nonlogician tends to view the syllogism as a complete argument unless he recognizes that it is, for him, most useful in identifying possible sources of disagreement. In such an instance, the syllogism can best be seen as a system of analysis, not as a system of proof.

One of the arguments Aristotle analyzed in his *Rhetoric* demonstrates such an application of a syllogism. A young man wrote to his father and requested permission to marry, his argument being:

All men should marry.

I am a man.

Therefore I should marry.

The father responded that both premises were in doubt. Some men, he maintained, are not fit to marry. The father had two comments about the predication of the major premise. He pointed out that it was twice incomplete: it should specify *when* they should marry and *whom* they should marry before the son could feel that he had won the argument. At the end of the argument the father might say, "Yes, I think you should marry. Now let's start talking about when you will marry and whether you have the right young lady as your intended." As Aristotle points out, the second premise is questionable as to definition and predication. The father said, "You will be a man when you are earning your own living."

In their last years, Alexander sentenced Aristotle's nephew to death for criticizing Alexander's desire to be worshiped as a god. Alexander defended the sentence with this argument:

A critic of the state must die.

Your nephew is a critic of the state.

He must die.

Aristotle and Alexander saw that this syllogism indicated where the argument should begin. The question was not whether the nephew should live; the issue was whether a critic of the state should die. Aristotle insisted that a state that encourages criticism actually profits from it. The syllogism was useful in finding where the argument really lay, though it did not spare the nephew's life.

Aristotle's last years were spent in the middle of a great controversy. As nearly as we can tell, Alexander had resolved that he would govern his kingdom according to the leadership most acceptable to the area. In Mesopotamia, and what are now Afghanistan, Pakistan, and India, he married his generals and himself into the satrapy families and ruled as they had ruled. In Egypt, he accepted the Egyptians' concept that a ruler must be a god, and the exhilaration of this experience was so heady that he returned to Greece expecting to be considered divine there. Aristotle refused to call him a god—and defended his own nephew who shared this opinion. Among the Athenians, however, Aristotle still defended Alexander as a great leader and became unpopular. In 323 B.C., Alexander died, and Aristotle had to flee to Chalcis where, within a year, he died.

Although Aristotle and Alexander, the prime creators and disseminators of Greek learning, were dead, the thrust of their efforts did not subside. The Romans, who soon conquered the Greeks, quickly became servants of Greek thought. For the next six hundred years the Romans took the Greek alphabet, and the architecture, art, and much of the knowledge of Greece to the farthest reaches of their own empire.

The study of logic is one of the most abstract and theoretical branches of learning. When a nation is at war it usually does not question its premises, and Rome was always at war. The major premise, the primary assumption, made at almost all times was that the State dominates all. All roads led to Rome: all culture, all books, all slaves, all booty, all responsibility went to Rome. The Romans did a great deal of thinking, but their thinking was characteristically deductive, that is, based on accepted assumptions. Thus it was that when Jesus Christ, in the Jewish corner of the Roman Empire, was faced with the famous dilemma whether taxes should be paid to Rome, his audience was receptive to a deductive syllogism:

Anything that belongs to Caesar must go to Caesar.

This coin (having a picture of Caesar on it) belongs to Caesar.

"Render therefore unto Caesar the things which are Caesar's." (Matthew 22:21)

When the Roman Empire became the Holy Roman Empire, about 1000 A.D., thinking continued along deductive patterns. Minds accustomed to accepting Roman authority quickly accepted Church authority. The belief was carefully nurtured that God directed man's intuitive thinking along right paths. Whatever was right God made seem obvious. This made unnecessary any epistemological questions about the source and nature of knowledge. Knowledge, it was believed, came primarily from God via either the Holy Bible or the teachings of the Church Fathers. The Fathers found their certainties either in the Bible or in the teachings of accepted mystics, the saintly persons who had some special channels of communication with God.

Convenient dates to limit the Middle Ages are 476 A.D., the fall of the Roman Empire, and 1492, the voyage of Columbus to America. During the intervening centuries the dependence upon religious absolutes and what is called a priori information was very great indeed. A priori knowledge is information that is supposed to be accepted by all as obvious and beyond question. At the end of the Middle Ages, Michelangelo was criticized for questioning the Biblically generated idea that man has one less rib than woman, since woman was created from Adam's rib. In about the year 1300, the great Italian poet Dante was asked whether water in its natural state was higher or lower than dirt. Instead of looking out his window and seeing the mountains near Florence towering above sea level, he began a tortuous examination of what seemed to him the absolutes relevant to the question. Two of his arguments were:

Noble elements are higher than less noble elements.
Water is nobler than dirt.
Therefore, water must lie higher than dirt.

An efficient universe is God's way.
Having water high is efficient. (It can run down to us.)
Therefore having water high is God's way.

Scholasticism and the question of reality

Although the Roman Church has been criticized for stultifying thought during the Middle Ages, credit must be given the Church for keeping *any* learning alive. Credit must also be given the Church for perpetuating an argument that eventually led to a vast improvement in the mode of thought. The great epistemological question of the medieval period had to do with the nature of reality. "What," men asked, "is reality?" They argued that it is foolish to think that a desk is real. All desks (or individuals or objects) are less real than the Idea which represents them. The philosophical belief that reality lies in the Idea is called *realism*. In the form most common today this concept is called *subjective realism* or *subjectivism,* the idea that true reality lies in the mind. It does not matter what a teacher *is;* what matters is what his students think of him. Today we call our mental perception of an object, person, or institution its "image." A university or corporation may actually decay, but if its image remains strong, it may operate or seem as effective as ever. Conversely, when the image of a country deteriorates, it loses power. Another school of philosophers also reject the reality of an object, but they insist that the perception of reality cannot be necessarily encompassed in the mind. Plato, who held this position, argued that reality lies in Universals which are always true and never changing. This belief is called *extreme realism* or *idealism*.

Opposing both forms of realism, *nominalists* maintain that general ideas are only conveniences; they hold no true reality. They argue that reality lies only in the individual person, object, institution, or concept. Such concepts as love, law, and learning, are reality only in the particular instances for which they were phrased. All universal or general ideas are merely names, and it is from this belief that the name was derived, *nominalism*, from the Latin word for "name."

The meaning of philosophical realism is hard to grasp because it contradicts the modern concept of realism. When we say today, "Let's be realistic," we mean, "Let's not fool around with dreams and theories. Let's look at things as they are. Let's look at *facts!*" In the Middle Ages many found realism comfortable. What they were told by the Church and what seemed obvious were their reality. Dante did not look out at the River Arno to see where water was; he looked into his own mind.

William of Occam, a fourteenth-century English philosopher, is often considered the outstanding nominalist, but many preceded him who questioned absolute belief based on realism. Whereas realists tended to support Church orthodoxy, nominalists tended to be heretics. In the twelfth century Peter Abelard (1074–1142), a brilliant teacher who is usually credited with founding the University of Paris, attacked the ultra-realism common at the time. Abelard is remembered today more for his pathetic and beautiful love letters to Heloise Fulbert than for his philosophy, but in his own time, neither was approved. After Heloise became pregnant, her uncle, canon of the Cathedral of Notre Dame, caused Abelard to be emasculated. Ill and in disgrace, Abelard became a hermit, but students sought him out even in his hermitage, and he lectured there to hundreds who were attracted to his heterodoxy. He rose again to prominence, but his nominalistic attacks on Church dogma became increasingly suspect. To show that mental perceptions are not realities, he wrote a book called *Sic et non,* a compilation of contradictory writings by various Church leaders. Abelard's purpose was not to expose the contradictions to ridicule but to provide his students an opportunity to reconcile them by logic and debate. However, Abelard's inclination to challenge realistic absolutes was considered heretical.

Although Abelard was forced to retire, his ideas were kept alive by his pupils, particularly Peter Lombard, and there was no peace between realists and nominalists for years. During the period of controversy the science of Aristotle was reasonably well known in Europe, but his logic was known only to Jewish and Arab scholars. In the mid-thirteenth century a Catholic monk, Thomas Aquinas (1225–1274) read the *Commentaries* on Aristotle by Averroës, a Spanish-Arabian lawyer and physician, who attempted to reconcile Aristotelian reason with the tenets of both Catholicism and the Islamic faith. Although Aquinas disagreed with some of Averroës's interpretations of Aristotle, he too recognized that Aristotle's emphasis on human reason did not necessarily jeopardize divinely inspired Church dogma. Aquinas, one of the world's greatest thinkers, steadfastly defended this point of view. To ease Churchmen's fears that human reason might threaten Church faith, he argued that Reason and Faith are equally valid channels to Truth and will never contradict each other. Aquinas presented this view so forcefully that Aristotle's logic, which had once been called heresy, was in 1270 found compatible by the Church. Although not recognized until 1879, Aquinas's synthesis and his other contributions led to his canonization in 1323.

Thomas Aquinas's synthesis and Aristotle's deductive syllogism together calmed philosophical turmoil, the former because Churchmen were comforted by the thought that nominalism (as the basis for Reason) and realism (as the basis for orthodox Faith) would arrive at the same conclusions and never contradict each other, and the latter because the deductive syllogism gave order to their thinking.

Church law is approved by God.

This is Church law.

This is approved by God.

The syllogism, interpreted as "Given A and B, C must follow," gave impressive support to a priori thinking, since A and B were often assumptions based on Faith, not on Reason or observations. However, not all Churchmen were satisfied, and a concern for right thinking was a major preoccupation of medieval clerics.

Eventually, perceptive thinkers came to realize that in welcoming Aristotle they were nursing a viper to their bosoms. Instead of Aristotle quieting dissent, his confidence in reason justified a long, skeptical scrutiny of dogma. A resurgence of interest in Abelard's *Sic et non* contradictions caused men to realize that, if some of the Church's assumptions were contradictory, some had to be wrong. The deductive syllogism raised in the late Middle Ages what it had raised in Aristotle's time, the possibility that major assumptions were in error. Humanistic logic could be demonstrated to be sound, but the starting premises could be questioned. Instead of Aristotle getting credit, he became the enemy.

The attack on deductive reasoning

In the fourteenth century, the rediscovery of classical literature fastened attention on the lot of man on earth and on the way his mind operates. As a hundred more years passed, new views of science posed new questions for the authoritarian deductive epistemology, but it was not until the sixteenth century that real opposition came to the deductive orientation of scholasticism. In France the scholar Petrus Ramus (1515–1572) falsely associated Aristotle with a priori thinking and wasted his time on an attempt to correct logic via grammatical and rhetorical principles, trying to clarify definitions by means of more exact language, much as Aristotle himself had done. He lost his life in the riots on St. Bartholomew's Day, and he is noted here only for fostering a brief interlude of opposition to Aristotle, an opposition best represented by the Englishman Francis Bacon (1561–1626). Bacon's father was a minor government officer and his mother a respected linguist and theologian, and the boy grew up surrounded by the excitement of the time. He heard of England's victory over the Spanish Armada, the flourishing new trade across the Atlantic, the circumnavigation of the globe, and the early colonization of America. He saw the new plays of Shakespeare, Christopher Marlowe, and Ben Jonson, and he read the translations of Greek and Roman classics, acquiring thus many humanistic ideas.

At twelve, Bacon enrolled at Trinity College, Cambridge, emerging three years later filled with hostility to the authority of Aristotle as taught at the time. The deductive syllogism, he was to complain later, "flies from principles, the truth of which it takes for settled and immovable." At sixteen he joined the staff of the ambassador to France and began to climb the political ladder. In 1606, he became Solicitor General, in 1617, Keeper of the Seal, and in 1618, Lord Chancellor. His climb was interrupted occasionally by bouts of spending that took him into debtor's prison and into public disfavor. Bacon opposed the insurrection of the Earl of Essex against the Queen, but when the Earl was captured, Bacon defended him in court. When Essex escaped and resumed war against the Queen, Bacon condemned the Earl and led the prosecution against him when he was recaptured. The fact that he was at one time or the other on both sides earned him a cluster of enemies who were pleased when he was accused of bribery and forced to retire in disgrace.

His busy political life was accompanied by great enterprise as a thinker. Socrates can be called the father of philosophy, Aristotle the father of logic, and Bacon the father of the scientific method, though he was not a great original scientist or a great innovator like his predecessors. The scientific awakening in Europe started in the thirteenth century with Roger Bacon (c. 1214–1294), moved along with the work of Leonardo da Vinci (1452–1519), and reached its peak in the astronomy of Copernicus (1473–1543), Johannes Kepler (1571–1630), and Galileo (1564–1642), in the research of William Gilbert (1540–1603) on magnetism and electricity, of Andreas Vesalius (1514–1564) on anatomy, and of William Harvey (1578–1657) on the circulation of blood. Nevertheless, Bacon was, in his own words, the "trumpeter" for a new method of thought. In *Novum Organum*, published in 1620 (the year the Mayflower sailed to America), Bacon attacked the epistemology and thinking of his time, claiming it was basically deductive and founded on premises that were not knowledge at all, but questionable assumptions. Before man could think properly, he said, he would have to expurgate from his mind all a priori assumptions.

There are, Bacon believed, four kinds of error, or "idols." These idols are false pictures of reality, notions or thoughts mistaken for things or truths. There are the Idols of the Tribe—that is, fallacies natural to man. For instance, man's desire for order and harmony may cause him to see more order in nature than there really is. He wishes to believe, for instance, that celestial bodies move in perfect circles. Because man is naturally concerned with himself, he sees the earth as the center of the universe and all of history as a record of man. There are also the Idols of the Cave—fallacies peculiar to the individual. "Every man has a cave of his own," said Bacon, and the way he looks out of his cave refracts and distorts the light of nature. Any rival is a bad man, any ally a good one. A law that helps him get food is a good law, even if it is unfair to someone else. There are also the Idols of the Marketplace. Man communicates with language, and language conveys, if not a distorted picture, certainly a limited one. There are also the Idols of the Theater, all the old myths, legends, and prejudices. Modern theologians would regard the fundamentalist interpretation of the Biblical story of Jonah and the Whale as an Idol of the Theatre. The explanations used by primitive people for thunder, lightning, and natural calamities would be Idols of the Theatre.

Once man has freed himself of these errors, he can turn to new, more dependable ways of thought. Bacon lamented that although the discovery of the compass helped man find new paths on the earth, "a new art of inventing and discovering the sciences remains hitherto unknown." The word *invent* at that time meant the coming-upon of a new idea. The "mental globe," Bacon believed, was still "shut up within the narrow limits of old discoveries. . . . The problem is that we still rely on dogma and deduction; we find no new truth because we take some venerable but questionable proposition as an indubitable starting point, but never think of putting this assumption to the test of observation or experiment." Bacon went on to describe the procedure that he thought should be used, the so-called scientific method. A man gets a notion from a simple experience, accident, or experiment. After the initial notion occurs to him, he then phrases it as a hypothesis and tests it under controlled conditions. In modern times, when someone got the notion that lung cancer might be caused by excessive smoking, scientists subjected lung tissue of rats not only to tobacco smoke, but to parts of the tobacco, for instance, nicotine, carbon, and even heat. They accumulated tremendous banks of statistics to see whether lung cancer occurred more frequently to excessive smokers than it did to nonsmokers or light smokers. This checking of the hypothesis is the second step in the scientific method Bacon recommended.

Bacon had a scheme to increase the likelihood of coming upon the first notion. He proposed that observation be stored in "tables of more or less." If any two qualities increase and decrease together, one may be the cause of the other. In his own tables Bacon noticed that whenever heat increases, motion increases. Freeze water and it becomes immobile; boil it and it bubbles. Chill animals and they huddle together, unmoving; heat their cages and they move apart and walk around. After long analysis he computed an exact correlation between heat and motion and concluded, correctly but superficially, that heat is a form of motion.

Aspects of modern thought

Francis Bacon was not one of the world's great scientists or philosophers, but he justifiably is recognized as a man who guided modern thought. Four of his basic ideas opened the four modes of contemplation that have characterized modern thought: (1) Bacon's concern for causality as demonstrated by his "tables of more or less" pioneered later studies by Blaise Pascal about probability, by John Stuart Mill about canons of cause, and by modern mathematicians about multivariate analysis. (2) Bacon's interest in the inductive method provided a base for empiricism and pragmatism. (3) Bacon's awareness of the Idols of the Cave and the Tribe provided a frame of reference for the studies of the subconscious by Sigmund Freud. (4) Bacon's fear of the Idols of the Marketplace was a prelude to the development of semantics and modern symbolic logic.

THE CONCERN FOR CAUSALITY

Almost all scientific laws and all beliefs are based on probability. According to legend, Chanticleer crowed in the morning to raise the sun; now we know what "causes" the sun to "rise." But we do not know that it will always rise. We know that two planets could crash together and put the earth or the sun out of its orbit, in which case the sun might not rise. But we know that is not "likely" to happen, and we are certain to a high degree of probability that the sun will rise. About other occurrences we cannot know as many of the attendant possibilities. When two young people marry, they may wonder about the probability of their staying married, and they may be sobered to learn that, in some areas, one marriage in four ends in the divorce court. They may conclude that their chances are rather small. But the theory of probability will provide some guides.

About 1650 a French mathematician, Blaise Pascal (1623–1662), formulated the theory of probability, presumably when requested to advise a gambler friend how to bet during a card game. Pascal theorized that, when drawing a card, the chances of getting the one desired vary according to the number of desired cards versus the number of total choices. A person trying to draw a spade from a fifty-two-card pack will have thirteen successes possible out of a possible fifty-two choices. Thus, his chances are

13/52 or 25 percent. If the card drawn is put back into the pack, the chances are again 1/4, but if the unsuccessful drawn card is not returned, the chances would increase to 13/51. Using a calculating machine of his own invention, Pascal devised a probability calculus that can determine the statistical probability or "probability coefficient" for any series of unrelated circumstances. For intsance, the chance of a player's winning with dice on the first roll is 2/9, and the chances of his winning at all are 244/495, or 49.3 percent. The chance of breaking even on "chuck-a-luck" is approximately 92 percent, and the chance of winning in roulette is even smaller.

Probability is also determined by factors that are so unmeasurable that they are considered pure chance. A housewife having a dinner party wonders how many rolls her guests will eat and is relieved to find that catering services have already determined the probability that each guest will eat a roll and a half. A military commander determines that he will lose one aircraft and one crew during every twenty sorties, so he orders a complete set of replacements (of men and matériel) for the appropriate number of missions. A chief of police who learns that there will be six hundred students at a parade assigns six police to keep order, because the one- to one-hundred ratio has kept previous parades in order.

The young couple distressed by the statistical possibility of their marriage ending in divorce can take comfort in studies that show that the following factors improve their chances of marital happiness: same religion, similar educational level, equivalent socioeconomic backgrounds, and freedom from financial strain.

Insurance rates are based on studies of "relative frequency." Because male drivers between the ages of 16 and 25 have many accidents, their insurance rates are high; girls of the same age and experience have a different—lower—relative frequency. Airline pilots and diabetics once had to pay higher insurance rates than the average person, but frequency tables have shown that they no longer die younger than the average, and their rates have been reduced. Nondrinkers can get considerable reductions in auto insurance. You might expect fire insurance to be cheaper for brick houses, and it is, but you may be surprised to learn that fire and theft insurance is 40 percent cheaper if the owner is a lawyer, doctor, or teacher.

The theory of probability has opened up many kinds of studies. Statisticians who develop these figures make no claim, as Bacon suggested, that "more or less" relationships suggest cause and effect. Many of their studies are based on completely uncontrolled circumstances, and they do not know what causes what. All they are quite sure of is that certain circumstances occur in certain patterns, and they are often willing to stake their reputations and their money on their predictions.

There are many sets of circumstances that do seem to happen together. Areas with a large proportion of Negroes, labor unions, and intellectuals tend to vote Democratic. Lung cancer occurs more often among excessive smokers. Christian countries in the temperate zones seem to have higher cultural and economic levels than non-Christian countries in the frigid and torrid zones. The question we must ask ourselves is whether there is a cause-and-effect relationship here or not. If we do not ask, we may unnecessarily ban cigarettes and build gigantic but useless air-conditioning systems in large Christian missions in Asia and Africa.

Computers are making Baconian tables of more or less more feasible. Information about education, income, accomplishments, population, voting, and interests can be fed into computers, which are then asked to indicate the factors that increase and decrease in relation to each other. When information about high-school students, including data about grades, religion, social status, ethnic group, social interests, extracurricular activities, car ownership, going steady, athletic ability, and hundreds of other observations, was fed into a computer, the educational researcher noted that low grades, car ownership, and an absence of extracurricular activities occurred together almost every time, and so he hypothesized that for a high-school student to own a car is almost a guarantee that he will have poor marks and that he will not be out for any sports or other extra-curricular activities. This hypothesis is now being tested.

The gigantic banks of computers that can deal with masses of information are a far cry from Francis Bacon's tables, but they demonstrate the significance that modern thought attaches to an understanding of causal relationship.

Bacon did not live to fulfill his dream of placing all data on charts to measure their relative increasing and decreasing. However, his idea that when two phenomena were observed to rise and fall at the same time there might be some relationship between them, perhaps one of cause and effect, has been very influential. In medicine, doctors at first sought cures for certain diseases; in modern times, attention has been placed on preventing them. We realize that when we find the cause of a disease, we can remove the cause and prevent the disease. Sociologists attempt to "cure" slums and poverty, which is as it should be, but even more effort is now aimed at eliminating the conditions that cause slums and poverty. The causes of earthquakes, cyclones, floods, crop failure, inflation, and many other natural and social evils are being sought in the hope of eventual prevention. Historians of Western civilization, when they seek to find a basic difference between the cultures of the East and West, have commented that the crucial difference is the preoccupation in Europe and America with cause and effect. One writer commented that this concern with causality has been the most important source of progress in the last two hundred years.

Proving cause is not easy. What seems to be cause and effect may actually be an illusion or superstition as when we seem to have bad luck after walking under a ladder or having a black cat cross our path. It may actually be chance. B may follow A a number of times and still be connected only by coincidence. Another possibility is that, although B follows A on every occasion, we may learn that they both are the product of a common cause. And there are many other explanations. Checking on these possibilities in a laboratory is difficult enough; in everyday life it is often nearly impossible. Facing up to this difficulty, John Stuart Mill in 1843 published his *A System of Logic,* which described the four tests that can be made to establish that A causes B. He called them "canons." These tests can be set up in the laboratory; they can often be used to determine cause and effect in society. In his discussion, Mill called the early occurrence the *antecedent;* the later occurrence, which seemed to be the result of the antecedent, he called the *consequent.*

The test of agreement. When a group of antecedent occurrences cause a certain consequent and the occurrences have only one quality in common, that quality may be assumed to be the cause. For instance, when a number of substances seemed to destroy odors, and they were all green, the "greenness" was assumed to be the cause; later chlorophyll was discovered in the green substance.

The test of difference. If a consequent occurs when an antecedent is present and if the consequent does not occur when the antecedent is absent, we may conclude that the antecedent is the cause or an indispensable part of the cause of the consequent. For instance, to use a very gross experiment, if we suspect that either fatigue, chill, or contagion is the cause of the common cold, we might subject a number of people to combinations of fatigue (F), chill (C), and exposure to other cold sufferers thus, FCE, FE, CE, and CF. If we find that our subjects never catch cold when one of the antecedents is absent, we may assume that this antecedent is a cause or a part of the cause of the common cold.

The test of residue. In a complex collection of antecedents and consequents, we may often know that some of the antecedents cause some of the consequents. By withdrawing known combinations, that is, by withdrawing A and then, as expected, seeing B disappear, by withdrawing C and watching, as expected, D disappear, and so on, we may end up with only one antecedent and one consequent. About this test Mill wrote in *Systems of Logic*, "This is the most fertile in unexpected results, often informing us of sequences in which neither the cause nor the effect is sufficiently conspicuous to attract by themselves the attention of the observers." The discovery of penicillin was a result of this type of test. Dr. Alexander Fleming remembered that bacteria had died in a culture, and he knew the consequence of everything but mold in the culture, so—using the test of residue—he inferred that mold destroys bacteria.

The test of concomitant variations. All the previous tests can usually be set up in a laboratory, but the appropriate combinations cannot always be arranged, especially in experiments involving people and expensive procedures. We cannot ascertain, for instance, if the moon causes the tides by removing the moon to see if we still have tides. But the test of concomitant variation can be applied. We can check to see the effect of varying degrees of a suspected antecedent. We can measure the tide and learn that when the moon is near we have higher tide, and that when it is farther away we have lower tide. When fluoride was suspected as a preventive of tooth decay, few people were enthusiastic about putting poison in their mouths to see whether sounder teeth would result. In areas that have fluoride naturally in their water we learned that certain amounts do prevent tooth decay—and do not cause any poisoning. People in areas that have too much fluoride in the water tend to have mottled teeth, and thus, before researchers ever went into the laboratory, they knew almost exactly what concentration of fluoride should be in the water. Similarly, after an election we cannot really assess the value of having national political leaders assist in local elections, but we can apply the law of concomitant variations: if there was much help in one area and the appropriate local candidates won, and if in the areas where a national candidate did not appear the party's local candidates lost, we have at least some evidence to determine the worth of national activity.

The test of concomitant variations can be applied as a substitute for all the other tests. The value of foreign aid, or military assistance, and a hundred other social, educational, governmental, military, and scientific procedures can be tested by seeing what happens when the antecedents are there in varying amounts and what happens when they are not present at all.

Strictly speaking, the social problems that have been discussed here are not pure problems of chance, and probability theory is related but not exclusively so. What probability theory has done for conjecture about cause and effect is to indicate that there is a statistical possibility for any two phenomena to happen simultaneously. Enough monkeys placed before typewriters for a long enough time *could*, by striking the keys at random, put together all the plays of Shakespeare. When a student sits down before a multiple-choice examination, if there are four choices, by sheer chance he should get about one-fourth of the answers right. Probability theory shows that the measure of his knowledge is actually shown by the number he gets right over 25 percent. Probability theory has thus refined our attempts to recognize causality. What we formerly thought of as cause we now may perceive to be chance. We can determine how much is chance; what remains may suggest a causal relationship.

EMPIRICISM

All this objective, almost bloodless scrutiny of how events happen raises questions about our perceptions of just what knowledge is. When we record "information" in tabular form and attempt to measure it, we are defining knowledge; we are stating a basic postulate of our epistemology. Francis Bacon had this definite idea about knowledge. He was not a mystic or a fideist; that is, he had no communication with any supernatural source of information, and he did not accept information on pure faith. He was not a rationalist; that is, he did not believe that man is born with any innate knowledge that only needs to be released in some fashion. Bacon was an *empiricist*; he believed that all knowledge must come from some perception of the senses. Since Bacon, Western civilization has been dominated by this concept. Although each of them had a different view of empiricism, Thomas Hobbes, John Locke, and David Hume were essentially empiricists, and their thinking has had a great influence on the thought of our time.

The thrust of the thinking of these men was to convert philosophy, especially epistemology, from a dependence on supernatural or other a priori assumptions to a reliance on premises grounded on observations. Renaissance thinkers had taken many of the questions of theology and placed them in the jurisdiction of philosophy. Now scholars took the philosophical questions and converted them to problems of sociology and psychology. In *Leviathan* (1651) Thomas Hobbes (1588–1679) based his perception of man and his way of thought on the "contention, enmity and war" he saw about him. He answered the question, "What is Man?," by looking at men. Hobbes tried to show that government historically is created by man's surrendering his selfish rights to government to achieve "peaceable, sociable, comfortable living." No one governs by divine right. Information comes to man as a by-product of his search for self-advancement. Thought cannot be objective but must always be colored by one's pride and selfishness. Logic cannot be an exact science, for it is basically a form of psychology; only by arrangement of men huddled together for mutual gain can it be sociology.

John Locke (1632–1704) questioned a priori considerations based on faith. In his *Essay Concerning Human Understanding* (1690), he rejected the existence of innate thoughts (thus condemning rationalism). Locke believed that man enters the world with his mind a *tabula rasa,* a sheet empty of any knowledge. From experience, man derives ideas that he refines by reflection. An interplay and nurture of experience and reflection yield very complex ideas, including such concepts as time, infinity, morality, and taste. For this interplay, man needs precise language to make possible the separation of parts of ideas and the logical interrelating of others. Ideas of right and wrong are neither innate nor the product of simple experience; they are derived from a complex of experiences and reflection. Locke's confidence in group reason was so complete that he believed governments should be replaced, by revolution if necessary, when they do not reflect the expressed will of the people. Locke's effect on the American Revolution was great, as might be expected. Thomas Jefferson thought Locke had one of the three most penetrating minds he had encountered.

George Berkeley (1685–1753), although an Irish bishop in the Anglican Church, was an associate of the English writers Richard Steele, Joseph Addison, Alexander Pope, Jonathan Swift, and other semi-skeptical thinkers. He was a follower of John Locke and, primarily, a subjective idealist. He denied the independent existence of matter. Its only reality is what we perceive it to be. It is meaningful only insofar as we realize its size, shape, color, and quality. Knowledge is the only reality, and it changes, grows, or deteriorates with each person's ability to appreciate it. Berkeley's importance as an empiricist lay in his confidence that man could arrive at this knowledge only by way of sense perceptions.

David Hume (1711–1776) helped introduce into England Jean-Jacques Rousseau's idea that government is a social contract. Hume comes to us more as an attacker than as a proponent, because he charged that the existence of miracles cannot be defended by any logical system. He relied upon sense perceptions as the only source of knowledge. This pattern of thought did not make him become an atheist, for he argued that there was so much need for religion that it inevitably develops. Even though man could have no proof or knowledge of what lies beyond human experience, he could still have strong belief in religions if they provide a useful morality. Hume divided perceptions into impressions derived from the senses, and ideas or thoughts, which were shaped by the mind according to defensible techniques.

In today's practical world, it is hard for us properly to assess the importance of this group of men, but we should not forget that at least two of them, Hobbes and Locke, shaped the thinking which led to the American and French revolutions.

Although there have certainly been influential and respected mystics and rationalists, the chain of thought linking Bacon, Hobbes, Locke, Hume, and Berkeley has been an important one in Western thought. With this objectifying of the concept of knowledge, another channel of thought became almost inevitable. Once man decided that he could trust only knowledge that comes via his senses, he began to evaluate it and to measure it. Throughout history there have been many ways of evaluating information. The hedonist says that that information is most valuable which brings the most pleasure. Jeremy Bentham and John Stuart Mill evaluated knowledge according to "utility," its ability to bring good to the greatest number of people. The early colonists in America evaluated knowledge according to its ability to "glorify God," specifically in the way knowledge could be used to shape history according to His plan. The strict Marxist evaluates information according to its use to further the Communist State.

The way of evaluating knowledge that has deeply influenced modern thinking began about 1890 with the writing of William James and John Dewey. James, the brother of the novelist Henry James, was a professor of psychology at Harvard Medical School. Dewey was a professor of philosophy and education at the universities of Minnesota, Michigan, and Chicago, and at Columbia University. Mutually they rejected any concept of a universal truth, that is, a truth that is always true. Rather than being absolute, complete, or fixed, truth is, they believed, changing and growing. It is developed or "carved out" by the human consciousness, which is active, selective, aggressive, and purposeful. Will and interest are thus primary; knowledge is their instrument. Truth is any "successful" view, idea, hypothesis, or belief framed for the accomplishment of our purposes. The popular idea of this school, *pragmatism*, is "whatever works is right." Dewey and James rejected any philosophical meandering or speculation that led to no useful result. In its ethical aspect, pragmatism accepts as real knowledge only that which can be employed to accomplish some good. Because of its practicality, pragmatism is often considered to be an American phenomenon, but its concepts appear in the writing of England's F. C. S. Schiller, France's Henri Bergson and Jules Henri Poincaré, and other European philosophers; it is a pervasive dogma. It was influential in the life of John F. Kennedy, who is reputed to have presented new appointees with these instructions: "We have no preconceived notion of how you should do your job. When you get an idea, try it. If it works, you will be a hero. If it does not, you will be gone before election day." At its best, pragmatism provides a vigorous, dynamic "can do" spirit and rationale for the common good.

On the other hand, pragmatism has been charged with a kind of godlessness. Rejecting any pretense of seeking any greater truth or objective reality, some pragmatists go so far in their search for a truth that works that they are more concerned with what has come to be called "image" than they are with what is behind the image. Pragmatism can be used as an excuse for shoddy but highly advertised merchandise, glossy but shallow political candidates, and glamorous but trashy Hollywood productions.

FREUDIAN AWARENESS OF THE NONRATIONAL

As concerned about objective knowledge as Francis Bacon was, he knew that, before it could be realized, the human mind had to be freed from the Idols of the Cave and Tribe. Man is not completely a rational being; he is influenced by his own interests and emotions. In addition, he will be influenced by the common characteristics of man—his selfishness, his fears, and his uncertainties. Systems of epistemology and logic must consider these Idols, and many of them have. Hobbes tried to make philosophy extremely practical, insisting, as Alexander Pope phrased it later, that "the proper study of mankind is man." When Hobbes scrutinized man intently, he found that man's ability to reason depended very heavily upon deep, subconscious underpinnings.

In 1879, the German psychologist Wilhelm Wundt established in Leipzig the world's first psychology laboratory, and soon almost every major European and American university developed facilities to study the operation of man's mind. The man who used these facilities to develop the deepest insights was Sigmund Freud (1856–1939). Even his critics would undoubtedly admit that Freud has enlarged our understanding of the thinking process. Freud, born in Freiburg, Moravia, received a degree in medicine from the University of Vienna and later studied in Paris. From 1902 until 1938 he was professor of neurology at Vienna, but he fled from Nazi persecution and became a British citizen.

Not many people have dismissed Freud as lightly as did Paul Elmer More: "Pretty much all the truth of Freudianism can be found in the Platonic and Stoic theory of dreams." Many, however, gave him more adulation than he deserved, as did Sherwood Anderson, who wrote in *Dark Laughter*, "If there is anything you do not understand in life, consult Dr. Freud." One of Freud's detractors was Alfred Kazin, who, in *On Native Grounds* (1942), wrote, "Freudianism, in its inception a clinical method for carefully trained and imaginative students, became—often quite unconsciously and unscientifically—the laziest kind of sophisticated small talk in criticism and a technique by which writers armed with nothing more than the debunking spirit as such could expose the conflicts between the apparent and real in every sphere."

Controversy aside, most agree that Freud's influence in dramatizing a new dimension in thinking has been very great. Prior to Freud, few people were aware of the tremendous hold that the subconscious aspects of the mind have upon the conscious, rational mind. Man liked to think that once he had all the "facts" and assuming he had the necessary "intelligence quotient" he could apply the rules of logic and come to sound conclusions. Freud demonstrated how rarely is the mind sufficiently free of encumbrances to permit this. More forcefully than Bacon's story of the Idols of the Tribe and Cave, Freud demonstrated that our subconscious is the product of feelings of insecurity or superiority, hidden motives, and scars and triumphs of our past; that we must seek out the sources of prejudices, fears, embarrassment, and uncertainties; and that we must recognize all kinds of emotional states before we can really think clearly. Even the metaphors and symbols we use are the result of our past inhibitions and traumas as often as they are objective vehicles of communication.

Freud was especially interested in the Idols of the Cave, but some of his followers were more interested in the Idols of the Tribe. C. G. Jung, for instance, noted several periods in the lives of most men when their conduct follows a customary pattern, not a logical pattern. Other schools of thought, influenced by Freud or not, have mentioned other Idols of the Tribe. Marshall McLuhan, in *The Gutenberg Galaxy* and in more recent books, has argued that man reacts according to the way that he receives information. Man at the time of the development of the printing press handled information differently from the manner of a generation brought up on television. Another Idol of the Tribe is called "territoriality." According to Robert Ardrey, neither man nor animal can act rationally when his home or land, or some symbolic version of it, is threatened or imagined to be threatened.

Since the existence of the deeper inner recesses of the mind has been so thoroughly publicized by Freud and his followers, almost everyone today is aware of the Idols of the Cave. Another Idol is today receiving a great deal of attention, the Idol of the Marketplace, the tyranny of words.

SEMANTICS

Man has long been concerned about the inability of his language to carry the burden of logical thought. We have noted Aristotle's great concern for definition, and he was not the first nor the last. Socrates incessantly demanded clarity in his dialogues; Voltaire said, "If you would speak with me, define your terms." Nevertheless, there was never a really systematic study of the meaning of words until the publication in 1897 of *Essai de Sémantique* by Michel Bréal, who had to make up a name for his new field of study—semantics. Primarily a student of etymology, Bréal turned his attention to the "tendencies of the mind" that go to work on the meaning of words. His first influence was primarily on literary criticism, and a rash of books came out trying to show the meaning of words as used by authors, with medieval French and German authors and Chaucer being early subjects. In 1922, *The Meaning of Meaning*, by C. K. Ogden and I. A. Richards, stimulated a great deal of interest in the problem of attaching meaning to symbols, and a host of writers followed in their footsteps. P. W. Bridgman explored the semantics of physics in *Logic of Modern Physics* and Thurman Arnold, in *The Folklore of Capitalism*, claimed that we are ruled by the manipulators of our symbols. Alfred Korzybski gave the study a therapeutic tinge in *Science and Sanity*. He suggested that many personal, national, and international maladjustments are caused by a tragic confusion of highly abstract and emotionally laden concepts. Since then, Wendell Johnson, Stuart Chase, S. I. Hayakawa, and J. Irving Lee have written less extravagant but very meaningful books on the subject.

The message of the semanticist is not new. Expressed in old terms like *denotation* or *connotation* or in the new terms *extensional meaning* and *intensional meaning*, the message is that a word has three levels:

1. a *signal* level of meaning—the sound of the spoken word or the look of word in print, as, say, mouse.

2. the *referent*, the actual, concrete object, the exact living rodent that the writer is thinking about, the denotation, or extensional meaning.

3. the intensional meaning; the connotation or recalled experiences of past mice or thoughts or stories about mice that are evoked in the mind of the reader. The reference may vary with the sex of the reader and certainly will vary according to the pleasure or unpleasantness of the past experiences.

The message of the semanticist in summary is:

1. The word is not the thing.

2. We must be very careful in distinguishing levels of abstraction, and use a word with as low a level of abstraction as possible.

3. Many of the barriers we encounter during communication are caused by confusion about words and things and by the sum of the emotions we have come to associate with words.

To revert once again to the ancient question of the nature of reality, realism versus nominalism, the semanticist is a nominalist in an unfriendly world of subjective realists who over-react to general concepts. He cries, "*Communism* is just a word. Plymouth Colony was communist; so was Brooke Farm after Hawthorne left it. Let's look at the thing we are talking about. Do not let your emotions reflect off the bad word onto what I am saying." Frequently we are pointedly aware that we completely fail to understand each other even though we converse in the same language. Thus we are comforted when some person in our midst soothes ruffled feelings by calling out, "Maybe we are not in opposition at all. Let's just get together and define our terms. Semantics, that's our problem!"

SYMBOLIC LOGIC

In an earlier chapter, the comment was made that language grows out of the needs and nature of the time and its people. The same is true of epistemology and logic. In the time of Aristotle, there was a need to collect and classify information—and Aristotle was primarily concerned with definition and predication. In the medieval period, the primary concern seemed to be an analysis of reality: is the thing real or is only our perception of it real? That thinking was primarily deductive. In the Renaissance the emphasis moved toward induction, to checking of assumptions and generalizations by direct observation of specifics. Bacon, the spokesman, sounded a strong note of concern for cause and effect. With his "more or less" tables he dramatized not the search for what *is*, but for what caused it to be that way. This preoccupation with cause and effect was refined by John Stuart Mill, whose four canons for causality provided the next step after Bacon's tables. The tables suggested that one occurrence might be an antecedent and another a consequent and that when p happens, q would occur, perhaps always, perhaps sometimes. Mill's canons provided a test for the degree of coincidence. Was p always found when q occurred? Does q occur when p does not? Does p ever occur when q does not?

Probably no time in history has been so systematically concerned with cause and effect as the present. What causes disease? What causes war? What can we do to bring about peace? What can we do to bring victory on the gridiron Saturday? How can I prevent acne? What can I do to lose weight? How can we win the election in November? How can we be sure this television program will be a success? What can I do to achieve happiness? What kind of education helps various segments of society? Will pouring money into the underdeveloped nations help them or debilitate them?

None of these problems is new. What is new is the determined, systematic way that we are attempting to discover what causes or influences what. There is a philanthropic foundation, a government agency, a college professor, or a professional researcher studying every one of the problems listed above.

This systematic attention to cause and effect has necessitated a whole new way of looking at the relationship between two incidents, or two groups of incidents.

Venn diagrams. Most of the heritage of logicians is verbal. Since Aristotle, deductive logic has been based on the syllogism and four types of propositions. The following deductive syllogism is perfectly clear.

Major   premise: Dogs are meat eaters.

Minor   premise: Fido is a dog.

Conclusion: Fido is a meat eater.

But the deductive syllogism is not always adequate to its task of defining, as this example shows:

Dogs are common.

Weimaraners are dogs.

Weimaraners are common.

To explain what is wrong with this reasoning would involve the application of a number of rules and would take several pages. The semanticist attempts to condense this involved analysis by pointing out that the abstract word *dogs* has two levels of meaning. $Dogs_1$ may be "all dogs," but $dogs_2$ may mean "a collection of species of dogs." The trouble is not only in the logic but in the confusion about what is meant by *dogs*.

Other logicians, working only with these limited sentences called *categorical propositions* (which deal only with the relationships possible between classes) utilize four standard forms:

Universal-Affirmative: All dogs are meat eaters.

Universal-Negative: No dogs are meat eaters.

Particular-Affirmative: Some dogs are meat eaters.

Particular-Negative: Some dogs are not meat eaters.

These four statements indicate the four possible relationships of one class with another. Clearly, if all four statements are made about the same two classes in the same order, not all of the statements will be equally true. Further, statements in these forms can be related as the premises of deductive syllogisms in a variety of ways, not all of which will produce valid (*formally* suitable) arguments. In order to test syllogisms visually, without necessarily working through some of the complex discussions required by some arguments, logicians have tried to develop diagrammatic methods. Two universal-affirmative propositions could be represented as in Figures 1 and 2.

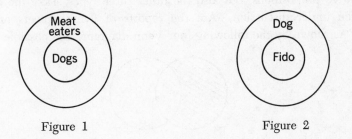

Figure 1   Figure 2

Figure 1 is read, "all things called dogs are in the class of things called meat eaters." (Note that the two circles are not co-extensive; all dogs are accounted for, but not all meat eaters. Formally, the subject term of universal-affirmative propositions is *distributed;* the predicate term is *undistributed.*)

Similarly, in Figure 2, Fido is all dog, but not all dogs are Fido. (Although distribution requirements are only one of the several rules regulating deductive syllogistic arguments, we mention them here because the most common fallacy is that of the *undistributed* middle term. See Figure 10, p. 290, for an illustration of the form such arguments take.)

If Figures 1 and 2 are combined, we have Figure 3:

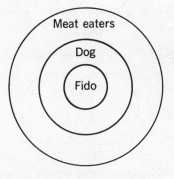

Figure 3

Figure 3 indicates that if Fido is a dog, he must have the characteristics of a dog.

Major premise: Dogs are meat eaters.

Minor premise: Fido is a dog.

Conclusion: Fido is a meat eater.

In the nineteenth century, John Venn, an English mathematician and logician, devised a system of diagrams to include not only universal-affirmative propositions, but also the other three types. Take the question so often under discussion, "Are the reports of flying saucers or UFO's true?" As shown by the following four Venn diagrams, the possible answers are:

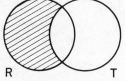

Figure 4

Universal-Affirmative: All the reports are true.

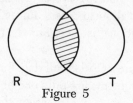

Figure 5

Universal-Negative: No reports are true.

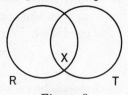

Figure 6

Partial-Affirmative: Some reports are true.

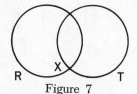

Figure 7

Partial-Negative: Some reports are not true.

A reader staring at Venn diagrams may have a feeling that he is back in kindergarten playing with blocks, but in a very graphic way the superimposed circles say a great deal about the nature of truth. The four diagrams testify to the open nature of the modern mind. Any statement must be approached with the possibility that it is or is not true. Although in Figure 4, that part of the R circle which is not in the T circle is shaded out—which means that the statement rejects the possibility—the shaded section is there instead of being eliminated; in short, the existence of the shaded section demonstrates that it was once considered. As we read the diagrams, we can make some other observations. If we look at the "predi--cate term," represented by the truth circle, we can see that we have never accounted for all of the truth. We can see that in all four cases, there can be other truths besides the reports. We have not accounted for, or "distributed," the predicate term. If the proposition were "All spaniels are dogs," we can picture a diagram like Figure 8.

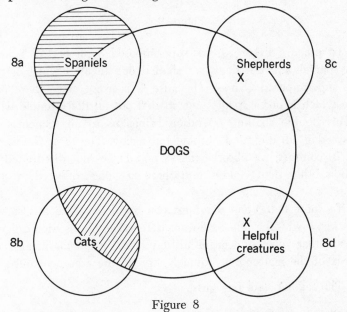

Figure 8

From this diagram we can make a number of observations. Figure 8a says that all spaniels are dogs; none is not a dog, although we considered that possibility. It also says that some dogs are spaniels; some are not. Figure 8b says that no cats are dogs; all cats are nondogs; and no dogs are cats. Figure 8c says that some shepherds are dogs; some shepherds are something else; some dogs are shepherds; some are not shepherds. Figure 8d says that some dogs are helpful creatures; some are not; some helpful creatures are dogs; some are not. Note that we have accounted for all spaniels and cats; those terms are "distributed." We have not accounted for dogs, shepherds, or helpful creatures. These terms are not distributed.

With these perceptions of Venn propositions, we can test syllogisms.

All spaniels are dogs.

Goldie is a spaniel.

Goldie is a dog.

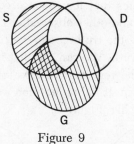

Figure 9

To prepare Figure 9, we superimposed S on D (all S are D). Since no spaniels are not dogs, we shaded out all of S which is not D. Then we superimposed G on S (because G is a S); since there is none of Goldie which is not a spaniel, we shaded out all the G circle which is not S. This double shading operation brings us to our conclusion that Goldie is a dog, all dog, and nothing but a dog. The term *Goldie* is distributed. In contrast, we observe that S and D are not distributed; there are spaniels other than Goldie, and there are dogs other than spaniels or Goldie.

To show that Venn diagrams can test logic, take this statement, "I do not know why the fellows do not date Susie. She is such a fine girl." You can see that you might argue all day about what *fine* means. To get to the crux of the matter more quickly, spread the argument out:

The fellows date fine girls.

Susie is a fine girl.

The fellows should date Susie.

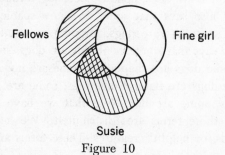

Figure 10

Part of the Susie circle in Figure 10 is clear in the Fellows circle, and some of it is shaded. Thus we can see that the fellows may or may not date Susie, and the speaker's conclusion that they should date her is not justified. Or take the lament, "I do not know why I do not get to play on the team. I attend practice while the fellows who get to play skip practice all the time." Whether his premises are sound or not, the player's argument is:

Football players attend practice.

I attend practice.

I should be a player.

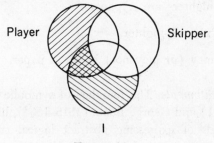

Player   Skipper

Figure 11

In Figure 11, we see that even though starting-quality players do not skip practice and even though our friend does not skip practice, he may or may not be qualified to play.

Or take this example: "Mr. Wilkins, I worked all night on this paper. I should have received an A." When one premise is missing from a syllogism, the result is called an *enthymeme.* The premise will have to be inferred, in which case the argument goes:

A papers take all night.

This paper took all night.

It should be an A paper.

In Figure 12, the argument is shown diagrammatically. What has our student in trouble is that she thought the major premise was reversible, that "All-nighters are A papers," whereas actually the predicate term was not distributed. An A paper may take all night to prepare, but not every paper taking all night deserves an A.

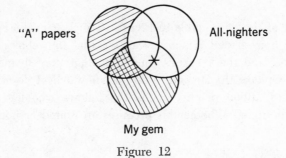

Figure 12

This brings up the importance of the qualified, or limited, particular, or partial proposition (known by any of these names). The argument produces no firm conclusion:

Some all-nighters are A papers.

My gem is an all-nighter.

My gem may (or may not) be an A paper.

Related statements. The founders of symbolic logic, Augustus De Morgan (1806–1871) and George Boole (1815–1864), like Venn, attempted to develop methods of expressing abstract logical concepts in symbols about whose meaning there could be complete agreement. Boole was especially interested in the interpretation of categorical propositions, especially particular affirmatives and negatives. One of De Morgan's chief interests was measuring probability in terms of degrees of belief. If an event was sure to happen, the probability was complete; as a result of partial knowledge and partial ignorance we might be less sure; to us the event is less probable. Both men were determined to find a way to express such logical concepts not in words but in symbols. Like Aristotle, Voltaire, Locke, and Bacon, they were suspicious of the Idols of the Marketplace.

The question at the base of the problem the symbolic logician faced is, as in the following sentences, what does *and* mean?

The whistle blew, and the game ended.

The Red Sox beat the Orioles, and there was an accident on El Camino Real, just south of San Francisco.

Fall faded, and winter arrived.

Supply goes up, and demand goes down.

Demand goes up, and price goes up.

I got a chill and caught a cold.

Reinforcements arrived, and the enemy was routed.

Medication was administered, and the infection disappeared.

In their need to consider, discuss, and communicate concepts of cause and effect, modern scholars need whole new approaches. They need to understand direct cause, common cause, and indirect cause. What causes influenza? That is easy, you say; a germ or a virus. Not so; there must be a complex of conditions. There has to be exposure to a certain virus, but the sufferer must also have had a condition of lowered resistance that *caused* the susceptibility. And what *caused* the loss of resistance? The teacher who assigned too much work? The girl friend? She may cause infectious mononeucleosis directly and influenza indirectly. Certain cigarette companies have noticed that college students can identify a group of students who are likely to get lung cancer—before they start smoking. Their hypothesis is that certain character traits, identifiable by college classmates, ultimately lead to lung cancer, but they do not speculate yet that the traits lead to smoking, which leads to cancer, or that the traits lead directly to high tension and/or cancer.

Conjunction. This awareness of the possible meanings of the word *and* leads us to the concern of the logician for the language to describe, without ambiguity, the relationships between two events.

The whistle blew, and the game ended.

Does the blowing of a whistle end the game? Our immediate affirmative answer is shaken a bit when we learn that, in the last moments of bedlam, the quarterback did not hear the whistle at all; he threw the ball away when he saw the official raise his hand. The other team stopped playing when the home quarterback threw the ball into the crowd. When we learn that in some games the end is announced by the firing of a gun, we realize that a whistle is not absolutely essential to end a game. The more we think about it, the more we think the question is unending. Actually the whistle or the gun are merely symbols indicating that many years ago, someone decided that a game would end in just one hour, not one hour after it started, but after one hour of playing time, no matter how many times it is interrupted. The ending time is continually changed, for instance to get in commercials if the game is televised. A Big Ten football game was once rushed because the officials had to catch a certain train. In view of all these influences, just what, exactly, is the meaning of *and* in the statement about the whistle and the game? The question boils down to the fact that there can be two kinds of causes, a *first* or basic cause, and an immediate or *affective* cause. The first cause was, in this case, the rule that a football game shall end after an hour of playing time, and the hour was up. The affective cause that actually brought this game to a close was the blowing of the whistle. There comes a time when the logician pointedly wishes to avoid calling something a cause because he wishes to avoid being caught in the question of whether p is the first cause or the affective cause. He may also wish to avoid indicating that p was a cause at all, even though p and q happened at the same time, or that p happened before q. In all such instances, he calls this co-incidence a *conjunction*. To express this relationship, the logician writes:

The whistle blew • the game ended

To reduce the sentence to its completely abstract quality, the logician substitutes p for the first statement and q for the second, thus:

$p \cdot q$

The logician is concerned with the possible truth of this compound statement, and he realizes that for the entire statement to be true, both components must be true, thus:

1. Where p is true and q is true, $p \cdot q$ is true.

2. Where p is true and q is false, $p \cdot q$ is false.

3. Where p is false and q is true, $p \cdot q$ is false.

4. Where p is false and q is false, $p \cdot q$ is false.

(1) The statement is true when the whistle blows and the game ends. It is not true if (2) the whistle blows and the game does not end; (3) the game ends without the whistle blowing; (4) the whistle does not blow, and the game does not end. We have not said that p causes q; we've only expressed the conjunctive concept—two events happen together.

Negation. A negative expression tends to be ambiguous. Expressed in words it has unintended overtones. "Tom is not a success" implies that Tom is a failure, whereas he could be something in between. To express the negation in a way absolutely devoid of implications the logician uses the curl ($\sim$) "Tom is not a man" implies he is a coward, but "Tom $\sim$ a man" expresses only the negation; it leaves open the possibility that Tom is a cat, or an infinite number of other possibilities.

Disjunction. Another ambiguous word that the symbolic logician tries to clarify is the word *or*. Note the meaning that follows.

The game will be played in rain or shine.

The sentence means that the game will be played if it rains, if it shines, or both. In legal documents, this inclusive meaning is shown by *and/or*. But note the different meaning:

With this suit you may have a second pair of pants or a vest.

Here the meaning is that you must take either one or the other. Legally this expression is shown by "either . . . but not both." You may have at least one, and at most one, but not both. The first meaning (and/or) is called *inclusive disjunction* and the second meaning (either . . . but not both) is called *exclusive disjunction*.

The inclusive disjunction of two statements is interpreted as asserting that at least one of the statements is true, and their exclusive disjunction asserts that at least one of the statements is true and at least one is false. This inclusive meaning of *or*, that at least one of the statements is true, is represented by the logician's symbol V.

We will buy stocks, or we will buy bonds.

This makes possible a *disjunctive syllogism:*

We will buy stocks V we will buy bonds.
We will not buy stocks.
Therefore, we will buy bonds.

These assertions do not, strictly speaking, indicate causality at all; they simply state the accepted relationship between two concepts. Still another type of relationship that borders on causality, but does not necessarily include it, is contained in these assertions:

If the solution is acid, then the litmus paper will turn red.

If you say that once again, I will scream.

If you do not hand over your money, I will shoot you.

If you do not get rid of this crocodile which just ate up our linoleum, I will go off and get married.

The last assertion, the ultimatum given to Dr. Dolittle by his sister Sarah, was demonstrated as inevitable when the indomitable doctor retorted, "All right. Go and get married. It can't be helped." The doctor could not bring himself to get rid of his animals, and he was willing to accept the consequences.

The relationship may be causality, "If you shake the bell, then it will ring," or it may be definition, "If it has six legs, then it is an insect," or it may be purely a matter of decision, "If I get my work done, then I will go to a movie." The logician shows all these meanings with a symbol called a "horseshoe," $\supset$.

It rains $\supset$ I will be angry.

This would be interpreted, "If it rains, then I will be angry."

The statement $p \supset q$ makes possible two fallacies. One might argue, erroneously, that if the consequent is denied, the antecedent would not be true; that is, if we see that q did not happen, we might conclude that the antecedent p had not taken place. This is called the Fallacy of Affirming the Consequent. Another fallacy occurs when we argue that, if we deny the antecedent, the consequent will not take place. For example:

If the barometer rises, rain will fall.

or

barometer rises $\supset$ rain falls.

If rain does fall, we cannot assume that the barometer rose, for the possibility of another cause is not ruled out by the original assertion. This would have been possible:

If the barometer rises or the wind shifts, then rain will fall.

or

Barometer rises $\lor$ wind shifts $\supset$ rain falls.

Therefore, the logician needs another term to indicate that q will occur *if and only if* p occurs. The symbol $\equiv$ means that p provides the necessary and sufficient conditions for q to occur. Thus $p \equiv q$ means $p \supset q$ and $q \supset p$. When a scientist can conclude his research with this symbol, he has discovered something very basic indeed.

This brief and over-simplified introduction to epistemology and logic may have helped you become aware of the problems that can best be explained more fully in a good course in the subject. After this discussion we cannot expect you to solve problems based on formal logic, but as a result of it, you should now have some perception of the reasons that modern logicians are spending time and effort attempting to reduce the confusion that is almost inevitable in language.

Logic and the student of writing

We now come to the crucial moment. The student of writing, having been confronted with all this information about epistemology and logic may well inquire, "But what is all this to me? Plato, Aristotle, Aquinas, Bacon, Mill, Dewey, Freud, Boole, *et alia*, what have they to offer to me?" We must sort out their contributions.

THE CANONS OF CONSTRUCTIVE THOUGHT

Canon one: get the facts. Basic to all consideration of epistemology and logic by all the theorists is a respect for accumulated, organized knowledge. As we noted earlier, Aristotle sent nearly a thousand young Greeks on the highways and by-ways of Alexander's empire to seek out factual information. He wanted all possible information, exactly stated, available in a meaningful, orderly manner. His system of classification was so sound and his information so conclusive that as late as 1628, when William Harvey began the research which determined that the blood in the human body circulates from the heart, he started with information Aristotle had supplied almost two thousand years earlier. Francis Bacon was just as determined as Aristotle to have the facts; he aspired to "take all knowledge into his province" and assemble it in his "tables of more or less."

Facts *can* be overemphasized. In the early part of this century, education was primarily a matter of memorization. Children earned pennies by parroting sections of the Book of Psalms. They took elocution lessons and learned literally hundreds of poems and monologues. They learned the multiplication tables up to the twenty-fives and could rattle off "18 times 17 is 306." College graduates memorized their senior orations. Soldiers memorized the entire Articles of War. So important was memorizing that schoolchildren played memory games to develop their powers of learning by rote. They filled their heads with mnemonics to help their memorization. Not long ago a college student was puzzled because he could not find out who St. Wapniacal was. He learned from an adult that this saint was never canonized; the name was an acronym to help students in the 1920s remember all the federal departments (State, Treasury, War, Attorney-General, Postmaster General, and so on).

Naturally a reaction set in, and under the influence of "progressive" education, memorization was thrown out. Teachers in Des Moines, Iowa, in 1926 were actually warned not to have their students memorize the alphabet in order. The ideal situation, of course, is somewhere in between, and memory learning is once more very much in favor, for we know now that one's mind has almost no limit. In the 1920s, the mind was often likened to a pitcher. "Don't fill your head with all that useless information," and "Anyone can fill a pitcher with water. The trick is to know how and where to pour it out." A more appropriate metaphor to describe today's learning is that of a cargo master loading a huge aircraft. He knows what he is required to deliver ("felt need"); he knows his load must be balanced properly to permit the plane to fly correctly ("orderly organization"); and he knows it must be in the proper packages for identification and utilization ("language"). He has a systematic checklist to make sure that he makes no mistakes ("fallacies"). This analysis is called the "motivated sequence."

Some learning will always be inevitable and disorderly. From reading newspapers, even if only headline deep, we pick up a world of information. The spin-off of the national "information explosion"—the proliferation of the mass media—pelts us incessantly. It is good that we learn as much as we do from this spray of information, but it also behooves each of us to choose his areas of competence. A college student accepts the fact that his college courses superimpose a "felt need" upon him. He should learn everything he can about them. He should get in the habit of doing reading beyond his textbooks; the syllabus or lectures of his course will provide a system of organization. Besides his course subjects, the college student will, almost automatically, be interested in a host of other subjects, about which he may either have a random gaggle of impressions or an array of facts and concrete information. About so dilettante a subject as football, some students can remember who beat whom and by how much, who the leading ground gainers were, how many first downs each team got in a particular game, and so on. Other students are highly informed about music, or books, or civil rights, or the opposite sex.

The college years are the time for the student to begin to select those subjects in which he wishes to become a minor authority. He will want to start now accumulating information about his profession. He will want to know how to manage money. He will want to know how to discipline himself to achieve success, whether he defines it in terms of morality, marriage, career, or finances. These are the years when he will want to shape his personal library in the direction of his interests, to subscribe to related magazines, to clip articles and toss them into appropriate manila folders. A distinguished college professor thought so highly of this discipline that he deliberately started a folder on a subject that he never expected to find interesting. He selected "ballet" and became an amateur authority.

His wife selected a little-known religious colony in Iowa, the Amanas, but spoiled her amateur standing by writing the definitive study of the group.

Matthew Arnold wrote that one should do what one thinks right; habit and success will make it pleasurable. The conscious acquisition of exact information is such a skill. Work at it and it becomes fun. No one likes prigs who parade knowledge, and there is nothing that stops a conversation as quickly as an ostentatious display of learning, but there are few ways to earn respect and advancement more quickly than by knowing a subject thoroughly.

The acquisition of exact information, then, is the first step toward sound thinking. As a corollary to consciously acquiring information, inventory your own epistemology. Ask yourself what sources of knowledge you accept. Your inventory should include these questions:

1. To what extent am I a mystic? Do I or do people I trust get information from supernatural sources?

2. To what extent am I a rationalist? Do I believe that my mind contains innate concepts that need, by some method, to be turned on or released?

3. To what extent am I an empiricist? Must all ideas be derived and supported by sense experiences?

4. How, in general, do I evaluate authorities? Whom do I trust on what subjects? How do I avoid bias, error, ignorance?

After this purely theoretical approach, write down ten ideas that you accept. Being as honest as you can, analyze just how you have come to have these ideas. If you are typical, you may be surprised to learn how much of your knowledge is based on non-empirical evidence. Usually a college student finds that he accepts his religion on faith or authority, his opinions on sex and morality on innate or a priori rationalistic bases, a very great percentage of his convictions from one authority or another, and relatively little on empirical evidence. Most students deny any allegiance to "rationalism," yet they say they want to "find themselves." What is this but rationalism?

Get in the habit of classifying your knowledge as you store it away. First of all, frankly face up to the fact that there are great areas of knowledge about which you know so little that you cannot have valid opinions. The purpose of your inventory is not to discourage your interest in any subject; rather, it is to perform an act of mental hygiene, to separate what you know from what you do not know. The inventory actually tends to turn on interests rather than turn them off. The areas of information we can master are almost limitless. A housewife with a college degree in dramatic arts, who avoided science courses all her life and who always thought herself completely stupid mechanically, was confronted by frequent crises in her domestic life: her electric appliances periodically broke down. After repeated failures with professional repairmen, she finally learned to repair an involved washing machine and frying pan herself. There exist in this world secretaries who can repair Volkswagens, bachelors who are skilled in raising house plants or cooking omelettes, and football players who know a great deal about art, mathematics, acting, or civil rights. Former Dallas Cowboy Halfback Jim Ridlon, for instance, now teaches sculpture at Syracuse University. Students who pursue an interest in fluoridation, the stock market, youth problems, powerboat navigation, or Japanese flower arranging find that in time their interests become more than that; because they require reading, discussion, and research, the interests become specialties.

Your inventory should inspire you to establish an objective attitude toward knowledge. Bacon talked about Idols of the Theater in the early seventeenth century, but there are just as many publicly held errors now. At the time of Leonardo da Vinci, it was believed that men had one less rib than women, because Adam had given one of his ribs to God to create Eve, but as late as 1933 some people believed that Negroes had one more toe bone than whites, which explained why they are such good athletes! Look around you and pick out some Idols of the Theater. On what evidence is the reputation of your own college built? Almost nothing is as subjective as the reputation of a college or university. When asked if he accepted Keynes's economic theories, a man responded that he did not. When asked to explain Keynes's general theory of employment, interest, and money, the man admitted that he did not know it. "But," added, "I am a rock-ribbed Republican." This man is chairman of the board of one of America's most respected corporations. What we have here is an Idol of the Theater; all the man knew was what theater he was in.

In your inventory, determine how many beliefs you hold that are the result of your color, your religion, your political party, the income level of your father, your school, the region in which you live, and your sex.

Canon two: keep your thoughts in analyzable, testable patterns. The value of taking time to sort out and organize one's ideas is partially demonstrated by an incident in the life of President Rutherford B. Hayes. Hayes, a straightforward, patriotic, not very complicated man, spent an evening in the home of Henry Adams in Washington. At that time Adams had surrounded himself with a group of dilettantes whose delight was to play catch with paradoxes and cynicisms. During the evening they bombarded Hayes with generalized criticisms of the United States and democracy, and he went home bewildered, unable to sleep. Hours after he went to bed, he clambered out again and sat at his desk. He jotted down some of the assertions he had heard, comments like, "Our system of government has failed utterly in many ways." "The House is not what it was intended to be, a deliberative body." "The majority can't control its actions." "Our navy is nothing." "In all ages the difficulty has been how to decide who shall be ruler. It is the same here. No means has yet been discovered of doing it peacefully. We have not got it." Once he had these remarks organized on paper, the President could see that some of them were contradictory and therefore of questionable validity. He determined which assertions needed qualifications and which were not supported by his own experiences. After staring at them for a while, he felt better, went back to bed, and slept soundly.

There is more to be gained than peace of mind from an orderly arrangement of thoughts. By classifying your ideas you can often see to what degree they are true. This is what modern logicians call "determining the truth function." When President Hayes pondered the assertion that the House of Representatives is a failure, he could see that he was merely confronting a definition. Henry Adams' guest had implied that:

> The House of Representatives, to be successful, is supposed to be a deliberative body.
>
> It is not a deliberative body.
>
> It is therefore a failure.

The question President Hayes had to face was whether he agreed with the definition of the duties of the House. You may find that you often deal with ideas that are ideas only because they are definitions. If you hear someone say, "That girl is a drip," you think poorly of her as a result. Under examination the assertion is true only by definition. You will find, perhaps, that your informant calls anyone a "drip" whom she dislikes. You may learn to refute such statements, perhaps silently, thinking, "This idea is a perception. It is not necessarily true by my definition."

Your inventory may help you to solve some problems that you did not even realize were solvable. A college student may dismiss frequent headaches with an airy statement, "Oh, you know how it is. Everyone has them." She needs to be reminded of Bacon's tables of more or less and to ask herself what happened before she got the headache. Headaches, sleeplessness, poor grades, feelings of social inferiority, poor leadership, and other phenomena that confront us every day are not something we have to accept. They may be cause, or effect, or both. We can avoid them or their adverse consequences by discovering and eliminating their causes.

Very often as you order your thoughts and beliefs, they fall into logical patterns, and you then know what to think, what information to assemble, and how much to trust the results. You may have observed that often a voter acts as though there is just one candidate running in an election: "I would not vote for that man because he is a Republican," or "I am going to vote for him because he is a veteran," or "I will not vote for him because he is divorced." Actually, since he knows he will vote for one candidate or the other, the decision confronting the voter is a disjunctive syllogism:

Either I will vote for A or I will vote for B.

The voter must compare the two candidates, not merely analyze the virtues of one candidate or the other. He must not ask merely, "Is A a good candidate?"; he must ask, "Which is the better candidate?" You will find it helpful, as you get into the habit of making decisions based on comparisons, to consider all possible alternatives.

1. If I do not get some sleep, I will get sick.

2. If I do not make up my mind, I cannot possibly succeed.

3. Either I will take American Lit 101 or Economics I.

4. Either I will go with Bill, or I will not.

5. Either I will go with Bill, or I will go with Bob.

6. Either I go into the service, or I go to law school.

The first question to be asked in all of the above cases is whether there are other alternatives. When this point is established, then you can make a comparison.

If your analysis reveals either a *sorites* or an *enthymeme,* you may be able to take appropriate action to help your thinking. A sorites is a chain of reasoning in which the premises in a later syllogism come from the conclusion of a previous syllogism. Often these chains get so involved that it is impossible to detect gaps in logic. Not long ago a newspaper article discussing an electronic company's financial difficulties reported that the corporation was seeking leadership outside its current personnel. A counsel for the board laid out the sorites in this fashion.

We are in difficulty; the difficulty is caused by our leadership; therefore, we must get new leadership.

Presently employed people will be influenced by present leadership; we want to avoid present influence; therefore we must
go outside the corporation for our new leadership.

All of these assertions were subject to question, and each subsequent sentence depended on a prior statement, but because the assertions were laid
out in an orderly way, discussion could be highly profitable.

Unraveling your thinking in this fashion will give you an opportunity to see where your weaknesses lie, and you may be able to remove
confusion. If your analysis reveals that you have a syllogism with a missing
premise, you have, as noted before, an *enthymeme*. A person phones a doctor's office and says, "Should I go to Dr. Howard for help with my impetigo?"
The receptionist responds, "Yes, Dr. Howard is a skin specialist." The complete syllogism would have been:

Impetigo is one of the interests of a skin specialist.

You have impetigo.

You should go to a skin specialist.

Although the receptionist had not stated the first premise, it was implicit
in her response.

As you analyze your thinking and find that you have an enthymeme, clarify your thinking, support it, or demonstrate a fallacy by supplying the missing premise.

The recognition and refutation of fallacy

People who have studied epistemology and logic do not find that
they always think more productively as a result, but they find that they do
tend to catch fallacies when they occur. The various kinds of Idols that
Bacon thought must be purged from the minds of men have not as yet been
so purged. We still encounter error. In general, fallacies fall into four
classes, those caused by *insufficient evidence,* by *irrelevance,* by *faulty
language,* and by *misuse of logic.*

ERRORS OF INSUFFICIENT EVIDENCE

Hasty generalization. This error occurs when we generalize on
too small a sample. You may meet a single Italian, think he is a jolly fellow,
and conclude that all Italians are sunny in temperament. You may purchase

a pair of shoes, find them too tight, and conclude that X Brand shoes are made on a last that does not fit your feet. You may read *The Golden Bowl*, find that it is too slow moving—and decide that you will read no more of Henry James's sixty-three novels. In all cases, you are guilty of hasty generalization.

MISS PEACH   By Mell Lazarus

Post hoc ergo propter hoc. Some of the fallacies have Latin or Greek names that have not been replaced by English. This Latin expression means, "after this, therefore because of this." This error occurs when we decide that because B happened after A, A must have been the cause. *Post hoc* reasoning is the cause of much superstition. A football coach wins two games and then decides his team won because he wore the same suit on both occasions. A student sits by the window in a classroom, does well in an examination, decides it is lucky for him to sit near a window. The Democratic party gets tagged with the title "War Party" because a war happens every time it gets into power. A Democrat would argue that this is *post hoc ergo propter hoc.* The cause for the war, he would maintain, lay in what the other party had done before the Democrats came to power. A corporation gets a new president. If its business gets suddenly better, is it cause and effect, or *post hoc?* Did business get better in general, or did the new president actually initiate effective new procedures?

Ad ignorantium. This is called the "appeal to ignorance." It assumes that, since a belief has not been proved false, it is true. A political candidate says, "I charged my opponent with embezzlement. Since he has not responded, it must be true." We accept in legal practice the theory that a man is innocent until proved guilty; in logic to do otherwise is to commit the fallacy of *ad ignorantium.*

Card stacking. The name is a metaphor, referring to the inevitability that if we could select only the cards we want, we would hold a winning hand. When Brother comes to Mother and complains, "Sister bit me," Mother may conclude that Sister deserves punishment—until she learns that Brother has withheld the information that he bit Sister first. Tourists in Pakistan at first become incensed at India, for the Pakistanis complain that India stole Kashmir from them. When the tourist moves on to India, however, he loses his warm feeling for the Pakistanis, for the Indians tell him how Pakistanis murdered Hindus in Kashmir. Then the tourist realizes, correctly, that there is a long history of abuses on both sides, which the contestants understandably tend to ignore. Very often this card stacking is unintentional because we are all often guilty of *selective recall;* we all tend to remember only what supports our convictions. Card stacking may be caused by viewing a problem or a statement out of context. We may read a single sentence from a long speech and get a misconception. We may not know what has gone before a situation, or what happened afterward. Since card stacking is, by definition, a *deliberate* withholding of evidence or a selection of evidence that supports the writer's conclusion, selective recall and perceptions out of context are not technically card stacking, but their results are the same.

REFUTATION AND CORRECTION OF FALLACIES BASED ON INSUFFICIENT EVIDENCE

When you encounter errors based on insufficient evidence (hasty generalization, *post hoc, ad ignorantium,* or card stacking), you can correct or refute them simply by asking for more evidence, or by producing evidence that is contradictory. In a case where cause and effect is claimed, you can apply the tests outlined by John Stuart Mill:

1. Agreement: Was the quality assumed to be the cause always present?

2. Difference: When the antecedent was there, did the consequent always occur? Conversely, when the antecedent was not there, was the consequent absent?

3. Residue: When the antecedent is surrounded by other qualities, can we determine all the consequences of the other qualities and thus end up with just one consequent, the one claimed for the antecedent?

4. Concomitant Variation: Does the consequent vary in amount as the antecedent varies?

In the case of *ad ignorantium,* look for the missing evidence. You can call your candidate and ask him to answer the charge his opponent has made. If this is impossible, for instance, if a maligned person is dead and unable to answer a charge, request fair play; you can ask that your reader not make up his mind until he has had an opportunity to examine more information.

FALLACIES OF IRRELEVANCE

Often when we are asked to make up our minds, the information we are supplied is not sufficiently related to the problem to be of value when we make the decision. Occasionally when we argue, we find that our opponent has presented as evidence some material that has simply nothing to do with the issues. Such information is called *irrelevant*, and it may appear in many forms.

Bandwagon. Most of us feel rather more comfortable when we are voting or running with the crowd, and many appeals are made to this understandable instinct. Being on the winning side can have many advantages. When the election is over, we may share the fruits of victory, and in any event, we will have the pleasure of having our opinion supported by the majority. However, if we voted in anticipation of the joys of winning or because we want to be with the pack, we have "climbed aboard the bandwagon" and thus committed a fallacy. A variant of bandwagon is *snob appeal*, which is a suggestion that all really distinguished and respectable people believe the assertion. Reverse "snob appeal" is called "plain-folks approach" when an appeal is made to everyday community life. The writer suggests that the reader should accept his assertion because good, common, unassuming people do.

Appeal to force. This fallacy of irrelevance is also called *ad baculum*. The force may be physical—"If you testify against Muggsy McGinnis you will end up in a concrete coffin in the East River"—or it may use other threats: "Unless you stop investigating auto safety, we will expose your personal life." It may be veiled, "Senator Touch, I represent three hundred contributors to your party treasury, and we . . . ." All these threats may be understandably persuasive, but they should be recognized for what they are. They should have no part in helping a man make up his mind.

Ad hominem. This expression means "to the man." In the midst of an argument a person may leave the issues and relevant evidence and point out alleged deficiencies in his opponent's character. In the investigation of Senator Joseph McCarthy that led to his censure, when a lawyer listed evidence of misconduct on the part of the senator, he countercharged that his accuser's partner had once been a member of a Communist organization. Whether the charge was true or not, it was not relevant to the study of McCarthy's own record. Senator McCarthy was guilty of *ad hominem*.

Tu quoque ("You did it too"). During an argument one member may respond, "Why are you charging me with this? You do it too." In the state of Massachusetts a group of Democratic investigators charged the governor of the Commonwealth with accepting campaign contributions from architectural firms and then giving them contracts for government buildings. The defenders of the Republican governor responded that the previous governor, a Democrat, had done the same thing. An old proverb, "Two wrongs never made a right," is appropriate here, but the main objection to the assertion is that it is irrelevant. The question was whether the practice was illegal or unfair; whether it was practiced by both parties had nothing to do with this particular question.

Red herring. In an oral examination, an instructor asked a student what person had most influenced a certain writer. Rather than say "I do not know," which would have been the direct truth, the student said, thoughtfully, "In the first place, it was not X." The instructor took the bait and said, "What makes you think that?" The student took five minutes answering the second question, and then it was another student's turn. The student had thrown out a "red herring," some information to throw the discussion off the track. A writer may spend paragraphs discussing the people involved in a problem or introduce any extraneous information he can think of in order to lead the discussion away from some damaging point in his case.

Fallacy of opposition. The fallacy of opposition is an attempt to condemn an idea by pointing out that the "bad guys" are for it. When a senator criticized a policy of the State Department, the Secretary answered, "That is certainly something that Red China and Hanoi would like to have us believe." The statement may have been true, but it was irrelevant and an attempt to curry emotional favor. In addition, it contained a veiled hint that the senator held a Communist viewpoint.

Inappropriate authority (Ad verecundiam). Advertisers often commit the fallacy of inappropriate authority. The "testimonial" provided by professional athletes, television comics, and Hollywood celebrities who swear that they could not live without certain brands of aspirin, mouthwash, deodorant, underwear, and gear shifts should only be ludicrous, but market analysts find them effective. An intelligent advertising man is aware that the celebrity is not used because of his testimony but because he attracts attention to the product. A man's attention is caught and held for a moment by a picture of Betty Bikini asking for a small cigar. After he reads the ad he is not convinced that Betty really does smoke cigars, but he has a favorable associative memory about the cigar, and he does know its name. When he sees the cigar at a tobacco stand, he has a pleasant memory, and he may buy the cigar. Irrelevant testimony is used frequently in court trials, in politics, and in literary criticism.

Appeal to pity. The appeal to pity is also called *argumentum ad misericordiam.* When a teacher grades a paper, he may be impelled to soften a grade if he knows the student is having family or financial trouble. This practice may be pedagogically sound, but the teacher should realize that his analysis of the paper has been affected by pity. Pity was an important factor in the senatorial election in Illinois in 1966. Voters recognized that both candidates were respected, both deserving. Voters who liked the Republican disliked voting against the Democrat because he had a long, distinguished record and they hated to turn him out to retirement. Just before the election, however, the daughter of the Republican candidate was murdered, and pity set in in favor of her father. At the same time in Massachusetts, two excellent candidates, both with extremely good records, were also running for the U.S. Senate. The strength of one man lay especially in his civil-rights record, but his opponent was a Negro, and, out of a hundred years of guilt, many votes that went to the latter might have gone to the former. Fortunately, all four candidates were unusually able and thousands of people voted objectively, but many voters were uncomfortably aware that their votes were cast on non-rational bases.

Ad populum. Ad populum is an appeal to the prejudices and biases of the reader or audience. A trial lawyer must be the master of this, and many lawyers have strong convictions about what biases or prejudices he can expect of jurors. Many lawyers prefer male jurors for women defendants. They prefer jurors who hold unimportant jobs if their clients have claims against large corporations. These are not the practices of unscrupulous lawyers; they owe it to their clients to secure sympathetic jurors. However, the fallacy must be recognized for what it is, an example of *ad populum.* The so-called glittering generality, that is, the phrasing of an idea in vastly favorable terms is often *ad populum,* as when a politician speaks of foreign aid as the "American policy of warmheartedness to its less fortunate neighbors." The use of "good" reasons instead of "real" reasons is also *ad populum,* as when a farm-state senator defends foreign aid because it is "humane for the underprivileged" when his real reason is that he wants to dump his state's farm surplus. There may be elements of truth in the glittering generality and the "good" reason may be part of the reason for a conviction, but when they are examples of muddy thinking or deliberate deception, they must be recognized as fallacies and treated as such.

Genetic fallacy. No matter how an idea is derived, it should be criticized on its own merits. An original idea may have come from coincidence, a whim, or a mistake. If the birth of the idea is attacked rather than the idea itself, a genetic fallacy is committed. When the ideas of Jesus Christ began to reach Jerusalem, scoffers said, "Nothing good can come out of Galilee." The criticism was a genetic fallacy.

REFUTATION OF FALLACIES OF IRRELEVANCE

Many of the errors of irrelevance (bandwagon, appeal to force, *ad hominem, tu quoque,* red herring, opposition, inappropriate authority, appeal to pity, *ad populum,* and genetic fallacies) originate in subconscious drives, emotions, fear, pride, pity, or competitiveness, and—as Freud has shown us—these forces are potent. When we detect these fallacies in ourselves, we can only back away and try to talk ourselves out of being swayed by our emotions. When we recognize them in the arguments of others, we cannot always succeed by saying, "But that's irrelevant!" More often we can succeed by suggesting, "Before we continue with our discussion, let's decide just what the issues are and what evidence we agree is acceptable. What authorities are we to trust? Are they experienced, free of bias, and supported by equally reputable authorities?" Still another procedure is to ask, "Would you mind developing that point further? In particular, will you tell me why it is relevant? Will you detail your argument a little more, perhaps spelling it out in a syllogism?" Occasionally you can get an opponent to talk himself out of a fallacious conviction.

An honest, responsible writer must confront himself with the question of whether he should use the emotional devices. He knows that in many cases to ignore emotion is to imperil his cause and that to be blunt is often to be tactless or unkind and thus to antagonize his audience. Pragmatically, however, he recognizes that he cannot depend on winning an argument every time if his case is based on purely emotional appeals. As you write, assemble the best possible case that you can. If your analysis is clear and your evidence is overwhelming, you will not need to appeal to the emotions of your audience.

FALLACIES OF AMBIGUITY

Francis Bacon referred to some fallacies in man's thinking as Idols of the Marketplace, the confusion caused by the shortcomings in language.

The English language is not perfect, and, intentionally or otherwise, its users can create wrong impressions.

Amphiboly. The fallacy of amphiboly stems from the fact that some constructions in the language permit more than one interpretation. Some of them are amusing, like the slogan during World War II that brought smiles when it appeared on signboards: "Save soap and waste paper." Some amphiboly is intentional, as when the Delphic Oracle told Croesus that if he went to war with Cyrus, he would destroy a mighty kingdom. Croesus went to war, and he destroyed a mighty kingdom, his own. Some advertisers exploit amphiboly and phrase slogans that are not dishonest, yet not honest either. For instance, an advertisement for Brand X aspirin may claim that, "Three out of four doctors recommend this type of pain relief." In the first place, the implication is made that three out of every four doctors were questioned, but if we look again, we realize this may not be so. Second, the implication is that Brand X is the "type" being recommended, whereas it is aspirin that is being recommended and there are dozens of brands of aspirin.

Equivocation. Equivocation is the intentional or mistaken use of a word in a sense different from that understood by the reader. William Wordsworth is supposed to have said, "I believe I could write like Shakespeare if I had a mind to try," whereupon his friend responded, with a smile, "Yes, all you need is the mind." Wordsworth obviously meant *inclination* for the word *mind*, but his friend equivocated and interpreted *mind* as *intelligence*. Benjamin Franklin used equivocation humorously when he wrote, "If we don't hang together, we will hang separately." When a candidate promises a supporter, "You will get what you deserve after the election," the supporter may find that the politician has equivocated. Another candidate is identified as "liberal" by his supporters, who later wonder whether the campaign oratory meant the opposite of stingy or of conservative.

The tyranny of the metaphor. Occasionally an inexact metaphor obscures meaning. For example, the term *Renaissance* imperfectly describes what happened during the years 1500–1660. The word means "rebirth" and, to be sure, there was a rebirth of interest in classical education and culture, but much that happened was completely new, a *birth*, rather than a *rebirth*. As a result many students have a misconception about the period. Henry Adams' use of the dynamo to characterize history since 1250 is unfortunate. We think of a dynamo as a creator of energy; Adams thought of it as something running down and losing its power. Other writers have adopted his metaphor and confused Adams' interpretation of history. The symbol of the United States as a bearded old man has caused foreigners to think of the U.S. as patriarchal and conservative. In order to understand national economics, students used to be encouraged to compare the federal government to a man who pays his bills at the end of the month; this comparison left a whole generation incapable of understanding Keynes's concept of deficit spending. Michelangelo's paintings of God have caused many to think of Him as a magnificent old man. When modern theologicians said that this was a faulty picture, the old man disappeared, and we were informed that "God is dead." What died was a God that never was.

REFUTATION OF AMBIGUITY

"If you would talk with me," the wise man said, "define your terms." This advice is good for the writer who would avoid the fallacies of ambiguity. A writer must be careful to proofread exactly to make sure that he has committed no amphiboly. He must avoid ambiguity.

FALLACIES BASED ON THE MISUSE OF LOGIC

A fourth class of fallacies is caused by mistakes in logic.

Complex question. Occasionally someone gets trapped into making a statement or implication that he did not intend. The classic example of this is the question, "When did you stop beating your wife?" Any response brings trouble. The question permits no direct answer that will indicate innocence. This sentence is considered comical, but James G. Blaine probably lost the 1884 Presidential election because he could not properly field a question by a New York clergyman, "Don't you think the Democrats are the party of Rum, Romanism, and Rebellion?" Blaine's attempt to untangle the question did not satisfy New York's Irish Catholics, and he lost their crucial vote. Liberal candidates are often embarrassed by the question, "Are you going to continue the trend to fiscal irresponsibility?" Either a yes or no answer involves damaging admissions; if the candidate tries to explain his position, an opponent may charge him with hedging or avoiding the question.

Begging the question. This fallacy, also called "circular reasoning," consists of restating one of the premises as the conclusion, albeit in different words. A college girl comes back to the dormitory enraptured about a new boyfriend. "Oh," she raves, "He is so grand." Her roommate asks, "Why do you like him?," and she answers, "I like him because he is so wonderful." This is no answer at all; about all it says is "I like him because I like him."

The garbled syllogism. A writer with a slight knowledge of logic can often phrase his argument in logical terms when his argument is not logical at all. He can toss around words like *premise, ergo, therefore,* and *recognized authority,* and make his argument sound much more convincing than it is. This technique, since it is an appeal to emotions and biases, is probably *ad populum,* but it often seems so reasonable that it can be untangled only by using the techniques of logic. Very often a syllogism will turn out to be faulty because it implies that one of the terms has been distributed when it has not. A student might not want to go to a college because it is not one of the "prestige" schools. His argument might go like this:

Prestige schools are worthwhile.

X is not a prestige school.

Therefore I will not go to X College.

The term *worthwhile* has not been distributed, which means that there are other colleges that are worthwhile. We can feel sympathetic to our student friend for the blow to his ego, but we could argue that his misfortune should not keep him from profiting from an education at X College.

REFUTATION OF ERRORS IN LOGIC

Very often you can straighten out your own thinking by taking out a scratch pad and jotting down your arguments. As you look at them you may recognize circular reasoning. The fact that grammarians have for many years defined an adverb as "a word which modifies a verb, adjective, or another adverb" and that in 1931 Calvin Coolidge announced that the only cure for unemployment is work indicates that begging the question can be hard to recognize. Sometimes faulty arguments seem so good that you may believe them yourself. However, if we recognize the possibility that circular reasoning, complex questions, and garbled logic exist, we can often eliminate them by learning to identify them. We can ask that arguments be spelled out more carefully, and we can use Venn diagrams and symbolic techniques to simplify and remedy arguments. In the case of the complex question, the best answer may be to ask for a restatement of the question. Another device is to slip between the horns of the dilemma: "I have never beaten my wife." In other cases, a careful response may work: "Your question is very complex. I cannot answer it with Yes or No."

Conclusion

The old battles of logic, epistemology, and psychology are still fought every day. Susie, in high school, asks, "Mother, may I wear a mini-skirt to school today? All the girls are wearing them." The ensuing discussion may open on three fronts. Mother may contest Daughter's statement on epistemological grounds: "I am sorry, Susie, but in this family we do not conduct ourselves on the basis of what others do. There is a right and wrong, and we think it is wrong for you to wear such a skirt to school." Mother may challenge Susie on the basis of the evidence provided: "I am sorry, Susie, but I drove by your school yesterday, and I observed that only a few of the girls were wearing such short skirts." Mother, without saying so, has accused Susie of the fallacy of card stacking. Mother must think of her daughter's emotions. If she responds, "I do not care what the other girls are wearing. You will do what I say, and I say 'No!'" Mother has forgotten the emotive aspects of the argument; if she is often in the habit of doing so, we can assume that she and Susie will be involved in all kinds of outbursts.

In your everyday life you will encounter problems of logic; very often you may not have the time to analyze the assertions and arguments. When you write, you will have time. Scrutinize every conviction you present to be sure that you have arrived at your conclusions soundly. Be sure that you provide your reader with the proper apparatus to check your logic. And, finally, be sure that you provide all the relevant evidence that he needs.

Projects

1. As a study guide, prepare a detailed outline of the contents of this chapter.

2. What are the contributions of the following to the history of epistemology and logic, and what are their approximate dates? Aristotle, Alexander the Great, Thomas Aquinas, Peter Abelard, Petrus Ramus, Francis Bacon, John Stuart Mill, Blaise Pascal, John Locke, Thomas Hobbes, George Berkeley, David Hume, Jean Jacques Rousseau, John Dewey, Sigmund Freud, C. K. Ogden, I. A. Richards, and the symbolic logicians. Part of the necessary information you can get from this chapter; the rest you can find in an encyclopedia or in a history of logic. Your instructor may ask you to make a report to your class or to write a paper about one of the figures.

3. Define and, where appropriate, illustrate the following terms: field perspective, wave perspective, particle perspective, logic, epistemology, deductive syllogism, major premise, minor premise, conclusion, deduction, induction, definition, predication, a priori information, realism, rationalism, nominalism, Idol of the Cave, Idol of the Theater, Idol of the Tribe, Idol of the Marketplace, tables of more or less, tests of causality, empiricism, pragmatism, emotive devices, semantics, symbolic logic, Venn diagrams, conjunctive syllogism, negation, disjunctive syllogism, sorites, enthymeme, hasty generalization, *post hoc ergo propter hoc, ad ignorantium,* card stacking, selective recall, bandwagon, appeal to force, *ad hominem, tu quoque,* red herring, inappropriate authority, appeal to pity, *ad populum,* good reasons and real reasons, glittering generality, genetic fallacy, amphiboly, equivocation, refutation, complex question, begging the question, and undistributed term.

4. What fallacies are illustrated by these sentences? In your discussion try to use terms explained in this chapter.

a. Did you see the way those Indians made it rain? Just as soon as they stopped dancing, it really poured!

b. All Germans are warlike and belligerent.

c. Democrats stand for freedom, liberty, equality, and prosperity.

d. Don't waste the evening listening to Schoenberg; everybody who's really "with it" will be down at the Unicorn listening to Oscar Schlopp sing Australian Aborigine protest songs.

e. God never lies. The Bible is the Word of God. The Bible clearly teaches that God exists. Therefore, God must exist.

f. I first met Baboon and Haggis cigarettes at the Henley Regatta. Where did *you* meet B & H?

g. "Neighbors, Ah growed up raht heah in Crockett County, an Ah knows that when yew make me yoah new govanuh, yew an me'll fahnd this heah state a better place to live in, her havin' a country born and bred, Godfearin' little old cowboy up theyah in the cay-upitl."

h. There are two philosophies—two ways of life—in the world today: the great capitalist free enterprise system and the godless, enslaving Communist conspiracy. We must choose today between them!

i. Why can't East and West live together in peace by joining in a federated world government where heavy industry would be state-owned, small commodities privately produced and marketed, and social legislation would ensure a decent standard of living to all without greatly vitiating the advantages of the talented and well-born?

j. Can I be trusted? Well, take a look at my autographed portrait of Cardinal Smith.

k. Consider joining the American Nazi Party. It is a small, fraternal group, permitting large individual participation. It is active, vibrant, alive; its objectives are clear and comprehensible.

l. Don't pay too much attention to Ustislav Keldysh's ideas on space flight; after all, he's a Communist Party member.

m. About a month after Uncle Ngobjebe refused to sacrifice to the Jujube, he was eaten by a lion. Impiety is always revenged by the gods.

n. Surfers of the world unite! History is a mighty wave, and we alone know how to ride it.

o. Joe Palooka says, "Gletch Slop-on Deodorant has made me the only clean-smelling boxer in the business."

p. Commitment to equal opportunity for all and human rights involves not only civil-rights action in America, but also immediate withdrawal of troops from Vietnam and recognition of Red China. Dr. Abernathy himself says so.

q. America is a nation governed by laws and founded upon a doctrine of human rights. Every American, therefore, tacitly assumes liberty and justice as the basis for his acts, abides by his understanding of the law, and respects his neighbors.

r. Better dead than red! (or Better red than dead!)

s. Love is Truth. I love all men, and therefore have all truth in my heart. Why, then, should I read books, which can add no truth to that absolute Truth which is mine?

5. Write a theme in which you present the case for the philosophical viewpoints of both realism and nominalism. For help, look up both concepts in an encyclopedia. In your theme cite people who in our time seem to be realists or nominalists.

6. An Episcopalian, a Mormon, and a Muslim were discussing their religions. The discussion was very gentlemanly and conducted in a spirit of honest inquiry, but in the course of the dialogue, the Episcopalian said, "I do not like to be critical, but I must confess that I have difficulty appreciating religions that were founded under the circumstances yours were. Mohammed was a poor camel driver who claimed the Angel Gabriel told him all about the Old Testament, but actually the report is more like the ideas held by the Jews in Medina at the time. The founder of the Mormons is supposed to have written his message down on gold plates, but the plates were lost." Almost in unison, the Mormon and the Muslim responded gently, "How can an Episcopalian talk thus? We all know that your church was founded so Henry VIII could get a divorce!" What fallacy did the Episcopalian commit, and with what fallacy did the other two respond?

7. A story is told about a farmer who bought an old horse from a backwoodsman. "Him no look well," the owner said, "but him plenty pull." Later the enraged farmer sought out the seller, exclaiming, "This horse is blind!" The response was, "That's what I told you. This horse, him no look well, but him plenty pull." Was the sales talk an example of card stacking or equivocation? Support your decision.

8. As an exercise in recognizing causality in the familiar social phenomena listed below, try to find areas where your antecedent is present in varying degrees or not at all. Check its relationship to the consequent that interests you.

a. The effect of U.S. foreign aid on new countries
b. The effect of U.S. military aid on new countries
c. Comparison of the effect of communism and capitalism since World War II on developed (industrialized) countries
d. The effect of a winning season on attendance at home professional sports events
e. The effect of night games on attendance
f. The effect of advertising on a company's gross sales (The Hershey Candy Company does not advertise.)

In class, report on how you will try to validate your results and cancel out all common causes and factors that might contaminate your results.

9. Write a theme analyzing the logic and use of emotive appeals of the following paid advertisement, which appeared in the Boston *Herald-Traveler*. Include the following considerations in your discussions: (a) What, exactly, is the central point of the article? Where is it stated? Why is it not stated earlier? (b) What rhetorical devices are used? (c) Do you find any fallacies? If you were talking to someone who was reading the article, how would you demonstrate that the fallacies exist? (d) Who are Ralph Waldo Trine and George R. Farnum? Why does the latter deserve to be called "Honorable"? (Look them up in *Who's Who in America* or the equivalent.) (e) Can you determine exactly what Mrs. Roosevelt was writing about in her letter to the PTA? (f) What can you find out about the practice of using animals for research? What is its value? Are there any legal regulations for this type of research?

SOWING THE WIND

Recommended Reading for Parents and Teachers

Be not deceived; God is not mocked: for whatsoever a man soweth, that shall he also reap.

Galatians 6:7

MANY CENTURIES have passed since Aristotle wrote, "All who have meditated on the art of governing mankind have been convinced that the fate of empires depends on the education of youth." Never has the truth of this utterance been seriously contraverted. Never can it be sincerely questioned. Not only is the peace of communities at stake and the solidarity of the family but the destiny of nations and the character of civilization themselves involved.

As we contemplate the ominous increase in crime, including juvenile delinquency, the breakdown of the traditional importance and blessed influence of the home, the inhumanity which governs such a large part of our relations with our fellowmen and characterizes to so great a degree our treatment of the lower animals over whom we have acquired dominion, we cannot escape the uneasy conviction that something is fundamentally and tragically wrong with our system of education. One perilous defect should be underscored.

Our schools are turning out annually uncounted numbers of students, no few of whom, regardless of intellectual training they have received, are moral adolescents. Many of these graduates will ultimately gain those material rewards by which the world measures success but far too few will develop into veritable men and women of God. The truth of the matter is that our schools are assiduously concentrating on the development of the minds of the students and blindly neglecting the cultivation of their souls. To strongly underscore this situation, let me repeat myself in somewhat different phraseology—that the student has an intellect of great potentiality monopolizes attention; that he has a soul of divine possibilities is largely ignored or forgotten.

We have a highly disquieting situation, indeed a veritable ominous one, in the biology classes of our secondary schools—public, parochial and private. Our science teachers are to an alarming degree betraying their sacred trust. Their immature and impressionable educational "wards" are being contaminated by the pernicious propaganda that vivisection—with all its revolting cruelties to defenseless animals, its demoralizing effect on human character, and its inevitable tendency to culminate in experiments on human beings—is an unobjectionable method of so-called "scientific research" and a necessary form of medical instruction, and, as such, blameless in the sight of the Creator of all life. In fact, its actual practice, long flourishing in many of our colleges for girls as well as for boys, is increasing to an alarming extent in these secondary schools.

What judgment shall we pass on the parents who are indifferent to the effect of this on the minds and hearts of their children? Indeed, in many cases and in one way or another, they have expressed their approval of this deplorable business. Irresponsible parenthood, adult delinquency!

Let us recall what Ralph Waldo Trine once wrote:

"*Another practice let us consider that is clearly hardening in its influence—a practice that children and older students are here and there called upon to witness. I refer to the practice commonly known as vivisection. . . . Personally, I should allow no child of mine to attend or remain at any school where it is carried on, and, moreover, I should raise my voice and exert my influence against it at every opportunity.*"

Also the forceful opinion of the late Mrs. Roosevelt, expressed in a letter to the President of the National PTA Congress:

"*I would like to join all those who sympathize with the principles of humane education and urge you to include a discussion on the vital matter and reinstate humane education on the program of the PTA.*

"*It seems to me of great importance to teach our children respect for life. Toward this end, experiments on living animals in classrooms should be stopped. To encourage cruelty—in the name of Science— can only destroy the finer emotions of affection and sympathy and breed an unfeeling callousness in the young towards suffering in all living creatures.*"

There is a profound truth stated in the familiar quotation: "Just as the twig is bent, the tree's inclined." To emphasize this thought by changing the metaphor, in our incredible folly we are blindly sowing the wind. Let us not be surprised, therefore, that the day has actually arrived when we are beginning to reap the spiritually devastating whirlwind.

The foregoing article is reproduced from *Reverence For Life Magazine* published by the New England Anti-Vivisection Society. It was written by Hon. George R. Farnum, the Society's President and Former Assistant Attorney General of the United States. It is offered to Boston *Herald-Traveler* readers as a few thoughts for serious consideration.

10. Write a theme analyzing the dependability of a news story. If the article is straight "news" you may wish to discuss the source. Is the author identified? Was the information approximately the same in several newspapers and in a weekly news magazine? (See especially "The Week in Review" section of any Sunday *New York Times*.) If known authorities are quoted, check their backgrounds in biographical reference works. (Are they properly trained and experienced? Do they have any reason for bias or prejudice?) If your article is an indication of recent trends, as suggested by such headlines as "Sharp Increase in Crime Rate," "F.B.I. Announces Increase in Violent Crime," "Public School Official Predicts Decrease in Enrollment," determine how the figures were derived, and by whom. For help in the analysis of such pronouncements, see *Social Indicators*, by Raymond Bauer, published by the M.I.T. Press, Cambridge, Massachusetts, 1966.

Further reading

BRINTON, CRANE, CHRISTOPHER, JOHN B., and WOLFF, ROBERT L. *A History of Civilization*. Vols. I and II. Englewood Cliffs, N.J.: Prentice-Hall, 1960.

COPI, IRVING M. *Introduction to Logic*. New York: Macmillan, 1961.

HALL, WALTER PHELPS, and ALBION, ROBERT GREENHALGH. *A History of England and the British Empire*. 2d ed. Boston: Ginn & Co., 1946.

SARTON, GEORGE. *A History of Science*. Vols. I and II. Cambridge: Harvard University Press, 1959.

TAYLOR, H. O. *The Medieval Mind*. Cambridge: Harvard University Press, 1949.

WHITEHEAD, ALFRED NORTH. *Adventure of Ideas*. New York: Macmillan, 1913. (Available in paperback under the Mentor imprint, 1955.)

"NUTS AND BOLTS"

III

Having a college education does not mean you have learned every-thing. It should mean that you have learned how to go about find-ing almost everything you do not know. . . . It should mean also that you know many of the ways society has of conducting its own busi-ness. FRESHMAN ORIENTATION, UNIVERSITY OF IOWA, 1937.

CHAPTER 9

THE LIBRARY
RESEARCH PAPER

There is more to college life than the routine of registration, paying fees, and even a dutiful attendance of classes and fulfillment of assignments. You do not really become a college student until you go, alone and because of some question of your own, to the library. . . . When days begin to pass in which you do no research, when you do not look up a new word in the dictionary or a new number in a telephone directory or you do not seek an answer to a new question, then you are beginning to die. I reemphasize my point: intellectual life begins and ends, if not in the library, at least in the research impulse. FRESHMAN ORIENTATION, BOSTON UNIVERSITY, 1967.

Research needs no defense. The most successful corporations today are the ones that annually allocate large portions of their budgets to research and development. In a recent study, a large number of Americans indicated that they regard research scientists second only to statesmen. Most of us are aware that the Western world leads the rest of the world in material well-being and armaments primarily because of the activities of its researchers and that the jeopardy to this lead stems from the research being subsidized in other countries. We have heard the romantic and dramatic stories of how penicillin and the polio vaccines were discovered.

321

Besides scientific research, we are aware of the research activities in social studies and of the polls that predict which candidates are most apt to be successful in the next elections, of the market analyses that result each year in new automobile styles, foods, fads, and fashions. When a community votes on whether funds should be appropriated for a new school building, citizens turn almost automatically to studies of population distribution, pupil counts, and transportation facilities. In short, research is an important and respected aspect of modern life.

The probability that a college student will at some time find himself doing research, professionally or nonprofessionally, is large enough to warrant his learning some basic techniques. Research is nothing more than a systematic method of problem solving. If a person decides to buy a new transistor radio, he has a need for information, but if he limits his information-gathering to reading a few magazine advertisements and listening to a television commercial or two, his effort is not worthy of being called research, and he deserves the trimming he will probably get. If he talks to a number of his friends, visits a number of dealers, and tests a number of radios, he is doing research, superficial research to be sure, but research. If he goes to a library and studies the numerous consumers' services that have analyzed, compared, and evaluated radios, he has done commendable research. He will probably save money and undoubtedly will get the radio best for its sound, range, durability, and beauty.

The high-school graduate wants to know what colleges will best suit his needs. He wants to know whether he can afford an automobile. He wants to know how to get rid of acne. How can he control his weight without starving? What church should he attend? What is the best way to study? What is the shortest, cheapest, and most interesting way to Chicago? Where should he go for his vacation? Can he afford to learn to ski?

The depth and significance of our questions vary with our interests and intellectual capacity. Some of us may wonder, for instance, how authentic a picture of life in nineteenth-century America we find in *Huckleberry Finn*. Others may want to know what makes an atomic bomb explode, what causes an infection, or what the difference is between naturalism and romanticism.

An attitude toward research

Perhaps no trait of the older generation is more distressing to the younger generation than the former's preoccupation with human values. "Things are not what they used to be," the oldster laments—and the college student sighs, annoyed not only by the banality of the truism, but more

by the implied criticism. One of the "things" that are different is the attitude of young people toward work. In an earlier day, work was glorified.
It was the foundation of our nation. Work won the West. When you were
hiring a man, you looked at his pants. If the seat was worn, you said,
"Don't call me; I'll call you." If the knees were worn, there was your man.
"Work is my salvation," a widow would say to indicate how she was able
to endure the loss of her husband. Work was even given a religious over-
tone. A man's occupation was his vocation, from the Latin *vocare*, the implication being that a man does what God "calls" him to do.

"Look at things now," the oldster says. "In my day, we thought
of a vacation as a reward for doing good work; now, you young people
think of it as a right. We used to think of retirement with regret—the day
we laid down our tools and could no longer help the world. I heard the ultimate a few days ago when a college graduate asked a personnel director,
'Do we get promotions, vacations, and fringe benefits automatically, or do
we have to work for them?' "

We will interrupt the oldster here, since you are undoubtedly wondering—with cause—"What on earth could this possibly have to do with
research?" The old fellow has something to tell some college students. Although there are many exceptions, some students think of college as
"work" and therefore as something unpleasant. For a student with this
viewpoint, a most onerous task is digging for information, the task we call
research.

Such an attitude is unfortunate, because it hampers the enjoyment
of some of the highest adventure open to man. Students of biography
often observe that men who have lived exciting lives will frequently
turn to—and enjoy—the life of the scholar. Presidents Thomas Jefferson,
John Quincy Adams, Herbert Hoover, and Harry Truman all assumed the
role of scholar-researcher after leaving the highest office in the land. Soldiers, young and old, have often found the transition from the battlefield
to the library an exciting one rather than a dull one, George Washington,
Robert E. Lee, and Dwight Eisenhower being only a few. Men whose
careers have bridged several fields—Dwight Eisenhower, five-star general
and university president, and Winston Churchill, soldier, diplomat, and
statesman—all have found the life of the mind challenging. John F. Kennedy
once confided to a friend that he hoped eventually to become a university
professor.

The point is that the process of research can be one of the most
exciting and rewarding of all occupations. The human organism has many
wants, and one of the most driving is the impulse to know. That student
is fortunate who has joined the large brotherhood whose members find
research, one of the most important aspects of education, fun instead of

work. The fun in this fraternity is a little like a mosquito bite: the feeling of not-knowing is irritating, but it is sweet torment to scratch.

Types of research

There are two ways to look at research. From one point of view, it is either pure or applied. Looked at another way, it is either original or secondary.

The distinction between pure and applied research depends upon why the researcher is asking his question. When Robert Boyle (1627–1691) experimented with the effect of pressure on a volume of gas, he was exhibiting a high type of curiosity; he observed that, temperature being constant, when pressure on a confined gas is increased, the volume of the gas decreases proportionally. A successor, Jacques Charles (1746–1823), was also interested in the effect of changed variables on gases. Charles discovered that, when heat is applied to gas, its volume expands proportionally. Neither Boyle nor Charles had considered how to use this information. Driven simply by the impulse to know, they were doing *pure* research. When Charles put these discoveries to use by heating gas in a balloon and getting himself yanked two miles into the air in the hope of producing a new method of transportation, he was doing *applied research.* Charles's contemporary, James Watt (1736–1819), also put research about gas to use and developed the steam engine by harnessing the energy of the expanded gas. This too was applied research.

Pure researchers often have great difficulty securing support for their work and acceptance of their discoveries. Galileo (1564–1642) earned the antagonism of his fellow scientists when his findings about the relative motion of bodies differed from the teachings of Aristotle, and the wrath of churchmen when his theory of the solar system seemed to support Copernicus and contradict Genesis. Pure research has made history, and it has made history possible. Adding to the work of Joseph Priestley (1733–1804), Antoine Lavoisier (1743–1794) isolated and named oxygen; Sir Isaac Newton (1642–1727) determined the laws of gravity; Michael Faraday (1791–1867) pioneered the transformation of mechanical to electrical energy; Marie Curie (1867–1934) isolated a radioactive substance; and James Van Allen, a professor at the University of Iowa, discovered a belt of radioactive material just outside the earth's atmosphere. All of these discoveries were the result of pure research, but every one of them is used in the applied research aimed at transporting man to the moon. The fuel used may be liquid oxygen; the rocket must blast out of the effect of earth's gravity; most of the controls will be activated by electrical impulse transformed to physical activity; the astronauts must somehow avoid the effects of the radioactive materials in the Van Allen belt.

Besides the differentiation between pure and applied research, there is a distinction between original work and secondary research. The original researcher takes the first look. He may work with manuscripts and published materials, but he will interpret them as no one else has or draw conclusions not reached by anyone before him. He may compare the prosody of Chaucer to that of Shakespeare, or he may observe the attention given by newspapers to sex (as measured in inches of column space in news and advertising). Another original researcher may study the effect of various ammonia ions on carbohydrates. Still another, by means of a series of interviews, may make a sociological study of man's reliance on God, the automobile, advertising, or tranquilizers. All of them may use highly intricate statistical procedures. These researchers are original because they make the first generalization or interpretation.

The secondary researcher uses the original reports for his own end. He uses encyclopedias, scholarly journals, diaries, and all manner of oral and published reports. If an archeologist pulls on his boots and pokes around the Mohenjodaro ruins, he is doing original research; if he goes to the library and scans scholarly journals about the diggings, he is doing secondary research. If a botanist takes notes on a diver's talk about flora at forty fathoms, he's doing secondary research.

The techniques of pure, applied, and original research will be discussed in chemistry, physics, biology, psychology, literature, and sociology courses. The instructors of such courses will assume that their students have mastered the techniques of library research.

We must emphasize the fact that college undergraduates can do original research. Several years ago a sophomore at Stanford University did some original research that set full professors at Harvard, in the Big Ten, and at Stanford itself back on their heels. At first they snorted with contempt at his discovery—and then they were humiliated. Henry James is the scholar's novelist. He is not popular with the average reader, but critics love him. Their favorite novel is probably *The Ambassadors*, and they have loved to write about little obscurities here and there that they think they can clarify. When the Stanford sophomore read *The Ambassadors*, he noticed that one sequence of incidents made no sense and wrote a paper insisting that the chapters were out of order. He suggested a re-arrangement that made the incidents clear. When he read his paper, his professor and his classmates smiled at his brashness. The general reaction was "Tut! tut!" When the persistent sophomore submitted his paper to a very scholarly journal, the editors sent back a mimeographed rejection slip pointing out that the journal was for experienced scholars. But the sophomore persevered. Acting on a hunch, he arranged by interlibrary loan to get a copy of an edition that had been published in England. Sure enough, he found the chapters in the order he suggested. He then dug back into the autobiography of the novel's publisher and found that Henry James had sent one chapter at a time via steamship to the American publisher—and that several chapters had got out of order. The sophomore could now produce irrefutable evidence to support his conclusion that every American edition of the book was improperly edited. You can imagine the embarrassment of the distinguished professors who had never noticed the error before.

The words *original* and *secondary*, unfortunately, have connotations that are undeserved. Secondary research has probably been as important as original research in the progress of civilization. To put it in its proper perspective, all research should usually be viewed as a combination of original and secondary effort. Charles Darwin is popularly considered the originator of the theory of evolution. Actually, however, the notion that man developed from simpler organisms goes back at least as far as Aristotle. Before Charles Darwin, the idea was suggested by de Buffon, Goethe, Lamarck, and Erasmus Darwin, Charles's grandfather. Darwin organized the theories of the earlier men—and buttressed them with his own observations.

Nobel prizes tend to go to researchers in applied sciences, the standard of judgment being that their contributions must do something to help mankind, but such contributions are usually based on the earlier efforts of "pure" scientists, who rarely are known, except by other scientists. Great thinkers are, in part, great because they are able to use the work of men who have gone before them. A cardinal principle of research is, in fact, that no sound scholar embarks on a research project before he has located and studied the relevant research that has preceded his own efforts. The earlier research, when published, is called the "literature" of the particular subject or field.

Much undergraduate research—indeed, much of *all* research—results in a report. A researcher surveys the available literature on a subject and then selects, organizes, and presents the information in a report. Though this report is valuable, it may have one shortcoming in the eyes of the college freshman. "Where," he may ask, "is my chance to be original?" The question is important, and the answer is complex. Before it is answered, however, the question must be put in the proper perspective.

By itself, originality is no virtue. If a man dreams up some idea and presents it as a "fact," he is being original, but his effort is useless and dishonest. A writer may have an original thought, but unless he presents it clearly, it will have little value. Thus an original idea must have worth in itself and be expressed clearly. Lacking significance and clarity, an original idea may be worth very little.

Of the famous team of Charles Darwin and Thomas Huxley there is little doubt about which was the more original and creative. Darwin was the collector, observer, and generalizer; Huxley was the expresser and popularizer. But the contribution of each is vitally important. Ironically, almost no one reads Darwin today, but Huxley is still read frequently. What Darwin created was science; what Huxley created was literature. Even Shakespeare was willing to profit by the efforts of his predecessors. He often demonstrated his creative genius by reworking a secondhand story, especially bits of history from Plutarch's *Lives* and Raphael Holinshed's *Chronicles*. The answer to the question of where originality lies in a research paper is that originality can play a part during the whole process. The selection of relevant material and its orderly presentation produce a work that has never been seen before, and this work can have value and excellence. In the process of finding, selecting, organizing, and writing, there is opportunity to be highly original.

The library tour

Of the many ways to become familiar with a research library, one of the best is the individual tour. Every student should read this section on the library and then, book in hand, make his own personal tour.

THE CARD CATALOGUE

Enter the library and look around. Make your way, first of all, to the card catalogue. Follow the alphabet from A to Z to be sure you know where all the drawers are. Pull out a drawer. Does it come out so that you can take it to a desk where you can write? How will you know how to return it to the proper place? Is the drawer numbered?

To give yourself some valuable experience, try a few operations. Select a famous person for whom there may be an author card, a subject card, and a title card, for instance, Ernest Hemingway, Thomas Jefferson, Adolf Hitler, Winston Churchill, Frank Lloyd Wright, or John F. Kennedy. As you leaf through the cards on your subject, notice that some of the cards are obviously books written by your man. This is an *author card*, an example of which is shown in Figure 13.

The information usually most important to you is the "call num-

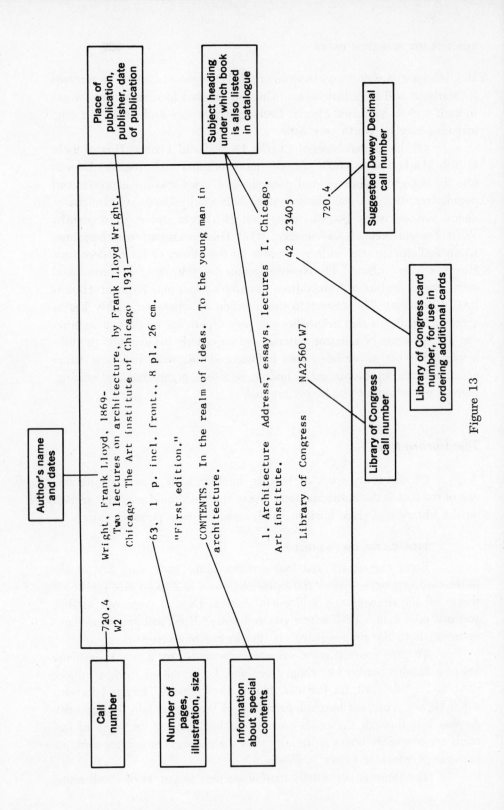

Place of publication, publisher, date of publication

Author's name and dates

Subject heading under which book is also listed in catalogue

Suggested Dewey Decimal call number

Library of Congress card number, for use in ordering additional cards

Library of Congress call number

Call number

Number of pages, illustration, size

Information about special contents

720.4
W2

Wright, Frank Lloyd, 1869-
    Two lectures on architecture, by Frank Lloyd Wright,
Chicago The Art institute of Chicago 1931

63, 1 p. incl. front., 8 pl. 26 cm.

"First edition."

CONTENTS. In the realm of ideas. To the young man in
architecture.

    1. Architecture   Address, essays, lectures I. Chicago.
Art institute.

Library of Congress   NA2560.W7

    42 23405

    720.4

Figure 13

ber" found in the top left corner. There are two systems of numbers used to provide the call numbers that tell you or the librarian where to find the book you seek. The sample card on page 328 has a number based on the Dewey Decimal System, still the system most frequently used, although more and more libraries are changing to the Library of Congress system because it has more divisions and more accurately covers the breadth of modern knowledge. The Dewey Decimal System has the following divisions:

Dewey Decimal System

000–099 General Works (encyclopedias, periodicals, bibliographies)
100–199 Philosophy, Psychology, Ethics
200–299 Religion and Mythology
300–399 Sociology (economics, civics, education, vocations)
400–499 Philology (language, dictionaries, grammar)
500–599 Science (mathematics, physics, chemistry, biology, zoology, botany)
600–699 Useful Arts (medicine, engineering, agriculture, radio, aviation)
700–799 Fine Arts (painting, music, photography, recreation)
800–899 Literature (novels, poetry, plays, criticism)
900–999 History, Geography, Biography, Travel

Each of the main classes is subdivided into the subjects appearing within the parentheses, and the smaller divisions are again divided. For instance, the numbers 630–639 represent Agriculture, which is subdivided into Field Crops, Garden Crops, and Dairy Products. When the classes become very fine, decimals are used: books on insects useful to agriculture are grouped under 638. If a library has many books on useful insects, those on beekeeping are kept under 638.1 and those on silkworms under 638.2.

The Library of Congress system is divided as follows:

Library of Congress System

A	General Works	M	Music
B	Philosophy–Religion	N	Fine Arts
C	History	P	Languages and Literature
D	World History	Q	Science
E	U.S. History	R	Medicine
F	Local History	S	Agriculture
G	Geography, Anthropology	T	Technology
H	Social Sciences	U	Military Science
J	Political Science	V	Naval Science
K	Law	Z	Library Science, Bibliography
L	Education		

Card information. The number underneath the classification number is the one by which the library stores the book within its class. Very often it begins with the first letter of an author's last name. On the specimen card, the Dewey number 720 stands for architecture, and the number 720.4 W2 indicates that the exact work is Wright's *Two Lectures on Architecture*.

Notice that the author's name, last name first, is on the top line. The dates after his name are his birth and death dates. Is your man alive or dead? Or was he alive when the card entered the catalogue? (Some libraries never catch up after an author dies, so don't rely on catalogue cards for such information.) Just under the author is the complete title of a book followed by the pertinent publication information: place, publisher, and date. The next line, *63, [1] p. incl. front. 8 pl., 26 cm.*, indicates the number of pages of text *(63)*, which, in this case, includes an illustration, a frontispiece, and eight plates. The final entry on this line, *26 cm.*, tells the height of the book. One centimeter equals about four-tenths of an inch.

The next line usually indicates whether there is a bibliography in the book; if there is, its page numbers will be indicated, as "Bibliography: p. 222–238." Next comes a list of subject headings under which a book may be found. The phrases, "1. Architecture Addresses, essays, lectures," and "I. Chicago Art Institute," mean that the book's card will be found under those two entries. Occasionally this entry will also indicate that a card is found under the name of a joint author or collaborator.

The next line is for librarians. The left number, "NA 2560. W7," is the number under which the book is classified if the library uses the Library of Congress system. The number on the right indicates the catalogue number of the card itself; it is the number by which the card is ordered from the Library of Congress. The number at the bottom right provides the suggested number for libraries which use the Dewey Decimal system.

Now look for a *title card*, that is, a card alphabetized in the card catalogue according to the book's title. Notice that the card is exactly like an author card, except that the title is typed or printed above the author's name. Look next for a *subject card*, also exactly like the title card except that the subject of the publication, for instance, "English language—Phonetics" is typed or printed at the top of the card, often in red ink. As you thumb through the cards you will notice that subject-card headings are often "inverted," that is "Photography, Aerial" and "Photography, Commercial." Subdivided subject headings also are inverted; you may notice something like the following.

Dancing

Dancing—Children's dances

Dancing—England

Dancing—Mexico

Another card you will find in the card catalogue is the *cross reference* card. Such cards suggest synonyms for subjects; for instance, under "Aviation," you will find a list indicating that there are also cards filed under *Flight, Aeronautics, Air Force*, or *Flying*. When an author has a pseudonym, there will be a cross reference for him, as in the case of Mark Twain, for whom a reference to "Clemens, Samuel Langhorne, 1835–1910" is given.

Union catalogue. Now that you know your way around the section of the library where the card catalogue is housed, check to see whether your library has a *Union Catalogue*. Usually the card catalogue indicates only those books that the library has on its own shelves, but some libraries have either a shelving system with cards for all the books in the Library of Congress and more than 700 cooperating libraries, or a copy of the Library of Congress catalogue (18 cards on each page, bound in a large volume). Using this catalogue, you can ascertain whether a book exists and then you can request that your library secure the book for you via interlibrary loan.

THE STACKS

If your library allows you to wander through its stacks, i.e., the area in which books are stored, secure a floor plan of the stacks and follow the classification system in order. Where are the philosophy, social science, natural science, literature, and history books located? A trip through the stacks with an eye to the classification numbers will give you some sense of the strengths and weaknesses of your library.

INDEXES TO PERIODICALS

Now that you know how to locate the books in the library, make your way to whatever facilities your library has to help you get at the information contained in magazines, journals, and other periodicals. Locate, first of all, the *Readers' Guide to Periodical Literature*. This multivolume guide indexes more than a hundred periodicals of a general nature, giving the author, title, source, and number of pages of information. It is indexed by subject, author, and title. To see how the entries work, look up several topics, for instance, *automation, existentialism, Winston Churchill*, and *Martin Luther King*. Near the bound volumes indexing periodicals of past years you will find paperback indexes for the current year. In the front of the *Readers' Guide*, check what periodicals are indexed. The *Readers' Guide* begins in 1900. For periodical literature prior to 1900 locate *Poole's Index to Periodical Literature*, which indexes by subject about 470 English and American periodicals of a general nature. It differs from the *Readers' Guide* in that it is indexed by subject only, and it includes fiction, poetry, drama, and book reviews, all of which are indexed alphabetically according to the first important word of the title. The dates of its coverage are 1802–1907.

While you are looking at indexes to periodical literature, check to see what other indexes are obtainable in your library. In general, periodical literature is divided into two classes, *general* and *professional*. While you are looking at general periodical indexes, see whether your library contains the following:

Biography Index. Gives birth and death dates, occupation of persons indexed, and shows where more complete biographies can be found.

Book Review Digest. Indexes and condenses reviews of current books, starting with the year the book was first published. A plus or minus sign indicates whether reviews are favorable or not. Author, title, pages, price, publisher, and dates for books reviewed are included.

Now turn to indexes of professional literature.

International Index to Periodicals. Indexes "scholarly and highly specialized periodicals in many countries."

Education Index. Begun in 1929; "a selected list of educational periodicals, books, and pamphlets," including publications from the U.S. Office of Education.

Almost every discipline has its own extensive bibliographic reference works, as is shown by these examples:

Fine Arts:	*Art Index* *The Literature of Jazz* *Music Index*
Literature:	*Cambridge Bibliography of English Literature* (cited as CBEL) *Abstracts of English Studies* (annotated fully) *Literary History of the United States*
Philosophy and Psychology:	*Dictionary of Philosophy and Psychology*
Religion:	*Index to Religious Periodical Literature*
Science:	*Guide to the Literature of Mathematics and Physics* *Guide to the Literature of the Zoological Sciences* *Industrial Arts Index*
Social Sciences:	*Guide to Historical Literature* *Public Affairs Information Service*

Obviously you cannot master all the information about biblio-graphic reference books, nor would you wish to do so, because they become obsolete very quickly. What you are learning on this trip is that, no matter what subject you have in mind, there is almost undoubtedly a reference work for it. There are even guides to guides, such as Constance M. Winchell's *Guide to Reference Books* and Robert Murphey's *How and Where To Look It Up.*

One of the tribulations of a researcher is that, after he finds an article that is exactly on his subject, he learns that his library does not subscribe to the periodical containing it. To help out in such a predicament, almost all libraries have what is called a union list of periodicals, a book that tells in what libraries your periodical can be found. There is now a union list for microfilms, newspapers, motion-picture films, pamphlets, and even advertising materials. If you happen to be doing your research in a large city you may be able to go across town and find your article in another library.

DICTIONARIES AND ENCYCLOPEDIAS

Now that you have checked your library's book and periodical bibliographic facilities, you can move on to the rest of the reference section, notably the dictionaries and encyclopedias. Since you are probably familiar with the second and third editions of *Webster's New International Dictionary,* look for the so-called *OED,* the thirteen-volume *Oxford English Dictionary,* which provides a history of English words introduced since 1150, giving the date each was first used and selective uses since then. Each use is illustrated with a quotation. Look up *bleed, nature, college, uncouth,* and *sanguine* to see how meanings change. Your library may have the two-volume shorter edition.

Your next stop may be in front of the encyclopedias. Take out a volume of the *Encyclopaedia Britannica* and note what edition it is. Note that most articles have a bibliography. Note also that the initials at the end of each article are decoded in a list at the beginning of Volume I, "Initials and Names of Contributors." Your library may have other general encyclopedias such as the *Americana* or *Collier's.* There is an encyclopedia for almost every subject; for example, your library may have:

> *Cyclopedia of American Agriculture*
> *Consumer Reports Buying Guide*
> *Crowell's Dictionary of Business and Finance*
> *Encyclopedia of Educational Research*
> *Grove's Dictionary of Music and Musicians*
> *Facts on File*
> *A Literary History of England*
> *Literary History of the United States*

Encyclopedia of Religion and Ethics
Encyclopedia of the Social Sciences
Dictionary of American History
New Dictionary of American Politics
New Encyclopedia of Sports
The Golden Bough: A Study in Magic and Religion (by Sir James
     G. Frazer)

Most encyclopedias are dependable, but if you think of them as a repository of absolute fact, you may disabuse yourself by comparing the entries under "Luther, Martin" in the *Catholic Encyclopedia*, the *Universal Jewish Encyclopedia*, and the *Encyclopaedia Britannica*. Also see the entries under "Abelard, Peter" for differences in interests and viewpoint.

HANDBOOKS, ATLASES, GAZETTEERS, AND OTHER TOOLS

By now you are probably mentally saturated, so take time for a cup of coffee, for there are many more important reference publications to become acquainted with. Besides the encyclopedias we have discussed there is an absolute myriad of works that condense a wealth of specialized information. In fact, there is a condensed reference work about almost every subject you can think of, the following list naming only a few.

American Universities and Colleges
Lovejoy's College Guide
American Library Directory
Oxford Companion to American Literature
Oxford Companion to English Literature
Familiar Quotations (John Bartlett)

A particularly important class of handbook is the *yearbook*, an annual compilation of general and special information. Many encyclopedias are kept up-to-date with an annual supplement, but the following annual publications provide information less fully covered elsewhere:

Famous First Facts (J. N. Kane)
International Motion Picture Almanac
Statistical Abstract of the United States
World Almanac and Book of Facts
University Debaters' Annual

You should look around also for atlases and gazetteers, especially:

Universal World Atlas
Commercial Atlas and Marketing Guide
Atlas of American History

BIOGRAPHICAL REFERENCE WORKS

Dictionary of National Biography (Dead British celebrities. Cited as *DNB*.)
Dictionary of American Biography (Dead American celebrities. Cited as *DAB*.)
Twentieth Century Authors

Webster's Biographical Dictionary

Who's Who, 1848–   . (Principally living British celebrities. The space after the dash indicates that the series is continuing to the present; if your library's holdings are incomplete, the actual dates held will be in parentheses.)

Who's Who in America, 1899–   . (Biennial biographies of living Americans. Also regional editions.)

Directory of American Scholars (Now divided into several fields.)

Who's Who in American Education

Biography Index: A Cumulative Index to Biographical Material in Books and Magazines

Current Biography: Who's News and Why, 1940–   . (Monthly with cumulative index to previous issues; discusses authors, foreign leaders, scientists, entertainment stars, and others.)

A last form of reference book you should know about and perhaps locate during your trip is a *concordance,* which explains allusions and terms in one particular book. A concordance of the Bible, for instance, lists important words used in it and tells where each word is used and what it means. Most important British authors, including Chaucer, Shakespeare, Milton, and later writers, have had concordances to their works prepared, as have such American writers as Emerson and Poe. Besides using the concordance to locate quotations, you can find where characters appear and also find explanations of confusing incidents and allusions.

Library usage projects

Your instructor may assign some of the following projects for individual students who will report upon them in class; if appropriate, the instructor may assign certain of these projects for discussion by all members of the class.

1. Indicate the meaning of all the information published on the library cards reproduced in Figures 14 and 15, page 336.

2. Your topic is "The Popularity of Charles Augustus Lindbergh." Find five newspaper articles that indicate what the public thought of him after his solo flight to Paris in 1927.

3. Your topic is "The Teaching of Rhetoric in American Colleges, 1850–1900," and you wish a summary statement about the effectiveness of instruction in that period. Report what Albert Kitzhaber said about the period in his Ph.D. dissertation, University of Washington, 1953.

4. What was the part played by Pete Martin in the preparation of Bing Crosby's autobiography, *Call Me Lucky?*

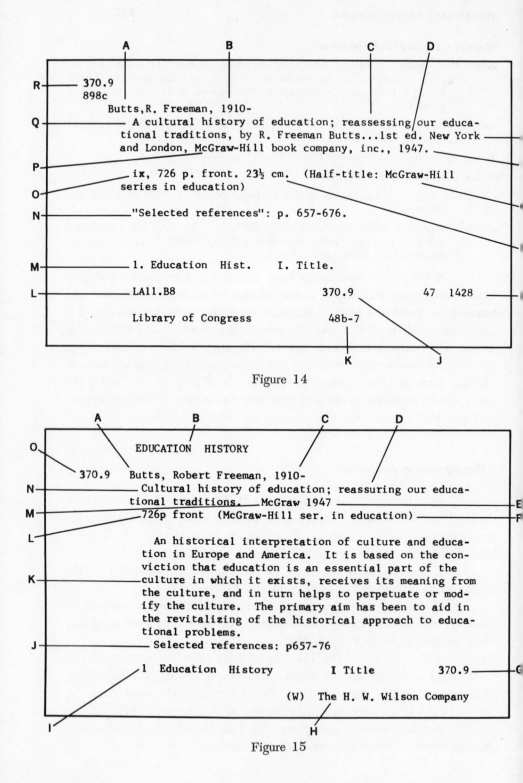

Figure 14

Figure 15

5. What is the home address of the linguist Mario Pei?

6. Is an organ a percussion instrument like the piano, a wind instrument like the flute, or a reed instrument like the clarinet?

7. Where did Arthur Mizener get his Ph.D., and when?

8. Your topic is "The State of the Stock Market Just Before the Crash of 1929." Check to see whether there was much evidence of fraud involving the New York Stock Exchange.

9. In a review of *Go Down, Moses* (New York, 1942), what critic wrote the following? "This is Faulkner at his best and worst—perhaps not quite his worst, for no loonies, degenerates, or gentlemen who fall in love with cows are major characters in these stories."

10. What anthology, published in 1962, contained Mortimer Adler's essay, "The Democratic Revolution"?

11. In the late 1930s and early 1940s there was some educational experimentation with a device called a "student interferometer." In what issues of what journal can you find a description of such experiments?

12. Where can you find a reproduction of Andrew Wyeth's "Lobster Pots?"

13. When was Dwight D. Eisenhower first commissioned as an officer?

14. You are writing an article about the part played by Italians during World War II. Where can you find an article, written during the war, about the Italian-American fighter pilot Don Salvatore Gentile?

15. What is the name of the article about George Santayana written by Malcolm Cowley in 1944? In what periodical was it published and in what issue?

16. Who invented the first fountain pen and when?

17. What was the name and occupation of the wife of the British economist John Maynard Keynes? What organization did Keynes establish and what building did he build as a result of his interest in her occupation?

18. On March 11, 1954, the Secretary of the Army charged that Senator Joseph R. McCarthy had tried to get "preferred treatment" for an army private who had earlier been the Senator's aide. What was the complete name of the soldier?

19. You have been asked to secure a prominent lumberman to give a speech and you have been informed that the "CRA" could recommend a speaker for you. What is the full name of the "CRA" and what is its address?

20. The editor of *American Heritage* has regretted that Clarence King is "the least known famous American in the 19th Century." Compare the coverage given King in the *Encyclopaedia Britannica*, the *Encyclopedia*

Americana, and the *Columbia Encyclopedia* for completeness, interest, and recency of information.

21. In one of Blackstone's famous legal tomes there is the sentence, "No man should be permitted to stultify himself." What did Blackstone mean?

22. What was the name, author, and publication information of an article written in 1960 defending crying?

23. Some readers of Matthew 3:13–15 are puzzled why Jesus had to be baptized. He was already pure, they say, and He had no sins to wash away. What explanation can you find?

24. How many Negro men were there in the United States in 1860? How many were slaves? How has the increase in number of Negroes compared to the increase in number of Caucasians since 1860?

25. Who is the author of the entry on "Grammar" in the *Encyclopaedia Britannica*?

26. The Lenin State Library is the largest in the U.S.S.R. and probably in the world. How has it come to be so large?

27. Where and when did the first tong war in America take place?

28. What did Edward Everett, the other speaker that day at Gettysburg, think of Lincoln's Gettysburg Address?

29. Have pajamas always been night wear? How was the word originally spelled?

30. In the *Encyclopaedia Britannica* several articles about money are attributed to "N.T.R." What are the name and qualifications of this authority?

31. In *Vanity Fair* (1848), Thackeray writes, "The little woman parried and reposted . . . ." What did Thackeray probably mean? Is the expression a metaphor? How would *reposted* be spelled now?

32. In Matthew 6:25 Christ admonishes his audience, "Be not anxious about your life," which is hard advice to take and difficult to understand. What did Christ mean?

33. When and where was the first church for Indians in New England and by whom was it established?

34. What was the particular contribution of "Mother Mary" Jones to labor agitation?

A PROJECT FOR ALL STUDENTS

Prepare a one-page checklist of information about the reference works in your library: where each kind is (floor plan), the name of the work, how to use it and what it contains. Your instructor may wish to see this list.

A college student prepares a library research paper

To be able to use a library efficiently requires a great deal of study. Graduate students usually take a course called, say, "Bibliography and Methods" and ten years later admit they are still improving their technique. In the life of a working scholar-researcher hardly a month goes by without his discovering some new reference facility or technique to make his work more thorough and efficient. Since some college freshmen have already used a library for elementary research, some of the suggestions in this section will be old hat. However, even the most experienced research-adventurer can learn something new.

Obviously, there are many ways to prepare a research paper. One hundred scholars have one hundred different techniques. But we believe that the best techniques have a similar origin. A tyro may blunder along and slowly patch a technique together, but it will rarely be a good one. The most efficient researcher can profit by the experiences of those who have preceded him. He will follow almost slavishly the technique devised by first one master researcher and then another. Having experimented with two or three systems, he will then devise his own system. Many learned men began their careers while writing their freshmen research papers; many even kept their notes and began a system of filing information that was to play an important part in their lives.

We suggest, therefore, that you go along with the routines outlined in the next few sections of this textbook. They may be the systems best for you—and you will not know whether to reject them or use them until you have tried them. On your next papers you may try other procedures, perhaps one described in more detail in one of the manuals listed in the bibliography of the chapter—and eventually you will develop your own system.

STEP 1. PLANNING

In this project your ally will be the library; your enemy will be the shortage of time. No matter how much time you have, it will not be enough. It will be disastrously short if you do not, at the very beginning, do the planning that will ensure the essential steps. The allocation of time varies with the nature of the project, of course, but a good rule of thumb is that you devote about one sixth of the time for preliminary steps, one third for research, one third for blocking and writing the first draft, and one third for revision. Yes, that is more than 100 percent of the time you have been assigned, but we hope you can find an extra weekend by knowing about the assignment well in advance. The first step is to sit down and prepare a schedule and resolve to follow it or you will get no sleep during the last three days of the assignment. The following model schedule is based on an assignment for which students were given three weeks plus a preceding weekend. At the risk of sounding a little too dramatic, we have used the military field order system to accentuate the passage of time.

The Preliminary Weekend D-Day minus 24–21 days	Select subject, prepare preliminary bibliography, do general reading in encyclopedia, prepare a prospectus.
First Week (Research) D-Day minus 20–14 days	Do the research: find books, periodicals, and other literature; start note-taking; determine issues or topics ("slugs"); begin "slug" outline; complete note-taking.
Second Week (Writing) D-Day minus 13–7 days	Complete outline, strengthen weak sections—or eliminate them; write first draft; insert footnotes and rudimentary transitions.
Third Week (Revision) D-Day minus 6–1 days	Verify all facts, quotations, and sources; tighten the organization; smooth out the prose; check for grammar, spelling, punctuation, and manuscript conventions. Type. Proofread, proofread, proofread.
D-Day	Submit paper, making sure that all requirements have been fulfilled.

STEP 2. WORKING OUT THE TOPIC

Selecting your subject may be your simplest problem, if your instructor makes the choice. Very often—perhaps because he knows what subjects are well provided for in your college library, or because he knows from past experience that some subjects yield good research papers and others do not—the instructor will pass out a packet of 3″ x 5″ cards on each of which is a topic and let his students take their pick. There is much to commend in this procedure. The function of the assignment is primarily to teach a student how to use the library and how to do research, and selecting a topic is a skill that is secondary to this assignment. Consequently if a student spends two thirds of his time on false starts, he will fail to accomplish the most important part of the problem.

Ironically, when an instructor selects the topic, unexpected benefits sometimes result. Often a person does not like ripe olives—until he forces himself to eat them—and then he loves them. Often an instructor introduces a student to an intellectual discipline that strongly influences him during the rest of his life. Various students of ours, because of research papers we assigned, have entered geology, speech therapy, play production, psychology, primary-school teaching, linguistics, football coaching, Canadian professional football, research in military ordnance, and physical therapy. Others have been converted to Roman Catholicism, to existentialism, to pragmatism, or to the religious position of John Dewey. One person was in a class where the teacher passed out subjects like a deck of cards. How he groaned when he drew "Nôtre Dame at Chartres." He wasn't sure whether his subject was a football game or a book by Henry Adams. By the time he finished his study of the famous French cathedral, however, he was fascinated by church architecture. During two trips to Europe he began a collection of color slides and a library about beautiful churches. Wherever he goes he visits famous churches and takes pictures of them. Thus, a lifetime hobby developed from an assigned topic for a freshman research theme.

Suggested topics. Some instructors prefer to leave the responsibility of selecting the subject to the student, hoping for greater interest and motivation. A student who is given an absolutely free topic will, in general, select his topics from the following groups.

1. Vocations. Subjects related to his prospective major in college or his prospective vocation: the pre-law student may study the contributions of Oliver Wendell Holmes or Sir William Blackstone, for example.

2. Current Events. Some students will look about them and see some topic currently of interest, and they may want to know how it came to exist. They may wish to study the roots of materialism, the background of pragmatism, existentialism, the history of bluegrass music, hotrodding, dianetics, cybernetics, cryogenics, or ulcers.

3. My Home Town. Very often students have lived all their lives in one place and yet know very little about it. These students are often eager to fill in the vacuum. Students of ours have written on "the history of the western trail leading to Bozeman, Montana"; "where Odebolt, Iowa, got its name"; "why Jasper and Newton appear so close on so many maps"; "the Chinese names in Illinois (Pekin and Canton)";

"the three Oskaloosas"; and "social structure in Enid, Oklahoma, from 1910–29."

4. Hobbies. Having dabbled in stamps, coins, jazz, or some other pastime, some students decide that since they have to do some kind of research, they might just as well do it in a field in which they have an amateur interest.

5. College Subjects. Often an instructor will encourage students to deepen their perceptions of materials they are currently studying. Students may select concepts (Utopianism, states' rights, symbolism, time and motion economy, double-entry bookkeeping), important figures (Iqbal, Sun Yat Sen, Keynes, a local politician, Enrico Caruso), a process (fractionation, modern math, silk screening, or dacron manufacture).

6. Language and Rhetoric. Many instructors prefer students to select subjects relevant to the study of writing, for instance, famous linguists, logicians, or rhetoricians; aspects of the new linguistics, dialects, slang, and jargon; public speaking; topics about mass communication, such as television programming, the power of the press, and the like.

The assumed audience. Fortunate is the writer who knows his audience. Unless your instructor specifies otherwise, you should assume that your readers will be the entire educated community, the people who read, say, the *Atlantic Monthly, Harper's Magazine,* and *Saturday Review.* Some instructors suggest that your class be your audience and that each student defend his topic orally before it. Each student must explain to the class why he thinks it will find the topic important and interesting. During this report he can get some idea of how informed the class is on his subject; he will thus know what vocabulary to use, and how much development is necessary. As has been mentioned many times in this book, the nature of the audience is one of the strongest generative influences on writing, and the writer who is writing for his class can be very exact. He can even read portions of his paper to his classmates to see how he is doing. The questions they ask will provide him with a guide to the topics he should cover in his paper, if he has not already done so.

Preliminary bibliography. An essential part of selecting a subject is the preparation of a preliminary bibliography. You cannot write about something for which you can find no material. Therefore, when you have a subject in mind, go to the library and read about your subject and its related fields in the encyclopedia. You will want to know the history and background of your subject, and you will want to know something about the key people who are involved in it. You will want to know the issues that are important in order to begin the process of narrowing from subject to topic. You will also want to know what the issues and questions are that will help you begin your organization. And finally, you will want to look at the entries in the encyclopedia to get your first bibliographic material.

Go to the card catalogue and find whether books are available on your subject. We use the word *available* advisedly. It is not enough to find that your library has the books, for all too often you will find that books you need are either out or on interlibrary loan or are at the bindery—and, having only a few weeks for your project, you are stymied. Take out the books you need as soon as you find them; if you wait a day or two, you may find that someone else has beaten you to them.

The next step is to go to the general index works, especially the *Readers' Guide, Poole's* (if your subject is pre-twentieth century), the *Education Index,* and the general encyclopedia index related to your subject. Check the list of reference works discussed in this textbook and refer to your own personal library guide.

Once you have your subject, some idea of the direction you will take, and a bibliography of several books and a number of periodical articles, you can prepare your preliminary prospectus and, if required, submit it to your teacher. This part of your project is extremely important. If you have a false start here, you are in trouble. You will be behind schedule, and your work will suffer. Worse, you may be tempted to take some shortcuts, the worst being the "borrowing" of a paper prepared by someone else. Remember, the Lord's Prayer not only says, "Deliver us from evil," it says "Lead us not into temptation." If your preliminary prospectus (see page 354) is adequate, you will not be tempted.

Narrowing. After selecting a broad subject, continue to the process of narrowing, which, as Jacques Barzun writes in *The Modern Researcher* (1957), "begins with the first steps of research and ends only when the last word has been written and revised." He defines topic as "that group of associated facts and ideas which, when clearly presented in a prescribed amount of space, leave no question unanswered *within* the presentation, even though many questions could be asked outside it."

From the very beginning a researcher should avoid the kind of topic that he can phrase as "I am going to prove that . . . ." This mind set leads to bad research. The student may slant his work, happily absorbing information that supports his intention and ignoring any that contradicts it. If the student is working on a controversial subject, he may profit from setting up a hypothesis, which he plans to prove or disprove. He should not make his own decision until he has surveyed all the relevant evidence he can accumulate. Even then he may decide that, at this time and place and considering his own competence, he cannot make a decision. Instead he will elect to present both sides of the question.

STEP 3. NOTE-TAKING, PRELIMINARY ORGANIZATION, AND BIBLIOGRAPHY REFINING

The next step is a multi-approach one. If you ignore any aspect, you will waste a great deal of time writing on cards you will never use. The temptation is great because it is satisfying to watch the pile grow. Nevertheless, you must constantly have in the back of your mind the nagging question: "How will I use this material?" Try to compartmentalize your mind during this part of the research. One part of your mind will keep thinking about the final thesis and the organization of the final product. At the beginning you will have in your mind a statement of purpose: "I am writing a report on ulcers." As you write, you will begin to develop a hypothesis that may or may not become the thesis of your article. You may start out to discuss the cure for ulcers, and later switch to the prevention. All this is fermenting in your mind as you take notes—and you take few that are irrelevant.

The slug outline. A helpful technique at this point in research is the use of the "slug." In the parlance of the researcher a slug is a temporary heading for a subtopic in the final paper. As a result of your preliminary reading, you begin to think of your topic in sections. Like so many aspects of writing, the topic itself is generative. By its very nature, it suggests certain headings. Almost any topic has certain "stock" subtopics, such as background, definition of terms, personalities involved, and current, timely developments. Keep your eyes open and notice how many researched articles, especially those in popular magazines, cover these subtopics. As you do your research, the "current," timely developments will become evident, and very soon you will have at least a feel for the major organization of your paper. As you take notes, you will begin to classify your cards under these headings.

The bibliography card. You will have two kinds of cards, the bibliography card, and the note card. Probably you will keep your bibliographic information on a 3" x 5" card, and it will exactly duplicate the entry that will eventually appear on the bibliography page of your paper.

A bibliography card for a book would appear:

Gilbert, John. <u>Scientific</u>
<u>Experiment</u>. New York:
("indent 5 or more spaces") Harcourt, Brace, and
Company. 1963.

A bibliography card for a magazine article would appear:

Bloom, Terence. "Science
or Culture?" <u>Saturday</u>
<u>Review</u> Lx11 (May 31, 1962),
pp. 27 - 28.

You may, with wisdom, decide to keep the call number of the work also on the bibliography card, perhaps putting it in the top left corner of the card, so:

901.
S413

Schweitzer, Albert. The
Philosophy of Civilization.
New York: Macmillan.
1949.

You may wish to indicate at the top right corner of your bibliography card a "short title." This may be your author's name or a key word from the title, for instance, either "Adams" or "Education" representing *The Education of Henry Adams,* by Henry Adams. Some students, in their zeal to cut down on motion, number their bibliography cards and use the number in place of a short title, but more often than not the number is forgotten or confused, and the system does not work. You will use the short title during your notetaking. Instead of laboriously writing out the complete bibliographic information to indicate the source of each note, use just the short title, thus, "Adams, p. 311."

The note card. Basically, your note cards will contain three bits of information: the source of the note, condensed to short title and page number; a hint as to the section in which the information will be used, condensed to a slug; and the information itself. Any direct quotation will be in quotation marks. All other information will be assumed to be a paraphrase. Some researchers put their paraphrases and editorial insertions in brackets or double parentheses to be sure to avoid accidental plagiarism.

3 by 5 bibliography

call no.

SLUG   SOURCE

Power   Adams   418
"Power is poison. Its effect on
Presidents hed [sic] always seen
tragic, chiefly as an almost
insane excitement at first, and a
worse reaction afterwards....
The effect of unlimited power on limited
mind is worth noting in Presidents
because it must represent the same
process in society"

Refining. For a while, many of your notes will not have slugs because you will not be sure of your subtopics. In the early stages of your
notetaking you will undoubtedly take notes that you will never use. As
your slug outline begins to form, you will take more relevant and valuable
notes. As you search, you should constantly revise both your slug outline
and your bibliography. As you watch your piles of cards accumulate, you
will keep them separate by slug title and probably keep them physically
separate with rubber bands. You will notice very soon that some of the
piles will grow quickly while other piles will be deficient. For instance,
in the research for a biography of Clarence King, the researcher quickly
found a wealth of material about King's life and acquaintances, but only
meager information about his career as a scientist. Up to this time the
writer's bibliography had been based on suggestions in the *Encyclopaedia
Britannica* and on several entries in the *Readers' Guide* and *Poole's.* When
he turned to the scientific indexes, however, he was referred to some articles
in geology journals and to some publications by the United States Geological Survey that were more fruitful. In fact, one of these sources opened
a whole new line of inquiry for the biographer when it made a reference
to King's Negro wife. Miscegenation was more rare in the 1890s than it is
now and the biographer could find no further mention of the apparently
secret marriage. Information of this sort does not customarily find its way

into a book of memorabilia collected by admirers, but the biographer was
sure that it would be available somewhere. He turned to the reputable newspapers of the time but found nothing. However, he kept at his search
and, sure enough, found a reference in the *New York Daily Tribune Index*
(1876–1907) to a mulatto son of the scientist who had sued for part of
King's estate. The biographer turned then to scandal sheets, the yellow-
journalism papers, and found a complete and morbid account in the *New
Amsterdam Times*. This illustrates how, as you add to your bibliography
because of holes in your research, the new sources may open up new questions and new avenues of inquiry to pursue.

Besides adding to your bibliography, you should refine it by
evaluation. Primary laboratory or field research is checked by caution and
replication; that is, the experiments are repeated under controlled conditions to corroborate all findings. Secondary research is checked by cor-
roboration with other authorities and by checking on the authorities themselves. If a number of authorities agree, you can have some faith that they
are right, but even when agreement exists, and always when you are depending upon one authority, check your references. There are several ways of
evaluating authorities:

1. In the first place, reputable encyclopedias list in their bibliographies the best and definitive sources for each subject. A "definitive"
work is one that is generally accepted by authorities because it is complete,
dependable, and recent—thus assumed to make use of the best of all
preceding studies. For many years the major source of information about
Clarence King was a book of memoirs about him, but no encyclopedia
listed the work because it was a collection of essays written by his friends,
many of whom had not bothered to check their facts, and most of whom
let their high regard for him color their memories. Articles listed in encyclopedias were short ones that had appeared in scientific journals. When
a full-length biography was written about King some time after the student
wrote his paper, subsequent editions of standard encyclopedias listed it.

2. Another check on an authority can be accomplished by noting
how many other books refer to it. When you go to the card catalogue,
note that, if the book has a bibliography, the fact will be listed on the
card. When you take the book out, check quickly to see which authors have
been depended upon by the author of your book. Often the bibliography
will be "annotated," that is, the author of the book will comment upon the
contents, dependability, and shortcomings of each entry in his bibliography.

3. Until now, your evaluation of your authorities has been rather
tenuous. Your hypothesis is that the author of the entry in an encyclopedia
or a book respected the sources he listed or he would not have included
them. For greater confidence, check to see if the books you are using

have been reviewed by competent authorities. If you are writing about Ernest Hemingway, for instance, and have come across *Hemingway,* by Phil Young, you can look in the *Book Review Digest* to see what competent critics thought of Young's book. Most scholarly journals have a number of reviews in each edition, and they are indexed yearly. Thus, if the book you are concerned about is literary criticism, you can examine the reviews in *College English* or find a review listed in the bibliography issue of *PMLA.*

4. A fourth method of evaluating your authority is to review his background yourself. By looking in the appropriate volume of *Who's Who* or the *Directory of American Scholars,* you can find his education, his training, and his experience. In *Twentieth Century Authors,* if your authority is listed there, you can find personal details about the author. The King biographer found that writers about the geologist fell into two groups. Ferdinand Hayden and King had been rivals for the leadership of the U.S. Geological Survey and the supporters of each became real enemies. Hayden supporters tended to be overly critical of King and to hold from him the credit he deserved for his important contributions to geology. On the other hand, King had such a vivid personality and was such a good story teller that he won many friends in nonscientific circles. He was overly admired, for instance, by Henry Adams and John Hay, whose writings about him are not objective at all.

You will be forced to make judgments about the value and objectivity of your authorities. A free-lance writer who contributes "medical" articles to a popular magazine may or may not be dependable, but Dr. Paul Dudley White writing on heart disease in the *Journal of the American Medical Association* will obviously be more so. The fact that your author possesses a doctor's degree means little in itself, for he may be competent in Greek literature, but not necessarily so in international affairs. If you are reading an article by him on the political vicissitudes of the United Arab Republic, evaluate it not by his reputation but by the force of his logic, the worth of his evidence, and the dependability and value of his sources.

Do not accept statistics uncritically. Check the qualifications of the compiler, but, more importantly, check the meaning of his statistics. Statistics about the crime rate, for example, can be almost meaningless. Compilers classify crime into various categories like major and minor crimes, and almost every year the definitions change. In one year, a fifty-dollar robbery might be considered a minor crime, but in the next year, if the robber is carrying a gun—whether or not he uses it—the crime might be recorded as major. Then too, crime rates are based on "reported" crimes. Only in very recent years have adequate reporting systems been developed —and even now, many villages and rural areas do not use them. A sound researcher learns to determine how his statistics were compiled, whether they are estimates, like future wheat yield, petroleum under the surface, and enemy armament, and whether they are sound. For instance, the small country of Kuwait has the highest per capita income in the Middle and Far East, but if you take away the income of one family, the family that owns all the oil, the per capita income is among the lowest in the area.

The result of Step 3 (note-taking, preliminary organization, and bibliography refining) is that you will have several piles of note cards, each headed by a slug that indicates approximately where the pile will be used in your paper. At this point in his research, the King biographer had his cards divided into the following piles:

Boyhood and education   (Educ.)

Early geological exploration in the west   (Early)

Political maneuvering in Washington   (Politics)

The U.S. Geological Survey   (U.S.G.S.)

Free-lance geology   (Free)

The decline   (Decline)

The words in parentheses are the words used as slugs at the top of cards. The biographer realized that six major headings might be too many for a 2,000-word essay, but he anticipated that he might be able to consolidate or even remove one or two of the headings if they did not prove profitable.

Each note card should contain only one bit of information—a quotation, a paraphrase, some statistics, a concise summary of an entire article, or a meaningful phrase. If the note contains a quotation by someone referred to by the author, the note card may identify the quoted person.

One's impulse is always to write too much and to write about matters extraneous to the topic. The sooner you have a sound group of slugs indicating the subtopics you will use, the less effort you will waste. It is difficult to accept the discipline of the slugs, but you must do so.

STEP 4. PREPARING THE SLUG OUTLINE, THE ROUGH DRAFT, AND THE MANUSCRIPT FORMAT

You are ready to move to Step 4 when you have exhausted your bibliography and feel reasonably sure that you have enough information for your paper. For some reason there is a tremendous psychological barrier at this step. Almost invariably you will prefer to stay in the library, shuffling your cards and perhaps even recopying some untidy ones. You do not want to start writing. However, you must eventually take the plunge. Since writing the introduction is almost impossible, start out by writing anything that comes to mind and work toward your statement of purpose. When you get this far, underline your statement of purpose or thesis, put a paper clip on that sheet of paper, and mark it "Introduction." Then, pause for a moment and think through your slug outline. The King biographer, although he had a great number of cards on King's boyhood in New England and his athletic prowess at Yale, decided to condense it all to a sentence or two and insert it when possible. The King story did not really get interesting until he went to California—and that, the writer decided, is where the story should start. He decided also that the last two slugs, "Free-lance geology" and "the decline," could be combined, partly because he did not have many "Decline" cards but mostly because the two were really all of a piece. His slug outline now read:

Early

Politics

U.S.G.S.

Decline

He began to write. He really was writing four brief essays rather than one long one, but at this point he did not worry much about transitions from section to section. Since he was following a rough chronological pattern, he put all his "Early" cards in order and read them through several times. A story and a rudimentary organization began to form in his mind: (1) King's decision to join Professor Whitney's party, which was to survey California, (2) the work of the various survey parties, (3) King's special interest in mountain-climbing, and (4) the success of the Whitney expedition. He scribbled down an outline, began to write, and several hours later had five pages of manuscript. Without stopping, he read the cards headed "Politics" several times after organizing them by date. Once again a skeleton organization began to form in his mind: (1) King's realization that there should be a geological survey of the entire West, (2) his efforts to get Congress to support one, (3) his surprise at being nominated to run it, and (4) his strenuous efforts to secure his election. Once again the student began to write. Since he had a pattern in his mind, the words flowed fairly easily. Whenever he came to information supplied by a card, he prepared for the eventual proper acknowledgment. If he used a direct quotation, he put heavy quotation marks in the proper places. Whether he was using a direct quotation or a paraphrase, he drew a line across the page, at the very moment he finished the reference, and inserted the footnote right in the middle of the page, thus:

Adams, p. 38.

There was no need to number the note since it was immediately below the reference. The student's major effort was aimed at getting all the parts to fit together, to add up to a total story; later he would come back to smooth out the materials and worry about effective transitions and better diction.

The student continued in this fashion until he had finished the body of his paper, the section on King's "decline." When he got to his conclusion, he was torn by his desire to explain why King was considered a failure, a magnificent one to be sure, but certainly a failure in the eyes of his friends, who had expected so much of him. The student decided that his thinking was not clear enought to hazard on explanation; instead he was content to summarize what he had written and for the moment let it go at that.

What he had at this point was a very rough draft. He read his product over with some satisfaction—it always feels good to finish with the first blocked-out draft—but he saw he had posed a question that he had not answered. Why had William D. Whitney, the Yale professor who had been King's superior on the California survey, opposed King as Director of the U.S. Geological Survey, to King's very great disappointment? Our researcher returned to the library to find a biography or an autobiography of Professor Whitney to see whether he could secure an explanation. He found the biography. In the index at the back of the book he found several references to Clarence King and Ferdinand Hayden, and he quickly found an explanation for Whitney's preference for the latter. Our researcher also secured an autobiography and articles by Alexander Agassiz that explained what lay behind the rivalry between Hayden and King. While he was at the library he read entries in the DAB about all the figures who appeared in King's life, even photographers, botanists, and senators. The redoubtable Senator Ben Butler, the so-called Beast of New Orleans, had been one of King's most intelligent supporters, and our biographer turned to the verbatim debates in the *Congressional Record* to see why Senator Butler was so well informed about geology.

The second deficiency at this point in the draft was the lack of a real introduction. The researcher was trying to demonstrate that Clarence King was too important to be forgotten and that his story cast real light on the period in which he lived. The introduction should therefore show that he indeed was important. Our researcher decided to go to the very heart of his story, cut out of it an incident that most sharply demonstrated the man's ability and courage, and include it in the introduction. In 1871, King had exposed a huge swindle based on a report that there were diamonds in large numbers on a mountain top in Wyoming. His exploits caught the fancy of eastern newspapers, and his story was on almost all the front pages of the time. Since locating the mine had required expert knowledge of geology, he was praised by leading scientists; since he had refused a very large bribe, he was commended from dozens of pulpits. He suddenly had a tremendous reputation. Our researcher told the story of the diamond swindle and ended his introduction with a summary of the praise. He then rephrased his purpose statement into a question, "Who was this man who had accomplished so much, and why is he now forgotten?"

Our researcher began to notice some discrepancies in dates. Events that were supposed to have happened to King in California in 1871 apparently occurred while King was actually in Washington. He realized that he needed to verify his evidence. First of all he rechecked his own notes and found that, except for two errors, they were accurate. He then traced two reports back to the memorial publication put out by King's friends at the time of his death—and decided that several of the chapters were written from memory by these friends, who had made mistakes. He made a decision as to which accounts were accurate, basing his judgment on government and newspaper reports that King actually was testifying before a congressional committee at the time in question.

Now our researcher had an authentic first draft, and he could begin the process of revision. Since the technique of revision is further dealt with by another chapter in this book, the remaining work on the paper will not be detailed, except for those steps that are particularly a part of a research paper.

STEP 5. REVISION

The processes of revision that are characteristic only of a research paper and that are therefore not discussed in Chapter 6 are related to verification and to manuscript techniques. Professor Jacques Barzun has estimated that 10 percent of all quotations in published works contain errors. In each new draft, check your quotations and statistics against your verified notes or against the original source. Watch numbers and publication dates in particular. Every time you verify a reference, put a small check mark in the margin to show what you have confirmed and what you have not. Check and recheck each and every footnote. (A suggested form for footnotes is given in Chapter 10, pp. 380–388). Each capital letter, period, comma, quotation mark, abbreviation, and underlining must be exactly right. When you proofread, read the capitals and punctuation out loud, preferably to another person who is looking at the verified draft. By now you probably have several dozen hours invested

in the paper, and it is simply foolhardy to skip this last-minute check, perhaps to lose full credit for careful, thorough research because of careless
presentation. If a typist has done the final draft for you, assume that she
knows nothing about manuscript form, typing, or your subject, and check
every mark on the paper.

STEP 6. THE FINISHED PRODUCT

Your instructor is not concerned only with the quality of the
paper; he is also interested in knowing how you accomplished every step
of the research and writing process. Unless he specifies otherwise, make sure
you have all of the following items ready to submit.

1. Planning prospectus. (Schedule of personal deadlines, preliminary bibliography, preliminary estimate of questions to be researched.)

2. Packet of bibliography cards in alphabetical order. (Some of
the cards will be for sources you checked but did not use. They
will not be listed on your bibliography page.)

3. Note cards, one pile sorted under slugs used as subtopic headings, and another pile containing notes you did not use.

4. Rough or first draft. (Your instructor may require you also to
submit the fair copy used by your typist.)

5. The final manuscript. (See pp. 379 ff.)

All cards should be right side up and secured by rubber bands.
The rough draft should be paper-clipped together, as should the final
draft. Never staple a manuscript.

On the following pages you will find the King researcher's final version. His format may clarify questions you still have; your instructor may wish
to point out strengths and weaknesses of the paper, and perhaps recommend
different methods of either research or presentation.

CLARENCE KING: THE FAILURE OF AN IDEAL

Stephen C. April

Rhetoric B

Section 16

March 28, 196—.

In October, 1872, severe storms drove Clarence King and his crew out of the Sierra Nevada Mountains where they had been conducting a geological survey for the United States government. As they were barged down the Sacramento River to San Francisco, they heard strange and exciting stories. Somewhere in the West, they were informed, some one had found a "mountain of diamonds."[1]

The richest and most powerful men in San Francisco, the story went, had secured control of a fabulous new mining company. William Ralston, the town's leading banker, was its head; Rothschild of London, Charles Tiffany and Horace Greeley in New York, and several senators in Washington were members of the company.[2]

Any mining discovery was heady news for a westerner at that time, so soon after the Rush of '49, but to Clarence King the rumor was disaster.

At this time only twenty-nine years old, and only nine years out of Yale University, King already had established a reputation as a leading geologist. During his three years as a volunteer with the Whitney Geological Survey of California, he had made its most highly publicized discovery; he recognized the nature of the gold-bearing strata, and made prospecting infinitely less

---

[1] James W. Wilkins, The Great Diamond Hoax and Other Stirring Events in the Life of Asbury Harpending (San Francisco: The James H. Barry Company, 1913), p. 245.

[2] Ibid., pp. 204-207.

hazardous. He was now the head of a survey of the 40th Parallel, a great honor for one so young, and he was the first surveyor to use contour marks instead of hachures. Already he was securing a reputation as a man of many parts. He had established a record for first ascents of American mountain peaks.[3] The Atlantic Monthly had recently published a series of his articles about life in the West, and at this very time, a publishing firm had accepted a book.[4]

His reputation would be smashed, however, if the rumor of the diamond bonanza turned out to be true. King and his company had already surveyed the area in which the diamond lode was supposed to have been located, and he realized that if there were any geological structures in the area which had permitted the formation of diamonds, much of the data for the eastern half of their survey was in error.

Within the next weeks, Clarence King performed one of the outstanding feats of scienic detective work in the history of science.[5] From hints dropped by members

---

[3] Francis Farquhar, First Ascents in the United States (Berkeley, California: privately printed), n.d.

[4] Francis Farquhar, "Introduction" to Mountaineering in the Sierra Nevada by Clarence King (New York: W. W. Norton & Company, 1935), pp. i-vi.

[5] T. A. Rickard, "The Great Diamond Hoax," Engineering and Mining Journal, CXIX (January, 1925), pp. 884-888.

of the mining company, he soon ruled out Arizona and New
Mexico as the locale of the find; one was too far and the
other unreachable because of flood conditions. Hearing
that the mining field was on a mesa near pine woods he
decided that the only place it could be was in the area of
mountains around Brown's Park, in Wyoming. He immediately
made his way to the suspected site and quickly found it by
marching up Green River Canyon and into Vermillion Canyon,
and into what is now northwestern Colorado.

He soon arrived at a gulch which had a notice stak-
ing out the mineral rights and signed by Ralston's chief
engineer. King brought his geological skill into play
and found all kinds of gems, not where nature would have
put them, but at the bottom of ant hills and the like, where
unscrupulous men would have put them. Within a week,
King exposed the whole affair and saved investors more
than twenty million dollars.

The fame King acquired was tremendous. The New York
Times, the Philadelphia Enquirer, and the Chicago News
gave him first page spreads, and he was eulogized from the
pulpits: "One scientific man, whose untarnished fame
alone is worth all the diamonds in the world, has found occasion to prove to the world the value of science and his
own moral worth."[6]

This kind of praise was almost Clarence King's lot

---

[6]S. F. Emmons, "Clarence King," Engineering and Mining Journal, XVIII (January, 1902), p. 9.

in life. Secretary of State John Hay wrote that "Clarence King was the best and brightest man of his generation."[7] Henry Adams, in his Education, wrote "One Clarence King only existed in the world. . . . Whatever prize he wanted lay ready for him--scientific, social, literary, political. . . . With ordinary luck he would die at eighty the richest and most many-sided genius of his day."[8]

Clarence King did not have that success, and he is forgotten today, but his story tells us much about his time.

Even the barest details about his life are impressive. While he was junior member of the Whitney Geological Survey he had located the first glacier in America.[9] During the same survey he was the first person to climb Mt. Tyndal, and one mountain even was given his name. His survey of the fortieth parallel provided valuable mining information, and it was completed on time and on budget without the political squabbles and suspicions of favoritism so common at the time. Its publications became models for government publications at the time.[10]

---

[7] Tyler Dennett, John Hay from Poetry to Politics (New York: Dodd, Mead & Company, 1934), p. 167.

[8] Henry Adams, The Education of Henry Adams (New York: Modern Library, 1918), pp. 311-312.

[9] Edwin T. Brewster, The Life and Letters of Josiah D. Whitney (Boston: Houghton Mifflin Company, 1909), p. 496.

[10] History of the United States Geological Survey (New York: D. Appleton and Company, 1918), pp. 3-6.

He left government geology for a time but was soon
drafted back to use his personal charm and organizational
ability to persuade Congress to create the U.S. Geological Survey, and he became its first head.[11] He
contributed articles, not only to geological journals
but also to Overland Monthly, edited by Bret Harte,[12] and
the Atlantic Monthly.[13] In 1872, he published a book,
Mountaineering in the Sierra Nevada, which Wallace
Stegner was to call, many years later, "in many ways the
most delightful book of its decade,"[14] a decade which saw
the publication of books by Mark Twain, Bret Harte,
William Dean Howells, and Henry James. William Dean
Howells called the book "so vivid that it all
seems an experience of the reader."[15] Thomas Wentworth
Higginson wrote, "I know no book of personal travel which is
today so fascinating. . . . I can still find myself turning
to it when other books fail, and there is no mood which it

---

[11] Ibid., pp. 4-6.

[12] James D. Hague, "Letter to the Editor," Overland
Monthly, XXXX (January, 1903), pp. 335-336.

[13] Atlantic Monthly, March, May, June, and July,
1871.

[14] Wallace Stegner, "Western Record and Romance,"
Literary History of the United States (New York: The
Macmillan Company, 1948), p. 865.

[15] King Memorial Committee, Clarence King Memoirs
(New York: G. P. Putnam's Sons, 1904), pp. 393-396.

cannot meet."[16] He became a member of the National Academy of Science.

In March, 1879, President Hayes appointed him Director of the United States Geological Survey.[17] In this position, King established four policies which were important. In the first place, he set a precedent for an alliance between government and science, which, before this period, was being largely developed in private schools and exploited by private industry. "It is true," King wrote in his first report, "that the practical genius of the people, acting in the political and social freedom peculiar to our system of government, is enough to insure the success of our industrial efforts."[18] But there were areas, King continued, where government must plan, supervise, and finance various enterprises to find the quickest, most equitable, and most efficient methods. Although he admired "the boldness of conception of engineering enterprises and the originality and ingenuity of the methods used in that industry," he felt disturbed by "the ill-advised, hopeless, and disconnected

[16]Francis Farquhar, "The Story of Mount Whitney," Sierra Club Bulletin (February, 1929), p. 3.

[17]"The Week," The Nation, April 10, 1879, p. 238.

[18]Clarence King, First Annual Report of the United States Geological Survey, 1880 (Washington: Government Printing Office, 1880), pp. 7, 14, 16, 50, and 57.

undertakings of the private mining companies."[19]

In spite of King's scientific, literary, and political triumphs, it was in society that he made his biggest splash. At the time that King accepted the position which made him the "geologist of the age,"[20] he was also a member of a special group which James Truslow Adams has called "the most noted salon this country has ever evolved."[21] In the year 1879, when King was director of the U.S.G.S., Washington, D.C., was just coming out of the mud. After the austere years of the Reconstruction, the city began to take on the beauty its designer, L'Enfant, had envisioned—and with the new beauty came a new social grace. Leaders of the new society were Henry Adams and John Hay, the former a descendant of two presidents and now a distinguished historian, and the latter an ex-protégé of Abraham Lincoln and now Secretary of State. Members of their circle were the publisher Henry Adams and John Hay, the former a descendant of two Schurz, artist John LaFarge, architect H. H. Richardson. Frequent visitors were President Hayes, James Garfield, the Theodore Roosevelts, Henry Cabot Lodge, John Sherman, and William Dean Howells. Eligible because of his wife's beauty and his own political power, Senator Don Cameron

---

[19] Ibid.

[20] History of the U.S.G.S., pp. 10-15.

[21] James Truslow Adams, The Adams Family (Boston: Little, Brown and Company, 1930), p. 327.

was one of the inner circle. But the core of the group were Adams, Hay, and Clarence King--and with their wives they earned the name of "The Five of Hearts."[22]

Of all the assembly, Clarence King was one of the most popular. John Hay wrote, "Once in a while he gives us a day, never more than that--in Washington, and then there is a Jubilee among the club members."[23] King was a brilliant conversationalist, according to Nicholas Murray Butler, president of Columbia University, one of the greatest of his time. His sense of humor was unquenchable. When Henry Adams' dog developed an eye disorder, King pronounced it a "tom cataract."[24] As he recounted his western stories, he brought the West to life, "A fresh mule and a lively man get along, to be sure, well enough," he commented, ". . . but when the high contracting parties get tired, the entente cordiale goes to pieces, and actual hostilities open in which I never saw a man come out ahead."[25] The assembly discussed art, sculpture, paintings, ceramics, tapestries, and carvings--with King the acknowledged authority because in his increasing travels he was accumulating a magnificent collection. He

---

[22] Dennett, op. cit., p. 156.

[23] Ibid.

[24] Ward Thoron (ed.), The Letters of Mrs. Henry Adams (Boston: Little, Brown and Company, 1936), p. 277.

[25] Clarence King, Mountaineering in the Sierra Nevada (New York: W. W. Norton & Company, 1935), p. 34.

provided primitive wood carvings and a silver and white
Aztec vase for the Boston Museum of Fine Arts. Now that he
was no longer in governmental service he was hired for
mining surveys all over North America. He was also
collecting memories, and all of them made fascinating
stories, about huge feasts with Hawaiian natives and
moonlit rides with bandits in Cuba, and shopping tours in
Mexico. When the company was exclusively male, he
described native girls who made cigars by rolling the leaves
up and down their bare thighs. As John Hay's biographer
put it, King's "glorious impulses were their vicarious
adventures."[26]

And impulses he had. When he had finished his task of
organizing the U.S.G.S. he resigned and became a
"geological Micawber" who tried to "rededicate himself
to geology"[27] but, perhaps as a result of his heady
acquaintances in Washington and New York, he needed money.
His tastes for good living were demanding. He could
command a fee of $5,000 for each mine inspection he made,
but he invested in a cattle ranch in Texas, and a bank
in El Paso. He went into partnerships with Alexander Agassiz
and Henry L. Higginson. Agassiz made enough money
on copper mines to replenish many old Boston fortunes,
and Higginson made enough to endow the Boston
Symphony Orchestra and Harvard Stadium, but King almost

---

[26] Dennett, op. cit., p. 156.

[27] King, Mountaineering, p. 174 and p. 193.

went bankrupt. His interests became so wide that he
could not tend to business. He made a Grand Tour of Spain
dressed in the manner of Don Quixote, and he helped
the Baron Rothschild stock his new mansion with treasure,
and he discussed art in Paris with Henry James, but he
could not stick to his own duties. In the space of five years
he plunged thousands of dollars (most of them borrowed)
in at least five mining corporations in Mexico and
the southwest, and one by one, all of them proved to
be failures.[28]

In the 1880's, wealth was the dream of America, and
King was not getting the dream. To add to his problem,
strange rumors began to be circulated about him—and a few
of his friends knew them to be true. Always fascinated
by native women, the darker-skinned the better, he became
enamored of a Negro maid in New York, and under an
assumed name, James Todd, married her. He could see her only
when he was in New York, and that in the dark of night.
He eventually had five children by Ada Todd, who did not
even know his real name. The demands of his extravagances,
the huge losses, made all the more unbearable by the
Panic of 1893, and the strain of his sub-rosa family began
to tell on him and a long series of illnesses developed.
The last decade of the century was also the last of Clarence

---

[28]G. E. Agassiz (ed.), Letters and Recollections of
Alexander Agassiz (Boston: Houghton Mifflin Company, 1913),
p. 12.

King, a series of illnesses, of indulgences in overeating
and overwork, and then rest periods, often at the
home of Henry Adams or paid for by John Hay, and then
the whole cycle again.

Clarence King died in 1901, alone, coughing up blood
in a hotel in Phoenix, Arizona. He was still hunting
for the fortune, and his friends had given up. "That
tramp," John Hay called him.[29]

The story of Clarence King is probably not so
important for itself as it is for what it tells about his
friends. The failure of Clarence King represented the
failure of a dream. In a surprising number of respects, he
resembled the figures glorified in Romantic literature,
by Byron, Wordsworth, Blake, Coleridge, Longfellow,
Thoreau, and Bryant. King had done the great feats necessary
for their heroes. Single-handed, dashingly, he had
thwarted the diamond swindle. He had almost been burned
by Indians, he had climbed America's highest mountains,
impulsive and daring. He had charted the Great West ;
he had triumphed over society and even its instrument, the
government, by his exploits with the U.S.G.S. He had
even demonstrated his affection for the brown and darker
races.

But when he turned practical, when he looked for
wealth, he was no longer Romantic. The need for money

---

[29] Harold D. Cator, Henry Adams and His Friends (Boston: Houghton Mifflin Company, 1947), p. 351.

defeated him. The "Byron" of his time was stilled,
and Romantics were saddened. At the end of their century,
their dream ended. Almost more than that of any other
figure, the death of Clarence King represented the passing
of an era, an era of impulse, individuality, and nature.
He was the failure of the Romantic ideal.

BIBLIOGRAPHY

Adams, Henry. The Education of Henry Adams. New York: Modern
    Library, 1918.

Adams, James Truslow. The Adams Family. Boston: Little,
    Brown and Company, 1930.

Agassiz, G. E. (ed). Letters and Recollections of Alexander
    Agassiz. Boston: Houghton Mifflin Company, 1913.

Brewster, Edwin T. The Life and Letters of Josiah D. Whitney.
    Boston: Houghton Mifflin Company, 1909.

Cator, Harold Dean. Henry Adams and His Friends. Boston:
    Houghton Mifflin Company, 1947.

Dennett, Tyler. John Hay from Poetry to Politics. New York:
    Dodd, Mead & Company, 1934.

Emmons, S. F. "Clarence King," Engineering and Mining Jour-
    nal, XVIII (January, 1902), p. 9.

Farquhar, Francis. First Ascents in the United States. Berk-
    eley, California, privately printed, n.d.

Farquhar, Francis. "The Story of Mount Whitney," Sierra Club
    Bulletin, February, 1929, p. 3.

13

Hague, James D. "Letter to the Editor," Overland Monthly,
    XXXX (January, 1903), 335-336.

History of the United States Geological Survey. New York: D.
    Appleton and Company, 1918.

King, Clarence. First Annual Report of the United States
    Geological Survey, 1880. Washington, D.C.: Government
    Printing Office, 1880.

King, Clarence. Mountaineering in the Sierra Nevada. New
    York: W. W. Norton & Company, 1935.

King Memorial Committee. Clarence King Memoirs. New York:
    G. P. Putnam's Sons, 1904.

Rickard, T. A. "The Great Diamond Hoax," Engineering and
    Mining Journal, CXIX (January, 1925), 884-888.

Stegner, Wallace. "Western Record and Romance," Literary
    History of the United States. New York: The Macmillan
    Company, 1948.

Thoron, Ward. The Letters of Mrs. Henry Adams. Boston:
    Little, Brown and Company, 1936.

"The Week," The Nation, April 10, 1879, p. 238.

Wilkins, James W. The Great Diamond Hoax and Other Stirring
    Events in the Life of Asbury Harpending. San Francisco:
    The James H. Barry Company, 1913.

Projects

Many college students begin their own private reference library while they have a good college bookstore available and when they often can take advantage of discounts to students. You may want to make a checklist of works you would like to own. Since your elders are often interested in contributing to such a worthy cause, you might make your list available to them. Although you should attempt to secure the most recent editions of the books you want, you may be able to find second-hand copies of earlier editions. From the list prices quoted below, you can determine how much of a bargain you are getting. We assume you already have a good dictionary.

> *Encyclopaedia Britannica* (24 vols.), approx. $350.00
>
> *Columbia Encyclopedia* (1 volume), New York: Columbia University Press. $49.50
>
> *Familiar Quotations,* by John Bartlett. Boston: Little, Brown. $10.00
>
> *Roget's International Thesaurus.* New York: Thomas Y. Crowell. Thumb indexed, $5.95
>
> *Bulfinch's Mythology.* New York: Thomas Y. Crowell. Paperback, .75
>
> *A Handbook to Literature,* by Thrall, Hibbard, and Holman. New York: Odyssey Press. $4.25; paperback, $2.50
>
> *A Research Manual for College Studies and Papers,* by Cecil B. Williams and Allan H. Stevenson. New York: Harper & Row. $2.50
>
> *Oxford Companion to American Literature.* New York: Oxford University Press. $10.00
>
> *Oxford Companion to English Literature.* New York: Oxford University Press. $10.00

Besides these you may eventually need a good history of the United States, a world history, the complete works of Shakespeare, a history of English literature, and a history of American literature. You will also wish to start collecting reference works in your major field. Your instructors in appropriate courses will have suggestions.

Further reading

ALTICK, RICHARD D. *The Scholar Adventurers.* New York: Macmillan, 1950.

BARZUN, JACQUES, and GRAFF, HENRY F. *The Modern Researcher.* New York: Harcourt, Brace & World, 1957.

WILLIAMS, CECIL B., and STEVENSON, ALLAN H. *A Research Manual for College Studies and Papers.* (3d ed.) New York: Harper & Row, 1963.

CHAPTER 10

MANUSCRIPT CONVENTIONS

Only those who have the patience to do simple things perfectly will acquire the skill to do difficult things easily. JOHANN CHRISTOPH FRIEDRICH VON SCHILLER.

Human beings are so different in their natures that, inevitably, their activities are different. If society is to succeed, it must, therefore, often standardize group activity. When the wheel was invented, each man made his own wheels to fit the cart he constructed for himself. Several thousand years later, wheels came to be made by mass production, and a carriage maker in Springfield, Massachusetts, could make wheels for a wagon in New York. The wheel, at that time, had to fit only reasonably well; if not, the blacksmith could warp it to fit. After the invention of the automobile, labor costs and the speeds the vehicle was capable of demanded accuracies within a thousandth of an inch. Now that mass production has become international, U.S. manufacturers have often had to improve their exactness by converting from inches and feet to the metric system.

The population explosion has been accompanied by a knowledge explosion and a communications explosion that have made standardized presentation essential. Laws must be written in a special jargon; it is not enough for a law to order someone to "stop" doing something, because he could stop, thus complying with the law, and then start again. The law must say "cease and desist" to mean "stop, and don't start again." Our study of language has shown us that language is an attempt by society

371

to standardize communication to make it effective. One aspect of communication that has also been influenced by the need to standardize is the matter of manuscript form. When a military field order goes from headquarters to a regiment, there must be no possibility of any misinterpretation. The field order therefore conforms with absolute rigidity to a prescribed form. A doctor's prescription, as illegible as it seems to the layman, follows a form about which the pharmacist can make no mistake. The list of prescribed forms is endless, order blanks, routing memos, maintenance records, inspection charts, and applications for government grants being only a few.

One of the most important communication formats is the one prescribed for what has come to be called a scholarly paper. When a chemist at Massachusetts General Hospital sends a report of an experiment to *Carbohydrate Review* in Brussels, he has no choice but to follow a prescribed form—not only insofar as the organization and style of the paper are concerned, but also in footnote and bibliogarphic information. In the early years of the information explosion, scholars could submit manuscripts in almost any form. Then, as time passed, each periodical began to establish its own rules, and an author had to get directions from each journal before he submitted an article. As related journals began to quote each other, it was only a matter of time before groups of journals cooperated to create form books or style manuals for several disciplines. A number of journals officially adopted *A Manual of Style,* published by the University of Chicago Press. This manual is now in its eleventh edition. It was not appropriate, however, for all branches of learning, and so the American Psychological Society, for instance, created its own form book, and the Modern Language Association prepared the *Style Sheet* whose conventions have been adopted by *American Quarterly, Comparative Literature, Far Eastern Quarterly, French Review, German Quarterly, Journal of American Folklore, Library Bulletin, Princeton University Library Chronicle, Romantic Review, Quarterly Journal of Speech, Studies in Philology, Yale French Studies,* and about seventy other journals. The thoroughness exercised by its distinguished author, William R. Parker, and the enormous prestige of the parent organization have made the *Style Sheet* the most influential in the field of humanities. Social scientists and scholars of educational disciplines are gradually agreeing on form books; recently, biologists prepared a *Style Manual for Biological Journals,* and British chemists agreed upon a *Handbook for Chemical Societies.* Other professional groups are developing their own manuals.

Today almost every person needs to master manuscript techniques. Not everyone, of course, is a publishing scholar, but almost every college student is required to prepare various kinds of term papers for which footnotes and bibliographies are necessary. Even if he does no research himself, almost every person today reads textbooks, technical manuals, scholarly periodicals, and other publications for which an understanding of the symbols and formats is necessary. Most important, everyone can profit from learning how to work with the ideas of other people, from being able to evaluate and mesh the thoughts of others, and from the training in honesty and responsibility inherent in the proper use of manuscript techniques.

At the outset it is well to remember that the purpose of manuscript techniques is not to impress the reader, though the following apocryphal conversation probably has some basis in fact:

"Well, I finished my term paper for Professor Slockrottem. I had fifty footnotes in it."

"Then you'll get an A, man; you'll get an A."

This student could have impressed Professor Slockrottem more if he had spent more time on his research and less on his footnote padding. In the Middle Ages, monks spent years preparing ornately beautiful manuscripts, an art called *calligraphy*. That day is gone, but often a misguided student demonstrates this same impulse by meticulously pecking out a design of typed x's and o's to form a silhouette of, say, Abraham Lincoln if his paper is about slavery. Such students should have spent their time on five last proofreadings.

There comes a time when plagiarism must be discussed. Almost all college students realize that, like other forms of property, ideas and expressions can be owned; to take them without authorization is, of course, to steal. But there is an indistinct line of demarcation. Taking an orange from a fruit stand is theft. That is clear enough. But if we *paraphrase* an idea we know to be commonly held, is that plagiarism?

It has been said that a college education is the only thing in the world that a person will pay for and then try not to get. There are some students who will submit a paper written for an assignment in another year, for another class, or another college. Setting aside the consideration of simple honesty, which is important in and of itself, we can easily see that such a practice defeats the whole purpose of a research assignment. The student is paying money and investing time to learn a skill; if he takes another student's paper, he is being more than dishonest; he is being stupid. A student receiving such help from another student deserves the penalty handed down at most colleges, instant dismissal. Fortunately, such plagiarism is easy to avoid; the intelligent, honest student would never use an assignment prepared by another student.

Less obvious than "borrowing" another student's work, and more difficult to avoid, is a more complex kind of plagiarism: taking material without proper credit or authorization from published materials. This practice infringes upon the provisions of the Copyright Law and is therefore illegal. Plagiarism is briefly defined by the *American College Dictionary* as "copying or imitating the language, ideas, and thoughts of another author and passing off the same as one's original work." Some colleges, in order to avoid any misunderstanding, say that any instance of a student using five successive words in the same way as his source is beyond the probability of chance, and such sections should be put in quotation marks. If the student paraphrases some writing, that is, if he expresses another's thoughts in his own words, he is still using the author's ideas, and he should make the appropriate acknowledgment. Certain factual information is considered to be in the public domain and does not have to be credited: birth and death dates of well-known figures; dates of military, political, literary, and other historical events; and statistics about population, national economy, and agricultural productivity. You can safely assume that any factual information found in a standard reference book is part of the public domain, but if you quote it in the exact words of the source, you must acknowledge your source. As a rule, the speeches of important public figures tend to be treated as public papers, and no source need be cited (although the speaker and date should be given). All illustrations, charts, and tables must be credited.

Acknowledgments, which are made either in the text or in footnotes, are governed by two principles. The first one, as expressed in the *MLA Style Sheet*, is, "Perhaps the only unchangeable rule is that authors must be consistent in their own practice." The second principle is pragmatic: footnotes and acknowledgments must accomplish their specific purpose. For that reason, we must understand what footnotes are supposed to accomplish.

Some footnotes are for a purpose other than acknowledgment. In times past, when printing costs for changing from one type font to another were less, and when readers could be more leisurely, footnotes were used to define terms and advance other explanations. Such information is now usually held to a minimum, the necessary explanations being included in the regular text. In textbooks and technical periodicals, footnotes are still used to show that the author has, for instance, surveyed all relevant or contradictory information on his subject and has deliberately decided not to discuss it in his article. Some textbooks use footnotes to suggest further reading on the part of the student. At the present time, however, there are usually just two needs which are likely to require any kind of notation, whether it be in the text or in a footnote. A writer, in an argumentative paper, may want to impress his reader with the weight of an authority or with statistics. In this respect, a footnote may make evidence more convincing. The second duty of the notation is simply to fulfill the requirements of honesty and law, to give credit where credit is due. In this case, the notation can often be accomplished in the text itself. A name can be mentioned or a book cited, and nothing more needs to be done. There are cases, however, when an article is so important that the reader may want to follow up the reference and see for sure that the original source, in the original context, was interpreted appropriately. Footnotes should be as easy to read as possible and as complete as necessary, and they need not repeat any information contained in the text.

From this pragmatic analysis of the function of footnotes you can understand that, ordinarily, a publishing writer tries to use footnotes as rarely as possible, if only because it is time-consuming for the reader to drop his eyes and adjust to the new type. If, on the other hand, and this is being very realistic, the writer is a student in freshman English, he has another purpose: he needs to show his instructor that he has mastered the footnote technique, and therefore when there is a question whether he should footnote, he does footnote. A freshman research paper with two or three footnotes and two bibliographic entries may be an excellent, original paper, but it certainly frustrates the teacher who is trying to determine whether his student has mastered footnote technique.

One of the numerous problems that students must solve is how to handle quotations effectively. The normal procedure is to put the information in quotation marks and to precede the quotation with a "tag," that is, an expression with a synonym of "say" in it, for instance, "Cardinal Richelieu responded," or "John Dewey wrote." Your reader must always know, without reference to a footnote, who is being quoted.

Procedure about the handling of long quotations varies markedly from one form book to another. Until recently, all long quotations—variously described as anything over three lines, over ten lines, or something in between—were put in smaller type and indented five spaces from left and right margins. When typed, long quotations were single spaced to resemble smaller type. For example:

```
Gobbledygook has become one of the real irritants

under the intellectual's hide. George Orwell
```

has led the fight against tortuous, jargonistic,
flaccid prose, but many others have joined the
fray. In a recent Harvard Alumni Bulletin, Richard
D. Fay translated Abraham Lincoln's Gettysburg
Address into "Faculty English":

> Eight and seven-tenths decades ago the pioneer
> workers in this continental area implemented
> a new group based on an ideology of free
> boundaries and initial conditions of equality.
> We are now actively engaged in an over-all
> evaluation of conflicting factors in order to
> determine whether or not the life expectancy of
> this group or of any group operating under the
> stated conditions is significant. We are met
> in an area of maximum activity among the
> conflicting factors.

Mr. Fay's translation continued, but our point is
probably made: gobbledygook can ruin good English
expression.

Form books

The problem boils down to a matter of following directions. The
two goals, consistency and efficacy, are easy to achieve if the writer will
almost slavishly pattern his notes and format after the rules and models
which are provided in one of the many complete form books set up by
scholars and publishers. Your selection of the appropriate form book will
depend upon your subject. If you were writing for a specific journal or
publisher, you would select the form book prescribed; most scholarly publications in their first pages tell how to submit manuscripts and what form
book is to be followed. The following are widely recommended.

GENERAL

Kate L. Turabian, *A Manual for Writers of Term Papers, Theses,
and Dissertations* (Chicago: University of Chicago Press [Phoenix Books],
revised frequently).

LITERATURE, MODERN LANGUAGES AND HUMANITIES

William Riley Parker, *The MLA Style Sheet* (New York: The Modern Language Association, 1951). Revised, and reprinted almost yearly.

SCIENCE

American Institute of Biological Sciences, *Style Manual for Biological Journals* (Washington, D.C., 1960).

SOCIAL SCIENCES AND EDUCATION

A Manual of Style (11th ed.; Chicago: University of Chicago Press, 1949).

The College of Education Style Manual (Columbus, Ohio: Ohio State University Press, 1960).

GOVERNMENT

U.S. Government Printing Office Style Manual (Washington, D.C.: G.P.O., revised and reprinted frequently. An abridged version is available).

As college freshmen turn to more technical research and reporting, they will want to secure one of the appropriate manuals listed above, but until then the conventions described in this chapter should suffice.

Manuscript terminology

Part of the ability to handle footnote and bibliography techniques comes from mastering the following terms:

anon.	anonymous, no author shown.
c. or *ca.*	*circa*, Latin for *about;* thus "*c.* (or *ca.*) 1610" means "about 1610."
cf.	Compare or confer.
ed.	editor, or edited by. Plural: eds.
e.g.	*exempli gratia*, Latin for *for example.*
i.e.	*id est*, Latin for *that is.*
f.	and following. Thus, "p. 16 f." means "page sixteen and the following." Plural: ff.
ibid.	*ibidem*, Latin for *the same as previously given*, or ditto; thus "from the same source as the one just cited."
ms.	Manuscript. Plural: mss.

n.d.   no date shown.

n.p.   no page numbers shown.

op. cit.   *opere citato,* Latin for *the work by this author already cited.* Thus, "Hemingway, *op. cit.*" means "the book by Hemingway cited in an earlier footnote."

p.   page. Plural: pp. Note: pp. 18–19 (not 18–9), and pp. 332–342 (not 332–42); but pp. 1127–31.

passim   Latin for *here and there.* Thus, "p. 16 passim" means "on page sixteen specifically and also in several other places in the work cited."

q.v.   *quod vide,* Latin for *which see.* Thus, the encyclopedia sentence "Napoleon's greatest disaster came at the Battle of Waterloo (*q.v.*) and from it he never recovered" means that there is further relevant information under the "Battle of Waterloo" entry which the reader is advised to consult.

[*sic*]   Latin for *thus.* This bracketed expression, inserted into a quotation just after a spelling, grammar, factual, or logical error, indicates that the editor has noted the error but has decided to retain it in the quotation. He wants the reader to know that the error occurred in the original passage.

text   The main part of the manuscript; it does not include the titles, footnotes, bibliography, etc.

trans.   translator, or translated by.

II:iv   About a play: "Act Two, Scene Four." About the Bible: "Chapter Two, Verse Four."

XXXII (September, 1968) 6.   "The September, 1968, issue which when bound is Part Six of Volume Thirty-two."

How to use a form book

The key to success in manuscript preparation is simply the ability to follow instructions. As you work on your essay or term paper, assume that you know absolutely nothing about footnote or bibliographic entries. Using the index or section headings, search through the form book you are using until you find an example that is exactly equivalent to the note you are preparing. If you wish to make a reference to an essay in an anthology that has two authors, scan the model footnotes until you find just such an entry. If you wish to make a reference to a pamphlet whose author is unknown, look for a model covering that instance. When you find the appropriate model, copy its form exactly, a capital where indicated, a comma here, parentheses there. There must not be a single mark of punctuation out of place. This meticulous care guarantees consistency and completeness.

If someone other than yourself types the manuscript, you and the typist should have a conference to discuss format, and the typist should be provided with a copy of the form book so she can check questionable items. In case of error, you will get the blame, since you are responsible for the final proofreading.

A manuscript form book for college freshmen

TYPE OF PAPER

Use white 8½" by 11" bond paper with a strength of at least 16 pounds. (Paper stronger than 20 pounds is both too expensive and too difficult to type through for carbons.) Do not use onion-skin or second-sheet paper.

TYPING

Any standard type is acceptable, but the type that resembles handwriting and the straight heavy Roman that has no lower-case letters are not recommended since they are distracting. Your typescript should be double-spaced except for long quotations (four lines or more), which will be single-spaced and indented five spaces from the left and right margins. Use black or very dark blue ribbon *only*.

HANDWRITING

Acceptable by only a few college teachers. Handwriting must be legible; paper must be wide-lined. Long quotations should be indented as above; if handwriting is sufficiently legible, the writer may elect to identify long quotations further by putting two lines of longhand between two ruled lines. Use only black or very dark blue ink.

CORRECTIONS

Erasures are less damaging than mistakes. Erase carefully or use correction tapes or fluids; insert corrections neatly. Do not use proofreader marks or marginal insertions; put corrections at the place of the error. If corrections are extensive, for instance if they involve three or four lines, re-do the page.

MARGINS AND SPACING OF TEXT

Title page (if required). Type title three or four inches from top of page, centered. Author's name should appear three line spaces below title, centered. Only author's name is necessary; the word "By" is redundant because of the position of name. Center the assignment number, course identification, date, and other information required by the instructor four line spaces below author's name. If there is more than one line of information, double space.

First page. Center title (if there is no title page) four to six line spaces (about an inch and a half) from top of page. Triple space and start text. Leave margins of one inch on bottom and both sides. If using *élite* (small) type, you may elect to triple space between paragraphs. Center page number at bottom of page, or omit.

Subsequent pages. Put page number four to six line spaces from top of page, consistently either centered or on right margin. Put no marks around the page numbers. Avoid *(10), -10-, 10.,* or */10/.* Simplicity and typist economy are virtues. Start typing the text three or four spaces below the page number.

FOOTNOTES

Footnotes may appear at any of three places.

1. At bottom of page. Triple space; type a line from the left margin fifteen spaces to the right. Double space and type the footnote, which is single spaced. Note position of raised figures.

Professor Turner seems to be in the main stream of education when he comments upon the "uniqueness of literature in the student's experience." He writes,

> The student discovers for himself that the sciences have no usable past; that the social sciences acknowledge only the present; but that literature encloses past and present and is the essence of prophecy. It is both timely and timeless, always

timely because timeless. Alone among the major
subjects in the curriculum, literature encompasses
both the understanding and the imagination and
at its best fuses them without joint or seam.[1]

He can hardly be included among the progressive,

however, when he discusses techniques of teaching. The

only visual aid he approves is the book.[2] He has no use for

such casebooks which "barricade" novels or short-stories

with a "tangle of brambles," by including a collection

of critical essays.[3] Nor is he conservative; he has only

scorn for the "collection of essays which were standard

in the freshman composition courses.

---

[1] Arlin Turner, "Literature and the Student in the
Space Age," College English, XXVII (April, 1966), 520.
 [2] Ibid., p. 521.
 [3] Ibid., pp. 521-522.

   2. At the end of the chapter, part, or book. Their form is the
same as it would be if they appeared at the bottom of the page. Technically, of course, they would be called "notes" instead of "footnotes."
   3. Immediately after quoted material, wherever it occurs on the
page. Again, use the same form. (This position is acceptable only if the
ms. is being prepared for publication *and* the editor or publisher requires
this practice.)

One of the primary findings of a study of comparative

religions is the relationship between other religions

and Christianity, particularly about how much of its

teaching will be tolerated. About Hinduism, Stephen Neill

writes,

   A Hindu, if he wishes, may accept in his heart all the
   tenets of the Christian faith; he may be regular

in attendance at Christian worship and may
contribute largely from his means to the support of
the Christian Church. He may even openly profess
himself to be a friend and follower of Jesus.
If he stops short of baptism, and is careful not to
offend against the rules of his caste, his position
in the Hindu community is unendangered and
unimpaired. But once let him take the fatal step,
and all is altered. He is at once cut off from
home and family, from all social ties, and from all
the ancient roots in the life of his community.
To his own people he is as one dead. It is baptism
alone that makes the separation irrevocable.[7]

---

[7] Stephen Neill, Christian Faith Today (Baltimore:
Penguin Books, 1955), p. 179.

The followers of Islam are permitted an even more

sympathetic relationship. Most Muslims respect all the

Both old- and new-style footnotes follow the same basic pattern:
Author's Name (first name first), *Title of Work* (in italics or underlined),
and page number. The differences between the two styles consist of (a)
what else should be included, and (b) the form of second and following
references to the same source.

OLD-STYLE FOOTNOTES: FIRST REFERENCES

Books (single author)

[1] Donald Lemen Clark, Rhetoric in Greco-Roman Education (New York: Columbia University Press, 1957), p. 66.

Books (two authors)

[2] Charles Brown and Ronald Cole, Understanding Science (Boston: Houghton Mifflin Company, 1960), pp. 251-258.

Reference to one volume of a multivolume work

[3] Thomas Mann, Joseph in Egypt (New York: Alfred A. Knopf, 1938), II, 383.

Edition indicated

[4]Will Durant, The Story of Philosophy (rev. ed.; New York: Garden City Publishing Co., 1938), pp. 1-19.

Editor instead of author

[5]Richard Ellmann and Charles Feidelson, Jr., eds., The Modern Tradition: Backgrounds of Modern Literature (New York: Oxford University Press, 1965), pp. 633-637.

Both author and editor

[6]Thomas Jefferson, Democracy, ed. Saul K. Padover (New York: Appleton-Century, 1939), p. 65.

Periodicals

[7]"Population Data on China Studied," The New York Times (October 2, 1966), p. 3, col. 1.

[8]"Larceny in Everyday Life," Time (September 9, 1966), pp. 26-27.

[9]Louis Seltzer, "Why I Went West--And Stayed There," Saturday Review (April 9, 1966), p. 68.

[10]Hanson W. Baldwin, "The Fall of Corregidor," American Heritage, XVII (August, 1966), 16.

Pamphlets

[11]Newton Buyers' Guide (Newton, Massachusetts: Chamber of Commerce, 1967-68), p. 18.

[12]Who Is Eligible for Welfare Benefits? (Washington, D.C.: Department of Health, Education and Welfare, 1964), n. p.

[13]Proscribed Commodities (Bellington, Massachusetts: Committee Against Un-American Activities, n. d.), n. p.

Dictionaries and Encyclopedias

[14] Webster's Third New International Dictionary of the English Language (1961).

[15] "Athens," Encyclopaedia Britannica, 14th ed. (1957) I, 678.

Selections from Collections or Anthologies

[16] Fyodor Dostoevsky, "The Legend of the Grand Inquisitor," A Casebook on Existentialism, ed. William V. Spanos (New York: Crowell Publishing Company, 1966), pp. 118-122.

[17] Emily Dickinson, "303," American Poetry, ed. Gay Wilson Allen, Walter B. Rideout, and James K. Robinson (New York: Harper & Row, 1965), pp. 532-533.

[18] Christopher Marlowe, Tamburlaine the Great, Elizabethan Plays, ed. Hazelton Spencer (Boston: D. C. Heath and Company, 1933), II:v., 11. 1-6.

Bible References. If the reference is to the King James Authorized Version (1611), information can be very brief; if reference is to a different version, more information is necessary.

[19] Luke, XXII: 1-8.

Stating the chapter in Arabic numbers is also correct and even preferable.

[20] II Kings, Interpreter's Bible, 4:i-iv.

OLD-STYLE FOOTNOTES: SUBSEQUENT REFERENCES

The conventional practice is not to repeat information. When a second reference is made to a work already cited, the abbreviations for either *ibidem* ("the same") or *opere citato* ("the work which was cited") are used. If a second reference comes immediately after the first, *ibid.* is used; if another work intervenes, the author's name is repeated with *op. cit.* and the page number. This sequence illustrates what might occur.

[21] David D. Anderson, "Pakistan's Search for National Identity," Yale Review, LV (Summer, 1966), 553.
[22] Ibid., 556.

[23] Mazheruddin Siddiqi, "Muslim Culture in Pakistan and India," Islam: The Straight Path, ed. Kenneth W. Morgan (New York: Ronald Press, 1958), pp. 297–301.

[24] Ibid.

[25] Anderson, op. cit., pp. 555–556.

[26] "Quaid-i-Azam's Contribution to Political Thought," Pakistan News Digest (September 1, 1966), p. 6.

[27] Anderson, op. cit., p. 552.

[28] "Quaid-i-Azam's Contribution to Political Thought," p. 8.

The article referred to in footnotes 26 and 28 had no author listed; the only possible subsequent note is to repeat the title, without *op. cit.*, of course, since that would be tautological.

NEW-STYLE FOOTNOTES: FIRST REFERENCES

The so-called old-style footnotes are cumbersome, often repetitive, and full of Latin expressions that some readers find unfamiliar or ostentatious. Also, some of the information they contain is unnecessary. Typists find them difficult to place in a manuscript, and publishers find the complex format an invitation to typographical error and the switching from one font of type to another expensive. Naturally there have been many attempts to simplify the system, the most extreme being by educational and scientific journals that wish to convey the most possible information at the least cost. *The Journal of Educational Research* requires its authors to number all the entries in their bibliography, which is printed at the end of their article. In the text, enclosed in parentheses, a number refers to the appropriate source; usually a second number indicates the page. In the example given (from the April, 1966, *Journal*, p. 366), (*6, 14*) indicates a reference to page 14 of the sixth entry in the bibliography.

> Using the California Test of Mental Maturity, Cook and Lanier found that the language IQ of dropouts was considerably below that of those who remained in school (6,14).

The impulse for reduced costs and simplicity has caused many publishers to ask that all footnotes be omitted and references be indicated in the text itself. Another condensation has been made possible by the general acceptance of standard abbreviations for many periodicals, thus, *Sat. Rev., C. E. (College English), PMLA (Publications of the Modern*

*Language Association), Amer. Schol. (American Scholar), JHE (The Journal
of Higher Education)*, and *Sci. Amer. (Scientific American)*. A code for
these abbreviations can be found in most libraries, encyclopedias, and the
publication using the symbols.

A standardized, new-style system that corrects at least a few of
the deficiencies of the more involved form has now been devised and is
recommended by many form books. Treat books, collections, pamphlets,
anthologies, and dictionaries the same as old style, but with publishing
company omitted. The reader will still be able to tell nationality and dates
of sources. Thus:

[1] Donald Lemen Clark, Rhetoric in Greco-Roman Education (New York, 1957), p. 66.

Treat periodicals, encyclopedias, and the Bible the same as you would
in old-style footnotes.

NEW-STYLE FOOTNOTES: SUBSEQUENT REFERENCES

The major difference between the new and old styles is the way
they treat subsequent references. With new style there are no Latin abbreviations: only the author's last name and the page number of the article
are cited, no matter whether the repeated reference directly follows the
previous reference to the same source or not. If there is no author shown,
the title is repeated. Footnotes 21–28 below represent references to the
same sources and pages as the old-style footnotes 21–28 on p. 385.

[21] David D. Anderson, "Pakistan's Search for National
Identity," Yale Review, LV (Summer, 1966), 553.

[22] Anderson, p. 556.

[23] Mazheruddin Siddiqi, "Muslim Culture in Pakistan
and India," Islam: The Straight Path, ed. Kenneth W. Morgan
(New York, 1958), pp. 297–301.

[24] Siddiqi, pp. 297–301.

[25] Anderson, pp. 555–556.

[26] "Quaid-i-Azam's Contribution to Political
Thought," Pakistan News Digest (September 1, 1966), p. 6.

[27] Anderson, p. 552.

[28] "Quaid-i-Azam's Contribution to Political
Thought," p. 8.

A form book, no matter how detailed, cannot list all possible types of footnotes, and there always will be problems that you must solve using your own judgment. Just remember to be sure to fulfill the demands of honesty and completeness. Your reader must know who wrote the article or book and where to obtain it.

EXPLANATORY FOOTNOTES

Although, as we have stated, most writers try to avoid explanatory footnotes, preferring instead to work the explanation smoothly into the text, there comes a time, particularly in a scholarly work, when they cannot be avoided. A writer, discussing a controversial topic, may wish to demonstrate in an explanatory footnote that he has read all the material both for and against his point. Or, he may want to explain a point to his reader when he doubts that the reader has the background information necessary to understand it. He thus presents the reader with an option: if the reader knows the necessary information, he ignores the footnote; if not, he reads it. The following appeared in the December, 1965, issue of *College Composition and Communication*, p. 237:

> In order to be of more than peripheral interest to rhetoricians and literary scholars, linguistic research must move beyond the sentence, even though passing over this threshold vastly complicates linguistic theory. However, the initial steps toward a theory of language which explains both grammatical and rhetorical patterns can probably be made by extending grammatical theories now used in analyzing and describing sentence structure. The purpose of this paper is to illustrate how one such theory, tagmemics, can be extended to the description of paragraphs.[1]
>
> [1] This work is the result of my collaboration with Kenneth L. Pike and Richard Young in research on rhetoric, sponsored in part by the Center for Research on Language and Language Behavior, University of Michigan, under a grant from the Language Development Branch, U.S. Office of Education. Tagmemic theory is developed in Kenneth L. Pike, *Language in Relation to a Unified Theory of the Structure of Human Behavior* (Glendale: Summer Institute of Linguistics, Part I, 1954; Part II, 1955; Part III, 1960). See also Robert E. Longacre, *Grammar Discovery Procedure: A Field Manual* (The Hague: Mouton and Co., 1964), and, for a brief description using English examples, Robert E. Longacre, "String Constituent Analysis," *Language*, XXXVI (1960), 63–68.

Later in the article, when the author, Professor A. L. Becker, refers to a theory that is not well known, even to the usual readers of the journal, he adds the note:

2 This three-part definition of a paragraph reflects the assumption in tagmemic theory that three perspectives are necessary to a complete description of behavior: a *particle* perspective, which views behavior as made up of discrete contrasting parts; a *wave* perspective, which emphasizes the unsegmentable continuum of behavior; and a *field* view, in which units are seen in context (sequence, class, or ordered set). This article focuses on paragraph tagmemes as particles in sequence. For a fuller explanation of tagmemic trimodalism, see Kenneth L. Pike, "Language as Particle, Wave, and Field," *The Texas Quarterly*, II (Summer, 1959), 37–54; and Pike, "Beyond the Sentence," *CCC*, XV (Oct., 1964), 129–135.

BIBLIOGRAPHY

Research papers customarily include a bibliography, that is, a list of all the sources to which there was reference in the text and which were, therefore, footnoted. On rare occasions, for instance, when a writer wishes to provide further reading on his subject, works appear in the bibliography that were not referred to in the text. The writer must always be scrupulously careful not to pad his bibliography to suggest that more work and learning were involved than actually were. Even when there is a reference to it, the Bible is not listed in a bibliography—unless the reference is to some nonstandard version. The bibliography is alphabetized according to author's last names; in the event there is no author, the item is listed according to the first major word in the title. If there are several items by one author, they are listed in alphabetic order according to their title, as demonstrated below. When alphabetizing by title, ignore definite and indefinite articles. *The Fall of the House of Usher* would be alphabetized under *Fall*, not *The*.

A bibliography entry resembles a footnote, with these differences:

1. Author's last name is placed first and is separated from the first name by a comma.

2. A period, not a comma, comes between the author's name and the book title and between the book title and publication information. (Article and periodical entries, however, use commas.)

3. Publication information is not placed in parentheses.

4. No page numbers are included for books.

5. Inclusive page numbers are indicated for articles and selections from anthologies, encyclopedias, and collected works. This means that, instead of listing only the pages to which your footnotes referred, list the inclusive pages, thus indicating the total number of pages in the article.

6. The identation is the reverse of the indentation for a footnote: the first line of a bibliography item is flush with the left margin; the second and following lines are indented five or more spaces. This "hanging indentation" causes the author's name and its place in the alphabetic order to be more noticeable.

7. Bibliography entries are usually not numbered.

8. Bibliography entries may be either single or double spaced.

SAMPLE BIBLIOGRAPHY

Anderson, David D. "Pakistan's Search for National Identity," Yale Review, LV (June, 1966), 552-569.

"Athens," Encyclopaedia Britannica, 14th ed., I, 677-679.

Becker, A. L. "A Tagmemic Approach to Paragraph Analysis," College Composition and Communication, XVI (December, 1965), 237-242.

Clark, Donald Lemen. Rhetoric in Greco-Roman Education. New York: Columbia University Press, 1957.

"The Crowded Left," Time, September 9, 1966, p. 46.

Ellmann, Richard, and Feidelson, Charles, Jr., eds. The Modern Tradition: Backgrounds of Modern Literature. New York: Oxford University Press, 1965.

Graff, Henry F. "The Wealth of Presidents," American Heritage, XVII (October, 1966), 4-5, 106-110.

Hartnett, Rodney T., and Stewart, Clifford T. "Final Examination Grades of Independent Study Students Compared

with Those of Students Taught by Traditional Methods," Journal of Educational Research, LIX (April,
1966), 354-357.

Jefferson, Thomas. Democracy, ed. Saul K. Padover. New York:
Appleton-Century, 1939.

——————————— Autobiography of Thomas Jefferson, ed.
Paul L. Ford. New York, 1914.

Marlowe, Christopher. Tamburlaine the Great. Elizabethan
Plays, ed. Hazelton Spencer. Boston: D. C. Heath
and Company, 1933.

Newton Buyers' Guide. Newton, Massachusetts: Chamber of
Commerce, 1967.

"Population Data on China Studied," The New York Times, October 2, 1966, p. 3, col. 1.

"Quaid-i-Azam's Contribution to Political Thought," Pakistan News Digest, September 1, 1966, pp. 6-7.

Seltzer, Louis. "Why I Went West—and Stayed There," Saturday Review, April 9, 1966, pp. 68-69, 81.

Spanos, William V., ed. A Casebook on Existentialism. New
York: Thomas Y. Crowell Company, 1966.

Webster's Third New International Dictionary of the English
Language. Springfield, Mass.: G. & C. Merriam Company, 1961.

Wilson, Gay Allen, Rideout, Walter B., and Robinson, James
K., eds. American Poetry. New York: Harper & Row,
1965,

Projects

1. For each of the following footnotes, explain the exact meaning of each item, i.e., raised number, author, title, publication information, and page number.

[1]Philip Hone, The Diary of Philip Hone, ed. Bayard Tuckerman (New York: Dodd, Mead & Company, 1889), II, 163.

[2]Ibid., p. 196.

[3]"Current Naval Court Proceedings," New York Express (December 17, 1842), p. 1.

[4]Hone, op. cit., pp. 165-167.

[5]Alexander Slidell Mackenzie, quoted in Proceedings of the Naval Court Martial in the Case of Alexander Slidell Mackenzie (New York: Henry C. Langley, 1844), pp. 1198-99.

[6]Ibid.; cf. "Triton, The Mackenzie Affair," New York Weekly Tribune (December 24, 1842), p. 3, for another view-point on the mutiny.

[7]Ibid.

[8]Proceedings of the Court of Inquiry (New York: Greely & McElrath, 1843), p. 31 in The Somers Mutiny Affair, ed. C. K. McElroy (Boston: D. C. Heath and Company, 1954), p. 6.

[9]Current Naval Court Proceedings," p. 3.

[10]William Shakespeare, A Midsummer Night's Dream, Shakespeare: The Complete Works, ed. G. B. Harrison (New York: Harcourt, Brace & World, 1952), III:ii, p. 519.

[11]Ibid.

[12]Robert Griscombe (ed.), Great Disasters at Sea (2d rev. ed.; Cambridge: Cambridge University Press, 1963), II, 19-21.

[13]Hone, op. cit., p. 167.

[14] Ibid., pp. 166-167.

[15] Griscombe, op. cit., pp. 22-23.

[16] Arthur Vanderbilt, "New Light on the Somers Mutiny Affair," American Naval Quarterly, XLVI (Spring, 1949), 16-18.

2. The author who prepared the manuscript below thought he was following directions for new-style form, but he obviously did not follow instructions carefully. Correct any errors you find.

According to foreigners traveling in England during the eighteenth century, the English had very simple foods which were not prepared very elaborately. Their many plain foods were in great abundance, however, and a variety of wines relieved the plainness of their fare.[1]

In spite of the opportunity to do so, the English did not really eat very much during the course of a day. For breakfast they had a few slices of bread with butter and tea, which meager nourishment had to last until tea at three or four in the afternoon.[2] "What would be scarce enough for a Frenchman of an ordinary appetite would suffice three hungry Englishmen."[3] The dinner meal was not heavy, but it was more varied than the breakfast. An eighteenth-century Englishman dining at home usually ate a dinner of half-broiled or half-roasted meat and cabbage leaves. The cabbage leaves were boiled in water and then served with a sauce made of flour and butter. In fact, most vegetables were served this way. The dinner meal was also accompanied by bread and butter and Cheshire cheese.[4] As for dinner in a tavern, the German

Charles Moritz reported that in London for a shilling
he got a meal consisting of roast meat and a salad. A
half-shilling tip to his waiter caused Moritz to declare
the whole meal too expensive,[5] and thereafter he dined
at home on pickled salmon.[6]

[1] George Christoph Lichtenberg, Lichtenberg's Visits
to England, As Described in His Letters and Diaries, trans.
Margaret L. More and W. H. Quarrell (Oxford: The Clarendon
Press, 1938), vol I, p. 49.

[2] Pierre Jean Grosley. A Tour To London; Or New Observations on England And Its Inhabitants, ed. by Thomas Nugent
(London: Lockyer Davis, 1772) vol. I, pp. 21-4.

[3] Grosley, ibid, I, 69.

[4] Moritz, Charles P. Travels, Chiefly On Foot, through
Several Parts of England in 1782 (London: Robinson, 1795)
pages 33-7.

[5] Ibid., 27.

[6] Ibid., 33.

    3. The bibliography below is in need of editing. Revise it to conform
to new-style conventions.

Aristotle, *On Man In The Universe*. Ed. Louise R. Loomis. New York: Classics
    Club, 1943.
Anderson, Wallace L. and Stageberg, Norman C. *Introductory Readings on
    Language*. (New York: Holt, Rinehart, and Winston, 1966.
Allegro, John Marco. Untold Story of the Dead Sea Scrolls, The. Harper's Maga-
    zine, Vol. 233, No. 1394. August, 1966, p. 46.
Blackburn, Ruth H., *The Bronte Sisters: Selected Source Materials for College
    Research Papers*. Boston: D. C. Heath, and Company, 1964.)
Milton, John. "Areopagitica." in Josephine Miles' *Classic Essays in English*,
    Boston: Little, Brown, 1961.)
Horgan, Paul (Pulitzer Prize Winning Historian). *Conquistadors In North*

American History. (Greenwich, Connecticut, Fawcett Publications, copyright, 1963.)

Sarton, George. *A History of Science.* (2 vols). Cambridge: Harvard University Press. (1959).

L. E. Steele. *Essays of Richard Steele.* London: Macmillan and Co., Ltd., 1937.

"The Meritocracy: Ability Testing and the American Spirit." Carnegie Quarterly, Volume XIV/Number 2, Spring, 1966. p. 5.

West, Robert J. "A Time of Exciting Ideas," *Stanford Today*, Palo Alto, California: Stanford University Press, 1940). pages 3–6.

Wright, Robt. "Education, Freedom, and the "Yes" Technique," *Education* vol. 72, no. 7 (March, 1952), p. 498.

CHAPTER 11

A HANDBOOK FOR
GRAMMAR, SPELLING, AND
PUNCTUATION

Formal written English is not the language; it is merely one type of English. Its rules are pertinent only to people studying or writing formal written English; other types of English have their own rules. JAMES B. MACMILLAN.

Language is an institution founded in man's social nature, wrought out for the satisfaction of his social wants; and hence, while individuals are ultimate agents in the formation and modification of every word and every meaning of a word, it is still the community that makes and changes the language. W. D. WHITNEY.

A defense of conventional usage

There is evidence today that we are living in a world of "anything goes." We are exposed to permissive education and nondirective guidance, to a God who is reputedly dead, and to a "situational" morality. Because the so-called revolution in language studies has disseminated the doctrine of usage and laid prescriptive grammar to rest, we might think that, insofar as language is concerned, this is also a time of linguistic chaos and grammatical freedom. This is not true. This is not a time of complete language laxity. Anyone who thinks so is ignorant of the nature of the American psyche and of the function of grammar.

Modern language research shows us that language is an arbitrary system of symbols set up by society. Research also shows us that within any given language there are dialects and jargons so specialized that dwellers in one apartment house or on one mountain top may not be able to communicate with their neighbors in the next street or valley. Nevertheless, a dialect must be used by a sizable number of people to be meaningful, for no one person can make up his own set of symbols and expect to communicate with his fellow men. Studies also show that languages change markedly and dramatically, though there is no indication that such change is, in and of itself, good. The ideal language would be one that would grow when necessary, but would mean tomorrow what it means today and be understood by all people.

Although it is not a perfect language, the spoken dialect that is most widely used in America is called Standard American, or General American. This dialect is thought of as the language of the Middle West, but it is used as far east as New York, Pennsylvania, and rural Connecticut; west of Iowa the area where it is used fans out to the southwest. It skirts southern influences in West Virginia, Arkansas, and southern Missouri. On the north, the region extends into Canada. Travelers in Quebec and the Maritime Provinces find English-speaking Canadians who sound more like Iowans than they do like nearby New Englanders or the British.

We have learned that languages follow the character of their users, and Standard American (Spoken) does indeed reflect the American character. It is easy-going, relatively informal, quick to change, and forceful. It is not, however, the language of "anything goes"; it is not linguistically chaotic. In its title, the operative word is "Standard." In Africa, Europe, and Asia it is rare indeed when every person living within any two-hundred-mile area can communicate with every other person in that area. In the United States and Canada, an area of language similarity almost 4,000 miles wide and 5,000 miles deep, a native of any point in this area can communicate readily with a native of any other, with the exception of some French Canadians. There is no other linguistic area as large anywhere in the world. Even minor differences are disappearing. The spread of education in America, the relative lack of social structure, the mobility of the American people, the proliferation of national publications, and radio and television all have worked to eliminate dialect distinctions.

Besides Standard American, there are two other spoken dialects.

Southern American and what has been called "Yankee talk," but their use is diminishing, perhaps regrettably. When an aspirant for stage or television of General American on Broadway and in Hollywood. When for-Tallulah Bankhead, the daughter of an Alabama congressman, spoke her version of General American on Broadway and in Hollywood. When foreigners are taught English by Americans they are usually taught General American. When the pronunciation of Bronx and Brooklyn children is corrected, they are given General American substitutes. Americans smile gently at ethnic jokes told with an appropriate Jewish or Italian accent, at a Boston twang, at a Southern drawl. They find amusing any deviation from General American.

The differences between Standard American and the other two dialects are colloquial, that is, they are found in informal spoken communication. A college freshman or a college professor from Georgia might say, "You-all come see us, y'heah?" but he would not use such an expression in a freshman theme or in an article for a professional journal. There are a very few dissimilarities in word choice: a southerner might refer to a "poke" of groceries, a midwesterner to a "sack," and a New Englander to a "bag." The Bostonian drinks "tonic," not "pop" or a "soft drink" as in other areas. Their spelling, grammar, and punctuation, however, show few dialect differences. It is almost impossible to detect any regional influence on the nonfiction prose of southerner Robert Penn Warren, midwesterner Adlai Stevenson, Bostonian Edward Kennedy, or southwesterner Barry Goldwater. In spite of some beliefs to the contrary, spoken dialect differences have had very little effect on American written grammar. Similarly, the influences that have made the American spoken language breezy and casual have had little effect on the construction of written American sentences. There have been many effects on word choice and idioms, but very little on grammar. For that reason it is important to keep in mind the fact that there are two pervasive American dialects: besides Standard American (Spoken) there is Standard American (Written), and in America written English is decidedly not a language of "anything goes."

An inflexible grammar may seem contradictory to the American character, but it has for many years been a characteristic of Americans. Americans, whether they be schoolteachers, writers, politicians, or what have you, have tended to be stricter with grammar than their English peers. So-called grammatical errors are easy to find in English literature:

Nobody will miss her like I shall. CHARLES DICKENS, *Letters.*

If it don't take, I will leave it off where it is. GEORGE GORDON, LORD BYRON, *Letters.*

Who has he come for?   GEORGE MEREDITH, *The Ordeal of Richard Feverel.*

Who are they likely to send down to examine us?   RUDYARD KIP-LING, *Debits and Credits.*

She did not know whom this strange young man might be.   HUGH WALPOLE, *Fortitude.*

He can't write like he used to.   GEORGE BERNARD SHAW, *Saint Joan.*

Hello, America, this is me.   WINSTON CHURCHILL, 1946.

Having no calendars, their only way of keeping track of the season was to notice and to remember which star-clusters rose just before dawn.   LANCELOT HOGBEN, *Wonderful World of Communication.*

Customarily when an "error" is called to the attention of a well-educated Englishman, he very likely indicates great tolerance. John Dryden spoke cavalierly about grammar. It should be handled, he said, "with well-bred ease." In 1761, Joseph Priestley commented that he knew of no surer way to indicate narrowness of mind than to exercise concern for grammar. "We have," he snorted, "infinitely greater things before us." Winston Churchill summed up the opinion of the cultured Englishman when he stated that he never let the rules of grammar get in the way of communication.

In contrast, American writers have almost invariably insisted on precise, parsable grammar. Benjamin Franklin forced himself to avoid questionable locutions. No one speaks better grammar than the noble savages in James Fenimore Cooper's novels. The prose of Washington Irving, Edgar Allan Poe, Ralph Waldo Emerson, Henry Wadsworth Longfellow, Nathaniel Hawthorne, Herman Melville, and William Cullen Bryant is grammatically immaculate; even the characters in their fiction tend to speak schoolteacher English. The early characters of Henry James speak grammatically; when he moved to England, his characters began to speak more colloquially. Huck Finn was almost the first character in significant American literature to use such constructions as "They was fetching a very nice-looking old gentleman along," and "So him and the dummy started off."

The stereotypes of the American as free, breezy, and informal and the Englishman as reserved, "correct," and formal are contradicted by comparing the language of the London *Times* and *The New York Times;* the grammar in the English paper is vastly more relaxed. The same impression results from a study of almost any equivalent British and American periodical. Likewise, B.B.C. broadcast speech is less grammatical than that of N.B.C. A contrast of British and American humor reveals that there are relatively few English jokes based on language; in America, "howlers," errors in grammar or diction, are frequently published, for they are found highly amusing in the United States. When the British object to American English they object to neologisms that duplicate already existing words, especially if they are longer or pretentious, such as *transportation* instead of *transport* and *motivations* instead of *motives,* or that are based on unsound historical principles, as when Americans use *hospitalize* to mean "send to a hospital," when etymologically the word should mean "convert into a hospital." It is small wonder that the British conceived a dictionary based on historical principles almost a hundred years before there was a similar project in the United States.

When an American deviates in any respect of his language, society whips him with its scorn. In 1928, voters had great difficulty taking Al Smith seriously as a Presidential candidate, in part because of his pronunciation, "*Tidday* I speak to you on the *raddio.*" In 1940, they were amused by Wendell Willkie, the "barefoot boy from Wall Street," who spoke to "Mah fella Amurrr-kins." When the mistakes are in grammar, the offender gets real abuse heaped upon him, as did Vice-Presidential candidate John Sparkman, who said, "Well, we run a good race." Sparkman was a Phi Beta Kappa from the University of Alabama, but many northerners considered him a country bumpkin because of his English.

Precise grammar has become in America the instant identification mark of educational, economic, and social status. College admissions officers, as we have noted earlier, admit that an application replete with grammar errors or misspellings gets almost no attention, the thought being that such errors reflect an absence of concern, teachability, and self-discipline. In a controlled experiment a group of college teachers was given a set of themes to grade. Unknown to the teachers, there were actually two sets, identical except that in one of the sets there were several grammatical and spelling errors. As might be expected, the second set received much lower grades—but, surprisingly—the papers with the errors were marked lower in content, organization, and style, in the apparently subconscious belief that an ungrammatical writer who can't spell can't organize or develop a thought either. Probably no other quality can so quickly undermine others' confidence in a person than for him to use such expressions as "he don't" or "they was."

The instruction in this chapter, which is an attempt to help students clear up difficulties with grammar, spelling, and punctuation, is based on principles that accept these mechanics as a product of logic and convention. These principles are:

1. If a deviation from conventions in grammar, spelling, or punctuation causes confusion, it should be corrected. The sentence, "John told Bill he had to go home" is indefensible, for the reader is left unsure whether it was Bill or John himself who had to go home. Prose must be clear. The reaction desired from the reader is "I understand," not "What's that again?"

2. Any deviation identified with the uneducated or the slovenly is rejected. Nothing is gained by "He swum to shore," "You was robbed," "He flang the ball." The reaction desired from the reader is "I understand," not a raised eyebrow or a snigger.

Admittedly these two principles may lead a writer to adopt an essentially conservative posture about punctuation, spelling, and grammar. Lord Chesterfield once advised his son that a gentleman is never the first nor the last to adopt a fad. The desired posture need not be one of conservatism, but it should be one of discrimination. A writer must develop a "feel" for the mechanics of writing; he must acquire "taste." About spelling, he has very little choice. There are almost no acceptable variations. He can use *centre* and *theatre* as proper nouns; a resident of Newton, Massachusetts, for instance, might walk down the *center* of *Centre* Street. He may use phonetic spellings in trade names or highway signs, such as "Nu-Lite," "Thru Street," or "Hi-Way 101," and he may take his choice about some words about which there is as yet little agreement; for instance, "programmed learning" or "programed learning." About punctuation, he has a great deal of choice, so much so that he depends as much upon the sound of his communication as he does upon arbitrary rules.

When he confronts a problem of grammar, however, his choices are limited. When two possible constructions occur to him and one is as clear as the other—and both are acceptable to popular usage—he may, quite frankly, turn to the one that is the more "proper." He will run into such problems rarely, but they do occur. Take these sentences, for instance:

1. All the students are here, but none of them are very happy.

2. I must say that he did good.

3. You will go!

4. The policeman said I should drive slow.

5. Ask him who he wants.

6. You are the person that I want.

7. I feel badly about this matter.

8. The document, hopefully, will provide the answer.

If we were to enter the mind of a writer confronted with these sentences, we might encounter responses such as these:

About #1.   Hm-m-m! Bergen Evans says that a majority of writers use *none* as a plural. There is a perverse kind of logic in their defense: after all *zero* is neither singular nor plural, and the sentence does have a plural ring, as though we are saying "All are unhappy," but instead say "None are happy." I guess either *is* or *are* would be satisfactory.

About #2.   This one has a kind of logic too. Strictly speaking, an adverb should be used, "He did well," but "He did good" is more forceful, as though we were saying "He went about doing good." However, even though I am attracted by the force, it does not sound right to me. Apparently "He did well" is more familiar, so I will stick to the strictly grammatical usage.

About #3.   Almost no one knows the distinctions between *shall* and *will*. Whether it is grammatically correct or not, I will use *will*.

About #4.   If I were quoting the policeman directly I would use quotation marks. Whether *slow* is proper is another question. Ironically, the policeman has history on his side. At one time "Walk slow" was as accepted as "Walk fast." Certainly there has never been a "fastly." Through the years, however, strict usage has favored "Drive slowly," one of the occasions where polite usage has been stricter than historical development. Okay, I will use the stricter form, "Drive slowly."

About #5 and #6.   The *who* and *whom* dilemma! *Whom* often sounds prissy, even when it is correct. Some "correct" uses of *whom* sound downright silly—for instance, "Whom's he seeking?" Even "For whom is he calling?" sounds a bit stilted. Settling the matter by using *that* is not very good, because it often makes a split construction necessary: you cannot say "You are the person for that I am looking": you must say, "You are the person that I am looking for." In this dilemma I guess I will stick to *whom* when it is appropriate; when I think *that* is better, I may be able to cross it out entirely.

Ask him whom he wants.

You are the person I want.

About #7 and #8.   Hm-m-m! There comes a time when a person has to draw the line. Ironically, "I feel badly" is used often by the semi-educated, rarely by the uneducated. Half-knowledge tells us that we should use an adverb after a verb, and adverbs have -ly endings. Ergo: shouldn't

I use *badly?* But there is also some rule about verbs of sense *(taste, smell, hear, feel)* taking adjective forms. If a fish smells badly, it means something is wrong with his nose. If he smells bad, he stinks. If I taste badly, there is something wrong with my tasting apparatus. I should use adjective forms, as I do when I use forms of the verb *be.*

> The fish smells bad.
> The fish is bad.
>
> I feel bad.
> I am bad.
>
> The meat tastes bad.
> The meat is bad.

Thus, "I feel badly" is a ridiculous affectation. I do not care who uses it. *I* won't.

About #8. There are some expressions that irritate me. If I use "hopefully" I should indicate who is doing the hoping. A document can't hope, as the construction seems to suggest. I will write, "We hope that the document will provide the answer we need so badly."

A student often comes to a kind of reluctant truce in the battle with grammar. He says to himself, "Okay, I will be pragmatic and go along. I will wear a tie at dinner. I will not pick my teeth in a café. I will try to write grammatically correct prose. My reader will think of me as an educated, stable, mannerly person, and I am more likely to convince him than if I violate the conventions of grammar." An experienced writer, on the other hand, more often has his respect for grammar based on real admiration. He knows that although his style may be the mark of his own personality, grammar is something invented and refined by society to make the best possible representation of a thought. He does not look at grammar as a discipline, but as part of freedom. Freedom, he reflects, is really only the privilege of exercising one's self-discipline. He concludes that the discipline of grammar is what makes it possible for him to exercise real freedom in thought and style.

A self-diagnostic review

Grammar, spelling, punctuation, and other conventions provide a dilemma for a college teacher. If he allots class time for instruction, those students who have already mastered the conventions are understandably bored and annoyed at having their time wasted. If class time is not allotted, some students will miss the opportunity to clear up a deficiency. The usual situation is that the average student knows most of the conventions but is uncertain about a few of them. Unfortunately these individual deficiencies have a way of besmirching an otherwise efficiently proofread theme. We urge, therefore, that you study the following sentences. Each sentence represents a convention that is often troublesome. If any of the conventions is unfamiliar, check the pages given in parentheses. Some sentences violate conventions; others illustrate them.

1. Date and bait rhyme with mate. (See *Italics,* p. 417)

2. *Man And The Mountain* and "Man and the Mountain" contradict each other. (See *Titles,* p. 436, and *Capitalization,* p. 408)

3. I wish I could go, I cannot. (See *Comma Splice,* p. 409)

4. When the President gave his speech everyone waved their hands. (See *Agreement,* p. 404)

5. He has an I don't care attitude. (See *Hyphen,* p. 415)

6. Dwight D. Isenhower [sic] was a very popular President. (See *Brackets,* p. 407)

7. The president announced at the White House today that the amendment would be dropped. (See *Capitalization,* p. 408)

8. The astronauts were ordered to test their oxygen equipment and other emergency devices and that they must be ready to go at once. (*See Parallelism,* p. 420)

9. There is a tax on food, gas, services, etc. (See *Abbreviations,* p. 404)

10. Before installing a television set, the appropriate antenna should be purchased. (See *Modifiers,* p. 418)

11. When it is time to go; we will be glad to do so. (See *Punctuation,* p. 422)

12. Shirley Temple became famous, in part because of the way she sang On The Good Ship Lollipop. (*See Italics* p. 417, *Titles,* p. 436, and *Capitalization,* p. 408)

13. 1,123 labor union members went on strike today. (See *Numbers,* p. 419)

14. "Knowledge is no knowledge without zeal;" wrote John Cotton, who continued, "zeal is but wildfire without knowledge." (See *Quotation Marks,* p. 427)

15. Life is action and love of a man it is required that he partici-
plate in both. (See *Run-on,* p. 431)

16. There are many people who lack the good things in life because they are the product of cowardly mentalities. (See *Faulty
Reference,* p. 430)

Common difficulties

ABBREVIATIONS (ABBR.)

As a rule, abbreviations are avoided in serious writing. Abbreviated titles of address, such as *Mr., Mrs., Dr.,* and *Lt. Col.,* are used in all
writing as are abbreviations for academic degrees and military honors.

Eugene Yarrington, Ph.D., is one of the poets mentioned in the
book.

Sir Colin Richardson, O.B.E., has just approached the rotunda.

Such abbreviations as *C.O.D., TV, U.N., U.S., JV, stereo,* and *hi-fi*
are currently so common that they are found in almost all publications,
but they still have a slightly colloquial tinge and should be avoided for
strictly formal writing. *Etc.* is not used in formal or semiformal prose.
Since it is often an indication of sloppy, inconclusive thinking, we hope
you will avoid it for reasons other than that it is an abbreviation. The
ampersand (&) is used only when it is part of a corporate name, for instance, *Harper & Row.* Otherwise, abbreviations should be restricted to
legal documents, form books, footnotes, bibliographies, informal letters,
and other writing in which saving space is essential or desirable.

AGREEMENT (AGR.)

Verbs and pronouns are alike in that they must agree in number
with a preceding noun or pronoun. A verb must agree with its subject,
and a pronoun must agree with its antecedent. Usually an error in agreement results from muddled thinking or slovenly writing, for instance,

If a rookie has any ability at all, Lombardi
will help *them* develop.

Flagrant examples of disagreement such as "they was" and "he
don't" are the marks of the educationally deprived. There are, however,
occasions when educated writers are puzzled about how to guarantee
agreement. The following suggestions may help.

1. The indefinite expressions *another, anybody, each, each one, either, everybody, everyone, neither, nobody,* and *no one* take singular verbs and pronouns:

No one *is* completely happy with *his* life.

If *anyone* objects, *he* must speak up.

Writers for informal audiences increasingly are following *none* with plurals, as:

None of the candidates *were* satisfied with *their* showing.

However, there are still enough discriminate readers that the careful writer may prefer to follow the stricter usage, being careful that a plural modifier does not confuse the issue:

None of the candidates *was* satisfied with *his* showing.

2. A compound substantive joined by *and* takes plural verbs and pronouns:

Babe Ruth and Gene Tunney were at the peaks of their careers in 1927.

3. After a compound expression joined by *or* or *nor,* the number of the verb and pronouns is determined by the nearer subject or antecedent:

The President or the Secretary of State is to give his verdict soon.

The President or the members of the committee are to give their approval soon.

4. Collective nouns take either singulars or plurals, depending upon the writer's intent. If the writer is thinking of an action by a unit, such as a committee, army, group, number, or class, singular verbs and pronouns follow:

The committee *has* finished *its* work.

The group *is* much smaller than *it* was.

Three-fourths of the land *is* in good shape.

If the writer is thinking of members of the group—that one, and that one, and that one—he will use plural verbs and pronouns:

Until the family settled the quarrel, *they* all *were* shouting at the tops of their voices.

When a *number* of the hoodlums arrived, *they* broke through the police lines.

After he gave his explanation, *three-fourths* of the audience *were* satisfied.

Pronouns provide an additional problem in that they must agree with their antecedent in gender as well as number. This is usually simple enough, but a problem is occasionally raised when the antecedent is both masculine and feminine. The inexperienced writer is tempted to use a double pronoun:

> The teacher asked that either the boy or the girl indicate his or her preference.

This is a stilted, unnecessary practice; in such cases a masculine pronoun is appropriate.

Care in agreement is a way in which a writer shows precision of thought. If his sentences get long, he still remembers what his subject is and uses the proper verb. When he writes a construction that permits loose agreement he rephrases it. Even a purist would hardly object to the use of *them* in the following newspaper account:

> When the President got off Air Force One, everyone in the audience cheered. He waved to *them*.

Nevertheless the careful writer would be uncomfortable with such an utterance and would probably condense the first sentence to "When the President got off Air Force One, the audience cheered." The writer would then have no discomfort with his subsequent use of *them*.

In almost no other aspect of grammar does simple common sense provide so good a guide. A writer can solve almost all problems of agreement by keeping pronouns relatively close to their antecedents and verbs close to their subjects.

In order to show yourself that you have mastered the problem of agreement, improve the following sentences and check your versions with the ones we have suggested.

1. Each of the coed group did his or her part.

2. Everyone did their job.

3. If one wants to get ahead, they would do well to become a dedicated worker early in life.

4. When the team finished the season, they were in fifth place.

5. The number of people in the club are quite inadequate for raising funds.

Our versions:

1. Each of the coed group did his part.

2. Everyone did his job.

3. If one wants to get ahead, he would do well to become a dedicated worker early in life.

4. When the team finished the season, it was in fifth place. (Plural verb would be contested only in strict usage.)

5. The number of people in the club is quite inadequate for raising funds.

Submit the following exercises to your instructor. Title them "Agreement" and indicate the theme or assignment in which you experienced difficulty with this particular point of grammar.

1. Make necessary improvements in the following sentences:

a. The family were tired of one another.

b. Everyone was waiting their turn.

c. Two-thirds of the grapes has been placed in the first vat.

2. Write a sentence demonstrating an error in agreement between subject and verb. Put one line under the subject and two under the verb. Then rephrase the sentence to correct the error.

3. Write a sentence demonstrating faulty agreement between a pronoun and its antecedent. Put one line under the antecedent and two under the pronoun. Then rephrase the sentence to correct the error.

BRACKETS [ ]

Brackets formerly were used for parentheses within parentheses; now they are used almost exclusively to indicate insertions by an editor in direct quotations.

> "It is his [the writer's] privilege to help man endure by because it cannot be educational." ALFRED NORTH WHITEHEAD.

> "It is his [the writer's] privilege to help man endure by lifting his heart, by reminding him of the courage and honor and hope and praise and compassion and pity and sacrifice which have been the glory of his past." WILLIAM FAULKNER.

Occasionally a writer comes across an error in a quotation he is using; often, if he is certain the error is unintentional, he corrects the error, but occasionally, especially if he is feeling snide, he inserts [sic] at the point of the mistake: "Recently I received a letter that said, 'When a studnet [sic] has been enroddled [sic] for four years, he graduats [sic]. . . .' By the time I finished the letter I was as 'enroddled' [sic] as the writer."

CAPITALIZATION (CAPS.)

The following are customarily capitalized:

1. The first letter of a sentence, quotation, or full line of poetry.

2. The pronoun *I*.

3. Interjections (Oh! Ouch!)

4. The first letter in each word of a salutatory phrase (*My Dear Sir*).

In addition, the first letter in titles is capitalized. The function of this convention is to indicate that the capitalized word is part of a traditional or official title. Do *not* capitalize such words as *college, union,* or *freshmen* unless they refer to specific groups. Do *not* capitalize directions unless they refer to recognized regions or cultures. Thus, you would have "Aunt Martha told me that the Senior Class of North Mason City High School officially cited the Dean of Men of Tulane University, one of the finest institutions in the South. For many years he has taught his famous course, 'Introduction to Philosophy'." But you would not capitalize similar words if they were not parts of titles, for instance, "When I was a senior in a high school on the north side of the city, my aunt introduced me to a dean from a nearby university. Before he was promoted, he taught a course in Eastern philosophy." In most countries, its president, monarch, or leader is accorded the respect of having all references to his title capitalized, thus, "The President announced today. . . ."

In titles with three or more words, it is not customary to capitalize articles (*a, an, the*), conjunctions, and short prepositions (three letters or less) unless they are the first or last word: *Pride and Prejudice, The World We Live In, Man Against Destiny, Once Upon a Dream, League of Women Voters, Tales of My Landlord,* and *God, the Redeemer.* Some titles have traditional short forms, for instance, the *U.N.,* the *Met* (the Metropolitan Opera Company in New York City), and the Y, and they are capitalized. One oddity is that although planets, stars, and galaxies are capitalized, *earth, sun,* and *moon* are not—except when they appear in a list, as *Mars, Earth, Saturn, Sun, Dubhe,* and *Moon.* Capitalize the titles or names of towns, cities, counties, provinces, states, countries, regions, officials, peoples, races, tribes, languages, books, poems, short stories, essays, months, days of the week, holidays, congresses, unions, clubs, political parties, treaties, laws, historical periods, literary eras, geological epochs, and celebrated events. Humorous, legendary, intellectual, sports-page, and honorific labels are capitalized (*Iron Duke, Thin Red Line, The Four Horsemen,* the *Crusades,* the *Middle Ages, Willie the Wisp,* the *Sultan of Swat*). Almost any reference to the Deity and organized religion or to any of its special teachings or traditions is capitalized: *Apostles' Creed, Holy Communion, God,* the *Prophet,* the *Lamb, Koran, Talmud.* Generic and directional terms are capitalized when they are distinctly part of the title, *Mahaska County, Commonwealth of Massachusetts, Gulf Stream, Labor Department, Atlantic Ocean* (but the *Atlantic coast*), *South Carolina* (but *northern Kansas*). Capitalize Latin names of classes, families, and genera, but not of species, like *Homo sapiens.*

When in doubt, the writer should ask himself, "Have I seen this concept given a proper name by a previous writer? Is it likely that it has an official name?" Thus, he would write about the Italian Renaissance, but he would write "The University of Chicago is having a football renaissance." Occasionally the writer will come across a word that was once a proper noun but is now in general usage. Reference to a dictionary will indicate whether it should still be capitalized, for instance, *English horn, French fries, Salk vaccine,* but *china tea pot, venetian blinds, pasteurized milk.* Individual letters, when they are grades on an examination, part of a title (*Model* A Ford), or parts of abbreviations, are often capitalized, for instance, *R.A.F., G.N.P., A.W.O.L., M.A.,* and *Ph.D.,* but a dictionary often will indicate exceptions, such as *i.e., mph,* and *f.*

COMMA SPLICE (c. s.)

The comma splice is an error in grammar and punctuation that should not appear in formal or semiformal writing. It often obscures meaning.

> I like studying but also pretty girls, strange to say, the pretty girls always win.

Does "strange to say" go with the first word group or with the second? Whether the comma splice is confusing or not, it is offensive to readers, who legitimately expect writers to show their education and manners by following certain social rules. The really skilled writer avoids the comma splice because it fails to take advantage of the real meaning of certain marks of punctuation.

Take the expression, "The sidewalk was slippery, I fell." which contains two complete sentences spliced together by a comma. Figuratively, the comma is the little brother of the semicolon and the period. If the writer wants to show his reader that he thinks of "The sidewalk was slippery" and "I fell" as two complete thoughts, he separates them with a period:

The sidewalk was slippery. I fell.

These sentences are now grammatically correct, but they do not show the relationship which the writer apparently tried to express by handling them as one sentence. To show a relationship, he can join them in either one of these balanced constructions.

The sidewalk was slippery; I fell.

The sidewalk was slippery, and I fell.

From this we can deduce that the semicolon is equivalent to a comma plus a coordinating conjunction such as *and, but,* or *or.* The semicolon is used to indicate either balanced ideas or markedly balanced structures. In revision, the writer will want to ask himself, "Just what is the relationship between the two sentences?" If the total idea is that the one caused the other, a word must be inserted which says more than "and."

Because the sidewalk was slippery, I fell.

He may have intended something else, for instance:

The sidewalk was slippery when I fell.

This sentence might be used in a court case when a plaintiff is suing for damages. He is primarily concerned with the ice on the walk, a fault, perhaps, of a property owner. Notice the meanings that are possible when one idea is subordinated to the other:

When the sidewalk was slippery, I fell. (Indicates point in time.)

The sidewalk being slippery, I fell. (Acceptable grammar, but possibly a little stilted; indicates that slipperiness caused the fall.)

The sidewalk was slippery since I fell. (A way of suggesting that we can assume the sidewalk was slippery because the writer fell.)

There is a rhetorical device used much in England that might be called the "literary comma splice." E. M. Forster, for one, used it: "The plot-maker expects us to remember, we expect him to leave no loose ends."

Julius Caesar's "I came, I saw, I conquered" has two characteristics: the clauses are short, and there is a rhythm to the parallel elements. There is little justification, however, for the sentence,

I heaved a sigh, I wept, I nearly expired.

Often the intentional comma splice has a noticeable rhyme. Punctuated thus, the units are forced together to enhance the effect of the rhyme:

I sighed, I cried, I almost died.

Test yourself on the following sentences. Not all are incorrect. If more than one correction is possible, choose the best one.

1. I will be at Filene's at three; wait for me.

2. Exercise is good, especially weight-lifting, although it is quite strenuous,.it builds the physique spectacularly.

3. Katie chose the red one, Edie selected the pink, Irma picked the rose number with the flounce.

4. I want you, I need you, I love you.

5. The light flashed red, I jammed on the brakes.

6. The batter gave a mighty swing, the ball went sailing over the fence.

7. The Great Wall did not protect China, he said, the DEW line will not protect America.

Suggested acceptable versions:

1. Since I will be at Filene's at three, wait for me.
   I will be at Filene's at three; wait for me.

2. Exercise is good, especially weight-lifting; although it is quite strenuous, it builds the physique spectacularly.

3. Katie chose the red one, Edie selected the pink, and Irma picked the rose number with the flounce.

4. All right as is.

5. When the light flashed red, I jammed on the brakes.
   or
   The light flashed red; I jammed on the brakes.

6. The batter gave a mighty swing, and the ball went sailing over the fence.

7. The Great Wall did not protect China, he said, and the DEW line will not protect America.

Correct the following sentences and submit them to your instructor. Title the exercise "Comma Splice" and indicate in what theme or assignment you had difficulty with it.

1. I will take the bus, you will drive, *and* he will fly down.

2. John came to school in shorts; everyone laughed.

3. *because* I knew the book forward and backward, I passed the test.

On the paper you submit to your instructor, write a sentence with a comma splice. Then rewrite, correcting it.

ELLIPSIS (. . .)

The ellipsis (three spaced periods) is used to indicate an incomplete element, usually in a quotation.

"Finally it is to be observed that Pater's work . . . is nevertheless creative in its own kind."

Here, the ellipsis marks the omission of, "critical and philosophical in intention". Note that the punctuation related to the omitted material must also be omitted.

If the omitted material occurs at the end of a sentence, a fourth period must be used:

"He believed that 'imaginative prose' was 'the special art of the modern world'. . . ."

FRAGMENTS (FRAG.)

The sentence fragment, as it often appears in student themes, is a construction that inadvertently omits one of the essential grammatical elements, often a finite verb form:

Colin and Mary, being too old.

Such a construction is often the result of haste, not ignorance, and the correction is simple: substitute a verb and punctuate appropriately. If the error occurred because the idea was not completed on paper (although it may have been complete in the writer's mind), then the correction merely requires that the idea be expressed:

Colin and Mary, being too old, were not included in the party.

A similar fragment—the afterthought fragment—can occur when the writer "tacks on" a qualifying clause without punctuating appropriately:

John rushed to the ticket window. Although he had no money.

Logically, the last clause cannot stand alone without the preceding sentence. Remove "although," and the meaning of the pair of sentences changes. Clearly, the writer intended:

John rushed to the ticket window, although he had no money.

On revision, this might better appear as

John, although he had no money, rushed to the ticket window.
or
Although he had no money, John rushed to the ticket window.

Carefully reread your papers to eliminate sentence fragments. If you discover that your current method of rereading does not catch these and other structural problems, try placing the index finger of one hand at the capital letter, the index finger of the other hand at the period, and reading slowly all the material between. Is this a sentence with a subject and a finite (limited in time) verb form? Does it depend grammatically or logically on a preceding or following sentence? Is it merely a clause with a subordinate relationship to another sentence?

Improve the following constructions, if a sentence fragment occurs.

1. The Red Sox now have a left-handed starting pitcher. Thus improving their chances.

2. The Rams need another quarterback. Although Gabriel does his best.

3. He would not get up for class. Because he preferred to sleep.

4. Many young men cannot decide whether to go to college or to fulfill their military obligation.

5. The current world situation sees two forces struggling for dominance. American democracy, characteristically free and individualistic, being opposed by Communism, characteristically rigid and collective.

Better versions:

1. The Red Sox now have a left-handed starting pitcher, thus improving their chances.

2. The Rams need another quarterback, although Gabriel does his best.

3. He would not get up for class, because he preferred to sleep.

or

Because he preferred to sleep, he would not get up for class.

4. All right as is.

5. The current world situation sees two forces struggling for dominance, American democracy, characteristically free and individualistic, being opposed by Communism, characteristically rigid and collective.

Spoken English makes much use of incomplete or fragmentary sentences, for the standard sentence order is so firmly fixed in our minds that we readily supply the missing elements. However, the best procedure for student writers is to be certain that each sentence is complete, both grammatically and logically. As you achieve more flexible skills in utilizing varied structures, you and your instructor may agree that an *occasional* incomplete sentence is effective.

Correct any deficiencies in the following and submit them to your instructor. Title the exercise "Fragments." Indicate the theme assignment in which you made the error.

1. American literature, now recognized as a major influence on world literature, was long thought to be merely a provincial echo of English literature. Melville, being ignored even in the United States, serves today as a warning to critics.

2. The "novel of manners" is a dying form. Society itself having withdrawn from public attention.

3. The two reasons for the Yankees' decline in recent years are quite obvious. Both their increasing average age and the failure of their farm system.

4. Political history in the twentieth century shows increasing governmental control. Both in democratic and in socialistic countries.

5. He could remember his first view of the city. How impressive the skyline and the smog.

On the same paper that you used for the exercise above, write three different kinds of sentence fragments and correct them.

HYPHENS (-)

Probably no other mark of punctuation is as slippery as the hyphen, its use varying widely from writer to writer and from formal to informal style. The following suggestions will help.

1. Use a hyphen at the end of a line when there is sufficient space for the entire word. Break between syllables; avoid breaking before a single-letter syllable:

> The most recent development in the study of English syntax has been the transformational analysis of Noam Chomsky.

2. Use a hyphen to avoid confusion.

> She recovered the sofa.
> She re-covered the sofa.

> I have a great grandfather.
> I have a great-grandfather.

3. When creating two-word adjective modifiers, hyphenate only if used before the noun:

> The rebellion was short lived.

> It was a short-lived rebellion.

If the modifier begins with an adverb ending in -ly, it is not hyphenated.

> He was an overly enthusiastic person.

4. Compound words customarily go through a routine. First they are written separately, then hyphenated, and then joined. *Drug store* became *drug-store* and is now *drugstore*. When in doubt check your dictionary.

5. The following examples will help you acquire a "feel" for hyphenation.

> a. *ultra-ambitious, re-entry, bell-like, re-elected, pre-eminent, pre-existent, fire-escape* (or *fire escape,* but never *fireescape*). Hyphens, in other words, are used to separate double letters at syllable breaks. Usage is divided with *co-, cooperate* and *coordinate* seeming objectionable to some writers who use *co-operate* and *co-ordinate,* or even *coöperate* and *coördinate.*

> b. *anti-American, ex-President Eisenhower, non-Birchite, conservatives.* Used to separate a prefix and a proper name.

c. *thirty-five, one hundred twenty-five, three-sixteenths.* (Usage varies greatly in the last.)

d. *president-elect, all-state, ex-singer, self-importance.* These four affixes (*-elect, all-, ex-,* and *self-*) are rarely joined to a noun without a hyphen.

IDIOMATIC CONSTRUCTIONS (ID.)

All languages develop characteristic usages that seem, to the non-native speaker, illogical and/or ungrammatical. In English, the *idiomatic constructions* that most frequently cause difficulty or uncertainty are those in which verbs require particular prepositions. Consider:

He is capable to do anything.

He is able to do anything.

Both sentences might look equally grammatical to a speaker of a language *other* than English. However, native speakers recognize that *capable* requires *of,* and that the sentence must be:

He is capable of doing anything.

Since there are hundreds of verbs with their attendant prepositions (some verbs taking several—and changing their meaning as they change prepositions), we make no attempt to list them. As a native speaker, you will automatically select the correct combinations most of the time—if you think through what you mean.

INCOMPLETE COMPARISONS (INC. COMPS.)

In their desire to intensify a statement, some writers will use incomplete comparative or superlative expressions that, in Standard Written English, must be completed.

She is such a good person.

I had more fun.

He was the best teacher.

All of the preceding statements need to be completed.

She is such a good person that I feel very humble in her presence.

I had more fun than anyone else.

He was the best teacher in the school that year.

Care in thinking out the meaning of your statements will enable you to avoid incomplete comparisons.

INCOMPLETE CONSTRUCTIONS (INC. CONST.)

Haste in writing, or careless thinking, sometimes causes a writer to leave out essential parts of sentences because he expects the reader to provide the preposition, or verb, or subordinating word, from a previously established pattern. In each of the pairs of sentences below, the second version is better than the first.

Dr. King long ago showed his concern and interest in civil rights. Dr. King long ago showed his concern with and interest in civil rights.

The prisoner's bonds were broken, and his freedom thus assured. The prisoner's bonds were broken, and his freedom was thus assured.

You should assume your readers are the entire educated community.
You should assume that your readers are the entire educated community.

Some instructors suggest your audience will be your classmates. Some instructors suggest that your audience will be your classmates.

Care in reading what you actually put on paper will aid you in avoiding incomplete constructions.

ITALICS (ITAL.)

Italics is the name of a font of printer's type used in contrast to Roman type, the type regularly used. This convention is represented in a typescript or manuscript by underlining and is used to indicate the following.

1. Emphasis: I will *not* go!

2. Titles of books, periodicals, theatrical productions, works of art, and vehicles: *Guard of Honor, Saturday Review, Guernica, The Sound of Music, Titanic.*

3. Foreign expressions used in English: *coup d'état, nouveau riche, Realpolitik, Weltschmerz, Weltanschauung.* Most dictionaries indicate with a double cross ($\ddagger$) or parallel bars ($\|$) which words have not become part of the standard English vocabulary and would therefore be underlined.

4. A word used as a word, not for its meaning: "I dislike *oxygen*, *cheese*, and *pastiche* because they are such harsh words." (The writer is speaking of the words themselves, not what they represent. If he had said "I dislike oxygen, cheese, and pastiche," he would have conveyed a different meaning.) This use is appropriate also for single letters and numbers:

> There are four *s*'s in *Mississippi*.

> Since the cartographer did not have an *n* in his type case, *Pago-Pago* has since then been misspelled.

5. Confusing sentences can be clarified by judicious underlining, as in the following example, where *had* appears eleven times:

> "Peter, where John had had *had*, had had *had had*; *had had* had had the teacher's approval."

MISPLACED AND DANGLING MODIFIERS (MOD.)

Misplaced and dangling modifiers have an unfortunate habit of causing confusion. Notice how modifying words, phrases, and clauses cause ambiguity in the following sentences.

> 1. D'Artagnan only challenged two people to a fight. (Does he mean, "All he did was challenge. . . ." or "He challenged only two people to a fight"?)

> 2. I like the painting that I told you about at your house. (Sounds as though the conversation took place at your house, but we suspect that it was the painting that was at your house.)

> 3. They went for a ride in a convertible with a dual exhaust that was flaming red. (Huh? Or was it the convertible that was "flaming red"?)

Occasionally a modifier placed between two elements may modify either of them: "Students who make good decisions without a doubt will succeed." The sentence could mean either "Without a doubt, students who make good decisions will succeed," or "Students who make firm decisions will succeed."

To avoid this confusion, good writers make sure that modifiers are placed as close as possible to the words they modify. They are careful, also, to have a word for the modifier to modify. This sentence is not sound: "To avoid defeat, Doolittle's campaign was called off." Doolittle, not the campaign, did the calling off, thus, "To avoid defeat, Doolittle called off his campaign." This error is called a "dangling modifier" because it modifies nothing; for example:

1. Walking down the hall, my eye was caught by the sign.

2. While painting the house, my brush dropped into the bushes.

To demonstrate your ability to avoid such mistakes, rephrase these sentences:

1. *Blast* Toothpaste has been effective against cavities in homes like yours.

2. Looking from the bridge, the first thing we saw was a yacht.

3. The band having finished that number, another piece was played.

4. Upon entering the museum, my eyes fell upon a small statue.

Better versions:

1. Tested in homes like yours, *Blast* Toothpaste has been found effective against cavities.

2. The first thing we saw, on looking from the bridge, was a yacht.

3. Although awkward, this sentence is acceptable. Better: Having finished that number, the band played another piece.

4. Upon entering the museum, I saw a small statue.

Rephrase the following sentences and submit them to your instructor. Title the exercise "Modifiers." Indicate the theme in which you had the difficulty.

1. While strolling through the park one day, my purse was stolen.

2. I delivered the message to the house where I was born this morning.

3. A person who is pleasant all his life will have friends.

Write a sentence containing a misplaced modifier. Correct it. Do the same for the dangling modifier.

NUMBERS

The question of whether to use Arabic numerals or to spell out a number in letters is now largely an arbitrary matter, but the conventions are based on an attempt to provide the information in a consistent and clear manner. A writer, first of all, should attempt to find what arbitrary rules exist in his writing circumstance. Rather informal periodicals, for instance, tend to require numerals if the number is larger than ten, and letters if smaller. More formal publications tend to require letters for round numbers (one hundred, one thousand, one million) and numerals for other amounts over one hundred, thus 101, 342, 4,555, and 1,002,897. Almost all publications and form books require figures for the following:

Mixed numbers: 6⅞, $4.32.

Dates: August 17, 1945. (Do not add suffixes to dates; say 17, not 17th.)

Percentages: 23 percent.

Addresses: 48 Ruthven Road; Apartment 307-1.

Page numbers and other references: *page 49; pp. 423–444;* and *Act IV, sc. iv, l. 22.*

Statistical information, especially if a series of numbers occurs: *The state legislature now contains 38 Republicans, 143 Democrats, and 7 Independents.*

Do not use numerals at the beginning of a sentence.

Not: 123 new officials went on duty today.

Acceptable: One hundred twenty-three new officials went on duty today.

Better to reword the sentence: Today a total of 123 new officials went on duty.

PARALLELISM (‖ISM)

Parallelism is a rhetorical device that a writer uses to demonstrate the equivalence of two concepts or two grammatical elements. If the parallel units are expressed in dissimilar structures, the result is called "faulty parallelism," which may confuse the reader or offend his sense of propriety and rhythm, as in the sentence, "I like hunting, fishing, and to swim." Caesar's "I came, I saw, I conquered" would not have been half so memorable had he written, "I came, observation was made, and conquest resulted." To make your parallel expressions effective:

1. Avoid a shift of subject or voice within the sentences: "The exercises were done by the student, and then he handed them to the

teacher." The sentence would be less awkward if phrased, "The student did his exercises and handed them to the teacher."

2. Avoid a shift in person: First the eyes close and then you shake your head. Better: Close your eyes and shake your head.

3. Avoid a shift in tense. "I came in and there is a teacher writing on the blackboard." Better: "I came in, and there was a teacher writing on the blackboard," or "When I came in, a teacher was writing on the blackboard."

4. Avoid changing grammatical structures in parallel: "The horse was sway-backed, uncomfortable to ride, and practically fell at every bump in the road." Better: "The horse, sway backed and uncomfortable to ride, practically fell at every bump in the road."

5. Be sure that constructions following such paired connectives as "not only . . . but also" and "either . . . or" are parallel. Avoid "She not only made us punctuate better, but also our style improved"; instead, say, "She improved not only our punctuation but also our style."

6. Avoid using "and who" to make elements parallel, not "The prize goes to a boy worthy of the honor and who shows true humility," but "The prize goes to a worthy and humble boy," or "The prize goes to a boy who is worthy of the honor and humble in receiving it."

7. Be sure that articles and prepositions govern all the elements in a series, or none. "I saw bell, book, and a candle" should be phrased, "I saw a bell, book, and candle," or "I saw a bell, a book, and a candle."

To demonstrate your mastery of this principle, construct at least one improved version of the following sentences. Compare your results with the suggested improvements.

1. They don't know whether to try harder or if they should give up right now.

2. The pamphlet describes the habits of rabbits, how to make them reproduce, and how to stop them.

3. Tom's grades in science have not progressed as well as he has in psychology.

4. This is for God, country, and for Yale.

5. The book was composed of exercises, and they were the best I have seen.

Possible improvements:

1. They don't know whether to try harder or to give up right now.

2. The pamphlet describes the habits of rabbits, their reproduction, and their restraint. (A parallel of "how's" is also possible.)

3. Tom has not improved as much in science as he has in psychology.

4. This is for God, for country, and for Yale.

5. The book was composed of exercises that were the best I have seen.

Do the following exercises and submit them to your instructor. Title the page "Parallelism" and indicate the theme in which your difficulty occurred.
1. Prepare improved versions of these sentences.

a. Ask not what your country can do for you, but ask yourself what can be done by you for your country.

b. He is a man above all others and who deserves promotion.

c. The papers were collected by the Brownies, and they stored them in the church basement.

2. Write a sentence with an error in parallelism. Correct it.

PARENTHESES ( )

Parentheses, which are always used in pairs and should be used seldom, are used in the following instances.

1. To enclose material inserted in a construction.

The thought process is important, not because the poet thinks and then seeks poetic expression for his thought (which is the recipe for bad poetry), but because the good poet is a thinker, a philosopher, and his thought takes poetic form during expression.

2. To enclose cross references: (see p. 29), (see *Encyclopedia Americana*).

3. To enclose letters or numbers in a list: (1) of items in a series, (2) of related items.

PUNCTUATION (PN.)

Punctuation is a decidedly imperfect system with which the writer attempts to communicate the meaningful juncture, intonation, and pitch that would be expressed by a speaker's voice. Punctuation thus has the responsibility of communicating meaning and preventing confusion. The so-called rules of punctuation were prepared after the fact; they are an attempt to describe certain vocal circumstances that can be represented in writing with the help of the marks of punctuation. The best way to punctuate effectively is to have a general sense not only of the function of each mark but also of the oral quality it attempts to duplicate.

1. The period ends an utterance that is complete structurally or that completes a thought; it represents the end of what we traditionally call a sentence. It reflects a terminal drop in the voice. Usually it is followed by a slight pause.

2. The semicolon is placed between units noticeably equivalent in meaning and structure and related in thought. The voice would reflect this relation not only by a shorter juncture than shown by the period but by an emphasis on the structures that are parallel.

John is going home; *Mary* will remain.

John is going to the *football game; Mary* is going to the *play.*

The semicolon stands between the comma and the period in ability to relate units. It can join complete sentences if they are related in structure and idea; the comma needs a conjunction to join complete sentences.

3. The comma is the weakest joiner of the marks of punctuation. Alone, it can separate only words and phrases; if it separates clauses, it usually needs the help of a conjunction.

4. The dash and the colon are contrasting separators. The dash looks backward as if to say, "As a result of what I have just said, you will not be surprised at what follows." The colon looks forward, as if to say, "See what follows."

The interruption—and that is the kindest thing I can call it—completely disrupted the meeting.

The meeting was disrupted for a number of reasons: it was too dull, it was too hot, and it was too long.

As separators, punctuation marks even have personality. The colon, with its air of careful explanation that seems best suited to wills and other legal documents, is somewhat stuffy. The semicolon has been called the mark of the intellectual, since it points out a neat balance of ideas, and since it often connects a series so intricate that internal commas are needed. An overuse of commas is considered the mark of the finicky.

Commas, when they enclose units within a sentence, have a quality of their own. The use of paired commas, if the unit is shown between other sentence elements, and the single comma, which isolates a structure at the beginning or end of a sentence, can be defined operationally by the fact that a distinct drop in the voice is indicated. Read these sentences aloud:

The agent who is in Moscow is our best.

The agent, who is in Moscow, is our best.

In the first sentence, the clause *who is in Moscow* apparently was thought necessary to identify the agent. In the second sentence, we can infer that the agent has already been identified, and the speaker has seen fit to give some further information about him. The first sentence means "The Moscow agent is our best." The second means, "The agent we are talking about is in Moscow. He is our best." Read the sentences aloud several times to get the appropriate intonation.

Even such enclosed units as years and states are in the category of the dropped-voice enclosure.

Montgomery, [which is in] Alabama, is a large city.

August 17, [which was in] 1945, was the date of the historic Regensburg Raid by the Eighth Air Force.

Modern speakers tend to run addresses and dates together somewhat, but the pause is still quite distinct after the state and year: "New York City, New York, is the second largest city in the world." "April 18, 1919, was the date of my birth."

After a writer understands the relationship between the sound and function of punctuation, he can usually punctuate a sentence properly if he reads it aloud.

If the following examples are read as illustrative of the principles discussed, a student can develop a "feel" for sound and sense that will make logical punctuation an instinct. The sample sentences should be read audibly.

The period is used:

1. To set off a declarative sentence.

2. With abbreviations and contractions: Mr., Dr., lb., etc.

The semicolon is used between independent clauses of a compound sentence when the independent clauses are not joined by a co-ordinating conjunction.

1. After a year or two he ran out of money; she left him.

2. At first I decided to go; later, however, I changed my mind.

A semicolon is used also when the independent clauses are joined by a coordinating conjunction, provided the clauses have internal punctuation.

> Although he had left them a considerable legacy, his wife's relatives were not satisfied; and, in an effort to mollify them, his son made them a further cash settlement.

Use a semicolon to set off sharply one independent clause from the other independent clause or clauses, even though the clauses are joined by a coordinating conjunction and contain little or no internal punctuation.

> The hastiness of his productions might be the effect of necessity; but his subsequent negligence could hardly have any other cause than impatience of study.

Use a semicolon as a kind of "supercomma" whenever the comma has already been used and a stronger mark of punctuation is required to show a larger unit of thought.

> His creed was simple: to believe in the Constitution, the Republican Party, and the Methodist Church; to work on six days and fish on the seventh; and to love, honor, and ignore his wife.

The comma should be used to set off independent clauses joined by a coordinating conjunction (*and, but, or, nor, for*).

> 1. I know he was there at two, and I am told he was still there at four.

> 2. The symptoms grew more formidable every day, for nothing would do but that we look at his flowers.

There are two exceptions to this rule. (1) If the independent clauses are short, no comma is used. (2) If the independent clauses are long or complicated, a semicolon, instead of a comma, is used.

Commas are used to set off *all* nonrestrictive modifiers, whether clauses or phrases.

> 1. The messenger, who had been five hours on the road, arrived shortly after dark. (Adjectival clause)

> 2. He spoke in a low voice, so that almost no one understood him. (Adverbial clause)

> 3. His first contention, that the penalty is too severe, is surely reasonable. (Noun clause)

> 4. The wolf, back-tracking quickly, shook off the pack. (Participial phrase)

5. The committee, on going into the matter thoroughly, decided that the charge was unfounded. (Gerund phrase)

6. We stopped there for the night, the hour being late. (Absolute phrase)

7. The house, old and deserted, stood at the intersection of the road. (Adjectival phrase)

8. Tom, my brother, was married yesterday. (Nonrestrictive appositive phrase) But: My brother Tom was married yesterday.

9. The class, naturally enough, felt bewildered. (All parenthetical phrases are nonrestrictive.)

Use a comma to set off such introductory elements as verbal phrases and clauses. Transitional words or phrases (*but, however, therefore*) and single introductory words are sometimes excepted.

Accordingly, the agreement was signed.

Taken aback, he fell silent.

If I come, I'll bring it.

If he refuses to obey orders, he will surely get into trouble.

Use commas to set off transposed elements occurring within the body of a sentence.

The narrative, as it progressed, became more and more incoherent.

Commas are used for direct address, mild interjections, and dates and geographical expressions.

For once, Tom, you are right.

Come here, you little devil.

Oh, what's the use!

The letter, dated March 1, 1889, bore his signature.

He went first to Portland, Oregon, and then to Pullman, Washington.

Commas are used between coordinate modifiers.

He lived in a cool, air-conditioned apartment.

Contrasting coordinate sentence elements require a comma between them, as do coordinate elements in a series.

I called him, not you.

He worked quickly, yet coolly.

The new models come in blue, red, green, and cocoa.

Finally, place a comma after a word or words which might be ambiguously read.

Below, the trail was no less difficult.

The colon is used before a formal statement that is pointedly explanatory of a statement immediately preceding.

I cannot but remark the respect perhaps unconsciously paid to this great man by his biographers: every house in which he resided is historically mentioned, as if it were an injury to neglect any place that he had honored by his presence.

Colons are occasionally used before a formal quotation, especially in expository writing.

The speaker began as follows: "I feel honored to have been asked to address you."

In formal writing, use a colon before a series.

There were three reasons for his dismissal: laziness, incompetence, and dishonesty.

The dash is used to indicate a break in sentence structure, especially in informal writing.

She's like—well, I won't be so catty as to say.

Dashes are used also to set off strongly parenthetical expressions.

Editorial writers have severely criticized our policy—or the lack of it—in this regard.

Quotation marks are used to indicate titles of poems, essays, short stories, and literary compositions not long enough to be published as a book.

In "How To Tell a Story" Mark Twain tells about a soldier who has been asked to carry an injured companion back to the field hospital. On the way a cannon ball decapitates his friend.

Use quotation marks to indicate an exact quotation, as in the same story by Mark Twain.

"Where are you going with that carcass?"

"The rear, sir,—he's lost his leg!"

"His leg, forsooth?" responded the astonished officer; "you mean his head, you booby."

Whereupon the soldier dispossessed himself of his burden, and stood looking down upon it in great perplexity. At length he said:

"It is true, sir, just as you have said." Then, after a pause he added, "But he *told* me it was his leg!"

Use quotation marks to enclose expressions that are not the writer's.

Henry David Thoreau wrote "There is no more Herculean task than to think a thought about this life and then get it expressed." This thought probably explains the effort he must have taken to devise such precious expressions as those he used to describe the weather, "fingering cold," "whitening snows," "moistening snows," and "remaining snows."

Quotation marks are also used to indicate expressions that have unfamiliar meanings or that the writer has coined for the occasion.

There are two types of reasons for doing anything. We have "good reasons" as when we tell a friend we did not attend a lecture because we disapprove of the speaker's conservative views. We also have "real" reasons, which we often do not admit even to ourselves. We may actually have stayed home because we did not have money for the ticket or because we wanted to watch some dumb television program. Good reasons are what we report to society, expecting its approval. Real reasons are often the product of our emotions and our prejudices.

I have observed that America is beset by a "paradox of opportunity": our economic system has given us enough money to buy almost anything good—but we can waste it on mere conspicuous consumption; our young people have so much entertainment available from so early an age that they are bored by the time they are teenagers; science has given us the tools for a perfect life—and the tool to blow us all up. This is our paradox of opportunity.

Note that after the writer uses the expression the first time he does not have to repeat the quotation marks.

Slangy and colloquial expressions in more formal writing require quotation marks.

We had a real "blast."

H. L. Mencken has referred to such quotation marks as "hygienic" because the writer seems to be holding his nose while he sneaks slang into his writing. Very often it sounds too clubby and self-conscious, and the writer is advised to stick to a consistent level of usage that makes the quotation marks unnecessary.

A quotation within a quotation is indicated with single quotation marks.

> My friend gave me some advice about how to join the "in" group in Cambridge, Massachusetts. "If you meet a student from Harvard," he said, "you ask, 'What house?' If you meet a girl from Wellesley, you ask, 'Did your mother go to Wellesley?' "

If a quotation is long, both margins can be indented and the quotation marks dispensed with. When typed, a quotation is usually single spaced to differentiate it from the rest of the text, which probably would be double spaced. Form books are arbitrary about when a quotation is "long," the most usual prescription being that if it is four lines or more, it is indented and single spaced. The best advice here is that you determine the will of the appropriate authority, including your own instructor. In all cases, it is important that you be consistent.

The notification that identifies a quotation, called the "tag," is variously punctuated. Ordinarily the tag is separated from the quotation with a comma, or with two commas if it interrupts the quotation. When the tag is a short introductory phrase or when the quotation is closely built into the structure of the sentence, no comma is necessary.

> In *Democracy*, Henry Adams had one of his characters say "You are all alike. You will grow six inches high and then stop. Why will not somebody grow up to be a tree and cast a shadow?"

> "I have always said," wrote Pascal, "that all of the troubles of man come from his not knowing how to sit still."

> My book says "War periods do not yield great literature."

> Our minister agrees with Mark Twain's belief that "Few sinners are saved after the first twenty minutes of a sermon."

A problem that is not really solved by the arbitrary decisions of publishers is how to handle the quotation marks at the end of a sentence. To achieve uniformity most writers follow these rules: periods and commas go inside quotation marks.

Montaigne wrote "The most manifest sign of wisdom is a continued cheerfulness."

"Life is action and passion," observed Catherine Drinker Bowen, "and it is therefore required that a man should share the action and passion of his time."

Semicolons and colons go outside the quotation marks. The sense of the utterance determines where question marks and exclamation points go. When the marks conclude the quotation, they are put inside the quotation marks; when they belong to the main sentence, the question mark or exclamation point goes outside the quotation marks.

Oliver Wendell Holmes wrote, "How good to hurl oneself against these magnificent heights, to put out all one's effort and feel body and soul respond!"

Who was it who said, "The Right Honorable gentleman is indebted to his memory for his jests and to his imagination for his facts"?

As is true of many of the conventions, there is considerable difference in the practice of different writers, but there are certain observable tendencies. Because many publications do not have an italics font of type and because typists wish to save the time that backspacing and underlining require, quotation marks or merely initial capitals are used increasingly for all titles, whether of books, works of art, airplanes, or ships. The practice of underlining or italicizing words used as words also is losing favor; instead, the writer puts them in quotation marks. For a while, many writers imitated the British who use only the apostrophe for quotations— the marks were called "inverted commas"—but opposition seems to have firmed up against the practice, and it has been largely rejected. The practice of indenting and single spacing long quotations is also decreasing, and often all quotations are put in quotation marks. In such cases, quotation marks are put at the beginning of every paragraph in the quotation, but closing marks occur only at the end of the long selection.

FAULTY REFERENCE (REF.)

Pronouns are handy words that can be substituted for substantive forms to give variety and tighten coherence. Since pronouns are substitute words, the reader must be certain of their antecedents. The following sentence is ambiguous, because the reader cannot be sure about the antecedent for the pronoun.

Tom told John that he was overweight.

Strictly speaking, every pronoun must have a single noun or another pronoun for an antecedent, but recently there has been a widely accepted practice of letting a pronoun refer to an entire sentence or paragraph, for instance:

The Board of Aldermen has recently acted on a simple voice vote. This is illegal.

The casual grammarian would be satisfied; the stricter one would not and would rephrase the latter sentence, "This practice is illegal."

RUN-ON SENTENCES (R. O.)

A run-on or fused sentence is a construction in which two complete sentences are punctuated as one.

We must watch the Red Dragon of China during this period of the Cold War he would love to carve up the United States and devour it with relish. (From a student theme.)

The writer must decide with which sentence the middle modifier should go.

We must watch the Red Dragon of China during this period of the Cold War. He would love to carve up the. . . .

We must watch the Red Dragon of China. During this period of the Cold War he would love. . . . .

The writer should avoid trying to separate the two units with a comma. He might, however, wish to subordinate one of the two elements:

Since the Red Dragon of China would like to devour the United States, we must watch it during this period of the Cold War.

SPELLING (SP.)

Everyone should and can learn to spell precisely. Fairly or not, poor spelling has come to be a mark of the uneducated, the careless, and the ignorant. Some people go through their lives ashamed to write letters to their friends because they have not mastered this simple technique.

Since many colleges and universities automatically fail all papers that have more than a very few misspellings, some students have their academic careers harmed by an easily removed deficiency. When a number of leaders in the business world were asked to list the types of instruction that they wished were given to all college students, spelling led all the suggestions. One respondee wrote, "Why in the hell don't you teach them to spell?"

Spelling can be mastered. In the first place, about 98 percent of the words in the English language follow simple phonic principles that a fourth grader can learn. Secondly, study at the University of Iowa indicated that better than 85 percent of student spelling difficulty can be eliminated by careful proofreading. For that reason, we suggest that you read or reread the section in this textbook on proofreading, p. 220. The Iowa test revealed that the words most frequently misspelled were not the terrors some students have come to fear, but, rather, words like *an*, *and*, *then*, *than*, *its*, *it's*, *have*, *to*, and *too*. Many experienced teachers claim that students spell as badly as they are permitted to spell. After students are informed that any paper with more than three spelling errors will be summarily failed, such errors almost invariably disappear.

Besides carelessness, two other causes contribute to spelling difficulty. Some students like to think of themselves as having some peculiar kind of mind that finds it impossible to spell correctly. Secondly, some students just do not take the time to learn the routine rules that clear up the spelling of some orthographic monstrosities.

Fortunately, the human mind can be trained in many ways. Some people admittedly do not have minds that remember pictorially. Some people can remember people's faces, word configurations, and symbols on maps, but the less fortunate lack that facility. They just cannot remember how a word should look; it looks just as good spelled one way as another. However, there are many ways to learn to spell, each based on a different ability of the mind. One approach is through sense perceptions. The eye "takes pictures" and stores them in the brain for future use. This is the facility used by a witness to identify a suspect in a police line-up. The ear also has a memory; in a sense, it makes a tape-recording and stores it in the brain ready for "playback" when needed. This is the memory that helps you recognize a tune you knew years ago.

The muscles also can "remember"; they remind you how to skate each winter and how to ride a bicycle when you have not ridden one in years. Besides these memory banks, we have a rational memory, which we use more consciously than we do the sense memories. The student of spelling must use all four memories.

Using your eye's memory. When you confront a word for the first time or when you look it up in the dictionary, use your eye's memory. Look at the word intently for an instant; then close your eyes and envision it as you spell it silently. Write the word, and, closing your eyes again, envision how it looks in your own handwriting.

Using your ear's memory. While you are training your eye, consciously help your ear remember. Many years ago, in spelling bees, experts often adopted an almost sing-song way of spelling such words as *Constantinople* and *Mississippi* without thinking at all: they just sang out the spelling. Em-eye-double-ess-eye-double-ess-eye-pee-pee-eye" they would chant in rhythm. Or sometimes they might use a syllabic approach; perhaps "Em-eye-ess-ess, Miss-, eye-ess-ess, Mississ, eye-pee-pee-eye, Mississippi." You can adapt this technique to your needs by audibly hissing out the spelling and getting your ear accustomed to how the spelling should sound. This technique is especially helpful when you are working on words that have an unaccented medial vowel, represented by the *schwa* (ə) in dictionaries, words like *sophomore, telephone,* and *attendance* in which the pronunciation does not identify the vowels. You can deliberately over-accent or even mispronounce the words to help your ear remind you that the letters are there: *soph-O-more, tel-E-phone, atten-DANCE, ATH-lete, con-fi-DENCE, cur-RIC-u-LUM, exist-ENCE, evi-DENCE, exper-I-ence, appear-ANCE, goverN-ment, main-TEN-ANCE, thor-OUGH-ly, prim-I-tive, def-I-nIte, femi-NINE, DE-spair, se-PA-rate, priv-I-lege, univers-I-ty,* and *DI-vide.*

Using your muscle's memory. Some writers use their kinesthetic memory bank by writing the word five or ten times, all the while sounding it and looking at it intently. Just as the muscles learn to swing a golf club, so can they learn to spell a word. This system is particularly helpful for the student who has the sloppy habit of writing "more then" or "would of." Train your muscle grooves by repeatedly writing "more than" and "would have." If you have the careless handwriting habit of misspelling "and" by leaving off the final letter, or if you have trouble with *its* and *it's,* write these words repeatedly in a context with other letters, for instance "more and more," "It's raining," and "its fur."

Using your rational memory. If a writer develops a sensitivity to language, he becomes aware of a host of spelling tips that appear in the fine print in the dictionary. Recently two surprising spellings have appeared in student themes, *chester drawers* and *foreign-hand tie.* These two spellings are logical enough, the one being analogous to another piece of furniture, the chesterfield or overstuffed sofa, and the other sounding as though the speller thought the tie was imported, as many are. A moment's thought or a glance at the dictionary would have cleared up the difficulty. The expression *chest of drawers* is completely meaningful, and the concept of a *four-in-hand tie* recalls that the knot is much like the one used by teamsters who held the reins of four horses in their hands, that is, "four reins in hand." The human mind is a wondrous thing, and you can turn on a part of it that constantly will police your spelling; it will say to you, "What does this word really mean?," and you will spell more carefully. This attention to word meaning will prevent such howlers as "At four, I was a toe-headed boy," and "He was a man of many faucets."

Keep yourself receptive to information about spelling. Often when you learn to spell one word you pick up some information about a Greek or Latin root or affix. *Manu-* means "hand," *auto-* means *self*, and *trans-* means "across," for instance, and these prefixes appear often in English words. Knowing *fini* means "end" or "limit" will clarify the spelling of *definite* and *infinite*. *Helios* is Greek for "sun"; *graph* is Greek by way of Latin for "writing," thus, a *heliograph* is a mirror-like instrument for sending messages using the reflection of the sun. Knowing these word units helps to spell their English derivatives. There are hundreds of such word sources, and the mind of a college student should be able to hold most of them.

Another sensitivity a writer must develop is the ability to distinguish between homonyms, words with the same sounds but different meanings and spellings. (*meat, meet; affect, effect; led, lead; accept, except; capital, capitol; compliments, complements; council, counsel; stationery, stationary; principle, principal; their, there; to, two, too*) If they stop to think, most college students know the differences. What they need when they write is a special awareness to flash a warning light when one of these words appears. If any of the pairs listed confuse you, look them up *now*.

There are some rules of orthography that might be helpful to you.

Rule One.

> Use *i* before *e*
> Except after *c*,
> Or when sounded like *a*
> As in *neighbor* or *weigh*

This old chestnut is surprisingly dependable. It indicates the proper spelling of *believe, retrieve, achieve, shriek, shield, siege, yield,* and *ceiling, conceit, deceit, receipt*. There are a very few exceptions; for instance, *foreign, forfeit, either, leisure, neither, seize,* and *weird*. If you wish, you can look up the etymology of these words and see why they violate the rule.

Rule Two.

Drop the final *e* before a suffix beginning with a vowel; retain a final *e* before a suffix beginning with a consonant. The words *accusing, aggravating, appreciative, commercial, conceivable, imaginary, medicinal, ridiculous, scenic* and *usual* drop the *e*. The words *accurately, achievement, adequately, advertisement, announcement, careless, likeness, suspenseful, useful, useless* retain their *e*.

An exception is *judgment,* although *judgement,* more common in England, is acceptable and sometimes used in the United States.

Rule Three.

The words *jot, tip, put, drop,* and *nap* all have a short vowel sound and end with a consonant. To keep the vowel sound short when you add a suffix beginning with a vowel (*ed, ing,* and *ance,* for instance), double the final consonant. Longer words whose last syllables have a short sound and are accented (*admit, permit, deter, propel*) follow the same rule. If you do not double the consonant, the vowel sound becomes long. Compare the following: *sloppy, sloping; tapping, taping; bitter, biter; tubbing, tubing; ridding, riding; planned, planed; cured, occurred.*

The Mnemonic System. Occasionally you will encounter words whose spelling you perversely cannot master. In these cases, you may wish to devise your own remembering system (*mnemonic*) to fix the spelling in your mind.

Examples:

    cemetery: You get to the *cEmEtEry* with *E's.*

    dispensable: Some girls consider SABLE indispenSABLE.

    friend: Be a fri*END* till the *END.*

    stationery, stationary: You get *stationEry* by going to a *stationER;* you cannot get it by *stAnding stationARY.*

Your own self-help program. The object of these suggestions is not only to help you spell the words used as examples; in addition, their object is to get you started on your own program toward perfect spelling. We recommend the following steps:

1. Keep a list of words you misspell or find difficult to remember.

2. Analyze the list to see why you misspell them. We predict that over 80 percent of your mistakes will be the result of careless-

ness or deficient proofreading. Follow the suggestions on page 220 for proofreading to eliminate this cause.

3. If any of the misspellings fall into a pattern, memorize the spelling principle that is appropriate. These rules can be found in almost any grammar book, for instance the ones recommended on page 440.

4. Use the various approaches recommended for exploiting the memory bank of your ears, eyes, muscles, and conscious mind. In particular, pronounce the word carefully as you write it, and then close your eyes and try to spell it and envision it at the same time.

5. Resolve to make yourself a perfect speller. There is just no point to wasting all your effort on a writing project because of a last-minute failure to be sure your words are spelled properly. Do not try to escape responsibility by claiming that some great men spell badly. We know that Abraham Lincoln misspelled *beginning, very, conferring, business,* and *privilege,* but we also know that he spent a great deal of time trying to improve his spelling. And don't wait for the day when you will have a secretary to correct your spelling. Forget it. Chances are you will have to correct hers.

SPLIT INFINITIVES (SP. INF.)

In the past, beginning writers were told, somewhat mindlessly, never to end a sentence with a preposition and never to split an infinitive. The first injunction led to such abominations as Winston Churchill's lampoon of this rule: "That is something up with which I will not put," and it is now reasonably acceptable to put a preposition at the end of a sentence. To avoid splitting an infinitive one has to forego the sentence, "If you wish to more accurately express your meaning, go ahead and split an infinitive," in favor of "to express your meaning more accurately . . . ," which is grammatically less sound because the modifier is farther from the word modified. However, since the rule has made split infinitives foreign to the ear, and because many purists are still offended by the split, you should, especially in formal usage, put the preposition and the verb next to each other, for instance, *to speak softly* and *quickly to retreat.*

TITLES

There are definite conventions about how to treat titles. The title at the top of the first page of your essays should have only the first letter of each major word capitalized. See p. 408 for conventions regarding capitalization of words in titles. Do not put the title in quotation marks unless you mean to show your reader that your title is a quotation from someone else. Underlining your title or putting it in quotation marks would be redundant, since its position on the page indicates it is your title.

When you refer to a title in your text, you should indicate the nature of the work you are citing. Underlining is comparable to italics in print, which usually indicates the title of a book, statue, painting, magazine, play, or the name of a ship. Putting the title in quotation marks indicates a poem, one chapter of a book, a magazine article, or an act in a play.

1. The *Queen Mary* is not the setting of *Ship of Fools*.

2. "Treasury of Words" is found in Margaret Schlauch's *The Gift of Tongues*.

VERBALS

A verbal is a form of the verb used as a noun or as a modifier. Three parts of a verb may be used as verbals: participles, gerunds, and infinitives. *Participles* are the past or present participle form used as adjectives.

1. They came *running* from the barn.

2. The *burned* house collapsed.

Gerunds are the present participle forms used as nouns.

1. *Walking* is a health-producing exercise.

2. John likes *swimming* more than Joe does.

Infinitives are the present forms of the verb used (with *to*) as nouns, adjectives, or adverbs.

As noun:	*To climb* Everest was his sole ambition.
	He wanted *to climb*.
As adjective:	We have much *to give* to others.
	He is our best choice *to win*.
As adverb:	She is too pretty *to lose*.

Verbals must always appear *in* a sentence; they cannot themselves provide the finite verb form required by all sentences, for they cannot—by definition—indicate time. Be certain that the main verb in each sentence is finite (shows a tense), and that you have not inadvertently mistaken a verbal (infinitive—indicated by *to*; gerund or participle—indicated by *-ed* or *-ing*) for the verb in the sentence or clause.

VERBS

All writers must pay considerable attention to their use of *verbs*, for, as the name indicates (it comes from the Latin word for *word*), in many ways the verb is *the word* in the sentence—that is, the verb can convey not only action and time, but also the tone, the pace, in effect the "flavor" of the sentence. Perhaps we have overstated the case somewhat. We are, nevertheless, convinced that effective utilization of various forms of verbs will add to a piece of writing much that can be achieved in no other way.

Elementary information about modern English verbs begins with the fact that there are now only two kinds or classes of verbs, regular and irregular. (Our remote ancestors dealt with seven classes of "strong" verbs and three of "weak" verbs; the process of simplification has aided us considerably.)

Regular verbs (formerly weak) are those—the vast majority— that form their past participle by *adding* a suffix (pronounced *d* or *t*) to the present tense form:

Present	Past	Present Participle
drop	dropped	dropping
carry	carried	carrying
walk	walked	walking

Irregular verbs are those that form their past tense by a change of vowel sound *within* the verb and perhaps other changes:

Present	Past	Past Participle
bear	bore	born
bear	bore	borne
begin	began	begun
bite	bit	bitten
choose	chose	chosen
do	did	done
run	ran	run
ride	rode	ridden
rise	rose	risen

There are about a hundred such verbs. In case of doubt about a verb form, see your dictionary. Avoid the attraction of the regular verb that young children and other illiterates often succumb to: I *drinked* it all up; the grass *growed* a foot.

Grammatical properties. Verbs possess the following grammatical properties.

voice: active and passive

mood: indicative, subjunctive, imperative

tense: present, past, future, and perfect tenses of each

The active voice is used when the subject performs the action:

John hit the ball.

When the action is received by or performed on the subject, the passive voice is used:

The ball was hit by John.

Ordinarily, student writers discover that their purposes are best served when they rely on the active voice. If you use passive voice at all, use it sparingly. Do not inattentively alternate active and passive voice passages.

Most modern, informal expository writing relies exclusively on the *indicative* mood. Spoken English finds considerable use for the *imperative,* as in "Look out," "Watch out for the overhang," "Duck!" and so on. The subjunctive mood, illustrated in the next sentences, is seldom used today except in a very limited number of constructions such as a statement that is contrary to fact.

1. If I were you, I would go.

2. If he were well, he might be a superb choice. (Colloquially, this would probably appear "If he was well . . . ," yet the preceding sentence, "If I were you," is colloquial: "If I *was* you" is widely recognized as a barbarism.)

Again, the error to be avoided is the incongruous mixing of moods, or the *inadvertent* shift from one mood to another.

English verbs identify, by means of tense, the *time* at which the action of the verb is said to take place. Of the six tenses usually recognized, the three simple tenses—past, present, and future—are most often used. The following paradigm shows the full conjugation of a regular verb.

Principle Parts

Present	Past	Past Participle
walk	walked	walked

Active Voice, Indicative Mood

Present tense	Singular	Plural
First person	I walk	we walk
Second person	you walk	you walk
Third person	he (she, it) walks	they walk

The third person singular present indicative final *s* is the remnant of a complex system of endings. In the subjunctive mood, this *s* does not occur.

Past tense

I walked	we walked
you walked	you walked
he (she, it) walked	they walked

Future tense

I shall walk	we shall walk
you will walk	you will walk
he (she, it) will walk	they will walk

The *perfect tenses* use past, present, or future forms of the auxiliary verb *have* with the appropriate participle: I have walked, I had walked, I shall have walked, etc.

Imperative: walk

Subjunctives: if he walk; if he be walked

Infinitives: to walk, to have walked, to be walked, to have been walked

Gerunds: walking, having walked, being walked, having been walked

Participles: walking, walked, having walked, being walked, having been walked

Emphatic form: I do walk

Progressive form: I am walking

Further reading

Grammars based on the more traditional concepts:

Buckler, William E., and McAvoy, William C. *American College Handbook of English Fundamentals.* New York: American Book Company, 1960.

Marckwardt, Albert H., and Cassidy, Frederick G. *Scribner's Handbook of English.* New York: Scribner's, 1967.

"Descriptive" grammars:

Curme, George O., and Kurath, Hans. *Grammar of the English Language.* Vol. I: *Parts of Speech and Accidence,* 1935. Vol. II: *Syntax,* 1931. Boston: D. C. Heath.

Jesperson, Otto. *Growth and Structure of the English Language.* Garden City, N.Y.: Doubleday–Anchor Books, 1955.

Grammars based on structural linguistics, as described on pp. 244–246.

Francis, W. Nelson. *The Structure of American English.* New York: Ronald Press, 1958.

Fries, Charles C. *The Structure of English*. New York: Harcourt, Brace & World, 1952.

Gleason, H. A. *An Introduction to Descriptive Linguistics*. New York: Holt, Rinehart and Winston, 1961.

Hockett, Charles F. *A Course in Modern Linguistics*. New York: Macmillan, 1958.

Sledd, James. *A Short Introduction to English Grammar*. Chicago: Scott, Foresman, 1959.

Grammars based on transformational or generative principles:

Bach, Emmon W. *An Introduction to Transformational Grammars*. New York: Holt, Rinehart and Winston, 1964.

Roberts, Paul. *English Sentences*. New York: Harcourt, Brace & World, 1962.

INDEXES

INDEX OF NAMES

INDEX OF SUBJECTS